T0329744

FROM RESIDENCY
TO RETIREMENT

Critical Issues in Health and Medicine

EDITED BY RIMA D. APPLE, UNIVERSITY OF WISCONSIN—MADISON,
AND JANET GOLDEN, RUTGERS UNIVERSITY—CAMDEN

Growing criticism of the U.S. health care system is coming from consumers, politicians, the media, activists, and health care professionals. Critical Issues in Health and Medicine is a collection of books that explores these contemporary dilemmas from a variety of perspectives, among them political, legal, historical, sociological, and comparative, and with attention to crucial dimensions such as race, gender, ethnicity, sexuality, and culture.

For a list of titles in the series, see the last page of the book.

FROM RESIDENCY TO RETIREMENT

Physicians' Careers over

a Professional Lifetime

TERRY MIZRAHI

RUTGERS UNIVERSITY PRESS

New Brunswick, Camden, and Newark,

New Jersey, and London

Library of Congress Cataloging-in-Publication Data
Names: Mizrahi, Terry, author.
Title: From residency to retirement: physicians' careers over a professional lifetime /
    Terry Mizrahi.
Description: New Brunswick: Rutgers University Press, [2021] | Series: Critical issues
    in health and medicine | Includes bibliographical references and index.
Identifiers: LCCN 2020031106 | ISBN 9780813570020 (cloth) | ISBN 9780813570044 (pdf) |
    ISBN 9780813591322 (epub) | ISBN 9781978822764 (mobi)
Subjects: LCSH: Physicians—Anecdotes. | Physician and patient—Anecdotes. |
    Residents (Medicine)—Job satisfaction. | Residents (Medicine)—Job stress.
Classification: LCC R705 .M59 2021 | DDC 610.92 [B]—dc23
LC record available at https://lccn.loc.gov/2020031106

A British Cataloging-in-Publication record for this book is available from the
British Library.

♾ The paper used in this publication meets the requirements of the American National Standard for Information Sciences—Permanence of Paper for Printed Library Materials, ANSI
Z39.48-1992.

www.rutgersuniversitypress.org

Manufactured in the United States of America

*To my inspiring grandchildren Zachary, Benjamin, and Anna—I wish you
a life as dedicated and purposeful as that of the doctors in these pages.*

Contents

FROM RESIDENCY
TO RETIREMENT

1   *Introduction*

Background

In the United States, becoming a doctor has long been considered one of the best career choices. In 2016 to 2017, according to the Association of American Medical Schools, approximately 52,000 people applied to go medical school (2017). In 2015 there were nearly a million licensed physicians in the United States (Statista, 2020). The people who go to medical school are generally young, recent college graduates, and the path ahead of them, once they finish their schooling, is filled with unknowns. Over the course of the last half-century in America, the country has undergone continuous and often large-scale changes to its health care system. Physicians must incorporate those changes into their medical practices, no matter their area of specialty, while also managing their own personal and professional lives.

In 1986 I published a book about the experiences of twenty-six American physicians who had recently graduated from medical school and were completing a postgraduate residency program in internal medicine. I observed those doctors over the course of twelve months, interviewing them and asking as many questions as I could about their work and professional experiences, as well as their emotional and personal experience as physicians. Five years later, I followed up with those doctors to learn more about their career trajectory, to see how their experiences over those several years had affected them and to understand how their experiences might shed light on the broader issues in America's health care and medical system (Mizrahi, 1986).

This book, which is being published more than thirty years later, is a continuation of that book's research project. In the years since that initial research, I stayed in contact with most of the physicians whom I first interviewed in the late 1970s, and for close to forty years I have continued to interview and gather information about their experiences as physicians. In the chapters that follow, I present the findings from this unique long-term study of these individuals, shining a light on their career-long medical experiences, while also revealing important information about the health care industry in America and how it affected their own professional lives and that of their counterparts.

From the 1960s until the late second decade of the twenty-first century, the medical profession in America underwent many turbulent changes. In this book, I look closely at how the career satisfaction of these twenty physicians evolved over the course of these decades, particularly in relation to their patients, peers, and practice. This in-depth longitudinal study builds on the research I conducted when these individuals were all in the same three-year internal medicine training program. It incorporates an additional five interviews I conducted with them during each decade until they were at or near retirement in 2016.

All of the physicians in this cohort were born and trained in the United States. However, despite differences in the organization, financing, and delivery of medical care, because the issues affecting physicians are similar to other Western countries (e.g., Canada, Germany, and Australia), the relevance of this study is much broader. (For Canada, see Hafferty, 2006; for Germany, see Gref, Gildemeister, et al., 2004; for Australia, see Lupton, 1997.)

In this introductory chapter, I present more broadly the early background of my pursuit to understand these physicians' career choices and those of their generation of physicians. I discuss my social activism in the 1960s related to health care reform before I became an academic and ever thought of this topic for a lifetime of scholarship. This broader historical and social context is essential for understanding the interrelationship between myself as the researcher and the participants in this longitudinal study. I also provide some background on the evolution of the study design components, along with a brief introduction to the methodological and conceptual framework. I also discuss important empirical connections to recent professional and policy literature, as well as the complexities, caveats, and caution associated with this—and any long-term—qualitative inquiry.

How It All Began

The research for this book first originated more than fifty years ago, in the late 1960s. At the time, I had recently obtained my master's degree in social work (MSW), and I was working as a new community organizer in a local civic association in a poor and working-class neighborhood of New York City. My beginning assignment was to organize a campaign for a new local hospital, which had apparently stalled after ten years of planning (Hall, 1971). As a result, almost by accident of this job, I became involved in the health care reform movement.

At that time, President Johnson's "Great Society" and "War on Poverty" had emerged as a compelling part of his liberal ideology, which promoted a proactive role for government in meeting human needs. Access to quality health care was one of his proposed solutions to achieving "equality of opportunity" and upward mobility for the disaffected and disadvantaged populations of this country (Chowkwanyun, 2018). His program included funding for community health centers targeted primarily to urban and rural communities deficient in physicians and other primary health care providers (Geiger, 2017). One of my job responsibilities was to assist three new federally funded community health centers (also known as FQHCs) in the neighborhood to get off the ground by providing relevant skill and resources working with residents and patients and other professionals. I am proud to say that the new hospital opened in 1974 (Chowkwanyun, 2011), and the three facilities are thriving to this day, providing health care with a social justice framework to thousands of individuals and families in that community.

Until the mid-1960s, there were no public federal funds available for health insurance coverage. As a result, a two-class health system existed in this country:

the poor and uninsured received their care from public clinics and hospitals to the extent they existed, while middle-class and more affluent patients received their care from private doctors and hospitals, paying either through some type of private insurance or out of their own pocket if they could afford it (Ehrenreich and Ehrenreich, 1970).

While a universal plan for health care for all U.S. citizens did not materialize under the Johnson administration, in 1965 Congress passed the transformative, national legislation Medicare (for the elderly and disabled) and Medicaid (for the poor) as amendments to the Social Security Act of 1935. Still, these monumental pieces of legislation were fought tooth and nail by the American Medical Association (AMA) and related medical organizations, who argued that these policies were an encroachment on private marketplace medicine (Marmor, 2000). Despite this organized opposition, however, these laws were viewed by many others as major steps toward the right to health care for all Americans.

'The Times They Were a Changin': The Advent of Patients' Rights and Consumer Power

In the years following the passage of legislation establishing Medicare and Medicaid, a number of other notable developments in American health care reform also occurred. In 1968 new federal legislation called the Comprehensive Health Care Act (PL 89-749) was passed. This legislation included the concept of "health care as a right" for the first time (Gawande, 2017). Not long afterward, in the mid-1970s, President Nixon proposed legislation to expand both federal health insurance programs. Although his bills were never passed, they might have become law had he not resigned from office to avoid impeachment.

Also in the late 1960s, citizen groups across the country began to demand more participation in, and even control over, the institutions designed to serve them. In the health care system, with the support of progressive doctors and other health care professionals as allies and instigators, local and state organizing built momentum. Many of the demands of these groups were born out of the civil rights movement and other movements for social justice that wanted a voice in organizational decision-making structures (Dittmer, 2009; Geiger, 2017).

A fundamental tenet of the demand for community control of health care institutions was a critique of professionalism, particularly the role of doctors. Medicine, touted as the quintessential model of a profession, was disparaged by consumer groups and health care activists, while a national mobilization for universal health insurance continued to gain popularity. Concomitantly, nurses, pharmacists, psychologists, social workers, and other occupations were also fighting against the physician monopoly for a greater and more autonomous role in health care decision-making (Freidson, 1970).

Additionally, a more intense patients' rights movement was picking up steam in the medical and psychiatric sectors. Groups advocating for women's health and mental health began to emerge in an effort to gain greater control of decisions that affected women's bodies and minds (Boston Health Collective, 1970). Mental health groups gained national attention with the Willowbrook exposé in 1971, in which Willowbrook State School, an institution in New York City for the "mentally ill and retarded" (as it was identified then), was exposed for its deplorable treatment of patients and residents. The campaign that brought that hospital's abuse to light was spearheaded by a young investigative journalist, Geraldo Rivera (Goode, Hill, et al., 2013). Other similar revelations of horrendous conditions in institutions across the country helped create a major movement toward "deinstitutionalization" in the "least restrictive environment" as a legal framework for patient-centered programs. These frameworks were based on class action lawsuits, specifically "Pennhurst," a class action suit against a state hospital in Pennsylvania (Geer, 1983), and "Wyatt v. Stickney," a class action suit against a state psychiatric hospital in Alabama (Leaf, 1977). The impact of these lawsuits would reverberate throughout the country.

In the 1970s state and federal regulations also began mandating various forms of consumer/patient participation in decision-making roles in a range of medical and psychiatric programs. This was based on an earlier government mandate to include "maximum feasible participation of the poor" that had begun as part of President Johnson's antipoverty program (Melish, 2010). At this same time, hospital patients' rights doctrines began to be codified into law and regulation, particularly after the American Hospital Association (AHA), one of the country's most prestigious medical organizations, approved the first such national document focused on this issue (AHA, 1992). The AHA's approval of this and other "bills" of patients' rights had a domino effect around the country. Most states passed some version of patients' rights mandates by the end of the decade for the first time in American history, all of which still exist today (Annas, 1975).

Once these patients' rights directives began to be put in place, there was a push among social workers and others, including myself, to make clients and constituencies aware of these transformative changes and to help organize their collective involvement in these accountability mechanisms, such as serving on boards of organizations and public commissions. A number of activist and social justice organizations were involved in this effort, led by the Medical Committee for Human Rights (MCHR), an organization that had been established to promote patients' rights and protections. Because of the work of organizations like the MCHR, the message of the patients' rights movement was spreading among health students and practitioners across the country.

Concurrently, Ralph Nader and his advocacy colleagues launched the broader consumer movement in the 1970s to protect citizens from the harm of unhealthy food and drugs and other products, including unsafe automobiles (Bollier, 1991). This consumer movement targeted the secrecy and lack of accountability of corporations that manufactured harmful products as well as physician groups who withheld vital medical information from patients. Many in this movement used Nader's strategies and platform to organize residents and health workers to demand their rights to participate in policy and program decisions.

Shifting from Consumer Advocate to Researcher

After participating in the patient rights movement as a consumer advocate and social worker, I expanded my focus to include that of researcher, academic, and writer. In the early 1970s, I moved with my spouse to the southern part of the United States, where, because of my work experience and MSW degree, I was asked to join the faculty of a southern school of social work. I became an "accidental academic," and my career trajectory changed. After a few years of teaching, I decided to pursue a doctoral degree to advance my career in a university setting. And that is where my passion for social work and health activism and my formal education merged.

Although I was steeped in the world of patient rights from a consumer advocacy perspective, when I began this new academic path, I realized that I didn't know much about those in charge of the U.S. health care system, including physicians collectively and their professional organizations. These professional organizations, including the AMA, had been the most influential players in preventing major changes in health care financing and delivery (Freidson, 1970, 1984; Harris, 1969). I saw that, in order to continue my goals of promoting a more patient-involved and consumer-led system, I needed to know more about how these powerful sectors shaped the American health care system. As a result, I decided to pursue advanced studies in the sociology of professions generally and in the history and structure of the American medical profession specifically (Dingwall and Lewis, 1983; Monteiro, 2015). I began to investigate the topic of physician socialization with the goal of understanding how neophyte medical students became the type of doctors they did; how they acquired their values related to, knowledge about, and skill for caring for patients; and how they learned the doctor-patient relationship.

During my studies, I pursued relationships with administrators and chairs of relevant departments at Southern Area Medical School (SAMS), a pseudonym of the medical school and hospital located in a southern U.S. city, the site of my book.[1] As a result of those connections, I was able to observe firsthand and talk with dozens of neophyte physicians over a full year while they pursued their three-year graduate medical training. This consisted of a one-year internship followed by two years of residency in internal medicine, a specialization that was, at the time of my study and historically, the largest and one of the most prestigious areas of medicine (Beeson, 1986). Based on this year of intensive participant observation research, I gained incredible insight into how these doctors acquired their professional identities, which I described in detail several years later in my book *Getting Rid of Patients: Contradictions in the Socialization of Physicians* (Mizrahi, 1986).[2]

The Evolution of the Study Design

During my initial study, the participant observation phase consisted of following individual "house staff" (a term used for those pursuing this combined three internship and residency program) around with their permission, through their work shift almost every day or evening for much of June 1979 to August 1980.

I took copious field notes behind the scenes after watching them each day interacting with patients, peers, superiors, and subordinates. During the same period, I conducted a series of in-depth interviews with many of these house officers, including the six chief residents who were completing their fourth year at SAMS, after their residency. I then randomly selected twenty-six individual physicians for follow-up. It happened that the individuals in the cohort were all White, all male, and had been educated in U.S. medical schools, typical for that time period.[3]

I used a combination of closed-ended and open-ended questions in each set of interviews to compare individual responses over time as well as similarities and differences within the cohort at each phase. I asked the physicians about general and specific aspects of their career trajectory. Many of the questions focused specifically on components of satisfaction, including *financial remuneration, intellectual stimulation, psychic/emotional satisfaction, satisfaction related to their own professional status,* and the *public's perception of the medical profession.* Other questions focused on how they viewed the future prospects for themselves and the medical profession, whether they would *recommend the practice of medicine to their children,* and their *optimism or pessimism about the future of the profession.*

As a result of this one year of intense scrutiny of their daily professional lives, I found that cultural, structural, and professional factors contributed to an antipatient and antisystem perspective among the house staff, which I documented in my doctoral dissertation and then later described in my book *Getting Rid of Patients,* published in 1986.

Extending the Research

In the early 1980s, a few years after receiving my doctorate, I gave a presentation on my study of these physicians from SAMS to some colleagues at work. After I completed the presentation, one colleague asked me, "Do you know what happened to those doctors after they completed the program?" This question and the conversation that followed would ultimately trigger a whole new vision for my research, and lead me in 1984, to interview those twenty-six doctors again five years after their SAMS residency, when they had entered the next phase of their professional lives.

In my follow-up study, twenty-five of the twenty-six physicians agreed to be interviewed again. Most of them had gone on to subspecialty fellowships within internal medicine and then into academic or community-based practice settings. A few remained in general internal medicine, and one left the specialty for another type of non-internal medicine practice. The topics of the interview questions focused on a beginning examination of their career trajectories as well as a retrospective look at their SAMS residency experiences from early practice. Those postresidency interviews resulted in a chapter in my earlier book. The positive response to the book academically and professionally, as well as my being a witness to vast changes in medicine taking place in real time, led me to continue the in-depth interviews over the next three decades, interviewing twenty of the twenty-five physicians four additional times; the interview sessions corresponded with critical junctures in their professional development.[4] (The interviews in 2011 and 2016 included only nineteen physicians because, sadly, one physician had died sometime after the fourth set of interviews.)

Over the course of this long period of time and the multiple interview sessions conducted in person or by telephone, none of the physicians refused to answer my questions or cut the interview short once they had agreed to a time and place. Indeed, some of the interviews went on much longer than the time verbally contracted for in advance. The relationships I was able to develop over time produced a level of comfort that allowed the cohort to engage in deep reflection and to care about the longitudinal aspects. For example, several wondered how their past answers compared to present ones; others asked about their fellow residents (which, of course, I could not reveal). This "prolonged engagement" (Padgett, 1998) and rapport (Corbin and Strauss, 2008) enhance the credibility of the findings.

It is rare to have a study that is both longitudinal over the professional lifetime of a cohort and qualitative, allowing for in-depth analyses. The few existing longitudinal studies of physicians' perspectives on their careers are for the most part based on self-administered surveys, which, of necessity, omit personal meaning and understanding of context (Durrington, Western, et al., 2006; Hojat, Gonnella, et al., 1995; Landon, Reschovsky, et al., 2006; Murray, Montgomery, et al., 2001).

Over time, researchers have established the importance of using qualitative methods to enhance survey research (Dumelow, Littlejohns, et al., 2000; Jovic, Wallace, et al., 2006; Konrad, Williams, et al., 1999; McMurray, Williams, et al., 1999). No study of physicians or other professionals has been found to incorporate both dimensions over such an extended time period. This book appears to be unusual also in that it examines both academic and community practitioners; the former group is usually omitted from or minimized in the physician satisfaction cohort studies (Chehab, Panicker, et al., 2001; Konrad, Williams, et al., 1999).

The Contextual Framework for the Career Trajectories

This longitudinal analysis is distinctive from previous research on career satisfaction because it reveals cohort trends as well as individual timelines. The years in which these twenty physicians were interviewed correspond roughly to six phases in the lifetime of a career, which I categorize as the six Es: *entry, early, established, entrenched, extended,* and *ending*. These phases also correspond, to a large degree, with major changes in the U.S. political arena that affected the organization, financing, and delivery of medical care and the role of physicians in society. Their career trajectories began with the administrations of President Carter (1976) when they were in medical school and, for most, terminated—or anticipated the end of their careers—in the last year of President Obama's second term (2016). (The interviews were conducted in the final year of each time frame.)

- The *entry* phase (1979–1980) represents the period of time near the end of the three-year internal medicine residency for fourteen physicians, and at the end of four years for the six members of the cohort who stayed an extra year as chief residents. As noted, their experiences as house staff at SAMS in this phase are captured in my book *Getting Rid of Patients: Contradictions in the Socialization of Physicians* (Mizrahi, 1986). This phase corresponded with the end of President Carter's administration.

- The *early* phase (1980–1984) refers to the five-year period after their house staff training, during which sixteen completed fellowships in various subspecializations and then started either academic or community practice careers. Three did not go on to formal postresidency programs and instead began careers in general internal medicine. One moved directly to a medical area outside internal medicine (NIM non–internal medicine). This phase corresponded with the beginning of President Reagan's administration in the early 1980s.

- The *established* phase (1984–1994) refers to the ten-year period (beginning five years after they had completed residency) when almost all had settled into an academic or community practice arrangement in the same setting or had moved to a different one. It corresponded to the first term of President Clinton in the early to mid-1990s.

- The *entrenched* phase (1994–2004) refers to the ten-year period (from fifteen to twenty-five years after their internal medicine residency) when most were embedded in the same setting, but a few had changed settings. It corresponded to the time of the administration of President George W. Bush.

- The *extended* phase (2004–2011) occurred in the first decade of the twenty-first century (interviews occurring thirty years postresidency), when almost all were still practicing full time. Only one physician was fully retired and two were partly retired, or using the preferred label, "semiactive." This was during President Obama's first term, when the country was in a deep recession. It was during this phase that the historic Patient Protection and Affordable Care Act (ACA) was passed in 2010 under his leadership.

- The *ending* phase (2011–2016) is the period thirty-five or more years out, when six of the cohort had retired, three were semiactive, and ten were still in fully active positions. Many had anticipated dates for leaving the field, while a few were still engaged in and uncertain about the end of their career. This phase corresponded with the implementation of and ongoing debates over the Affordable Care Act, or "Obamacare," as it is known.

These six Es serve as a framework for analyzing the physicians' career trajectories and help place each phase within the physicians' broader professional context. Originally my plan was to conduct the last set of interviews with the cohort during 2011 and 2012, which I characterized then as the *ending* phase because many of the physicians in earlier stages of their careers had anticipated a slowing down or retiring by this time period. However, all but one were still working at the end of 2011. In 2015 I decided to reinterview the cohort for a sixth and presumably final time. All agreed, and these conversations by phone were completed in early 2016.

The phase labeled *ending*, originally used for the fifth time frame, was changed to *extended*, with so many of the participants' expectations of ending their careers not coming to pass. By 2016 most of them viewed themselves in the final phase of their career, although many of those at or near retirement were still involved in "things" medical. Out of the twenty original physicians, fourteen are still practicing part or full time, although each of those is contemplating retirement within the next five years or so, with varying degrees of ambivalence, trepidation, and vacillation about this last career phase and beyond.

Analytical Insights

Given the breadth of data collected over the course of this research, a methodology that addresses the complexity and nuances of longitudinal analysis is essential. Johnny Saldana's *Longitudinal Qualitative Research* (2003) provided the primary framework for describing the analytic processes I used.

What qualifies this research as longitudinal? According to Saldana (2003), there is no definitive amount of time at which point a research study becomes longitudinal. Saldana defines longitudinal studies as one of three different formats: "1) continuous research in the same small society over a number of years; 2) periodic restudies at regular or irregular intervals; and/or 3) returning after a lengthy interval of time has elapsed since the original research" (p. 2). Arguably, this study encompasses all three formats—the cohort of doctors from the same community (SAMS residency) was interviewed six times at fairly regular intervals over the course of the lengthy interval of almost forty years. In this case, the longitudinal approach has revealed which aspects of these doctors' careers changed, which remained the same, and which shifted back and forth over time.

Qualitative analysis values what is cumulative, idiosyncratic, contradictory, and interactive (Corbin and Strauss, 2008; Padgett, 1998; Saldana, 2003). Saldana (2003) provides a framework for examining life rhythms through time: phases, stages, cycles, and multiple rhythms although without rigidity. Independently echoing Saldana, Corbin and Strauss (2008) suggest that "a researcher might think of process in terms of phases, stages, levels, degrees, progress toward a goal, or sequences of action" (p. 261). As Saldana suggests, I searched for patterns and themes as well as examined the variations and consistencies and inconsistencies within their responses.

Fundamentally, Saldana's (2003) methodology is about understanding the impact of *time* on change. Longitudinal data collection is about treating time as an integral aspect of the data itself. In analyzing the interview transcripts of the doctors in this study, the question of time has often been in the foreground— what is it about *a particular period of time*, characterized in this study as one of six career phases, that contributes to the conditions, experiences, and perspectives the doctors have about their careers? How have these conditions, experiences, and perspectives changed or remained firm from the beginning of their career (entry and early phases), to the middle (established and entrenched phases), to the end (the extended and ending phases)? Essentially, when analyzing longitudinal data, Saldana (2003) argues that the researcher must consider the ways time may be felt, interpreted, or understood differently by different subjects.

As time is considered contextually, so is *change* as another unique variable. While it is important to define in a longitudinal study what constitutes a change (e.g., an increase or decrease in career satisfaction from one phase to the next), Saldana (2003) emphasizes that researchers may not know from the beginning how to define the change they are looking for. Building on a grounded theory approach, Saldana (2003) pushes for more complexity and nuance in longitudinal analysis by acknowledging multiple theories of change and allowing for increased flexibility in the process of interpreting the data.

For Saldana (2003), what is most useful in grounded theory is the task of coming up with a "through-line," which explains an overarching theory or narrative of the participants' experience or of the data (p. 49). However, one narrative or through-line is often not enough given the complexity and quantity of data in a longitudinal study—as is the case here. In examining the doctors' experiences over time, an overarching theory about their experience was not the focus; instead the analysis focused on trying to understand the complexity of what it means to be a doctor: whether and when it goes beyond a job and becomes an all-encompassing identity. Ultimately, it was critical to demonstrate how changes in the context have affected their identity, their perceptions (attitudes), and their practice (behavior) in each time frame. And finally, one of the study's central goals was to examine what sustains the doctors through time as they attempt to control or adjust to major, even transformative, external forces impinging on their professional lives.

Data Analysis

The interview data were transcribed and analyzed using constant comparative analysis, which includes open coding associated with grounded theory (Corbin and Strauss, 2008). An inductive approach was used to code the open-ended questions, identify themes, and then deductively return to data to see which applied and where there were variations or negative cases (Corbin and Strauss, 2008; Padgett, 1998). Saldana (2003) emphasizes the importance of analyzing data for context—the larger sociopolitical structure and its impact on these physicians' experiences.[5]

After intensively reviewing each physician's multiple transcripts on their overall satisfaction and dissatisfaction, I with two colleagues assigned each participant to one of three categories—satisfied, mixed, or dissatisfied. This was based on an exacting scrutiny of responses to seven questions dealing with different facets of satisfaction (financial, psychic/emotional, intellectual, public recognition, and status for self and for the medical profession, recommendations of medicine to their children, and their optimism or pessimism about the future for their profession).

Independent external assessments of each physician's overall career satisfaction score were done by the three researchers. This was an attempt to cluster and interrelate discrete indicators of satisfaction and to identify inconsistencies, constancies, and contradictions between an insider's self-reporting and an outside interpreter's views of the situation. As Saldana (2003) suggests, an effort was made to identify patterns without using rigid markers, which hopefully increases the credibility and trustworthiness of the data.

A similar technique was used by David C. Dunstone and Harold R. Reames (2001) in their more limited qualitative study of a cohort of nineteen physicians over two time frames, the study of physicians that comes closest to this one. In Dunstone and Reames's study, and in this study, the questions generally focused on three broad topical areas about the physicians' satisfaction relating to the type of and relationships with patients, their practice including workplace conditions, and their relationship with peers, which included colleagues both junior and senior to them and those both inside and outside their setting or institution. These categories—patients, practice, and peers—were applied to this cohort in each career phase.

Empirical Connections

In the almost forty years since these physicians completed their residency training, drastic changes in financing, delivery, and organization of health care affected their career satisfaction as well as their attitudes and behavior toward their patients, peers, practice, and the medical profession.[6] Yet there remain differing perspectives among scholars about the quality, extent, and impact of corporate, government, and broader societal changes on the medical profession (Domagalski, 2005; Hafferty, 2006 Light, 2005; McKinlay and Marceau, 2005; Schlesinger, 2002; Starr, 2004).

Most studies that have examined physician satisfaction have not referenced the sociology of professions literature; conversely, those engaged in the study of the medical profession and theories of professionalism have not sufficiently grounded their conceptualizations in the real world of physicians' careers (Abbott, 1995; Hafferty, 2006). Mine is one of the few longitudinal studies that capture the changing perspectives of practicing physicians about the medical profession and, in particular the impact of historical political, economic, and social changes on their individual and collective career trajectories and practice over time.

Given the magnitude of changes in technology, and in the organization and financing of health services, along with the growing criticism of the health care system generally, the medical profession has been under intense scrutiny by different groups: sociologists and political scientists (Hafferty, 2006; Hartley, 2002; Light, 2005; Stevens, 2001), policy-makers and the public (Schlesinger, 2002), and by physicians themselves in many countries (Dunstone and Reames, 2001; Horowitz, Suchman, et al., 2003; Lupton, 1997).

Many scholars also argue that the status of physicians has deteriorated and the influence of physicians on policy has decreased as corporate power and government control have increased (Jasso-Aguilar, Waitzkin, et al., 2004; McKinlay and Marceau, 2005). Others assert that physicians still maintain a measure of legitimacy and countervailing power independent of those two dominant forces (Coburn, Rapport, et al., 1997; Freidson, 2001; Light, 2005). Regardless of which perspective is adhered to, the levels of stress and burnout among physicians have surely increased (Henry, 2004; Murray, Montgomery, et al., 2001; Shanafelt, Hasan, et al., 2015).

In 1979, Mawardi compared the career history of a sample of U.S. medical graduates from 1935 to 1945 with those from 1956 to 1965 and found that there were categories of satisfaction that endured over time. Accurate diagnosis, successful treatment, and patient appreciation gave greatest satisfactions for both groups, suggesting that these may be enduring categories. Since then, studies have provided indicators that may explain changes in outlook for physicians' career satisfaction (O'Rourke, 2014; Shanafelt, Hasan, et al., 2015) during the last several decades.

Research indicates that an increasing percentage of physicians in the United States and elsewhere have seen their professional lives deteriorate; the extent of deterioration has been associated with such issues as practice setting, age, practice arrangements, payment method, geographical location, and subspecialty with little unanimity over the most salient dimensions (Arnetz, 2001; Bury, 2004; Chehab, Panicker, et al., 2001; Dunstone and Reames, 2001; Jovic, Wallace, et al., 2006; Landon, Reschovsky, et al., 2006; Leigh, Kravitz, et al., 2002; Linzer, Gerrity, et al., 2002; Murray, Montgomery, et al., 2001; Zuger, 2004). All told, there is no one set of characteristics that by itself predicts positive or negative reactions to professional practice as noted (Dunstone and Reames, 2001; Nixon and Jaramillo, 2003).

Results of studies conducted in countries other than the United States also focus on gaps in physician well-being as negatively affecting career stability and satisfaction: for example, Sweden (Arnetz, 2001), and the United Kingdom (Yamey and Wilkes, 2001). These studies have found that there is long-term job satisfaction among physicians, indicating that for many, the payoff of this increasingly difficult career is still viewed positively: for example, Brazil (Gouveia, Barbosa, et al., 2005) and Australia (Durrington, Western, et al., 2006). Schlesinger (2002) in the United States and Bury (2004) in the United Kingdom highlight changes in professional practice that suggest a fundamental shift in the social relations of health care and the role of medicine. Hafferty (2006) identifies putative loss of public confidence in the medical profession and the authority of science, an increased role of the media and internet in informing patients, and a change in government's relationship with health care professionals as dimensions of professional challenge. Clearly these macro level changes in career satisfaction and trajectory are reflected in the views and reported actions of this physician cohort.

At the micro level, time conflicts between needs of work and family surfaced at each career phase, reflecting the findings from other studies in the United States and other countries (Dumelow, Littlejohns, et al., 2000; Jennett, Kishinevsky, et al., 1990; Murray, Montgomery, et al., 2001; Williams, Konrad, et al., 2002). Before those studies, physician vulnerability and family dynamics were often omitted or limited in career research with a few important exceptions (Appold, 2016; Charon, 2008; Ofri, 2013a; Weiner, 2017). These physicians were asked and sometimes volunteered information about aspects of their personal lives that affected their professional choices. Several of them revealed personal struggles (marital problems including divorce, coming to terms with homosexuality, drug addiction, heavy drinking, and serious illness for themselves or their wives). Given the scope and the depth of the information disclosed over a professional lifetime, this study offers powerful new insights into key questions that physicians are facing in their careers. These insights help shed important light on the broader medical field at a time when transformative new health care policies are once again being debated by politicians, patients, the public, and health care professionals in the 2020 presidential election campaigns.

Complexity, Caveats, and Cautions

Researchers from the United States and abroad concur that it is difficult to deconstruct the interrelated factors related to career satisfaction and dissatisfaction. There still is a lack of consensus on the nature of this multidimensional construct. Konrad, Williams, et al. (1999) attempted to develop a more complex and nuanced physician job satisfaction instrument that could assess the quality of work life across medical specialties and settings over several years, but one that would still be discriminating enough to capture different aspects of physician opinion on the rapidly changing practice environments in which these physicians find themselves. Their work is categorized into several "domains," which include autonomy, relationship with colleagues, patients and staff, personal time, intrinsic factors, community, pay, administration, resources, and then three related to global issues: global job, specialty, and career. Other studies classify similar factors using different categories (Jovic, Wallace, et al., 2006; Konrad, Williams, et al., 1999; Nixon and Jaramillo, 2003; Williams, Konrad, et al., 2002).

For the study on which this book is based, I use three broad themes extracted from the physicians' responses—patients, peers, and practice. Although these themes provided a useful model for this study, there is still some difficulty in reconciling inconsistencies and gaps in the categorization of physician satisfaction among researchers. For example, Williams, Konrad, et al. (2002) place long time relationships with patients under a category of physician characteristics, while they omit a separate category for colleague relationships. Thus their findings may overly emphasize practice characteristics as a rationale for whether physicians in their study are satisfied or not. Indeed they conclude that patient characteristics are not as important for physician satisfaction as other factors (which is different from my findings). Moreover, to the limited extent that Williams, Konrad, et al. (2002) factor in colleagues, the colleague category appears to be related to those outside the physician's setting and to administrative personnel. However, I found relationships with internal peers to be an important component of job satisfaction, something which was omitted in their study. Furthermore, Williams, Konrad, et al. identify but do not report on categories such as "respect," "status," and "community," which relate in this study to "the public recognition of physicians" category; neither do they distinguish between personal/individual and professional/collective perspectives. McMurray, Williams, et al. (1997) include "intellectual stimulation" and "case mix/patient variety" under a category labeled "day-to-day" practice characteristics, whereas I classify the former under peer relationships and the latter under patient-related factors. Given these differences or gaps in the meaning of career concepts, greater consensus on the content and dimensions of the career satisfaction construct is needed to allow for better comparison and interpretation of data.

The type of research methodology used in physician studies must be also considered. Different data may be gleaned from different methods, as I found in the beginning phases of this study (Mizrahi, 1986). As an example, qualitative data based on in-depth interviews (Dunstone and Reames, 2001; Horowitz, Suchman, et al., 2003; Lupton, 1997) and focus groups (McMurray et al., 1997) yield more complex and nuanced responses than survey instruments do. This is particularly true for questions regarding affective areas such as psychic/emotional satisfaction.

As will be presented in depth in the following chapters, these physicians' cumulative experiences over close to forty years, as reported during lengthy interviews, reveal consistencies and changes over time as a result of numerous factors, including external conditions, their own maturation, and fluctuating personal and family circumstances. Nevertheless, this study is limited by the fact that interviews, no matter how in depth, can only reveal the self-reported accounts of these physicians' attitudes and behavior. It is not possible to know whether and how the data collection methodology affects the accounts of their career satisfaction over time.

While the results of this study are limited by the small size, sampling technique, and the homogeneity of the cohort (White cisgender males), the rich descriptions of physician satisfaction that it yields indicate a promising direction for future studies of career trajectories and satisfaction. Ideally, mixed-method research designs with large groups of physicians are necessary before reliable and trustworthy results can be achieved (Dumelow, Littlejohns, et al., 2000), which accurately portray the career satisfaction and dissatisfaction for U.S. physicians as a whole.

Also noteworthy is the fact that neither Saldana nor other methodologists emphasize enough how the research process can affect data gathered or ignored. It is important and necessary to examine that the way a researcher poses questions, the order the questions are raised, and the omission or follow-up to a line of inquiry may affect the outcome of any study. It is essential for the researcher to be self-reflective and even self-critical. It will be evident that my bias and lack of awareness of certain issues and time constraints affected my role as a researcher, and these shortcomings inevitably affect the quality and depth of these physicians' responses. For example, I regret in hindsight not focusing more on the role of their spouses in their professional decision-making, which a few of them had identified early on. Moreover, I omitted a question about the role of religion and spirituality in their lives, which was pointed out to me critically by one of the participants in the ending phase. On the other hand, there were numerous times when the connections between myself and these physicians resulted in surfacing some intimate revelations, whether they offered those spontaneously or whether in response to a question I posed.

In reporting on this cohort's journey, I believe I was perceived as a dispassionate outsider and strongly feel that these physicians used the opportunity to explore and analyze their experiences emotionally as well as intellectually (Ruspini, 2000; Westervelt and Cook, 2012). In the early phases of the study in particular, some would ask, "Where did you get that question?" or comment, "No one ever asked me that before." They revealed deep-seated insecurities, admitted serious mistakes, exposed vulnerabilities—along with long exhortations about their pride, dedication, and sacrifice in service of their patients and students. They often felt maligned but were also quick to be self-critical and not afraid to critique their profession and peers in their roles as informants. The readers will decide for themselves as to the accuracy, completeness, and authenticity of what is presented in this book.

Chapter Outline

Chapter 2—Meet the Doctors: Career Choices in Their Own Voices

Chapter 2 presents these physicians in their own voices. It includes the choices they made on their career path beginning with their choice of medicine, internal medicine, SAMS, subspecialty, practice, institutional or community setting, and workplace changes over time. It ends with some surprising revelations about their choice of medicine.

Chapters 3 and 4—Satisfaction and Strains: The Ups and Downs of Being a Doctor, Parts I (Early to Mid-Career) and II (Mid-Career to Retirement)

Together, chapters 3 and 4 examine patient, practice, and peer components of their professional lives. Physicians are classified as positive, mixed, and negative based on a Satisfaction Index comprising seven factors in the six time frames (intellectual stimulation; psychic satisfaction; financial remuneration; professional status for themselves and more generally; recommendation of medical to their children; optimistic or not about future of medicine). Consistencies and fluctuations as well as trends are presented.

Chapter 5—"Speaking of Their Own": Relationships with Peers, Partners, and Protégés

Here the focus is on their interactions as house staff with their fellow residents and faculty attendings in real time and as they recall them over time. It also presents their perspectives on the peer culture inside and outside their practice setting at each career stage. Finally, the way they perceive and experience "the new generation of physicians," meaning those who are still in training or are younger practitioners, is depicted.

Chapter 6—Mistakes and Malpractice: The Bane of Physicians

This chapter presents the way these physicians define and defend mistakes they and others made during house staff training and in practice at various time frames. The relationship between their perspectives on and experiences with malpractice lawsuits and mistakes is revealed; in particular, how they attempt to prevent adverse outcomes whether defined by themselves or adjudicated by external reviewers inside and outside the medical profession. Their perspectives on and encounters with "peer review" are presented, touted as the method for ensuring patient and public protections from harm they might cause. Finally, the chapter concludes with how they respond as "expert witnesses" in cases against other physicians.

Chapter 7—The Physicians on Health Regulations, Reimbursement, and Reform

This chapter presents the physicians' views of the rules and regulations governing their practice from the early phase (1980–1984) and their experience with government and private insurers imposing constraints on their autonomy for the sake of accountability. It also documents how the various presidential proposals for health care coverage and insurance were received in different decades as they anticipated changing policies and procedures, experienced them in real time, and projected solutions for health care reform.

Chapter 8—Vulnerability from Within: Hidden Revelations about Disillusionment, Cynicism, Fear of Failure, and Self-Doubt

This chapter is a deeper, more intimate examination of cynicism and self-doubt, topics that are rarely found in the literature. It includes a probing in-depth focus on the role of the hospitalist position and the advent of the electronic medical record not only on their own academic or community practice but also more broadly. It also examines how these structures have affected their doctor-patient relationship, their subspecialization of internal medicine, and the new generation of physicians.

Chapter 9: The Personal and the Professional: The Interaction between Private Lives and Public Postures

This chapter probes the cohort's private lives, with an emphasis on how personal relationships affect their professional development and career trajectories. It emphasizes their domestic and family life over time. By the ending phase (2011–2016), it scrutinizes the role of their wives in affecting their decisions about their residency program, setting, community, and practice. And finally, it presents their self-admitted illnesses and disabilities they or their spouses have suffered as they aged, sometimes revealed long after those first occurred, and sometimes newly acquired in the decade when they were being interviewed.

Chapter 10—Physicians' Happiest and Unhappiest Times, and Their Wishes and Misses throughout Their Careers

This chapter reveals their emotional state beyond satisfaction and dissatisfaction at all six career phases. Looking back from later vantage points, what were the highlights, pinnacles, and nadirs as they experienced them and as they put them in perspective later? The chapter also explores their existential responses to their feelings about "the roads not taken." By choosing medicine in general and their particular career path, what do they miss, and what do they wish? What were the things they omitted, sacrificed, ignored? And finally, this chapter explores their responses to questions asked at the ending phase (2011–2016), about any regrets. Ultimately, at or near retirement, their reflections are telling and, at times, poignant.

Chapter 11—Conclusion

The conclusion chapter recaps some of the key findings, lessons learned, and broader implications of this project.

Meet the Doctors

How do these physicians trace their career trajectory? What are the major factors that affected their chosen professional paths? How many of their short-term and long-term goals were based on deliberate, proactive decision-making (made by design), and how many were fortuitous, based on a chance encounter or a particular circumstance (made by default)? Were there any patterns to this cohort's choices based on their personal or academic background, family circumstance, or external societal events?

This chapter presents their brief biographies in their own words. Their career choices will be presented in a Q&A format so that readers can get to know them personally and answer the following questions:

- When and why did they choose medicine?
- Why did they choose the specialty of internal medicine?
- How important was their choice of SAMS as their internal medicine residency program?
- When and why did they choose a subspecialty (or why did they not choose one)?
- Why did they select an academic or community medicine setting?
- Why did they change locations or institutions at various career stages (if they did)?

The cohort was also asked to identify milestones in their professional lives at different stages. Here the reader will learn about those transformative moments that may be linked to circumstances and opportunities in their careers or beyond. Finally, they were asked at different phases if they could picture themselves doing something else as they looked back over their careers. Their responses reveal a sense of their commitment to medicine as well as fantasies about alternative lifestyles and pathways. They also reveal some of the motivations behind their choices, and the meaning and consequences of those choices for their career trajectories.

The physicians are presented alphabetically by last name—the academic physicians (AP) are presented first, and then the community practitioners (CP) are presented. The comments from the physicians are drawn from different interview cycles. (The corresponding date for each comment is presented in parentheses before the related text.)

At the end of the chapter, I analyze in more detail some of the notable revelations that surfaced in later stages of their careers as they discussed their motivations and the reality of their professional lives. (The names of the institutions have been disguised, and the locations where they settled have been generalized to a region of the country. Their specialties are real because these relate directly and indirectly to the choices they made.)

The Physician Cohort

Table 1 describes the subspecialty and setting for each physician over the six phases of their careers. Their names, cities, and other institutions are disguised. However, their specializations and type of settings are factual because these factors are essential for understanding the evolution of their career tracks. The term *practice* is used to connote their sets of job responsibilities. The term *community* is preferred to *private* practice, because the former connotes the setting where they practice medicine outside a university/academic institution. *Private* is inaccurate since most of those in community settings receive many of their fees and funding from the federal and state governments.

Academic Physicians (AP)

Kyle Annas (AP, Cardiology)

Choosing medicine? (1984) I have a framed essay hanging in my office that I wrote in the third grade: "I want to be a doctor." I had no idea what that meant at the time; I never went through that phase of wanting to be a fireman or a policeman. I always wanted to be a doctor. In college, I took premed courses and applied to medical school. It was pretty straightforward.

Choosing internal medicine? (1984) I flirted with surgery in medical school; it seemed glamorous, but then I realized thinking was more fun. I found pediatrics depressing. I liked the intellectual stimulation of internal medicine, and I liked the faculty and peers I worked with. The attendings [faculty physicians] were down to earth, not mean or derogatory compared to surgeons, who were just doing it without thinking.

Choosing SAMS? (1984) My first choice was a medical school in the same state where SAMS was located. But I didn't get in. Not sure if it would have made a difference if I went to another institution. I wanted to go to the other school for the wrong reasons—for prestige—and my friends were going there. (1994) The cost of an in-state school was hugely advantageous. SAMS didn't prepare me for academic medicine, but I would recommend SAMS, absolutely.

Choosing cardiology? (1984) I like pathophysiology, and at the time cardiology was a discipline that had a clear, defined one. Plus, I enjoyed my experience on that rotation.

Choosing an academic setting? One milestone was the offer I received from an academic department of medicine in a university in the Midwest after I did a fellowship at SAMS that I couldn't resist. There was no way I could have gotten the facilities, staff, and grants at SAMS, but it was difficult for my wife to move

Table 1   Career Stages of Physicians: Subspecialty/Setting

Physicians	Practice Setting	Entry Phase (1979–1980)	Early Phase (1980–1984)	Established Phase (1984–1994)	Entrenched Phase (1994–2004)	Extended Phase (2004–2011)	Ending Phase (2011–2016)
Annas	AP	Cardiology[a]	Cardiology/A	Cardiology/A/M	Cardiology/A	Active	Active
Boswell	AP	Rheum[a]	Rheum/A[a]	Rheum/A[a]	Rheum/A[a]	Active	Active
Finast	AP	Pulmonary[a]	Pulmonary/A[a]	Pulmonary/A[a]	Pulmonary/A[a]	Semiactive	Retired
Lash	AP	GIM	GIM/A	GIM/A[a]	GIM/Acad.Admin[a]	Active-M	Active-M
O'Brian	AP	Nephrology	Nephrology/A	Nephrology/A/M	Nephrology/A/M	Active	Active-M
Paul	AP	GIM[a]	GIM/A[a]	GIM/A[a]	GIM/Acad.Admin[a]	Deceased	Deceased
Polikoff	AP/CP	ID[a]	ID/A[a]	GIM/C (HMO)	GIM/C (HMO)	Active	Active
Rosen	AP	Nephrology	GIM/A[a]	GIM/AM	GIM/A	Active	Active-M
Strelko	AP	Oncology[a]	Oncology/A	Oncology/A	Oncology/A	Active-M	Active
Allen	CP	Cardiology[a]	Cardiology/C	Cardiology/C	Cardiology/C	Active	Active-2016
Beech	CP	Nephrology[a]	GIM/Nephrology/C	Nephrology/C	Nephrology/C	Semiactive	Semiactive/2016
Cahn	CP	GI[a]	GI/C	GI/C	GI/C	Active-M	Active

Conley	CP	GI[a]	GI/C	GI/C	GI/C	Retired (2010	Retired
Jarvis	CP	GI	GI/C	GI/C	GI/C	Active	Retired (2015)
Johnson	CP	Oncology[a]	Oncology/C	Oncology	Oncology	Active	Semiactive
Lynch	CP	Oncology	GIM/Oncology/C	Oncology/C-M	Oncology/Hospice/C	Active-M	Semiactive-M
Melone	CP	Nephrology	Nephrology/C	Nephrology/C	Nephrology/C	Active	Retired (2013)
Nolan	CP	GIM	GIM/C	GIM/Geriatrics/C	GIM/Geriatrics/C	Active	Semiactive
Ross	CP	Oncology	GIM/Oncology/C	GIM/Oncology/C	GIM/Oncology/C	Active	Active
Mahoney[b]	Non-IM	Non-IM	Non-IM	Non-IM	Non-IM	Active	Retired

Note: A = academic; C = community; GI = gastroenterology; GIM = general internal medicine; ID = infectious disease; M = moved (either changed position or setting or both); Rheum = rheumatology.

[a]Southern Area Medical School (SAMS) is the institution where these physicians did their fellowships, and some remained in an academic career track. Superscript "a" indicates that they did their fellowship in an academic institution other than SAMS, or left academia.

[b]This physician left internal medicine for another type of medical position.

since we always lived in the South. Other milestones were my decision to choose clinical medicine rather than an NIH-funded research career and getting my first paper accepted for publication.

Career changes? (1994) By 1990, I had moved from the university in the Midwest to a university in the northern Midwest in another state, which was a transformative moment. I needed to make the change. I wanted to make a name for myself.

Choosing an alternative career path? (2011) Architecture. I've always enjoyed drafting. Just a fantasy.

Peter Boswell (AP, Rheumatology)

Choosing medicine? [Not revealed.]

Choosing internal medicine? (1984) When I started Central State Medical School in the Midwest, I thought I was going to be a family doctor in a small town back in a plains state where I am from. Then as a third-year student, I met a guy who was in the medical school program. Until I met him, I thought internal medicine people were arrogant jerks. He was reasonable and bright. I decided it was the most intellectual of the subspecialties.

Choosing SAMS? (1984) SAMS made a difference in my career choices. If I stayed at that prestigious medical school in the Midwest, I might have been turned off to academia—too high pressured, too competitive, and cutthroat. Here at SAMS, you could have intellectual stimulation and still be a nice person! I would choose SAMS today because there are younger, more diverse attendings. At SAMS I received good training in general internal medicine. (1994) Going into research and the lab was a milestone. My choice of academic medicine happened during residency. I had lots of fun as a chief resident.

Choosing rheumatology? (1984) It is close to the field of immunology in terms of basic research. Getting a fellowship in that subspecialty at SAMS was a milestone. I like the long-term patient relationships and the ability to apply immunology to a particular field of medicine. There was no role model. I also considered nephrology but ruled it out because of the uncertainty of research and the time demands of patients on dialysis. I ruled out the intensive care unit, thinking it would be mostly having patients die. At least with rheumatology, the disease may not go away, but some patients get better. I have no regrets.

Choosing an academic setting? (1994) When I was an intern, I thought I'd go into general internal medicine. But then I became turned off because of the demands of patients. In Central State, general MDs have no life at all, on call twenty-four hours a day. Academic medicine is most intellectually satisfying and a better lifestyle. My home life is more satisfying. I can do reading at home, rather than being in the hospital sixty to ninety hours per week. In the middle of my second-year residency, I chose academic medicine. (2004) I became division head at SAMS and have stayed here. (2011) My career at SAMS has gone downhill. It's painful.

Choosing an alternative career path? (2004) I could have seen myself being a history professor.

Jacob Finast (AP, Pulmonary Medicine)

Choosing medicine? (1984) My vision when I chose medicine was that I could be like my doctor, who used to take care of me as a kid. He was a GP. All I remember was him coming to my home and giving me shots. I guess that was preventive medicine. The image remained.

Choosing internal medicine? (1984) As a medical student, by the third year, I was going around saying, "I don't like this or that specialty." I chose internal medicine because the role models were closest to what I saw in myself. For example, I saw a surgeon walk into a patient's room and say, "I'm Dr. X and I'm going to cut off your leg!" I couldn't identify with that. I appreciate doctors who contemplate how something affects patients. The drama of surgery was an attraction, but I like the other approach better. OB-GYNs demean their patients. Pediatrics is too frightening; those kids are so sick. The peers that I loved in internal medicine all seemed happy with their lot and genuinely compassionate. I said, "I want to do that."

Choosing SAMS? (1984) I joined a medical organization and went to investigate lung diseases among coal miners for two years. (2011) I shifted to SAMS city, partly because my wife was looking for a town that had a graduate program in her field. We weeded out the big cities; fortunately, SAMS wanted us.

Choosing pulmonary medicine? (1984) I first got interested in pulmonary medicine in Appalachia. When I got to SAMS, there was a good teacher in pulmonary medicine who made it very exciting. It was fun to think about taking care of people who were critically ill and bringing them back to health, saving their lives. And the team concept working in an ICU was very attractive. And the hours didn't seem so bad. (2011) Another milestone was my participation in a pulmonary organization that has been supporting patients for the last ten years. (2016) I also became interested in terminal ICU care because of end-of-life conversations with patients or families.

Choosing an academic setting? (1984) I became a chief resident at SAMS. It was an honor and formative in my career path. The best part was working with the house staff. It was lots of fun, and I got another year's experience. A lot of people in private practice don't have the opportunity to bounce ideas off and share thoughts with peers and those more experienced. Community practitioners spend so much time going from exam room to exam room—I don't think I ever considered that strongly. Academic medicine is intellectually stimulating. I enjoy teaching and recognizing when the students and residents see the light.

Choosing an alternative career path? (2011) My original plan when I first started was to work until I was fifty-five and then establish a second career. Well, fifty-five came and went a long time ago. No, I couldn't imagine doing anything else. I think I made the right choice.

Douglas Lash (AP, no subspecialty)

Choosing medicine? (1994) I was a psychology major in college in the Vietnam era. It just seemed like the world was a garden, and I could choose anything

I wanted to do. Little did I know I couldn't. There were too many temptations in college; I didn't get into one public southern medical school, but I got into another one in that state, although it was not as prestigious.

Choosing internal medicine? (1984) The first milestone was in my third year of medical school; I figured out that I could communicate, plus I had ideas for primary care. My lifestyle made me feel comfortable in internal medicine. I chose it because of my peers. What they did outside of medicine was important—they played instruments, hiked; their humor was my humor. I couldn't get surgeons' jokes, plus, outside, they liked to repair cars. When you are spending 120 hours per week with peers, you want to fit in. (2011) I love the field itself: I like puzzles, thinking strategically, and making diagnoses.

Choosing SAMS? (1994) I was at another public southern medical school, and I wanted to stay, but I didn't do that well. SAMS was my second choice. Years later, I was asked to be chief resident at SAMS. It wasn't a popular job, but I knew I didn't want private practice, or a subspecialty, and you did have some power in that role. I liked that. It was a milestone where I honed my skills in communication media and resurrected my interest in behavioral health.

Choosing an academic setting? (1984) Sometimes I wish I did choose a subspecialty. I'm not sure I would have enjoyed anything more than internal medicine. I thought I wanted academics or to hit the road and work in an ER. Now I'm realizing that I have some skills in leadership and administration. I could have gone into practice right after completing the chief residency. I was single and footloose and didn't care about money or the future, so I did this fellowship at another southern medical center. That was a milestone. (1994) When you met me at that public medical center in 1984, I was resistant to becoming an administrator. There was responsibility with no authority. It was stressful, but then I had a child and my wife wanted to move. I was offered a leadership job at SAMS in 1990 and so I went back there.

Career changes? (2004) I have been back at SAMS for many years using my strengths as an administrative leader. Then this opening came up at SAMS to direct a group practice, a real power position. I love my job and my personal life a lot. (2016) A few years ago I left SAMS. I took a position at a statewide health system in a midwestern state. They made me an offer I couldn't refuse.

Choosing an alternative career path? (1984) I'd choose something that allowed me some freedom. The grass is always greener.

Harry O'Brian (AP, Nephrology)

Choosing medicine? (1984) I became interested in premed in college as I was interested in science, but I really was unaware of what doctors actually did. I thought it was an interesting profession, and then once I got to medical school I was hooked.

Choosing internal medicine? (1984) It was the role models. I liked the people. I liked the thinking that went into internal medicine, the problem solving. I also liked surgery and being in the lab, but I liked the intellectual aspects of medicine more, plus I liked caring for patients. As my career developed, I grew to like taking care of patients longitudinally.

Choosing SAMS? (1984) A milestone was at the end of my residency when you feel like a doctor and then you pass the internal medicine boards. That's a milestone as a recognition of what I accomplished. (2016) Looking up and down the East Coast, SAMS was my second or third choice, and that's where I got matched. SAMS influenced my career in that I interacted with a couple of faculty who influenced my decision to go into nephrology. SAMS did not hurt my career path, and it helped me learn to be a doctor. A milestone was finishing as a chief resident; I was proud of what I had done at SAMS.

Choosing nephrology? (1994) I got interested in nephrology because of the specific role models in nephrology. I liked the science. Then I got interested in a specific kidney disease because of those role models and mentors. I linked my clinical interests with my research interests and that led to my career development.

Choosing academia? (1984) As far back as residency training, I got interested in being an academic. After SAMS, I did a fellowship at a university in the Northeast and stayed there for three years. That was a milestone.

Career changes? (1994) I moved over to another university in another northeast city as a junior faculty member after three years. I was there through the 1980s, and then I moved crosstown to another academic university medical center to be chief of nephrology. (2011) After a few years, I moved to a southern state medical academic complex to become chairman of medicine, a final milestone.

Choosing an alternative career path? (2016) Now that I've been leading a department, I could see myself doing management in a field outside medicine. Twenty years ago, I really didn't know what I was getting into. But, once I got into medicine, I liked the administrative aspects.

David Paul (AP, Oncology)

Choosing medicine? (1984) I was in college, and it was the Vietnam War. I was making private agreements with God that if I got into med school, I would devote my life taking care of African tribes. I was a Peace Corps–type liberal. I looked down my nose at academics and subspecialists. I thought office-based general practice was where it was.

Choosing internal medicine? (1984) When I came to medical school, I thought I wanted to be a primary care practitioner, and that never changed. My first two years in medical school, I was miserable. I wasn't an academic type. (1994) My first milestone was in my third year of medical school when I got my confidence up and I made my decision. I was born an internist. I feel strongly that every specialty has certain requisite personality traits, and you gravitate toward that specialty that suits your temperament. Internists tend to be careful thinkers to the point of being overly compulsive. They tend to be broad minded, liberally educated people who like dealing with patients. It's like being a detective and it is for those who don't like to use their hands.

Choosing SAMS? (1984) I chose SAMS because it was heavily oriented to patient management. Coming from another medical school in a different state, SAMS was my third choice. I would choose SAMS again, but I wouldn't have anticipated doing administrative tasks. I was asked to be chief resident when I finished. My first milestone was my residency years. I wanted a med-peds (pediatrics) residency program but didn't get in. Next was the chief residency year, a milestone. It was the best year of my professional life in every way.

Choosing an academic setting? (1984) I got the reputation in my junior residency for being a teacher. Choosing an academic setting was not so much against private practice, but a move more toward academic administration. I never had the confidence in my own knowledge. I never thought I could be a good teacher and would not have stayed in academia except for the dean who said my talents would be wasted in practice.

Career changes? (1984) I'm getting tired of being responsible for other people, and I'm going to decide whether to keep this administrative job. I'm being put on the spot to defend myself. The system is highly politicized. (1994) I was told my services are no longer needed as director of the

SAMS residency program. A milestone was heading a special VA program. I learned how hospitals worked. I became a member of the national program directors' program to get a wider perspective. The next milestone was this prospective deanship. It's going to be a big one. (2004) That's been the history of my career, cycles when I lay low and just practice, and then come back into a leadership role in the future.

Choosing an alternative career path? [Dr. Paul never discussed this in his interviews.]

Bill Rosen (AP, No Subspecialty)

Choosing medicine? (1984) In the second or third year in college, when I was working with emotionally disturbed children, medicine crossed my mind. I saw what doctors could do to make a difference. (2011) It was probably a combination of wanting to do good and not wanting to go to Vietnam as to why I'm a doctor. I was deferred, but that was absolutely a factor. Everybody my age who doesn't say that is pretty dishonest.

Choosing internal medicine? (1984) In third-year medical school at SAMS I found out I was an internist. Five days into my medicine rotation, I fell in love with it because of a resident who was a role model. It's a chance to be a detective, a therapist, and do something different every day. I can't imagine anything else as satisfying both intellectually and emotionally. But I also wanted to study kidney diseases, and I got a renal fellowship at another southern medical center but realized my mistake in six months. I disliked the research, so my first milestone was to follow my own instincts then. I decided I want to work with people, so I quit the fellowship and returned to SAMS in general internal medicine.

Choosing SAMS? (1984) SAMS was the best house staff program I could get into and I wanted to stay in the SAMS city since I moved there at sixteen. Being at SAMS made all the difference in my career track.

Choosing an academic setting? (1994) After that research experience, I worked in an ER for a while and came back to SAMS as a chief resident. For sure that was a milestone. I became an academic general internist by default. (2011) I found out that primary care medicine is a great field. At SAMS I became program director of house staff training and division director and assistant professor of primary care—those were all milestones. I have done research since in one specific primary care disease that made me famous.

Changing career? (2004) Moving to another southern state medical center was another milestone in 1994. I received an offer to go with the chair of the department of medicine to that other state. It was good for my mindset and everybody else's. The day I went to that program, people looked at me differently. I became a dean at one of its branches in 2004 and have been there until now. (2011) Moving to this southern state was one of my big milestones.

Choosing an alternative career path? (2016) As you well remember, when I was applying, it was medical school or the jungle. I can't tell you how much I disliked the first two years of medical school. But then in my third year, I found out I was an internist five days in. I can't imagine anything else.

Benjamin Strelko (AP, Oncology)

Choosing medicine? (2011) There are no MDs in my family; I've never been sick. I gravitated to science and chemical engineering in college. Then I took summer jobs at a hospital, first as a janitor with real mops, and then as an orderly. I did a lot of enemas and catheters. The hospital environment was fun and interesting. So, I switched to premed, and I never looked back.

Choosing internal medicine? (1984) In medical school, I liked surgery but didn't like surgeons. I couldn't picture myself with that identity. There was a certain locker room mentality with obnoxious attitudes. The medicine guys seemed much more intellectual and more interested in teaching and viewing patients as people. I concluded that my personality was more suited to it.

Choosing SAMS? (1984) I got accepted to an elite residency program in the Midwest and considered it because it had a better reputation. Then a friend told me about SAMS. I visited it, enjoyed it, and stayed. At the program in the Midwest there was too much theory and research and not much practicality—a true ivory tower. SAMS had more general medicine. The interns of the midwestern elite school were always swallowing down Maalox and worrying about where they would do their fellowships. At SAMS people worked hard but seemed to enjoy themselves more. The SAMS residency program as a whole was a milestone, a very intense three-year period where I gained confidence in myself.

Choosing oncology? (1994) Many people pick a specialty based on a small number of role models. The same doctor role model who influenced me to go into medicine influenced me to do oncology. I liked that it combined clinical research with seeing patients. As house staff, you defer your maturity by choosing a subspecialty fellowship. After the SAMS residency, I spent nine months as an instructor at SAMS. The frustrations were that every patient had social problems that I couldn't fix. So that's when I decided on oncology and got a fellowship in a New England medical center and stayed there for twelve years.

Choosing an academic setting? (1994) I thought after the fellowship I'd go into private practice, but then I realized that private practice oncology was not good for the treatment of most common cancers. I couldn't imagine charging a lot of money for toxic ineffective drugs. I was invited by the oncology division director to do research at the New England program. Then a faculty position became available in the Midwest, and I went there in the late 1990s.

Career changes? (2004) I've been at this New England medical center for twelve years; I'm not sure if I want to continue. There are frustrations, low salaries. I am getting other offers from some prestigious programs in the Midwest, where I would make twice as much money with less hassle. (2011) A milestone was my recruitment to this Midwest medical center to be head of a national clinical trials cancer group. I took it and became a specialized cancer doctor, also running the fellowship program, and stayed for seventeen years. (2016) I moved back to a different state in the Northeast to take an academic position at a cancer center a few years ago, where I still am.

Choosing an alternative career path? (1984) I could see myself doing surgery or outside of medicine, teaching German. (1994) From an intellectual perspective, I could do psychiatry. Or education administration. (2016) I think I'm at an age where I could picture myself doing things not related to medicine, like volunteering in a literacy program or Habitat for Humanity.

Community Practitioners (CP)

Michael Allen—(CP, Cardiology)

Choosing medicine? (2011) In college as a chemistry major, I thought I could become a chemist, but then maybe I'll go to medical school and become a research doctor in chemistry. With a draft number of sixty-five, if I didn't go to medical school, I'd go to the Army, and that played a bit of a role, honestly, in my career choice.

Choosing internal medicine? (1984) My wife always teases me that I had a hero of the month. When we were doing OB-GYN, I'd come home and say, "I want to be an OB-GYN doctor." And then the next month I'd be doing gastroenterology, and I'd say, "I want to do GI." And that's when I decided on internal medicine. It was so broad. My first night on call by myself was a milestone. I look back and say, "I survived that and I'm still there." You build character in those nights.

Choosing SAMS? (1984) I did my internship, residency, and fellowship all at SAMS because my wife had a teaching job in the SAMS city. We had a house, family was nearby, so I didn't want to leave the state. I looked at another residency program which was my first choice, but I wasn't accepted. My expectations at SAMS were pretty much what I anticipated.

Choosing cardiology? (1984) When I came out of medical school in 1980, heart catheterizations were going crazy. Doctors were opening up heart cath labs all over the place, which patients wanted in the SAMS city. I didn't want to do caths, so pretty much nobody wanted me there.

Choosing a community setting? (1984) Another city in the SAMS state where I grew up had a 350-bed hospital and no cardiologist for sixty miles. The administrator called me to come and look around. So that's how I ended up here, and I've enjoyed it. (1994) That was the biggest decision, coming back to my home community. I joined one guy who was by himself with another doctor, and then he added a couple more. The deal was really ugly for us and really good for him. After several years we broke away and formed our own group. That was a big milestone.

Choosing an alternative career path? (2016) Twenty or thirty years ago, I'd probably be a lab geek. I always said I could be a teacher except for when the students didn't do what they were supposed to. I'd go berserk! Still, teaching patients is the only other thing that I've really enjoyed.

Timothy Beech—(CP, Nephrology)

Choosing medicine? (1984) I don't know why I became a doctor. My father was a doctor. I wanted to be a marine biologist, but there weren't many doctoral programs in that field, so medical school was the only other option. I wish I had a better inkling before I became a real doctor. Not sure I would have chosen it, but I'm not sure what else I would have been doing. (2011) By the time I was getting ready to graduate college, grants for marine biology dried up, so what else do you do with a biology degree? I could be a teacher or go to medical school.

Choosing internal medicine? (1994) Early on I knew surgery was not for me. I'm not good with my hands, and rounding until 10 at night and then beginning at 4 A.M. was too much. I remember on one surgical rotation, finishing after midnight, and the resident said without batting an eyelash, "OK let's begin morning rounds." I didn't like babies so that left out obstetrics and pediatrics. Medicine was cerebral. A surgeon is all blood and guts, but the real doctor was Marcus Welby (a TV fictional personality) who could look at a patient like a puzzle and put it together.

Choosing SAMS? (1984) There's a thing called matching. I chose some higher- and some lower-ranked residency programs than SAMS, but SAMS chose me, so I went there. I was happy because I had some friends going there. I've seen my confidence grow as I gained more experience. But in some ways, I've been short changed. For example, in learning about the business side of medicine. If it wasn't for my partner, I would be lost. SAMS was a milestone. I stayed at SAMS from medical school through a nephrology fellowship. I remember the first night in the intensive care unit taking care of patients who were really sick. That was a milestone.

Choosing nephrology? (1984) I chose nephrology because of some interesting lectures and role models. That was a milestone. Nephrologists were welcomed by both surgeons and internists and in critical care units. I wanted to keep general internal medicine first and be a nephrologist second. It was the puzzle solving. I always thought you had to be a good generalist to be a good nephrologist. There are so many kidney diseases that affect other body systems.

Choosing a setting? (1984) I picked private practice instead of academics because my father was in private practice. I wanted to get out into the real world. I got my compassion and caring values from my dad. I moved back to my city in SAMS state where I grew up. My real confidence came when I began my private practice. It transforms you. That was a milestone.

Choosing an alternative career path? (2011) Doing nothing if I win the lottery or being independently wealthy. I don't know what else I would have done, to be sure.

Daniel Cahn (CP, Gastroenterology)

Choosing medicine? (1984) I knew I wanted to be a doctor for a long time. I went to a small college in the North because it had a high rate of acceptance to medical school. I got into a prestigious mid-Atlantic academic medical school where I was extremely happy. And I got married in my last year in medical school to my first wife.

Choosing internal medicine? (2011) I wanted to be a pediatrician, and then I went through a pediatric rotation, and I realized you weren't taking care of the children, you were taking care of their parents—bad news. And then I thought I was going to be a surgeon, and I realized that I didn't want that stress of having to make on-the-table decisions. In med school, there were GI specialists who were my role models. I was a frustrated surgeon, so I liked GI because it had procedures. I liked cardiology, but it's a pressure cooker to make life-and-death decisions so quickly. In GI you have time. I never wanted general medicine with all those runny noses.

Choosing SAMS? (1984) I did it for my first wife's career. She needed a professional program, so when I matched for SAMS, we went there reluctantly. I had no idea where it was, but it turned out to be a fantastic part of my life. (2004) A medical school in the mid-Atlantic offered me a residency, but my wife couldn't get into a program there. I knew I wanted GI, and an advisor told me SAMS had a good GI program. I knew I'd have a better chance of getting a GI fellowship if I went to SAMS for the residency. (2011) The SAMS residency was negative; I was away from family. I faced economic pressures, so I had to moonlight in a hospital, and that had a negative impact [on my experience].

Choosing gastroenterology? (1994) To become a gastroenterologist, you have to become an internist first. In my GI fellowship, I realized I didn't want to be in a lab for all my life. That was a big milestone because I was headed for academia; it was a tremendous maturing experience, although teaching was negative. My GI role models had been clinicians, not researchers.

Choosing a community setting? (1984) I was devastated, going from top of the heap at the mid-Atlantic med school to the bottom at SAMS, but it converted me from an academician to a non-academician, and from an idealized Marcus Welby (TV physician) to the practical business side of medicine. But my dream to remain at the mid-Atlantic school had been taken away. The next milestone was coming to this southern city in another SAMS state to practice GI. (2011) Next milestone was leaving that first job after six months and setting up my own practice in the same city. The next were taking my first partner, expansion into capitation, my divorce, the incredible growth of the practice, and a second marriage. I've been financially successful with a lifestyle I never would have had in academics; (but this southern city where I practice) is not the best place to live.

Choosing an alternative career path? (1994) Nothing else outside of internal medicine, but if not medicine, I'd probably be a lawyer.

Dennis Conley (CP, Gastroenterology)

Choosing medicine? (1984) My grandfather was an army doctor and my inspiration. I disliked biology and science. But I admired my grandfather. So, I eventually chose medicine and was accepted to a university in a southern state. (2011) I knew I wanted to be a doctor when I was a teenager.

Choosing internal medicine? (1994) It was the process of eliminating specialties that I didn't like. (2011) When I was a medical student at a university in a southern state, I wanted to go into surgery, and then I thought I wanted to go into OB-GYN. I rejected the surgical rotation when I saw what they did and how long they worked. I decided I wanted to do internal medicine.

Choosing SAMS? (2004) I applied to many residency programs in the South and was matched to SAMS—my second or third choice. It had a fairly good department of medicine that was improving. Also, there was a lot of pathology there. Getting through the internship was the biggest milestone in my life. After that, you feel like you can do just about anything, though I still have a lot of self-doubt.

Choosing gastroenterology? (1984) I did a year of a GI fellowship at SAMS. I learned early that GI is not all fun and glamor. I went from idealism to realism. I chose GI out of the process of elimination. I didn't like leukemics or people with COPD. I thought I could do a lot more for GI patients. General internal medicine didn't appeal to me—too broad. I also liked the GI faculty and fellows in medical school. They were role models. (2011) There were more organs to learn about—the liver, the intestines, the stomach. More interesting than just the heart. This whole idea of being able to use an endoscope was new back then and was fascinating.

Choosing a community setting? (1984) I had a two-year medical obligation in the military in another southern state, where I did some teaching and enjoyed it more than I thought. I did some clinical research, but my primary responsibility was for patients. I knew I was going into private practice and got a flavor of private practice in the clinics. (1994) My residency roommate was from my southern city, where his dad was a medical administrator. He told me there was someone practicing GI by himself who was looking for a partner; my dad wanted me to come back near home, so it all worked out. But it was a big adjustment. Patients can be very demanding, and the buck stops with you. No going home at 5 P.M. like in the military. Getting through the first year of private practice when you realize you're over the hump was a big milestone.

Choosing an alternative career path? (2011) I remember thinking back then I was going to be a forest ranger or have some kind of outdoor job. As a kid, I always wanted to play professional sports. At that time, I couldn't have pictured myself as a doctor. (2016) Now I could picture myself doing something in the business world. Maybe I would have gotten an MBA instead.

Monty Jarvis (CP, Gastroenterology)

Choosing medicine? (1984) I was a biology major in college in a big northern city and decided pretty much from the get-go to be premed. I'm someone that doesn't like change, so I never changed! The first decision was where to go to medical school. I knew I wanted out of a big city, so I went elsewhere in the Northeast. It was important to get out of the house! (2016) I still remember the conversation with the draft board when I got a low number. My answer to having to report for the draft was, "I am in medical school." That wasn't the motivation, but it sure was a good deal! Finishing my second year in medical school and celebrating was another milestone.

Choosing internal medicine? (1984) I wanted to do peds, but I had a miserable rotation with creepy interns. I couldn't stand the people. Then I found camaraderie with people in internal medicine.

Choosing SAMS? (1984) SAMS was no better than any other place in terms of getting a job. You can be the best resident ever to come out of a training program, and it makes no difference when you go to practice. SAMS would have been a tremendous disadvantage for me if I wanted to go into academia. Finishing internship and residency were milestones. After having the hell knocked out of you, you actually have some time off. (2011) I wound up at SAMS by chance. I ranked it fifth, but now I'd rank it first. The South turned out to be a great experience. (2016) There was great training and great people at SAMS.

Choosing gastroenterology? (2011) You're exposed to certain people as a house staff. My chief of medicine was a liver doc, plus there were a lot of high-powered attendings in GI in the SAMS city. I was offered a fellowship at SAMS. I liked the idea of doing technical procedures; it was fun, plus the cognitive stuff. I almost did rheumatology, but GI had more interesting diseases. The next big milestone was to go to a medical center in the Midwest for a GI fellowship.

Choosing a community setting? (1984) Like anything else, it was pure chance. I wrote to every GI practice in the SAMS city. I could have practiced in the South, but they didn't want me. I'm like a chameleon, I can go anywhere. Then I received a letter from a solo physician saying he was looking for somebody in a Midwest city. So that's where I went. That was a big decision—a milestone. Over time, I was influential in growing our practice to be the biggest in that Midwest state. (2011) There were practice milestones along the way, helping to create a reputation and then becoming a big GI group, bringing together many small ones. We're better together, rather than competing.

Choosing an alternative career path? Driving harness horses! And within medicine, probably rheumatology.

Mark Johnson (CP, Oncology)

Choosing medicine? (2016) I probably chose it because of my mother's poor health. I was always taking her to the doctor, and she had great respect for physicians. I originally was interested in law, and she would frown. When I talked about medicine, she would light up. My wife also encouraged me. My number in the Vietnam draft was in the middle of the pack, but you weren't one hundred percent safe until you could get a deferment, which I did.

Choosing internal medicine? (1994) When I got up in the morning, I either looked forward to a rotation or hated it. I decided on internal medicine in my third year of medical school. (2011) As I was coming up, all the smart people went into internal medicine. Not to sound so egotistical, but I found that attractive. Now, smart people also choose dermatology because it's something you do during the day, then go home. People choose medicine based on lifestyle now. When I was coming up, internal medicine residencies were very competitive; now it's dermatology and ENT (ears, nose and throat) specialties.

Choosing SAMS? (1984) My lack of resources compelled my going to school in the state where SAMS was located and where I am from. I chose SAMS medical school and stayed in the city where SAMS is for personal and financial reasons; my wife was finishing up professional school in that city.

Choosing oncology? (1994) I made the medical oncology decision the same way—in my third year of medical school. There were role models, and I liked the challenge of taking care of cancer patients. It was a milestone. (2011) One of the reasons I went into medical oncology was because it was a new thing and there was a lot of research. President Nixon had declared a war on cancer. They were spending a whole lot of money, and it looked like treatments would get better.

Choosing a community setting? (1994) The next big milestone was to decide whether to do academics with another fellowship or private practice. I chose private practice because I liked the autonomy. I was tired of the institutional medical center. I settled on another city in the same state as SAMS because it had a medical community that was cooperative compared to the city where SAMS is located. And my wife's license was only good in that same state. I wanted to live close to where I worked and where my kids could go to public school. That was a major milestone, as was joining an oncology practice, and then the practice took off in 1986. There are also milestones in the treatments in medical oncology, like breast cancer, that changed my practice to an outpatient one.

Choosing an alternative career path? (2004) I started practice at twenty-nine years old, and the idea of doing it for many more years is questionable. Still, just because I've been at it for so long is not a reason to do it again. Lots of people change careers. I don't think I'll be in medicine in ten years.

Samuel Lynch (CP, Oncology)

Choosing medicine? (2011) Medicine was always an idea in my head from grade school. So by the time I was a junior in college, I took the MCAT, did reasonably well, and was accepted at a med school in the Midwest. I also thought about becoming a teacher because everybody in my family is in education, but it didn't click, so I started thinking more about medicine.

Choosing internal medicine? (2011) My decision to go into internal medicine was made when I was in medical school. I thought I'd be a family practitioner, taking care of kids and obstetrics—maybe with a little surgery. Then I started my clinical rotation and realized that I was only interested in adults. I was meant to do internal medicine by looking at other specialties, which were all negatives. I liked the intellectual side of internal medicine; it just fit with my personality and my needs. I liked thinking rather than doing.

Choosing SAMS? (1984) SAMS was my first choice of residencies because there were a lot of acute medical patients there, and that's where I matched. In medical school, there were an awful lot of esoteric problems as a big referral center. But a major deficiency was the lack of acute medicine, ICU care, and emergency room patients, so SAMS complemented med school. It worked out very well. (1994) I look back on three years of boot camp. Chronically fatigued, depressed, overworked, and overwhelmed. (2011) Having been at SAMS I got adequate training, but now I'd look for a residency with faculty who have a greater interest in teaching and patients than they did at SAMS.

Choosing oncology? (1994) I developed an interest in oncology because a couple of attendings whom I respected were excellent role models. Although I was angry all the time at SAMS, I learned a lot from them. (2011) The oncology faculty seemed to be the kindest, the smartest, and the best overall doctors. I wanted to be like them. I applied for a cancer fellowship in the West.

Choosing a community setting? (1984) I did a year of clinic and a year of research in my fellowship in the West. I decided I didn't like academics, so the only other alternative was oncology private practice, and I liked the patient contact. I liked living in the West, so location was part of my decision. I liked the people at the Western Academic Medical Center. I found a practice opportunity and stayed.

Changing settings? (2016) Since early on I've moved to more than three different practices. Moving to this western state and to different cities in the same state were all milestones. I tried different kinds of practice settings from a multispecialty group to solo practice to a single specialty group, to being a medical director of a hospice. They've each had pros and cons. Oftentimes it was frustrations with system or personality conflicts that caused me to move. Now, at the end of my career, I'm just part-time in a private practice, which I like at my stage.

Choosing an alternative career path? (2016) I don't know what else I could do. It was just the right thing for me. I kind of fell into it, and it worked out the way that it was supposed to.

Frank Melone (CP, Nephrology)

Choosing medicine? (2011) I decided to be a doctor when I was five years old. I made an early decision about becoming a surgeon before med school. I chose to become a surgeon because of a bad internship. (2016) With a low draft number it was important I get a deferment. Vietnam wasn't the reason to choose medicine, but it certainly made it easy to stick with.

Choosing internal medicine? (2016) Choosing internal medicine over surgery was a milestone! I decided against being a surgeon after a year because I thought most surgeons were idiots with hands. I couldn't stand anybody thinking about me, what I thought about most surgeons. Now that turns out not to be true, but that was my take on it then.

Choosing SAMS? (1984) When I came to SAMS, I intended to do primary care. SAMS made a difference in that a large university hospital made me feel good about my training compared to others trained in a small hospital. It did a lot for my ego. But objectively it is too much work for what you get back. I drove into the parking lot of the SAMS hospital one day, and admired all the classy cars, and then I thought, "It's 3 A.M. and every one of the MD owners is in the hospital!"

Choosing nephrology? (1994) I had a friend with end-stage renal disease, and I got interested in kidney diseases and dialysis. I went to another southern state program for a nephrology fellowship. That wasn't a good choice, in retrospect, since I wanted more clinical than research. (2011) I was interested in nephrology and cardiology, but I can't hear heart murmurs very well, so I nixed cardiology. I was too chicken to go out into private practice since I didn't know enough, so I continued with a renal fellowship with the idea of becoming a better internist.

Choosing a setting? (1994) I didn't want to raise my kids in that city of my fellowship. The force to choose private practice was that I always wanted to be my own boss. That was a milestone. The SAMS city was a good choice because I had been there before. (2011) A nephrologist who had been one of my professors heard I was in the SAMS city and asked if I would cover for him. When he wanted to sell his practice a few years later, I bought it and opened my own little shop. I was making a dollar and ninety-eight cents a year for several years! It was five years of slogging until I hired my first partner. And then the practice exploded. I realized that you could make a living doing "blood laundry." Renal took up more time and primary care less over time. (2011) There are financial milestones, such as signing with a lucrative dialysis firm. Then, when they needed a medical director here, I said, "OK."

Choosing an alternative career path? (2011) If not doing nephrology, I'd do any branch of internal medicine or invasive radiology. It has the appeal of surgery but is more nine to five and hospital based. Not sure I would do anything outside medicine, maybe teaching English in a liberal arts college.

George Nolan (CP, General Internal Medicine)

Choosing medicine? (1984) Being a doctor wasn't something I always wanted to do from the time I was little. But at some point, I applied and was accepted to SAMS

Medical School. The hardest part of going to medical school is getting in. (2016) It was graduate school or medical school. I majored in biology, but you can't do much with a BA in biology. And there was the Vietnam War with my high number—no good. And one exception to the military was medical school. There was a big call to produce more people in science. Having the Vietnam draft blood on my neck was significant in making me pick medicine.

Choosing internal medicine? (1984) As you start your clinical rotations, you realize what's interesting and what's not. I found pediatrics to be exceedingly depressing, all those dying kids with their incredibly stressed parents. Then I did my internal medicine rotation, and it was much more about problem-solving, a lot more fun and interesting. (1994) Many milestones: Setting foot in medical school, then working in a biochemical lab, doing my internal medicine rotation, graduating from medical school—choosing SAMS.

Choosing SAMS? (1984) When I looked at residencies, I wanted a place that was busy where I could teach and do things. It was a comfortable place having been there for medical school. I knew people, so I stayed. Milestones were getting accepted into the SAMS residency program and then getting asked to become chief resident. That was something special.

Choosing general internal medicine? (1994) When I left SAMS, I went into internal medicine practice. I did that for the first few years and then realized that the only part I really enjoyed was the older patients. At that time, you didn't need to be board certified in geriatrics. Eventually I took those boards, passed them, and limited my practice to geriatrics. I then started going to nursing homes as well; that was probably the biggest milestone. The attraction wasn't money since Medicare was a lower-payer provider. If you go into pediatrics or cardiology, there are a lot of smart people already. That's not the case with geriatrics.

Choosing a community setting? (2016) My wife is from a nearby city in the SAMS state, and at that time there was a placement service that matched physicians. I interviewed, liked the situation, and joined a small practice in that city. Another important milestone was surviving the first year, trying to build the practice, including coming here to this city and staying all this time.

Choosing an alternative career path? (2016) No, I couldn't imagine doing anything else. I think I made the right choice. You don't have to worry about anybody laying you off in private practice. It's a good career as long as you can manage the bad parts, like being on call.

James Polikoff (CP, Infectious Disease, General Internal Medicine)

Choosing medicine? (1984) My father was a doctor, and I always assumed I would be a doctor. I went to college to be a doctor; it was a natural thing for me to do.

Choosing internal medicine? (2011) When I had to choose a residency, I liked internal medicine. I didn't have the personality for surgery. I didn't like obstetrics; then I thought about being a pediatrician, but it's hard enough to see children suffer with diseases, and I was bothered by the effect on the parents. What drew me to medicine? I liked adults. I liked the puzzle solving and thinking. It fits my personality.

Choosing SAMS? (1984) I went to SAMS Medical School and stayed at SAMS. I ranked it seventh, but I didn't want to leave the SAMS city. I felt comfortable here. When I went to SAMS I was single, and my personal life was dictated by my work. If I was married and had kids, I would not have felt the sacrifice was worth it. Finishing internship was a milestone because of fears about whether I could handle the demands. (2016) I had very good training at SAMS.

Choosing infectious disease? (1984) I did an infectious disease fellowship at SAMS. Glad I did it to become really good in something. There was no reason to leave SAMS again. Infectious disease was a conscious choice because I liked the people in the department, and infectious disease involves every subspecialty in medicine, surgery, and OB-GYN.

Choosing a setting? (1984) I never imagined myself in this role as an infectious disease academic attending. I think everyone envisions going back to their hometown practicing medicine. Being a faculty member is a very high ideal, but I'm still not sure I feel it. If this position wasn't available, I'm not sure what I would have done. I might be leaving to join a large IM group practice. I don't like writing grants, seeing patients five days a week, plus presenting lectures and teaching. My wife wants to leave and find a place closer to her family. But if I go into private practice, I'll have less time, and I'll be working longer and harder.

Changing settings? (1994) I realized that I wasn't going to make it on an academic track, so I decided to look elsewhere in a community. (2011) My wife saw an ad for this HMO group in the New England area. She had family in that region. I ended up joining that group and inheriting a practice of one of the partners. I've been with that group ever since, and happy as ever.

Choosing an alternative career path? (2016) I haven't thought about it. I'm not a businessman-type. Medicine was the right thing for me; it fits my personality.

Richard Ross (CP, Hematology/Oncology)

Choosing medicine? (1984) I'm not sure how I chose medical school. I was an engineering major but didn't like that. I saw the Donna Reed TV show with an MD who I thought was a neat guy. There were no doctors in my family. I became an orderly in a hospital, and then I changed to premedicine in my third year of college. I got accepted to a university medical school in the South, and it didn't make a difference whether I went to a prestigious place or not. (2011) It was an interesting time—it was Vietnam draft time. Everybody was getting drafted, so I had to make an adult decision. I didn't want to be in the Army ROTC, and I thought I could get into medical school. In those days, it was a much larger decision than today. Getting into medical school was a milestone; that was the largest hurdle of all.

Choosing internal medicine? (1984) IM was my first medical rotation, and I knew I wanted it. Not sure if I did it because of a particular person or because I knew what I didn't like. I liked the brainy part of it. I liked to be one of the smarter guys. It is more intellectual; there were more thought processes than in a lot of other specialties.

Choosing SAMS? (1984) I applied elsewhere, but I didn't like them or else I had a crummy interview. SAMS was third on my list, but my only match, so I went by default. I was at another southern college medical school. SAMS made a difference, because I would have considered an academic track elsewhere, but not at SAMS. A milestone was finishing my internship; "I made it!"

Choosing hematology/oncology? (1984) I liked hematology a bunch, and my mentor in medical school was a hematologist. At the beginning of my third year in medical school, I finally decided. So, even before I knew what I wanted to do within internal medicine, I was interested in hem-onc (oncology).

Choosing a setting? (1984) After my residency I had aspirations of becoming an academic, but I wanted to come back to my southern city because of my mentor and because it was a nice place to live. In the middle of my fellowship, I realized I needed to get out of academics. I figured out I've been in school for twenty-four grades and had enough! A friend knew a physician looking for a partner. The irony is that I settled thirty miles away from where my wife and I grew up. My fellowship in that southern city, going into practice and figuring out where to settle were all milestones. (2011) I've stayed in this city, but now I do more internal medicine than hematology.

Choosing an alternative career path? (2016) I could have been an engineer. I aspired to that when I was younger.

Dennis Mahoney (Non–Internal Medicine)

Choosing medicine? (1984) I knew I wanted to be in medicine since the sixth grade. So, college and medical school were all in the cards since then. I went to medical school in a large northeastern city. (2016) Vietnam had an effect, although medicine was already my career path. In my junior year, I got a very low draft number. I was sure to go since five of six medical schools already rejected me; I got the draft mailgram August 28 from Uncle Sam—I still remember the day. I was set to report when I got the acceptance letter from the sixth northeastern medical school. Imagine!

Choosing internal medicine? (1984) One of my decision points was as a third-year medical student. I was thinking about surgery, but a surgical attending said, "You'll never be a surgeon; you're lefthanded—wrong side of the table." I know now that was not true, but he burst my balloon. I thought internal medicine would be a good place from which to start.

Choosing SAMS? (1984) SAMS was not my first choice for residency. It was fifth. I wanted the West Coast, but it didn't want me. I chose a hospital-based residency program in the same large northeast city as my medical school, but there were some administrative issues, and they rejected me. SAMS worked out for the best. I wouldn't have met my wife or had the kids if I went elsewhere.

Choosing a non–internal medicine career path? (1984) During medical school, I gravitated to the non–internal medicine services. If I had nothing to do on a

Saturday night, I would go to the hospital and volunteer. Then I got a moonlighting job working in a clinic, which I found dismal; I did not want the practice of medicine in an office. No way! I wanted to get out from under the wing of "mother institution" and out from under an academic center. (1994) A milestone was when I was fresh out of internal medicine residency and beginning practice when I passed the non-IM boards.

Choosing a setting? (1984) At twenty-five years old, our roots started to grow in the city where SAMS is located. I had been in school since age four or five, and I viewed residency like being in school. I wanted more independence. I got it at St. James Hospital in that same city; that was a milestone. And being in non-IM, I could go where I wanted. (1994) Getting through last year's contract dispute, without getting fired, were also milestones. (2004) I moved to LG Hospital because there was a medical change at St. James. I was dissatisfied, but I was living in the SAMS city and didn't want to move. I found LG Hospital. We agreed on a contract, and so here I am.

Choosing an alternative career path? (2011) I would have pictured myself doing something else in the field of medicine, twenty-five years ago. If I lost my legs or my hands and became disabled, I'd choose radiology, but still in medicine. Even earlier than twenty-five years ago? Maybe teaching.

The Timing and Rationale for Choosing a Medical Career: A Closer Look

Choosing Medicine

When examining the profiles of these twenty physicians, I noticed that decisions about their medical journeys did not seem to be predicated on when they decided to become a doctor. Six of the cohort (Drs. Annas, Conley, Melone, Polikoff, Cahn, and Finast) knew they always wanted to be doctors from an early age, although admitted they didn't understand the ramifications, while almost half didn't decide until their late college years (Drs. Beech, Rosen, Nolan, Mahoney, Allen, O'Brian, Ross, and Strelko). Most of this group had a predilection for or were on a science track. Drs. Johnson, Jarvis, and Lash, Lynch, and Paul were not fully committed to the medical profession until the time or even after they entered medical school.

For some of these physicians, the process of becoming a physician began when they were children, as Dr. Annas described. As they were growing up, Drs. Ross, Cahn, Beech, Finast, and Boswell had an idealized image of a physician based on fictional TV characters or their childhood memories of their family physician. Some mentioned specifically that they had their families invested in their decisions (Drs. Johnson, Cahn, and Mahoney). Seemingly unusual, a few identified a subspecialization they wanted to pursue so that internal medicine became a means to that end (Dr. Cahn, GI, and Dr. Ross, hem-onc). For Dr. Mahoney it was the path to a specialty outside of internal medicine once he was dissuaded from surgery. For the most part, their recollections about the reasons for their career decisions were remembered the same way throughout their career with one exception. As will be detailed later on in the chapter, an additional if not central rationale for a medical career included the possibility of being drafted for the Vietnam War.

Choosing Internal Medicine

In general, their choice of internal medicine was made both by default and design. More of the community practitioners seemed to emphasize their selection was made by rejection; that is, there was something off-putting about pediatrics, OB-GYN, and/or especially surgery. It was interesting that several were attracted to surgery at first and then rejected it because of the lifestyle and culture of the surgeons, rather than, or in addition to, the demanding multiyear residency program. Several mocked surgeons even to the point of caricature ("mechanics"; "doers not thinkers"). Their ridicule described by so many in the entry phase (1979–1980) and early phase (1980–1984) was still repeated by some when asked about their choice of internal medicine at the end of their careers. However, a few admitted that they had modified their views of surgeons in their later years to be more accepting, but not all of them. Those who had reasons for eliminating pediatrics all focused on the negative aspects of dealing with distressed parents as much as not wanting to handle dying children. "Too depressing" was a common lament. When asked at the end of the interview about alternative careers, only a few mentioned other subspecialties in medicine as a possibility.

Almost verbatim, all the academics and many of the community practitioners focused on the intellectual aspects of internal medicine, choosing it deliberately for the "thinking rather than doing" aspects of that discipline. They commonly likened the specialty to playing "detective" and being a problem-solver. And for many, it was this aspect that kept them wedded to the specialty (as described in many of the subsequent chapters). Among those who chose general internal medicine, like Drs. Rosen and Paul, the sentiment "I was born an internist" was commonly expressed.

Many admitted to having little to no sense of the scope and specifics of this large specialization until they were in their third year of medical school. It was often happenstance as to whom they interacted with on those clinical rotations that led to a specific field, with a few exceptions. Dr. Allen referred to having positive impressions about a number of specializations—what his wife described as him liking "the specialty of the month." Almost half specifically used the term "role models" or mentors as a major or compelling reason for choosing a specific subspecialization. The choice was based on personal interactions regardless of the subspecialization for Drs. Rosen, Finast, O'Brian, Strelko, Beech, Conley, Cahn, and Johnson. There seemed to be a "goodness of fit" in choosing internal medicine and/or one of its subspecializations.

Choosing SAMS

In terms of choosing SAMS for their residency, SAMS was not the first choice for most of the cohort, and for some, it wasn't any choice; rather SAMS chose them as part of the national residency matching programs (NRMP). Surprisingly, perhaps, a few found themselves at SAMS or in SAMS city, happy or not, because of their wives' professional education or career needs (Drs. Finast, Cahn, and Johnson).

In real time and in hindsight, many were satisfied with the SAMS selection because of the type of residency, defined collectively as one that was academic based but did not prioritize research over clinical training. Looking back, so many identified the opportunity to have a measure of autonomy to make patient care decisions as paramount, even though the trade-off was trepidation and the stress of being too much on their own. Given the fact that some merely accepted the idea of going to SAMS, while others felt relief at receiving any bid for a university-based internal medicine residency program, it is notable that very few vacillated or changed their minds once they got accepted. And over time, in the main, their recollection of how much they learned at SAMS improved. For the academics who oversaw residents as part of their job responsibilities, they began to empathize over time with the attending physician dilemma of needing to mediate between oversight and autonomy of house staff.

The importance of choosing SAMS was evident: it directly affected the long-term subspecialty outcome for so many who were exposed to myriad opportunities by their second year of residency. With the exceptions of Drs. Polikoff and Rosen, the subspecialty stuck. Dr. Polikoff left a SAMS academic infectious disease position after the early phase (1980–1984) for community practice, and Dr. Rosen left a renal research subspecialty fellowship after six months for an academic general internal medicine position back at SAMS. SAMS clearly had an impact in both directions—positive and negative—as to their choice of a university versus community setting. Some did not like what they were witnessing or experiencing at SAMS and so pursued a community practice path, including Drs. Lynch, Cahn, and Ross, while Drs. Boswell, Paul, and Strelko, who had envisioned a community setting before going to SAMS, ultimately decided on an academic career track. Dr. Lash was an outlier in not pursuing a specific medical area after SAMS residency, although ultimately he chose an administrative medical center track that brought him back to SAMS in a variety of roles for most of his career.

Choosing Subspecialty

For the many who completed a subspecialty fellowship by the early phase (1980–1984), there was an identity change as they shifted from calling themselves "internists" to identifying as a subspecialist (e.g., cardiologist, oncologist [Mizrahi, 1986]). They also reported losing their internal medicine acumen quickly postresidency as they concentrated on acquiring the competencies of their subspecialty through a fellowship; that is, they traded breadth for depth. And those who tried to do both found themselves quickly dropping one; Drs. Melone and Beech transitioned to a full-time nephrology career, while Drs. Ross and Polikoff transitioned to general internal medicine. Dr. Nolan narrowed his area to geriatrics, which became a recognized subspecialty after he had moved into practice in the early phase (1980–1984).

In looking back on their subspecialty choices at the ending phase (2011–2016), many reported how much more specialized their subspecialization had become, whether oncology, cardiology, or gastroenterology. They acknowledged that if they were beginning now, they would have to narrow their choices within their subspecialty even further. As they were ending their careers, many felt that they were losing ground and were out of touch even within their own discipline.

Choosing a Setting

Their choice of settings—whether academic or community—reflected a set of trade-offs and priorities. Most of the cohort recognized the balance among competing priorities. There were a few unanticipated career shifts for both trajectories. Most of the academics changed their setting to advance their career or seek other opportunities, including assuming administrative and leadership positions. However, at the beginning of their careers, hardly any academic identified an administrative or leadership role for themselves; Dr. Paul was an exception. Yet as they progressed, many more assumed those academic management roles (Drs. Rosen, O'Brian, Annas, Strelko, and Lash). At the same time, there were a number of community practitioners who also moved into managerial positions within their own settings—which was unanticipated by them and not revealed in the literature—as late as the entrenched (1994–2004) and extended (2004–2011) phases (Drs. Johnson, Melone, Cahn, Allen, Nolan, and Jarvis). Conversely, some gave up that role by the ending phase (2011–2016). They cut back on their management responsibilities as they moved toward retirement or became increasingly disaffected.

The proximity of their setting to SAMS, and to the city and state where SAMS was located, was notable; one could draw concentric circles around them with SAMS in the center. Drs. Paul, Boswell, Finast, and Lash stayed at SAMS for all or most of their career in a variety of positions. A few remained at SAMS, in the SAMS city or state for the early part of their careers (Drs. Rosen and Polikoff), and several others for their whole working lives remained in the SAMS state (Drs. Melone, Mahoney, Allen, Johnson, Nolan, and Beech). Dr. Allen located his practice back to his home community, because he could limit his practice to a type of noninvasive cardiology with no competition. Some went back to places they had lived earlier (Drs. Rosen and Cahn) or moved to other southern states (Drs. Ross and Conley). The rest (one-quarter) went to other parts of the country, usually beginning with the institution in which they did their subspecialty fellowship (Drs. Lynch, Jarvis, Annas, O'Brian, and Strelko). Dr. Lynch remained in the same western state but moved to several different practices and settings within it over his career.

Milestones

In looking back over their milestones, doctors expressed differences as to whether they incorporated their wives' lives or circumstances in their own decision-making. Several of the cohort went back to or settled near their home community in SAMS or region of the country because of their or their wives' family connections—sometimes by design and some by happenstance (Drs. Ross, Beech, Allen, Conley, Nolan, Johnson, and Polikoff). This was a particularly interesting revelation as the role of their wives was not directly asked until the ending phase (2011–2016). At times, their spouse was a determining factor in where they settled or whether they changed settings, notably for Drs. Finast, Cahn, Johnson, Rosen, Mahoney, and Polikoff. For some, changing practice settings conjured up important domestic deliberations. In a few cases, it clearly caused tension and even conflict, whether or not their spouses' views were a determinative factor in where they settled, especially for Drs. O'Brian, Cahn, Rosen, and Nolan. (The role of wives and family is discussed more fully in chapter 9.)

About two-thirds of the physicians incorporated personal and family factors in response to a question about professional milestones. Dr. Cahn commented, "My wife dragged me into going to SAMS reluctantly." Dr. Nolan also included his wife's short-lived career in his decisions: "A milestone during my OB-GYN rotation was meeting my wife. She worked as a nurse practitioner before the kids, and then stopped." Dr. Mahoney elaborated further: "I wouldn't have met my wife and had my kids if I went somewhere other than SAMS. And there were considerations of my wife who was working and wanted to stay in the SAMS city." Dr. Allen was emphatic: "My girl was born in 1979 when I was in my residency and my boy three years later at the beginning of my practice. That was more life changing than becoming a doctor." Dr. Beech, when asked about milestones, rather casually replied, "Well, your usual things: You get married. You have children."

The Role of the Vietnam War: The Big Revelation

In the extended phase (2004–2011) the spontaneous revelation about the role the Vietnam War played in the cohort's motivation for going into or remaining in medicine was astounding. More than one-third identified the prospect of being drafted as contributing to, if not a major reason for, becoming a physician. Except for Dr. Paul, who was the only one who suggested in 1984 that he was consumed with draft considerations in college, it had never been identified in earlier phases when general questions were about why they chose a medical career. I missed its significance at that time. Since I did not pick that up early, I did not ask a question to the cohort until the ending phase after it emerged extemporaneously in the extended phase (2004–2011). Numerous other doctors expressed similar sentiments, particularly as their careers moved toward final phases. Several of them, like Drs. Rosen and Ross, even acted as informants for their peers. Dr. Ross asserted that it affected every man's decision-making in that era, "whether they confessed it or not."

Chance clearly played a role as to whether they received a low or high draft number, and those draft numbers in turn affected the decisions for at least nine of the twenty, including Dr. Paul. A number of the doctors had low draft numbers, which meant a high likelihood of being drafted. Dr. Allen, who had the low number of sixty-five, said, "That probably played a considerable role, honestly," in his decision to pursue medical school. His use of the word *honestly* may be indicative of at least a modicum of shame that self-interest played a part of the enticement for a medical career, especially for those who had not thought of it seriously until then.

Because this added rationale was offered by almost half the cohort during the extended phase (2004–2011) as to why they chose medicine as a career, a specific follow-up question was added in the ending phase (2011–2016), if it was not volunteered: *Did the Vietnam War play any part in your decision-making?* Many responses were again unexpected because more of them denied the Vietnam connection, including some of those who had revealed it five years earlier.

Nevertheless, almost fifty years since medical school, the entire cohort recalled during the final interviews in 2016 their draft status and specifically their draft number, as well as other military-related experiences (e.g., the reserves, ROTC). Dr. Jarvis vividly recalled, "I was number fifty-one for the draft. While that wasn't the motivating thing, medical school was sure a good deal and a relief that I didn't have to go." Dr. Mahoney offered a passionate response as he recalled the anxiety associated with his low draft number. Like Dr. Jarvis above, his low number confirmed his choice of a medical career: "Vietnam was always there as the draft was instituted. Remember? I think I told you this. My lottery number was thirteen, so it was certain. I didn't decide to go into medicine in order to avoid the draft, but it was either go into medicine or get drafted." (He thought that he had described it to me before, but he hadn't.) Dr. Mahoney further recalled with precise detail and with emotion that particular day: "I had received rejection notices from five of the six medical schools in the summer of 1971. Then I got a mailgram notice from the military, 'Uncle Sam is calling you. Report for your preinduction physical.' I was in the process of getting drafted when Northern Medical School called with a spot for me. I remember the day because I was considering fleeing to Canada. We were either going to be drafted or got our 2S deferment for medical school, which I did."

It remains puzzling as to why only one of the cohort (Dr. Paul) raised the Vietnam War as a factor earlier in their career, or why there was a fluctuation in their memories in the way they interpreted the impact of that event on their decision-making in the later part of their career. It remains an area to explore further; perhaps the concept of "selective memory" is relevant for why there were varying interpretations of that same event when asked at a time period of more than forty years. Perhaps there was guilt involved, given that almost all of the cohort had been either alarmed or relieved about the prospect of going to war or not, depending on their draft status. It is likely that they recognized their privileged status in being able to opt out of the military, while so many other young men could not. Only one of the doctors asserted that he might have considered serving despite the draft deferral—Dr. Lynch, who had a brother in the military. He admitted that if he wasn't 4F (rejected) because of his asthma, he might have considered serving. Still, when he got a low draft number, he pointed out that "it took the pressure off."

Whether or not the possibility of being drafted into the Vietnam War played a critical or major role in their decision to pursue medicine at the beginning of their careers, once these doctors were in medical school, other important factors would continue to emerge to influence and impact their professional lives as they moved along their journeys toward physicianhood within the American medical system.

Each of the following chapters takes up in detail other important aspects of their professional lives while also highlighting how their careers intersected with the changing macrocosmic societal and professional environments in which they were embedded. What kept them engaged in such a demanding field throughout transformative and sometimes tumultuous times? Using their own words as much as possible, in the chapters that follow I provide the context, themes, and interpretations of their attitudes and self-reported actions over almost four decades.

3   *Satisfaction and Strains*

THE UPS AND DOWNS OF BEING A
DOCTOR, PART I (EARLY TO
MID-CAREER)

The next two chapters examine the overall career satisfaction and dissatisfaction of the physician cohort from the time they completed residency (1979–1980) until they were at or close to retirement almost forty years later. This chapter looks at the overall career satisfaction and dissatisfaction during the entry (1979–1980), early (1980–1984), and established (1984–1994) phases of their careers, while chapter 4 discusses the overall career satisfaction and dissatisfaction at the entrenched (1994–2004), extending (2004–2011), and ending stages (2011–2016). In addition to discussing the doctors' satisfaction and dissatisfaction as they moved through these phases, to help provide important historical context each chapter also examines some of the major and, at times, transformative changes in the medical profession that occurred around the timing of each interview cycle. In each chapter, that contextual framework affecting the medical profession is presented first, followed by a discussion of common patient-, peer-, and practice-related themes—similar to the three broad topical themes used by Dunstone and Reames (2001)—that emerged from the interviews.

These twenty White male physicians consider themselves to be largely reflective of the population of the U.S.-trained internal medicine house staff at the end of the 1970s. They are also typical of a group of physicians who chose a public, academic-based residency program like SAMS that focused on clinical practice and hands-on learning more than it did on large-scale academic research. By 2016 these academic and community practitioners were at or near retirement with an end in sight. Their individual and collective journeys in many ways tell the story of White male physicians' experiences in American (internal) medicine in the last third of the twentieth century through the first decade and a half of the twenty-first century.

Satisfaction and Dissatisfaction Themes

Over the last four decades or more, drastic changes in the financing, delivery, and organization of health care have affected physicians' career satisfaction, as well as their attitudes and behavior toward their patients, peers, practice, and the medical profession itself (Arnetz, 2001; Bury, 2004; Chehab, Panicker, et al., 2001). Yet differing perspectives remain about the quality, extent, and impact of corporate, government, and broader societal changes on the medical profession and on the lives of physicians who came of age during this period (Domagalski, 2005; Hafferty, 2006; Light, 2005; McKinlay and Marceau, 2005; Schlesinger, 2002; Starr, 2004). The cohort was directly and indirectly affected by the myriad societal and professional changes that were occurring and by projected trends.

The physicians regularly reflected on which and how macro level conditions affected their practice environment and, ultimately, their satisfaction and dissatisfaction with their career choice. Beginning with the early phase through the ending phase, they were specifically and systematically questioned in depth about the overall positive and negative aspects of their practice and asked specific questions about their satisfaction with five components of professional life: financial remuneration, intellectual stimulation, psychic/emotional satisfaction, satisfaction related to their own professional status, and the public's perception of the medical profession.

Queries were also made about whether they would recommend the practice of medicine to their children and whether they were optimistic or pessimistic about the future of the profession, both of which would be further cues to gauge their feelings about their career track and their profession more broadly. These seven factors constitute a Satisfaction Index that I with two colleagues calculated for each physician at each phase. These were then assigned to one of three categories—satisfied (positive), mixed (a combination of positive and negative), or dissatisfied (negative) as a result (see table 2).

Futurist questions, such as whether physicians would recommend medicine to their children or pursue it themselves all over again, as noted by Elliot (2006) and Zuger (2004), help gauge the extent and intensity of their perceived feelings about their own career choices and the future of their profession. A negative response as to whether they would recommend a medical career to an offspring could be viewed as a profound sense of disillusionment or lack of optimism about the future of medicine and its next generation. Unlike other questions, that one forces some self-reflection since all but one (Dr. Paul) had children. It was not merely hypothetical.

The questions were posed with the hope of uncovering their perspectives on their career trajectories at the time of the interviews, revealing their perspectives on this when looking into the past (retrospectively), and disclosing how they anticipate their own futures and the future of medicine at each time period (prospectively). They were always asked, "Was [a given topic] better or worse—or did it happen more or less—than in the preceding ten-year period, and do you anticipate that [a given topic] will move in a positive or negative direction in the future?" I also examine whether their predictions came to pass and whether these were consistent with how they viewed a situation in real time compared to how they viewed it at other stages in their careers.

The Entry Phase (1979–1980)[1]

The Context

When the physicians were nearing completion of their three-year residency at SAMS, President Carter's administration, with its low popularity rating and the country in a general malaise, was coming to an end. During his term, President

Carter had introduced one of the first hospital cost-containment bills. This occurred after the passage of Medicare and Medicaid more than a decade earlier, which had transformed American health care financing and delivery. Although Carter's legislation did not pass Congress, it was a harbinger of the turmoil that would follow in the next decades (Blumenthal and Morone, 2010; Starr, 2004). As mentioned in chapter 1, the decade of the 1970s was one in which patients' rights and protections came to the forefront in state law and public discourse, right at the time when this cohort was going through medical school. The role of the physician in controlling health care decision-making on an individual and collective level was already being questioned as emerging consumer and patient advocacy groups critiqued the organization, delivery, and financing of American medicine (Bollier, 1991; Dittmer, 2009; Haskell, 2014).

By the 1970s medical education encouraged specialization and subspecialization; fellowships were abundantly available from the federal government for postgraduate medical education. These opportunities were reflected at SAMS in the many choices the cohort had beyond general internal medicine, including pulmonology, cardiology, nephrology, and gastroenterology. Subspecialties of internal medicine were spurred by the growth of technology, such as dialysis, increasing the need for nephrologists, catheterizations and CT scans for interventional cardiology and pulmonology, and "scopes" of all kinds, enlarging the field of gastroenterology.

At the same time, in spite of this subspecialization wave, a counter trend to increase the number and type of generalists in primary care was also beginning to surface on the national scene. This was reflected at SAMS with the creation of a general internal medicine career track during this same time period.

As part of the context, the history of hospital segregation played a factor in the training of SAMS residents. As recently as the early 1960s, the SAMS system had been racially segregated by law (de jure), and remnants of a system divided by race and class still remained more than a decade later at the time they entered the residency program (Ubel, 2014). Virtually the entire cohort's view of the patient culture was shaped by the myriad patients they encountered, disproportionately Black and low income.

The Cohort

Cultural, structural, and professional factors contributed to an antipatient and anti-SAMS system perspective among these house officers in the late 1970s. I characterized this perspective by their attitudes and behavior as "getting rid of patients" based on a year of observation, multiple interviews, and self-administered questionnaires. This experience became the title of my earlier book, *Getting Rid of Patients: Contradictions in the Socialization of Physicians* (Mizrahi, 1986), which began this study.

As a cohort, these newly minted internists were leaving SAMS satisfied with the amount of learning they had acquired and their ability to practice internal medicine with a fair degree of confidence overall. At the same time, given their grueling residency training regimen, long hours, and inordinate amount of responsibility (by the design of the program), the house staff assumed a posture I characterized as one of survival. Most believed that the only redeeming value of the majority of SAMS patients were their illnesses and disabilities; in other words, interesting patients were those that they had the ability to learn from because of their medical conditions. And they happened to be a predominantly poor, uneducated, and disproportionately Black population.

Certain patient types by their own admission were disparaged, including substance abusers, homeless people (termed "trolls"), people with sickle cell anemia (identified as drug seeking), among others. While these neophyte, all White male, generally middle-class U.S. physicians belittled these patients' lack of education, culture, and behavior in the extreme, they made exceptions for the patients they personally took care of in the outpatient clinics over their three-year tenure (Mizrahi, 1984a), types of patients they described as "solid citizens."

A satirical novel had been published a couple of years earlier titled *The House of God* (Shem, 1978), characterized as a comedy-of-the-absurd examination of an internship at a fictional hospital in the Northeast. Many of these house staff called the book to my attention. They expressed, often spontaneously, that they were living the experience in real time described by Shem, the pseudonym for the physician author. The fictional patients were the butt of jokes and snide remarks, which has been labeled elsewhere as "gallows humor" (Watson, 2011). "The only interesting patient is a dead patient" was a popular slogan quoted from Shem's book. Several mentioned it as an exaggerated caricature of their experience; others joked that it was pretty accurate ("Except for the amount of sex the intern in the book had!" one doctor admitted [Mizrahi, 1986]).

These disparaging sentiments were captured in response to my question, "How closely do you anticipate SAMS patients will be to the types of patients in your anticipated future practice?" Most were repelled by that notion, typical of this comment by Dr. Annas: "No way! I'm dealing almost exclusively here with indigent people and alcoholics—that's not in my future." Drs. O'Brian and Johnson, who were moving into different subspecializations and career tracks (nephrology and oncology), nevertheless reflected similar sentiments. "At SAMS and in the VA," Dr. O'Brian stated, "Patients are lower SES, not representative of the patients I will go out and practice with. That's not necessarily a negative. I don't feel comfortable, either, with middle-class patients, who are more complex and neurotic. Class differences are more apparent than race differences, but both impede patient care." Or, as Dr. Johnson described, "Here (at SAMS) they are alcoholic, low SES, low IQ, with a long list of neglected problems. Hardly any will correspond (to my future patient population). That's negative in that you are not getting practice experience like you'll have in the future, but you're learning to manage different diseases. Rich people get diabetes too, so I'm glad I learned to handle that common disorder at SAMS."

As they contemplated their future, several already expressed resignation about their anticipated patient mix, regardless of which subspecialty they choose or whether they selected an academic or community practice setting. While most planned to eschew the patient mix at SAMS, they identified two caveats, as seen in the quotes by Drs. O'Brian and Johnson above. The first was that the middle-class patient population whom they aspired to treat would have its own set of challenges, and the second, that they probably could not avoid accepting all patient types, including some with similar attributes as the SAMS cohort in their anticipated future practice. More likely, auspice, financial arrangements, and geography would dictate their practice. Dr. Boswell, who remained at SAMS to pursue an academic practice in rheumatology, still assumed his patient population would be different: "I probably won't see so many alcoholics or COPD'ers [people with chronic obstructive pulmonary disease] in my academic practice. The patients may be a little younger. I don't know if that's a plus or minus. Addicts are more common than I thought in the patient and general population."

Dr. Paul, who was moving into an administrative and teaching role in general medicine at SAMS, ironically identified some benefits of taking care of an "indigent" population: "I think there will be more patients like that in my practice, but it's even worse handling the upper classes. It will be much harder to pull the wool over their eyes and say, 'It's just nerves.' I don't think there's going to be anything rewarding about lower-class patients, except they'll keep coming back here to SAMS because they trust us."

In additional queries about the pressures they felt from SAMS patients and whether they anticipated more or less pressure in the future, most of them predicted that there would be continuing, if not increasing, but perhaps a different type of pressure from a different class of patients. Dr. Beech, who would pursue community-based nephrology and general internal medicine (GIM), described his views: "Sure, there is pressure now; patients always want to get better faster or ask why they are not getting better; it puts pressure on you, but I suspect there will be more in the future." Or, as Dr. O'Brian responded, "Yes, there will be lots of pressure from patients: those with a difficult diagnosis; patients who try to manipulate you for drugs, whether it be from a forty-five-year-old housewife or a drug addict executive."

As Dr. Conley moved into his GI subspecialization fellowship, he summarized, perhaps in an exaggerated way, his already cynical sentiments echoed by many of his SAMS peers: "In the beginning, you envision patients who think you are great doctor; you're more idealistic. And later you realize that's not the way it is. I am cynical. It's a big hassle; people are after doctors; the government is out after the medical profession; you see it in the press, and you hear it from patients. It's a pain in the butt; I'd just as soon go fishing and enjoy myself."

In answering the question about what they were looking forward to and not looking forward to in the next five years, most made comparisons between their experiences of the last three years as residents and the projected next phase of their careers. Dr. Strelko, who was moving into an oncology fellowship, anticipated that in his future setting, "This sloughing at SAMS [a cavalier treatment of patients] doesn't occur as much in private practice." Still, he gave several examples of the phenomenon of "getting rid of patients" by "disposing" of them one way or another. Then he provided a lengthy tirade about lower-income, alcoholic patients in particular: "At SAMS there are so many indigent patients who don't follow up. I'm looking forward to taking care of 'real' patients with real problems. In oncology, a real plus is that my patients will have a definite disease. I don't want people who have destroyed themselves or who need a therapist."

Dr. Polikoff, who had just moved into an infectious disease subspecialization fellowship at SAMS, was almost despairing: "If it's anything like the experience we've had at SAMS as residents, I don't have anything to look forward to. My frustrations here were with the clinic, the labs, families trying to get rid of their old relatives. You're stuck with disposition problems, alcoholics, and more." In anticipating the future, other academically oriented physicians who were ending their residency discussed additional aspects of their career choice that they were not looking forward to. Dr. Paul was concerned about "not keeping up, not getting the whole picture." Dr. Rosen echoed his sentiment: "[I'm] afraid of getting out of date, getting behind."

While the cohort faced the future confident in their intellectual abilities, many were not satisfied with the "price they paid" for getting to this stage. Nevertheless, whether they were beginning a subspecialized fellowship training, as most were, or directly entering the world of community practice for a few, they expressed assurance with the knowledge and skill they acquired, as exemplified by Dr. Paul: "I'm looking forward to being recognized as being good, whether it will be in education or as dean, or writing a paper—something noteworthy."

Dr. Mahoney, who was leaving internal medicine and SAMS, was grateful to be exiting: "I'm looking forward to getting out from under the wing of mother institution. When you're twenty-nine, married, and have been going to school thirty percent of your life with people telling you what to do, it's enough. I'm looking forward to getting away from the government for a while, plus having a little more free time."

Most of the cohort believed they were on top of their game in internal medicine (Mizrahi, 1986), with private doubts buried deeply under the eagerness of moving forward to the next career phase. They had survived grueling house staff training and were proud of their achievements, notwithstanding their struggles, although deeper doubts and uncertainties would emerge (which I discuss more in chapter 5 on their relationships with peers, in chapter 6 on mistakes and malpractice, and in chapter 8 on disillusionment).

The Early Phase (1980–1984)

The Context

President Reagan was elected in 1980 on a conservative platform that was both philosophically and fiscally against government "entitlements." He did not believe that people had a right to benefits and services, although advocating a "safety net" for the "truly needy." When he won reelection in 1984, his administration implemented a prospective payment system (PPS) for hospitals known as diagnostic related groups (DRGs) under the Medicare program. This projected cost savings program provided a lump sum payment to hospitals for a particular patient's medical diagnosis rather than reimbursing hospitals for the traditional per diem rate paid retroactively, also known as "fee for service." This model would forever change the way medicine was practiced in hospital settings and began a fundamental shift in the way both academic medical centers and community practices would operate (Light, 2004; McKinlay and Marceau, 2005).

No longer was the physician's clinical judgment the only criterion used in decision-making (Freidson, 1984); instead, Medicare rules (to be followed by private insurance policies) intervened in determining hospital length of stay, access to invasive procedures, and coverage for office/outpatient visits. At this time, the AIDS crisis was beginning to be identified in medical circles. I overheard several private discussions over the year among the house staff at SAMS based on articles they were reading about this unusual infectious disease emanating from medical clinics in San Francisco with the implications that it was "gay related." (Indeed, for the first few years in the early 1980s, the new diagnosis was actually called "GRID," for gay-related immune deficiency.) Yet there were no public pronouncements about the advent and seriousness of this infectious disease from President Regan until 1986 after the death of his friend, actor Rock Hudson. These issues would have an important impact on medical practice and the cohort's professional experiences during this era.

The Cohort

By 1984, the doctors were in the early years of establishing a community practice or an academic career path. Fifteen out of the twenty physicians had, within the last year or two, completed a fellowship in a range of subspecializations at SAMS or elsewhere (see table 2): pulmonary (Dr. Finast), nephrology (Drs. Ross, O'Brian, Melone, and Beech), oncology (Drs. Johnson, Strelko, and Lynch), gastroenterology (Drs. Cahn, Conley, and Jarvis), cardiology (Drs. Annas and Allen), infectious disease (Dr. Polikoff), and rheumatology (Dr. Boswell). Within their subspecialization, six chose academic practice, which included teaching, service, and research responsibilities, and nine chose a specialized, referral community practice usually in single or multispecialized group settings. Of the other five, four chose general internal medicine—three in academic settings (Drs. Paul, Lash, and Rosen) and one established his practice in another city in the SAMS state (Dr. Nolan). Dr. Rosen flirted with a research-based nephrology fellowship in a medical center in the South, but within a year came back to SAMS in GIM. Dr. Mahoney, as noted earlier, who had immediately left internal medicine for another medical career track, remained working in a hospital setting in the SAMS city.

Satisfaction Index

Based on the physicians' responses at this early stage in their careers, and using the Satisfaction Index I created with colleagues, twelve physicians were categorized as positive, two were negative, and six were mixed (with some positive and some

Table 2   Satisfaction: Consistency and Changes Over Time

Physician ID #	Time Frame				
	Early	Established	Entrenched	Extended	Ending
Positive					
AP Annas	Positive	Positive	Positive	Positive	Positive
AP Lash	Positive	Positive	Positive	Positive	Positive
AP Rosen	Positive	Positive	Positive	Positive	Positive
CP Allen	Positive	Positive	Positive	Positive	Mixed
Trending positive					
AP O'Brian	Mixed	Mixed	Mixed	Positive	Positive
AP Strelko	Mixed	Positive	Positive	Positive	Positive
CP Polikoff	Mixed	Positive	Positive	Positive	Positive
Fluctuating					
AP Finast	Positive	Mixed	Negative	Mixed	Mixed
CP Jarvis	Mixed	Negative	Mixed	Positive	Mixed
CP Johnson	Positive	Mixed	Positive	Positive	Mixed
CP Lynch	Positive	Positive	Negative	Positive	Mixed
CP Melone	Mixed	Mixed	Mixed	Negative	Mixed/ Negative
CP Nolan	Positive	Positive	Negative	Mixed	Mixed
CP Ross	Positive	Positive	Mixed	Mixed	Mixed
NIM Mahoney	Negative	Mixed	Mixed	Mixed	Mixed/ Negative
Trending negative					
AP Boswell	Positive	Positive	Mixed/ Negative	Negative	Negative
AP Paul	Mixed	Mixed	Negative	Deceased	Deceased
CP Beech	Positive	Mixed	Negative	Negative	Negative
CP Conley	Positive	Negative	Negative	Negative	Negative
Negative					
CP Cahn	Negative	Negative	Negative	Negative	Negative

negative aspects; see table 2). Of the twelve who were classified as positive, five were in academic practice (Drs. Boswell, Finast, Lash, Rosen, and Annas). Of the six who were mixed, three were in academic practice (Drs. O'Brian, Strelko, and Paul). Dr. Mahoney, who had left internal medicine, and Dr. Cahn, who opened up a specialized GI community practice in another city in the South, were classified as negative. By and large, their choice of subspecialty did not seem related to their satisfaction score, although, in terms of setting, a notably higher number of physicians classified as positive were situated in academic institutions.

Satisfaction and Dissatisfaction Themes

The physicians' responses at this early phase (1980–1984) were used to classify their general levels of satisfaction into three themes relating to patients, practice, and peers. The next set of interviews were conducted five years after the physicians had completed working as house staff at SAMS.

Most were generally positive about beginning their professional life's journey, more than they and I had anticipated at the end of their residency training five years earlier. Although they were working hard—some working harder than they had imagined five years earlier—most felt the benefits outweighed the negatives.

The single highest cluster of satisfaction responses for the academics fell under practice-related factors; almost all specifically used the terms "balance" or "mix" when referring to the satisfying aspects of their practice. Dr. Strelko, who did his oncology fellowship and began his academic career in the Northeast, noted the combination of responsibilities as his reasons: "I'm satisfied to watch interns become residents, seeing the patient care they provide and having assisted in their development. I also enjoy being on the frontier of new cancer treatments. My life is better than I imagined in a university setting with no night call, contrasted with my time at SAMS. And I'm satisfied with my clinical research so far." Dr. Finast, who specialized in pulmonary medicine at SAMS asserted, "I have more time now for my personal life. Teaching is most satisfying although research is presenting a challenge." Others also commented on the relative ease of pace and intellectual stimulation they received, with the challenge of establishing funded research as the one downside.

Spontaneous comments about the status, class, and even race of the patients were all too common, especially when they were in settings that contrasted with SAMS. Dr. Strelko admitted, "Here in this rural area, it is mostly White patients. I get satisfaction from the occasional patient I cure. I spend more time talking about relevant research to them. They don't throw chairs or come in with guns, which was my image of many SAMS VA patients."

For the community practitioners with mixed responses, patients were almost always their one source of satisfaction. As Dr. Jarvis noted, "Patients are the reasons why I am in this profession; money doesn't justify the time or commitment or effort, but my relationship with patients does." This was also the view of Dr. Melone: "It's fun to make patients better. They come in sick as a goat—and go out smiling. It's a power trip—playing God." The term "fun" began to be used by many of the physicians

Table 3   Components of Physician Satisfaction Over Time (by percentage)

	1984	1994	2004	2011	2016
Financial remuneration	74	63	42	83	88
Psychic/emotional satisfaction	70	61	58	72	50
Public recognition: self	Not asked	66	72	83	83
Public recognition for profession	20	06	05	Not asked	12
Optimistic about future of medicine	39	28	33	40	60

beginning in the early phase as a particular way to characterize their practice experience. It appeared more and more over time and came to be used as an evaluative criterion as to whether they were satisfied or not. Comments such as "It wasn't as much fun anymore" reflected increasing dissatisfaction.

Almost all the community practitioners made comparisons with SAMS patients. Dr. Nolan described his experience like this: "I feel closer to the patients now than I did at SAMS. They're more like me, and I'm on a first name basis with many of them." Dr. Allen commented on his changing view of patients by referencing a slang term for undesirable patients found in *The House of God,* the satirical book about interns (Shem, 1978): "I went from being in awe of patients, to being uncomfortable around them, to calling them 'GOMERs,' [slang for Get Out of My Emergency Room] to seeing them as people now. My patients are lower or middle class, White, hardworking, and honest."

Components of Satisfaction

With respect to specific components of satisfaction (see table 3), three-quarters of the cohort were generally satisfied with their *financial remuneration*. Virtually all the community practitioners were enthusiastic. As Dr. Allen put it, "I'm very tickled. It's more than I ever thought, and it's just my second year." The few not satisfied with their remuneration were academics. As Dr. O'Brian reflected, "I could do better; that's the major drawback to the academic lifestyle. I am still paying off loans."

During the interviews in 1984, *psychic satisfaction*—which I define as the internal subjective pleasures they receive from their work—was at a high level (about seventy percent among the physicians). Still, there were some mixed reviews. As Dr. Jarvis reflected, "Sometimes yes to psychic satisfaction, and other times I feel like I am just a technician and a mindless idiot." Dr. O'Brian and others were less satisfied than at the entry phase: "Yes, but less here [an institution in the Northeast] than at SAMS. You have to be more aggressive now; there's more competition. You get fewer compliments for a job well done, and that affects my emotional well-being."

The biggest difference that varied by practice setting was, not surprisingly, in *intellectual stimulation*. All those in academic settings were more than satisfied. As

Dr. Paul emphasized, "I've never been bored a single day." But many of the community practitioners were not as satisfied. Their anticipated worries at the entry phase (1979–1980) came to be realized at the early phase (1980–1984). Dr. Beech's feelings were typical: "[Intellectual stimulation is] not as great as it used to be. It's a challenge to keep up, see patients, and get things done efficiently." Dr. Melone directly commented, "I get less than when I was at SAMS."

At the end of this early phase (1980–1984), the physicians were also asked their opinion of the *public's view of the medical profession*. At this moment when they were settling into their chosen careers, only twenty percent thought the public had a high regard for their profession. Some of the comments regarding public recognition were directly related to the context of this era, in which they already felt restrictions being placed on their practice. Dr. Melone lamented, "High esteem was an important reason for my going into medicine, but in reality, docs put up with a lot of crap now." Dr. Nolan, a generalist community practitioner, complained that he felt affected by restrictions that negatively impacted his image of the medical profession: "Now, if patients have a cold for a week, they call and want to see you. All that will change with managed care. If I am on a salary, I will go home after eight hours, regardless of whether a patient is sick or not."

Anticipating the Future

It is surprising that, in these early years, only five of the doctors were enthusiastic and positive about *recommending a medical career to their (then young) children*. In general, across the different career stages, the number of physicians who would recommend a medical career to their children would notably fluctuate. In 1984, however, about half of the cohort had qualifications and reservations, in addition to five who emphatically declared "No!" they would not recommend it.

Dr. Annas, who was otherwise positive about his work life, reflected, "When I was done (with residency), I was very enthusiastic about medicine; it was lots of fun. Now I see other career choices as financially rewarding. I had the view that if you were intelligent and wanted a high-paying, prestigious job, you had to become a doctor. I've drastically changed my ways." Dr. Conley also was less sanguine: "With all the rules and regulations, it's been disappointing—so much government interference, paperwork. I grew up with images of Marcus Welby and Dr. Kildare [fictional MDs portrayed on TV] that were so positive."

At this stage, five years postresidency, despite most being personally happy with their career choices, almost two-thirds of these physicians were already pessimistic or mixed in their prognosis about the future of medicine. They expressed several reservations, most frequently related to the increasing encroachment on their professional autonomy and an anticipated fear of malpractice, especially the community practitioners like Dr. Conley: "Moving forward, I'll make a good living, but it's not going to be as much fun. It won't be as enjoyable with so many people looking over your shoulder." Dr. Finast, an academic practitioner, who was otherwise enthusiastic until the end of his career, projected in this early phase: "I'm optimistic medicine will continue to improve quality of life, but I'm pessimistic about finances, practice styles, competitions, and social issues." (These sentiments are discussed more in chapter 6 on mistakes and malpractice and in chapter 8 on disillusionment.)

Most of the academics were also optimistic about the research potential (theirs and others), but they, like community practitioners, also mentioned costs and fears of government intrusion in their institution, if not on their own practice. Dr. Strelko expressed his ambivalence: "The DRGs (diagnostic related groups) are going to put some financial constraints on things. Research funds are drying up. You have all these oppositional interest groups—the Catholics on abortion, the antivivisectionists on animal research. The flaw with DRGs is you are penalized if patients live!"

The hardships of residency expressed five years earlier appeared to have been modified. Although they recalled sleep deprivation and undesirable patients, they believed that they acquired their medical competency because of the autonomy they were granted by the structure and culture of the SAMS system. They were now ensconced either in academia, where they chose their own disease subspecialty, or in a community setting, where they chose their patient population for the most part.

While most are positive about their practice overall, there were chinks beginning to form in the armor, especially for those who remained at SAMS. External scrutiny, especially for community practitioners was, in their collective view, already being fueled by lawyers, political/government watchdogs, and private insurance companies, and many felt it would only get worse.

The Established Phase (1984–1994)

The Context

In the established phase (1984–1994) of their careers—ending fifteen years after the doctors had finished residency—another fundamental shift in health care occurred that was beginning to severely impact their practice. The election of Bill Clinton as president in 1992 led to the anticipation of major health care reform under his leadership with an increased role for government (Gorin and Mizrahi, 2013). His proposal was followed by a year or more of public hearings, alternative proposals, and debates under the leadership of his wife, Hillary Rodham Clinton.

The American Medical Association and other physician organizations provided different reform proposals while trying to stem the diminishment of their professional autonomy and influence (Skocpol, 1995; Surowiecki, 2016). Most physician organizations opposed the Clinton proposal to create conglomerates, which were a combination of public and private insurance known as "managed competition." No health care insurance group nor conservative political organization was happy with this compromise plan (Skocpol, 1997).

The ultimate failure of the Clinton administration's efforts to reform health care contributed to the Republican Party landslide in the 1994 midterm elections. That resulted in the election of a Republican majority in Congress (Johnson and Broder, 1996). The conservative Congress with a right-wing agenda in opposition to any government intervention signaled the demise of any major health policy (Gingrich, 1994). This shift to a conservative market-oriented agenda dominated the nation's political life, although President Clinton won re-election for another term.

At the same time, the proliferation and dominance of corporate entities influencing health care which began in the 1980s ratcheted up in this time frame. The 1990s became known as the era of "managed care" (Jasso-Aguilar, Waitzkin, et al., 2004; Light, 2005). Managed care (also characterized by some as "managed costs") meant that insurance companies primarily determined which physicians their insured patients could see, and how many visits and procedures would be authorized for payment. These corporations became major gatekeepers, making decisions about clinical care, especially for patient access to specialty care and medical procedures. Moreover, limitations were imposed differentially on physicians' clinical judgment and reimbursement for services, similar to the restrictions placed by the implementation of DRGs in the 1980s. These trends, combined with continued reductions in Medicare payments to academic medical centers, were the broader context for both the academic and community practitioners of this cohort during this career stage (Sturm, 2002; Tyrance, Sims, et al., 1999).

The Cohort

Forty percent of the cohort made major changes in their careers during the established phase (1984–1994). Dr. Polikoff left academia for a health maintenance organization (HMO) community practice, and five other academics moved to different institutions in different cities (Drs. Annas, Rosen, O'Brian, and Strelko) or back to SAMS (Dr. Lash) in the ten-year period from 1984 to 1994. Drs. Lynch and Mahoney also changed locations in the same city but remained in a similar type of practice.

Satisfaction Index

By 1994, applying the Satisfaction Index we developed, a fewer number of the cohort (ten) were positive about their careers (see table 2) than ten years earlier. Six of those ten were in academic practice—the same five who were categorized as positive in the early phase, plus Dr. Strelko, who moved into a positive classification after changing institutions and position. Seven of the cohort now scored mixed in their views of their career, including Drs. Finast and Paul, both academics, who moved from positive into that category. Drs. Conley and Jarvis were ranked totally negative at this stage, joining Dr. Cahn, with all three working in a subspecialized community practices. The overall trend was toward a more mixed and negative cohort.

Satisfaction and Dissatisfaction Themes

With fifteen years of experience now behind them, they compared and contrasted what was positive and not about their career during this time span. Those who stated that they were satisfied overall or on balance identified one or more factors that contributed to that view. This is exemplified by the perspective of Dr. Strelko, an academic who moved to a new setting in the Midwest to receive more support: "I am more satisfied here. I am doing useful things. We have politics here, but we have a lot better research going on. There is a collaborative atmosphere on campus; people work well together here."

Overall, patient-related themes were again the most frequently cited sources of satisfaction by community practitioners and even academics. Dr. O'Brian, working in an academic setting, commented, "Patients [compared to SAMS] are now well informed. They are grateful. You don't have to talk baby talk to the patients here; they know a phenomenal amount," while community oncologist Dr. Johnson lauded, "The patients I have seen for a long time are like friends. These people have a sense of decency about them. And I enjoy seeing them." Although they were fifteen years beyond residency, so many of their views of patients, in general, or their specific patients, were still colored by their negatively experienced SAMS situation.

The academic physicians additionally continued to describe the mix of responsibility and the balance of their work life positively (teaching, research, patient practice). They cited peer-related rewards that emanated from having become mentors and teachers to current house staff and medical students. For the community practitioners, the colleague-related satisfaction included the ability to influence physician decision-makers such as hospital executives, while for the academics, colleague-related satisfaction came from their work as department chairs and deans (discussed more in chapter 5 on peer relations).

There were also challenges that affected their levels of satisfaction. For example, Dr. Rosen, who moved to another academic medical institution in a different southern state, reflected his mixed sentiment: "I love taking care of patients, especially those who present an intellectual challenge. I have a mix of patients— millionaires and indigent of all races. Teaching students, seeing the light bulb go on is great. But negatives are creeping in. Dealing with the system here is frustrating; insurance companies are encroaching much more than ten years ago. I spend too much time with bureaucratic idiots."

Community practitioners also pointed to having less ability to contain or avoid the managed care companies and other corporate pressures as affecting their satisfaction. Dr. Lynch lamented, "It's too much. Patients who want extended care are increasing. You have to put up with a lot of crap, such as pressures to remain current, plus a very busy call schedule, communicating with patients with high expectations, and stressful meetings about business-related matters." Dr. Allen responded similarly: "Massive paperwork, lots of death and dying people with heart disease; it wears you out. But I'd rather deal with cardiac patients than these nebulous, redundant complaints from the many undiagnosable patients of old at SAMS."

There were more mixed and negative physicians than in the previous decade. Dr. Jarvis summed this up: "The Golden age of medicine is finished." Some dissatisfaction emerged even among the positively classified physicians. Most of the discontent among academics ironically centered around competition for patients from doctors in community hospitals. As Dr. Finast, who remained at SAMS, alluded, "We've trained ourselves out of a job. A pulmonary group just opened up in town, and they are our graduates!" He and others related this to the financial pressures that their institutions were facing, which affected his department and his and others' individual incomes. Dr. Paul added, "Competition for patients is leading to cutting our prices. Now decisions are based solely on whether it is going to bring in money and not whether it is good for patient care or society. We worry about who's going to pay for medical education."

Dr. Lash, who moved back to SAMS into an administrative position, also identified challenges with reimbursement for outpatient services: "Funding is going to inpatient care, so how do you train for primary care? Faculty have to see patients every fifteen to twenty minutes. Where is the time to teach, let alone research? There is also political stress, jockeying for power in a complex competitive institution."

Dr. O'Brian, having experienced three different academic medical centers since he was chief resident at SAMS, complained, "There is too much government control. The threat of Clinton's proposal has transformed medicine. Now there is a bureaucratic system with competition in the community among dialysis providers. Patient care suffers—no reimbursement, no care." The issues Dr. O'Brian raised—previously thought to be limited to the community practitioners—had crept into academic medicine. Even Dr. Annas, perennially positive, described competition at the hospital level, but coped by "keeping out of it. It's above my pay grade."

Universally, these physicians felt strongly that external forces impeded their ability to practice successfully. It is hard to convey in writing the passion of these widespread sentiments. Dr. Lynch was typical: "Bureaucracy and insurance companies, lack of control, pre-authorizations galore all drive me crazy." Dr. Cahn ranted and raved: "The volume of stress and anxiety is so overwhelming now. It doesn't compare to ten years ago. I'm working harder to make the same amount of money. And the people running the system just aren't as smart enough to be decision-makers." Dr. Beech added the patient component to the stresses he believed were getting worse: "I've less tolerance for these Clinton era uncertainties; maybe I'm entering pre-burnout. Patient expectations are much higher; with the advent of technology, knowledge, and Marcus Welby TV shows, the tendency is to blame us for bad results. There are too many unappreciative patients."

Components of Satisfaction

Financial remuneration still gave satisfaction to almost two-thirds of the cohort, although less than in the early phase (1980–1984) of their career. For the academics, it was about expectations and trade-offs. As Dr. Finast acknowledged, "I am comfortable even though I am not going to make as much as people in private practice. But I make more than ninety-five percent of Americans and drive a nice car; got kids' college paid for. I can't complain." Dr. Strelko, who had moved to another academic institution a second time, commented, "My income is okay; it's less than private practitioners, but more than I made in my prior setting, where I was underpaid."

While most community practitioners added that they were making more than they had anticipated, others commented that they were less satisfied than they had been. A few were comparing their compensation to the past and their earning potential in the future; typical was Dr. Ross: "It's about the same as earlier. They say it will increase, but I don't believe it. Never happen!" Some, like Dr. Conley explained, "Our compensation is eaten away by the Medicare schedule. If all fees were set at that level, I doubt I would be compensated enough."

A majority (sixty-one percent) still reported on receiving *psychic satisfaction*, but fewer than ten years earlier: " It is absolutely and always enough," commented Dr. Annas, while Dr. Rosen emphasized, "If you mean total strangers coming in and adoring you and putting you up on a pedestal, yes I have it. If that doesn't make you feel good, you are brain dead."

Community practitioners received less emotional fulfillment than academics down from the early phase (1980–1984). To the extent that it existed, these physicians pointed to patients for that emotional element: "The patients really appreciate what you do for them, and even if the patient dies, the family does," noted Dr. Johnson, while Dr. Nolan qualified his satisfaction with a caveat: "It's still fun when I am not sleep deprived." Most community practitioners, however, were outright negative, as found in Dr. Jarvis' lament: "There are no emotional rewards. My generation has been in medicine in its 'glory days,' when there wasn't competition, malpractice, or the government intruding." Note the nostalgia embedded in that term he used.

Intellectual rewards were still viewed positively by a majority (sixty-one percent) of the cohort, about the same as a decade earlier. This component, not surprisingly, was important for almost all of the academics, as per Dr. Rosen's comments: "I like imprinting my style on others, being a role model and mentor; at the same time, I learn from the house staff. Teaching is most stimulating for me intellectually." For a generally dissatisfied physician like Dr. Paul, this was his salvation: "The whole reason I went into internal medicine was the joy of patient problem-solving. It is endlessly stimulating."

The intellectual component was still satisfying for some community practitioners but waning for others: "It's more than enough. I get it with my partners, plus I read and take a few courses," says Dr. Jarvis. However, as illustrated by nephrologist Dr. Beech: "It (intellectual stimulation) has dropped off dramatically. I come home more beat up and then I want to spend time with the kids, so I spend less time reading medical stuff. There is no way I can work twelve hours a day and then read." Dr. Johnson explained why he was disappointed: "Oncology hasn't improved as rapidly as I thought it would when President Nixon declared a 'war on cancer.' We thought we would be pumping out cures."

In this stage, the theme of *professional status* included two questions: one on the profession's impact on themselves—that is, whether they personally received enough professional recognition, and for the first time, their views of the status of the medical profession. Two-thirds of the physicians felt that they were highly regarded personally as physicians in their own environments, regardless of setting or subspecialty. Dr. Paul, although in academia, noted that his personal satisfaction came through his volunteering in a community clinic: "I've seen how university people like me are appreciated as experts as I am the only physician board member. It's fun."

Dr. Johnson, sounding like a celebrity, commented, "I could actually stand a little less recognition. I'd like to be able to go to the mall without talking to three patients and their families." Dr. Allen reported, "Sure, when they call me 'doctor.'" There were a few exceptions like negative Dr. Cahn, who reported, "No I don't receive it; for example, we treat many physicians' families in this community, but they don't send their patients to us. Respect has dropped off."

Multiple reasons for the falling status of their profession and for the seeming erosion of public trust were described by the cohort and in the literature: managed care, the media, and unrealistic patient expectations (Mechanic, 1996). Dr. O'Brian, speaking for academic physicians, identified several misconceptions that he thought had contributed to its lower status. "Academic physicians are an anomaly. The public thinks we earn the same as plastic or cardiac surgeons. I don't think I'm held in any high regard in the community for being an academic physician." Dr. Strelko lamented his current situation: "I was more starry-eyed as a resident. Now you feel the pressure; people are more demanding. You have to prove yourself every day, more than in the past." Nevertheless, some qualified their negative responses by expressing the view that, compared to other professions, physicians were still highly regarded, as Dr. Nolan did with a bit of irony: "Our status is down some, but being a lawyer is much worse in the public's eye."

Anticipating the Future

In spite of their reservations about the state of the medical profession at this established phase (1984–1994), there were eight affirmative responses related to whether they would *recommend medicine to their children*, up in the last decade from about one-fourth to one-third of the cohort: "Medicine has a considerable amount of job security, and you get paid well. It's intellectually challenging. What else can you really ask for?" queried Dr. Conley. Even Dr. Mahoney, who stated that he is pessimistic about the future for himself and the profession, asserted, "Yes, I would recommend it, with all its sacrifices and limitations."

For several of the physicians who said they would continue to recommend it, their answers had a relativistic quality: "Compared to what?" or "By what criteria?" were questions they posed. Hardly any of the cohort were enthusiastic—the positives were that medicine was a good living or a relatively secure one, while the negatives grew over time. As Dr. Boswell lamented, "I would recommend it less. There is higher debt from medical school. There is a lot more stress than I anticipated, and opportunities for research are much more limited." Dr. Paul, the only one of the cohort without children, went even further: "If I had to do it over,

I'd become a nurse practitioner. There's almost as much prestige, less training, and it's a seller's market. They don't take their responsibility home with them."

The number of mixed and pessimistic responses regarding the *future of medicine* also increased. There were inconsistencies and ambivalence, or just plain resignation, as Dr. Paul continued to lament: "I'm more pessimistic than most. My private practice colleagues seem to get more pleasure. I'm optimistic because of technology, but MDs are losing prestige and income. I miss the excitement. The thrill is gone." Contradictions abound. In spite of still recommending the profession to his children, Dr. Mahoney expressed caution: "Today people who enter medicine have to jump through hoops to get their patients treatment. They have to answer to other powers—government, lawyers. I'm scared that the health crisis will lead to mediocracy as corporations are taking over."

No one indicated that medicine was a "calling" or a noble endeavor anymore, yet that was an important reason why so many chose medicine in the first place. Dr. Conley explained his mixed review: "I'm optimistic about the future. There will always be medicine and only MDs can do it. But medicine as we know it will cease to exist in fifteen to twenty years. It already has changed; it's less of a profession." Even generally positive Dr. Polikoff, who moved from an academic subspecialty to an HMO practice, said he was "pessimistic, but not panicking. There is lots of publicity about high MD salaries, but they are not paid as much as CEOs in business. I predict lots of big changes on the horizon. None good."

Many separated their personal futures from their generalized view of medicine, as did Dr. Boswell in sync with his recommending medicine less than in the past: "Things are so bad they can't get worse in medicine. But things are looking up in my own career. I have a pretty good life and real balance." While many of the academics were leading comfortable lifestyles doing research, teaching, and practicing clinically part time, their expectations about the future for the profession were less sanguine.

Conclusion

From the time of their residency to the time they had been in one or more settings for more than a decade and a half, the cohort as a whole appeared to be surviving by adapting to their circumstances in various ways. The excitement of moving into a community or academic setting was tempered by the bureaucracies they experienced and the stress of building their patient base to sustain them financially and intellectually. Almost half of them had changed locales or institutions by the established phase (1984–1994). Patients were the redeeming aspects of their careers for the community practitioners, and an important one for the academics, especially when compared to their memories of the SAMS patient cohort.

They recognized that the whole practice of medicine had changed toward one of complexity, which included outside actors if not intruders. It was not returning to a more autonomous framework that they had envisioned, but ironically, had never actually experienced. Even more telling was their overall uniformly negative perception that the status of the medical profession had declined in the public's eye, whether justified or not. They were less optimistic about the profession's future while hopeful about scientific and technological discoveries that they believed would benefit society generally and their patient populations specifically.

Considering they began medical school in the early/mid-1970s, by the time they finished the established phase (1984–1994), the physicians were nearing the midpoint of their careers. The next chapter, using similar criteria and questions used during the interviews in the phases above, looks at the second half of their careers, focusing on the entrenched phase (1994–2004), extended phase (2004–2011), and ending phase (2011–2016).

Satisfaction and Strains

THE UPS AND DOWNS OF BEING A
DOCTOR, PART II (MID-CAREER
TO RETIREMENT)

Building on the last chapter's discussion of physician satisfaction and strains during the entry, early and established stages of their career, this chapter looks at the same issues in the physician cohort's professional lives in the later stages. It focuses on the time when they were more entrenched in their careers until the time when they were at or near retirement, almost forty years after they had been house officers at SAMS. Specifically, this chapter looks at the entrenched (1994–2004), extended (2004–2011), and ending (2011–2016) career phases. Similar to the findings in chapter 3, contradictions and tensions appear throughout their complex professional lives during these later stages. In this chapter, I discuss the motives and rationales underpinning the physicians' decision-making strategies as they coped, adapted, and endured in their professional lives during a time period that saw continuing major changes in the medical and health care industry.

The Entrenched Phase (1994–2004)

The Context

In the entrenched period of their careers, conditions and expectations were changing yet again for physicians, particularly in relation to an increasingly important corporate role in the health care system. Preoccupied with the aftermath of 9/11 and with two ongoing wars in full force, the government was not focused as much on a domestic agenda. Only one significant national health-related change was completed under President G. W. Bush: the passage of a complicated and costly prescription drug benefit to the Medicare program (known as Medicare Part D). Concerns about the rising cost of health care, the proliferation of internet-based information in the hands of patients, and competition within the medical profession combined yet again to alter the relationship among physicians, patients, and payers. Without a major federal government health reform agenda, corporations reigned supreme over health care decision-making. Attempts to bring so-called "efficiencies" to the system were based on business models to health care. These resulted in an emphasis on pay-for-performance, evidenced-based medicine, and treatment protocols (Domagalski, 2005; Light, 2005), while insurance companies and for-profit hospitals continued to expand and consolidate their power (Potter, 2010).

The Cohort

While this career period is characterized as "entrenched," it turned out to be less stable than had been anticipated from earlier periods. In the previous ten years or so, almost half the physicians made career changes: three academics (Drs. O'Brian, Lash, and Paul) and one community practitioner (Dr. Lynch) moved to new settings, and Drs. Johnson, Allen, Melone, and Cahn took on major administrative roles in their group's practice (see table 1 in chapter 1).

Satisfaction Index

There was less satisfaction as a cohort as they moved into the entrenched phase (1994–2004). Dr. Cahn was the only wholly dissatisfied physician in 1984, whereas by 2004 there were six additional dissatisfied physicians based on the Satisfaction Index (Drs. Finast, Nolan, Lynch, Beech, Conley, and Paul). An additional five were moved to or remained in the mixed category (Drs. Mahoney, Ross, Melone, Boswell, and O'Brian). These physicians fluctuated from the established phase (1984–1994) or trended negative, indicating an increasingly adverse view of their practice environment from a decade earlier. Of the seven physicians who remained positive based on their overall score, five were in academic practice.

Satisfaction and Dissatisfaction Themes

In 2004 responses regarding overall satisfaction and dissatisfaction were more similar among the physicians than previously. Their use of the word *fun*, identified in the earlier years in the previous chapter as one barometer for what is still pleasurable (or was lost), accelerated in these later phases. Almost three-quarters of these physicians referred to their experiences at least once using this term. External circumstances with respect to managed care, hospital competition, and mergers negatively affected most physicians' practices and continued to dampen their enthusiasm. Dr. Melone labeled this period as "cover-your-ass medicine." Even Dr. Polikoff, who was positive overall, noted, "You have to work much harder for your patients to get certain things done because you have to justify the claim to insurance companies."

Patient-related themes continued to be associated with satisfaction, especially for community practitioners. As Dr. Allen commented, repeating a theme he first identified a decade earlier, "Seeing people get better and showing their appreciation, plus teaching them how to keep themselves well, are all still satisfying." Half of the cohort emphasized the emotional connections they had with at least some of their patients.

Nevertheless, more than in prior stages, limitations on positive patient feelings surfaced, linked to external attacks on them by the legal profession and the public, and the advent of technology. Dr. Mahoney expressed those sentiments: "I'm dissatisfied with the use of technology—more testing, longer patient waits; you get backed up and now you need to practice defensive medicine because of lawyers and the media." Similarly, Dr. Melone connected patient expectations and the information technology revolution: "The families tend to be more demanding now. Lots of internet-driven information. Many show up with sheets of paper from both genuine and bogus websites. You spend a lot of time, saying, 'That's baloney.'" Community practitioner Dr. Beech lamented, "Patients are more demanding and more adversarial than before. Expectations are out of line. You deal with older and sicker patients with unrealistic expectations. They become litigious with bad outcomes."

Fewer mentioned finding satisfaction with making a diagnosis or effecting a cure than they did previously. Several in both community and academic settings suggested that there were fewer unknown diagnoses to uncover. Nevertheless, many were sanguine about both diagnostic and therapeutic technology overall in spite of the limitations noted earlier; for some, scientific advances continued to be one of the very few positive factors on the horizon for the profession as they anticipated its future.

Satisfactory peer relationships were confined mostly to those working in academic settings in their teaching and research roles. For example, although Dr. Paul's career track was frustrating and difficult in this time period, he found some pleasure in "curriculum and teaching. I like using web-based learning. Teaching other faculty and house staff is still very rewarding." Dr. O'Brian, who attempted but failed at this juncture to move into medical academic administration, still found satisfaction in the teaching environment in spite of increasing demands: "What turns me on is all the variety in academia like I told you last time; my lab and funding grows and shrinks, but the work is still interesting and enjoyable. I love mentoring junior faculty; it's fun because my research attracts trainees."

The physicians perceived much more competition and a less collegial environment, specifically between referral-based specialists and primary care practitioners. The demands and frustration of practice were almost unanimous; the major differences were only whether the physicians felt that the satisfactions outweighed the stresses and strains. Dr. Nolan said it succinctly: "I'm dissatisfied with the progressive decline in reimbursement. I'm working harder for less. And the malpractice crisis is getting worse; it only depends on outcomes, not the physician's practice." Dr. Johnson focused on time and costs: "Medical care has gotten more expensive due to insurance companies. We're not making a whole lot more than ten years ago, yet hospitals, drugs, insurance, equipment are more expensive. I've had to hire an RN to handle all the paperwork. What's worse are the number of people who need help paying for their care. It's not as much fun anymore."

Components of Satisfaction

Given the emphasis on government and corporate infringement on their reimbursement and lifestyle at this stage, less than half were satisfied with *financial remuneration*, not surprisingly, down significantly from a decade earlier. This was split proportionally between academics and community practitioners. The topic of student debt surfaced predominantly for the first time. Dr. Conley gave a complex answer when asked if he was satisfied with his compensation: "I am receiving less, but I am certainly not suffering. But ask someone coming out of residency with $125,000 of debt, and I bet he would say, 'no' unless you were comparing his salary to a plumber. I don't think I am getting paid what I should." Dr. Nolan was more succinct: "Not even close!" Dr. Cahn's response was explicit: "My malpractice insurance was $11,000 ten years ago; today it is $50,000. Moreover, when I came to this state, I got reimbursed $1,200 for doing a colonoscopy; today I only get $247."

Psychic satisfaction also continued to lessen from the early phase (1980–1984) to the entrenched phase (1994–2004) in their careers; the eleven who said they still received psychic satisfaction were almost evenly divided between the academics and the community-based practitioners. Dr. Polikoff affirmed, "It comes from a great group of doctors and a highly educated clientele, who most of the time are very appreciative. It's a lot of fun coming to work. I love my job because of my patients and my colleagues." Although Dr. Allen was satisfied in his patient educator role, he lamented, "It's still fun, but I don't get paid for the time I spend on teaching patients how to stay healthy." And in the academic sphere, Dr. Annas commented, "Yes [for psychic satisfaction] there are rewards and benefits for doing a good job that are still in place. It is always gratifying to see people you trained getting good jobs and doing good."

Dr. Beech echoed the view of many of his colleagues as to why many community practitioners received less emotional gratification in this time period: "It's not enough now. If you could remove malpractice threats, I would stay in practice longer." Dr. Strelko remarked, "Some days are better than others, but it's not as good as it was."

By contrast, *intellectual stimulation* continued to be important in this phase of their careers and was a positive feature for almost seventy percent of the cohort, an even larger percentage than ten years earlier. This was somewhat surprising, since there were so many complaints of external restrictions on their ability to exercise their clinical judgment. For the academics, intellectual activity remained an essential aspect of their relationships with peers, students, and mentors. For example, Dr. Annas, an academic physician, noted, "Interacting with the fellows, residents, and students is satisfying. It's the mix that is attractive." Or, as Dr. Rosen, another academic physician, described it: "Yes, that is one of the reasons I have stayed here. The combination of working with outstanding people and training young people on their way up is positive."

Interestingly and somewhat unexpectedly, intellectual growth became more important for many of the community practitioners over time. In 2004, for instance, Dr. Melone described what sustained his satisfaction: "Having interesting patients and having intelligent colleagues is a nice combination." Dr. Allen replied, "Yes, and it's gotten better since I went from no partners, to two, to five. It's stimulating having five peers to bounce things off." Dr. Johnson and others also obtained intellectual growth through educational activities in person and online, separate from their practice: "That's one of the good things. I get it through listening to tapes; learning is fun. It's a little better than ten years ago because residents rotate through our practice now."

In this entrenched phase (1994–2004), once again, only one physician was positive about the *public recognition given to the medical profession*. Not surprisingly,
several blamed external forces with even more vigor, as did Dr. Nolan: "Physicians have dropped in esteem; they are tarred with the brush meant for insurance
companies." Dr. Melone explained, "I think the profession is only regarded as
tolerable now. It's the media, trial attorneys, and the internet bringing it down."
Moreover, he saw a shift in the larger society with more exposure and less tolerance for abuse: "It's a triumph of democracy. Now you can prove that Catholic
priests are toads just like the rest of us. Doctors have always had a privileged
place, but respect for medicine by society is being eroded a lot."

They continued to distinguish between themselves personally and the profession as a whole, being much more favorable about the former than the latter,
which matched past comments in previous time frames. Dr. Ross noted, "Generally, people hate the health care system but still like their doctor." A few more in
this time frame provided mixed responses or a qualified "yes" as to whether they
were personally satisfied with the recognition they received from the public. As
Dr. Jarvis reflected, "Yes and no. In my practice, there are a lot of grateful patients
but also a lot of adversarial ones who call us 'providers,' not doctors." Overall, the
public sentiment for our profession has declined with many more demanding
patients than before." Nevertheless, for a substantial majority of the community-
based cohort, the personal support from their patients and local communities
were the only satisfying elements of practice as they matured.

Anticipating the Future

In this entrenched phase of their careers, they were once asked about whether
they would *recommend a medical career to their children*. Responses varied in the
same way as ten years earlier. Six were totally against promoting it to offspring;
only two said they would recommend it more than they would have in the past.
Almost all of them in this phase had grown children who already had chosen their
career paths. Ironically, two of the five who had children becoming physicians
gave medicine mixed rather than totally positive reviews. As Dr. Melone said,
"Yes, I would recommend it, but less than in the past because of the borderline
incomes. Malpractice rates negatively affect the reimbursement I receive. Still,
most doctors make a wonderful living today. But I bet twenty years from now,
fewer will be in medicine, and those in the field will have more and more debt."

Much more than in the prior stage, the physicians who were still somewhat
favorably disposed to medicine, or at least had positive things to say about the
field, tended to assess their rationale for recommending the medical profession to
their children by highlighting the way the field had changed. Dr. Boswell, an academic practitioner, said he would have to explain to his children that "medicine
will be different for you than it was for me." Several discussed the changing
"mindset" of newer doctors as well as the organization of practice, which included
that more physicians at that time were salaried, had less responsibility, and
worked nine to five. Dr. Allen, who had been classified as a positive physician

until this phase, was ambivalent: "I'd tell my children to find a day job. So, I would recommend it less now. It's more risky. If you go in thinking you're okay as a salaried kind of guy and not being your own boss, with that realization, fine. Someone's got to do it." Dr. Paul, who did not have children, was philosophical and took the opportunity to reflect on his own career. He would not recommend it, he said, because "it was not worth the encroachment on my personal life and development." (This issue is also discussed in the next chapter on relationships with peers.) Most of the physicians seemed to view medicine through this new practice paradigm, and only in that sense did they think the next generation (including their children) could be content with that career choice.

In this career phase, a majority gave the *future of medicine* a pessimistic prognosis overall, as typified by Dr. Jarvis's comment: "The future of medicine is in jeopardy until the malpractice issue gets resolved. Insurance companies are raking in all the profits and cutting fees. It will get fixed only when middle-class voters can't find doctors to deliver babies, fix their head traumas, and dialyze a family member." Many concluded that the attacks on medicine from all fronts made him pessimistic about medicine's future. As Dr. Beech stated, "Less money and less insurance for more and more people who are older and sicker; fewer people becoming MDs; somebody will hope you die before you need a new hip. Health care will be rationed. You will pay privately or stand in line." Dr. Melone believed "it will be a lot less rewarding intellectually, less prestige, and lower quality of folks going into it. As a career, it's all going downhill."

Dr. Strelko, as an academic physician, came to a different conclusion than Dr. Melone, although he cited many of the same problems and made a radical prediction: "Lots more people are going into radiology, leaving a gap for those of us in internal medicine who like to talk to patients. Cost of drugs will continue to be a lightning rod, especially for older people; medical networks will continue to dominate. Doctor-patient relationships will be okay, but there will be lots of patient cynicism about the system. I predict a form of national health care eventually ironically." (See chapter 7 on health care reform for more detail.)

After a quarter of a century since completing residency training, the only area they continued to be most optimistic about, albeit with more caution than in the past, were major advances in diagnostic and treatment technologies, ranging from imaging to pharmaceuticals. Several mentioned genetics for the first time as the key to the future. Dr. Johnson was in awe of its medical potential: "With the human genome, we will be able to prevent for example, hardening of the arteries—like what antibiotics did for infections." Dr. O'Brian expressed, "One of the positives of my job is being privy to what's happening biologically, and it's exciting."

Yet there was a downside even to technological advances expressed for the first time by a few. Dr. Strelko, as an academic oncologist, warned, "Although some technological advances are spectacular, the public has been oversold—for example, on the value of a mammography." Dr. Allen also raised moral, ethical, and political reservations: "I'm concerned about using DNA and genetic testing to predict the future. If you are a twenty-one-year-old patient, insurance companies will be able to cancel your insurance, and employers could fire you if they uncover diseases you may have."

Ultimately, a few of the physicians struggled to find meaning in their own professional lives even as they predicted a bleak or mixed future. As Dr. Mahoney reflected, "I'm pessimistic (about the future of medicine). The priorities of the country are out of whack. No one cares, so government and insurance companies can do what they want. They are eroding the stature of medicine. But I'm happy and sufficiently challenged." Dr. Allen put it this way: "When I get up in morning, I can't wait to go work. It's wonderful and rewarding, but I'm pessimistic in that patients won't do what you tell them to and then complain. Managed care will always beat up on you, and the media will always make you sound bad."

And even a generally optimistic academic like Dr. Rosen worried for the profession: "Lawyers, insurance and managed care companies are putting the squeeze on internists. Physicians will stop taking private insurance and Medicaid because of low reimbursement." Still, he ended by saying that "this crisis period will eventually end, and the pendulum will ultimately adjust."

Overall, the notion of the physician becoming a "shift worker" was worrisome, and some believed it would negatively affect the quality of care and the doctor-patient relationship. Clearly the cohort in at this entrenched phase (1994–2004) had complex and at times competing or contradictory responses depending on the connotation or context of a question. For example, dissatisfaction with peer relationships was on the increase, while intellectual satisfaction with peers remained high. Pessimism about the profession was on the rise as the issue of medical debt, which was first identified ten years earlier, increased in a serious way. Yet what had been a trend toward an increasingly negative perception of their profession would, as I discuss below, begin to shift as they transitioned into the next phase of their careers.

The Extended Phase (2004–2011)

The Context

In 2011, more than thirty years since the cohort completed their work as house staff at SAMS, I interviewed them for a fifth time. In the seven years that had passed, there were major political and policy changes as the country shifted from the second Bush administration to the historic election of President Barak Obama at the end of 2008. The dire predictions for managed care from the "right" and the "left" did not come to fruition; it neither fully controlled costs through the marketplace nor did it end the fee-for-service model. It was neither a destroyer nor savior of medicine (Brill, 2015).

During this period, these physicians experienced a historic event resulting in the most monumental change in the health care system since the passage of Medicaid and Medicare in 1965. President Obama promised and delivered on his pledge to reform health care and move the country toward universal coverage. The political process that occurred in 2008 to 2010 to attain this reform involved was in serious contention, with opposition to the Obama proposals both from Republicans and conservatives on the right and from liberal progressives on the left who wanted a "Medicare for all" system (Brill, 2015). This dynamic tension led to a compromise bill that became the Patient Protection and Affordable Care Act (ACA), which President Obama signed into law on March 23, 2010 (Kirsch, 2011). While most of the ACA had not been implemented at the time they were interviewed at the end of the extended career phase (2004–2011), it was already being criticized by Republicans, who disparagingly called it "Obamacare" (Manchikanti, Helm, et al., 2017).

In the years leading up to the ACA, however, there were other notable issues that physicians also had to contend with. Medicare and Medicaid rates and regulations, for example, continued to negatively impact the physician community overall. Payments by public and private insurers were reduced and accountability requirements increased, resulting in a tightening of restrictions on prices and coverage. Furthermore, for the first time, the introduction of the mandated electronic medical record (EMR) and the new position of the "hospitalist" (a full-time physician hired by a hospital to take care of all inpatient services) surfaced as major structural changes in medical practice. These were raised by most of the cohort spontaneously and both were depicted overwhelmingly in an unfavorable light (Gunderman, 2016; Omotosho and Emuoyibofarhe, 2014). (For more details on the EMR and hospitalists, see chapter 8 on disillusionment.)

The Cohort

The term originally assigned to this career phase in 2011 was "ending," because it was around this time period that the physicians had earlier predicted that they would retire or significantly cut back by 2011. However, hardly anyone ended their career during the entrenched-phase interviews occurring seven years earlier. Consequently, the term given to this career phase was changed to "extended," because all but one of the physicians (Dr. Conley) were still working. Most remained in full-time practice, while a few had cut back to what they described as semiactive (Drs. Finast and Beech), which, for them, meant working only four days a week or giving up an administrative or hospital role. One community practitioner moved to a new practice setting (Dr. Lynch), while another changed his practice priorities in the same city (Dr. Nolan). Three academics ascended to new positions of managerial responsibility, two at new institutions in different cities (Drs. Lash and O'Brian), and one within the same system in a different southern city (Dr. Rosen). The other eleven physicians remained in their same setting or institution. Sadly, during this period, one of the physicians, Dr. Paul, died, having left SAMS and academia a few years earlier. He apparently moved to a community-based clinic practice some years after he was last interviewed in 2004. (This information was revealed when his obituary was located years later.)

Satisfaction Index

Until this period, the trend in career satisfaction had been toward a more mixed and negative direction. Now, in this extended career phase (2004–2011), the overriding shift was in the direction of increasing satisfaction as they looked back over their thirty-plus year career track. Many more of the cohort were classified as positive based on their overall descriptions of the aspects of their career that gave them satisfaction and in their responses to the seven specific components of satisfaction (see table 2 in chapter 3).

Of the eleven community practitioners, five were positive at this stage (Drs. Johnson, Lynch, Allen, and Polikoff, and Dr. Jarvis, who trended in a positive direction). Drs. Ross, Nolan, and Mahoney (who was outside internal medicine) were classified as mixed. In addition to the three who remained negative (Drs. Cahn, Conley, and Beech), Dr. Melone moved into that category. All but one of the remaining seven academic physicians were either positive (Drs. O'Brian, Lash, Rosen, Annas, and Strelko) or moved from negative to mixed (Dr. Finast). Dr. Boswell, the one academic exception, emerged as a fully negative physician in this phase, despite only giving hints of dissatisfaction in the earlier periods of his professional life.

Satisfaction and Dissatisfaction Themes

For three of the positively disposed academics (Drs. Annas, Rosen, and Lash), I apply the term "super satisfied," given their fervent enthusiasm for their career at this stage. Dr. Annas was typical of those academics: "I enjoy it all. I'm at the point in my career and a place in the administrative structure where I get to define my job description; patients are rewarding, and we have a collegial bunch of people." Nevertheless, for the first time, he introduced a touch of negativism into the group of academic physicians—a negativism that was already full blown among the physicians in community practice—regarding the EMR. "Very little frustrates me except the switch to EMRs, which changed the workflow, not for the better."

More generally, however, the academic physicians remained positive. Dr. Boswell, who was a notable exception among academic practitioners, was so despondent about his practice that he rejected an in-person interview and instead sent me a lengthy written diatribe via email, which clearly documented just how painful his career at SAMS had become. Here are only a few excerpts to illustrate his seeming despair (with some details omitted or disguised): "I am sorry to disappoint you, but it is clear that my department chair regards me and my division as a complete failure. While quite a few people nationwide in my field know I did a pretty good job, there has not been one positive word for years from above. This institution is in crisis with an atmosphere of mistrust, and it lacks understanding of and discounts what clinicians do." He went on to provide what he considered to be unethical and perhaps illegal actions by the SAMS administration that will not be repeated here. He ended the email with this response: "It's too painful to talk about. Please understand that this upsets me too much to go into." Dr. Boswell was the outlier, however.

Among the community practitioners, several—more than in the past—praised most of the components of being a physician, as exemplified by Dr. Polikoff: "It's great work; you interact with people, you do good things. It's fascinating; you learn something every day. I truly enjoy going to work every morning. It's hard and I work my butt off. Even though I'm always behind, I absolutely love it. I'm enjoying it more now and having more fun than twenty years ago."

As in the past, relationships with patients were still the most common and important source of fulfillment for the community practitioners. In some instances, these interactions could override many of the externally imposed negative factors that caused them dissatisfaction and stress. As noted by community practitioner Dr. Melone: "Seeing patients who I've been seeing over the years still gives me pleasure. They've become friends. Even routine internal medicine patients without kidney intrusions are still pleasurable." Dr. Allen rejoiced as in past stages: "Seeing really sick patients get better and leave the hospital when I know they are going to stay out of trouble is still the best. The thing I like best is talking to and educating patients and staff."

Dr. Lynch, who had moved to practice in another oncology setting for a third time a few years earlier, resumed his positive views about his career with a few caveats: "I always love what I do: taking care of cancer patients and being the best communicator in a challenging and rewarding field." He expressed what the core of being a physician meant to him: "The politics change, the reimbursement changes, the drama of working with insurance companies certainly changes, but the basics of human encounters are always rewarding and satisfying." What upset him, he said, was "getting approvals, which takes away from patients." He noted, as did several other community practitioners, that his practice needed to hire two full-time people to deal only with finances.

In addition to the trend of deriving satisfaction from work with patients, many of the academic physicians, and a few of the community practitioners, pointed to the education/teaching aspect of practice and peer interaction as having given them the most fulfillment in the last five years. Dr. Rosen, an academic physician, concluded, "I get pleasure working with the residents, but the most satisfaction now is working with medical students, helping them grow up, nurturing them to become great doctors." Patient teaching was also an area of increasing satisfaction for community practitioners, and it was mentioned much more often in this extended phase (2004–2011) than previously. Similar to Dr. Allen, Dr. Ross, another community practitioner, described it this way: "Teaching residents and medical students gives me the greatest pleasure. I just got a lifetime achievement award for teaching. That's the single thing that gives me the most enjoyment; plus, the camaraderie of interacting with my new partners."

Dr. Lash's comment was typical: "I like counseling patients; plus, we have a terrific group of nurses and just generally everybody around is good. It's a fun place to work." On the contrary, in describing negative factors, the lack of "fun" was also invoked by a few of the mixed or negative subcohort, particularly with regard to the impact of hospitalists on medical practice and physician relationships. For example, despite deriving satisfaction from teaching and his new partners, Dr. Ross still fell into a negative category overall: "I miss the fun of medicine. It's a business. I desperately miss the collegiality with a group of doctors on a daily basis, talking about patients. We don't have it anymore; the hospitalists have killed it."

Components of Satisfaction

In spite of their overall criticism of payments and fees, satisfaction with *financial remuneration* was surprisingly the highest ever, double the percentage who were classified as satisfied in the entrenched period (1994–2004) seven years earlier, a seeming contradiction. Ironically, although the academic physicians' incomes were probably less than those of the community practitioners, the academics seemed more content with or accepting of their compensation. Dr. Rosen was typical: "It's more than adequate, and because of my leadership roles I do better than the great majority of internists. It's not why I do what I do, but it's a nice side effect. It's better than ten years ago, and I was perfectly satisfied then." Dr. Strelko confided jokingly, "I do receive enough, but my wife will kill me if she heard me telling you that. I'm not overpaid, but it's all relative." He then criticized the medical profession more generally: "Some internists and family practitioners are grossly underpaid compared to specialists; but for subspecialists you have to ask, 'How much is enough?' Studies show even the lowest paid rheumatologists are in the top three to 4 percent of this country's earners. Big salaries in medicine have been a mistake and problematic; there's a sense of entitlement now."

For the community practitioners, there were fewer complaints than expected. Dr. Allen echoed Dr. Strelko's sentiment: "Some of my partners never make enough. But in my first year I made $40,000 and I thought I'd struck it rich! I'm working less now and making more money." Also like Dr. Strelko, Dr. Nolan admitted, "I guess the standard answer is supposed to be 'no,' but I do receive enough compensation. I'm more satisfied now than ten years ago, but the hours I'm working are harder and longer." Dr. Melone also noted the relativism in responding to the question, echoing others: "I made more money than I ever thought, but now I'm making less because I've backed off night call."

Psychic/emotional satisfaction was positive for almost three-quarters of the cohort, back to where it was in the early phase (1980–1984). A majority of the physicians indicated they received more psychic/emotional satisfaction than ten years ago, while a minority said they received less or that it had stayed the same. Dr. Finast, who was semiactive at this point, said he enjoyed work more at this stage: "I'm glad to be coming here, going into clinic to see patients, and working with my colleagues, thinking about medical problems. It's better now because I don't have the same physical demands to be here at odd hours. And not being in charge of the pulmonary service now I can say, 'Sorry, that isn't my job.'" Dr. Rosen recalled his answers as in times past: "I always tell people how lucky I am. I have the best job in the world. You've interviewed me before; I'm an eternal optimist." He repeated all the areas that give him satisfaction: "helping patients, solving problems, teaching residents to be their best."

The community practitioners pinpoint different reasons for the emotional satisfaction. Dr. Cahn, in spite of his negative responses to almost all the components of satisfaction, noted, "I still get tremendous emotional satisfaction with big cases that go well. It's a rush. And I've been blessed; I haven't been sued in thirty years. But psychic satisfaction isn't as much these last ten years because of the bullshit we have to go through with EMRs and hospitalists."

To the contrary, Dr. Jarvis mentioned the reasons he was getting more emotional fulfillment than ten years earlier: "Because my terrific wife lets me spend my energy on medical stuff, and I'm more secure in what I do. I get a lot of positive feedback from lots of people at work, so it's very gratifying."

Intellectual stimulation was at its all-time high, almost double from the entrenched phase (1994–2004) phase less than ten years prior. Doctor Annas continued to view the cerebral aspects as a significant part of his professional life: "I receive more than I can handle being surrounded by a very bright group of residents and fellows who are inquisitive, curious, and hardworking."

The surprise was that most community practitioners concurred with the academics for the first time, although they perceived learning in different ways. As noted by Dr. Mahoney, "Intellectual prowess is still there. What keeps me going is the strides in medicine that translate into problem-solving." Or, as Dr. Lynch described it, "There is plenty to learn from every new patient. You have to review the literature, and due diligence by consulting experts to give state-of-the-art care. Plus, I go to professional meetings." Dr. Lynch also expressed that patients' access to information on the internet was a positive development, a sentiment that made him one of the outliers in the cohort: "Patients now bring me new information based on their research, which makes it more stimulating than ten to fifteen years ago." But most identified patient access to the internet as a reason why the doctor-patient relationship had deteriorated.

Nevertheless, in touting the positive scholarly aspects of keeping up with the rapidly changing scientific aspects of medicine, a few of the community practitioners were conscious of falling behind the new trends, like Dr. Jarvis: "The field of GI has grown geometrically. Now I'm the dinosaur. We hire sub-sub-specialists in GI. I'm the way it used to be—a generalist GI guy. Now I need to be on the internet all the time to keep current." This was a sentiment expressed by many; it was worrisome because not keeping up could be grounds for a lawsuit if something went wrong with a patient.

A positive perspective on *personal status and public recognition* also soared in this extended phase (2004–2011) for almost all of them. It is the one component that kept moving in the positive direction over time. Several of the cohort identified the sources from where their gratification came: patients, their geographic community, professional organizations, and/or peers in their subspecialty. Dr. O'Brian responded in the second person as an informant: "[As physicians,] we are pretty egocentric people; there's never enough praise. It manifests itself by leaders acknowledging you, and by success when you see your residents mature."

At the same time, most of them also downplayed it for the first time, saying they either didn't seek personal accolades or didn't care about them. It is not clear what brought about that significant change in their reaction to the question. Perhaps it was the longevity of their career and their maturity in not needing external approval as much. Dr. Ross, in a characteristically sarcastic tone, noted, "I don't get much, but I don't want much. The next time I want my name in the newspaper is when I'm dead! But in my community, us doctors play golf on Thursday, and I get to choose who plays with whom; that's the extent of my status."

For most, this downplaying of personal status in their responses did not seem driven by "false modesty" or "sour grapes," but rather a genuine humility. Dr. Johnson's comment was typical: "I actually get more than I deserve. It's embarrassing going to the mall or eating out. People stop you. To tell the truth, I certainly wouldn't say I need more than that." Similarly, Dr. Strelko commented, "I don't need a lot to keep me going. But nationally, I got an award last year for a significant contribution I made to training residents. That was nice."

Dr. Cahn, clearly an outlier on this issue, confessed that he had been worn down: "I used to care, but I don't anymore. I was voted the best GI in my area for many years. I don't read social media now. And as for the profession, I became a doctor because of Dr. Kildare and Dr. Casey [two popular TV shows about doctors]. Nothing like that exists for physicians now."

Anticipating the Future

Another surprising change from the entrenched to the extended phase was the physicians' responses as to whether they would *recommend medicine to their children*. For almost all of them, the question had a different meaning now since their children were grown and most of them, with a few exceptions, had chosen careers outside of medicine. Many were already grandfathers. Still, the number of "yes" responses to the question (with or without qualifications) more than doubled in less than a decade. Dr. Lynch's enthusiasm was typical: "Not only would I recommend it, but I think it's an absolutely spectacular career. I tell them (his two grown children) all the time it's intellectually challenging and prestigious. When I come to work, the first person who says, 'Good morning, Doctor,' still gives me a chill. It takes a huge commitment caring for someone. I tell them not to do it for monetary gain, but medicine will always provide a comfortable living."

Even the retired Dr. Conley, who almost always received a negative satisfaction score, spoke more positively, albeit with caveats, at this stage: "I wouldn't try to dissuade my children because the opportunity to make a difference could be rewarding, which is the reasons most doctors are still in medicine. I wish there were a way to get rid of some of the hassles. Ten years ago, I might have been more cautious about recommending it; when you are in the thick of it, the hassles get you down."

There were qualifications in contemplating their recommendations to their children. Dr. Jarvis, being positive, reiterated a common theme that different expectations will produce different outcomes for physician satisfaction: "My daughter chose medicine. It was her own decision, but if she asked me, I would have been encouraging. I would say, 'Do it wholeheartedly.' It's more than a job, it's gratifying and challenging.' Still, I'm jealous of what my younger-generation partners are getting in terms of benefits. We senior guys made that happen for them, but we didn't get it for ourselves. The expectations are very different now."

The minority perspective expressed by two negative physicians included their pessimistic assessment of the *future direction of medicine*. Like Dr. Jarvis above, Dr. Melone who also has a physician son, compared his own "coming of age" with his son's "new generation," but came to a different conclusion: "I'd recommend it less than 10 years ago; it's getting worse. Physicians have too large a target on their backs today. The idea that doctors should be giving up their time, their reimbursement, their respect, as opposed to everyone else in the country is too much. My son is now in medical school. It's easier for his generation. I could do their sixty-hour-a-week job now in my sleep. We worked a lot harder and we were much tougher."

A sizeable minority were still *optimistic about the future of medicine*, but the number was smaller than those who would recommend the profession to their children. As a cohort, however, they rebounded to almost the same percentage of optimism as when they were in the early phase (1980–1984). In reaching their conclusions, they looked back over and assessed their own career trajectory as well as over past and future trends for their profession. Dr. O'Brian, who became an academic administrator in this extended phase (2004–2011), projected a mixed perspective about the future: "I'm on the optimistic side. I think in my position I can still influence change. My pessimism comes from a lack of finances. I'm using better fiscal management skills, but if there's no funding, there is only so much you can do."

Ironically, while many were cautiously optimistic about the future of medicine for themselves, they were less sanguine about the profession as a whole. Interestingly, many interpreted the question about the future of medicine as being about the future of health care reform. Dr. Lynch and more than half of his peers were not positive, even with the newly passed ACA. Dr. Lynch said, "I'm pessimistic about health care reform. I'm concerned about decreasing reimbursement and fewer physicians going into primary care. It's tragic when people go without care because they can't afford it or lose their insurance." Ironically, it was Dr. Conley, who retired because of those negative experiences, who predicted an eventual radical move to a single-payer system with salaried physicians financed or run by government: "Negotiating with 150 different insurance companies is not worth it. I'd take one government payer. The future depends on how many hoops you have to jump through. We need a simplified system." He and others called for even more extreme proposals than President Obama's ACA. (See chapter 7 on health care reform for more details.)

Almost all predicted a continuation of cutbacks and "rationing" on the patient side, consolidations or mergers on the facility side, less autonomy of decision-making for practitioners, and more competition from nurse practitioners and from subspecialties like surgeons. Almost unanimously, they forecasted less payment or reimbursement for physicians, even though most were cautiously sanguine about their own finances, perhaps because they were at this late career stage.

The minority of negative and mixed satisfied/dissatisfied physicians saw uncertainty ahead and were not sure in which direction the country would go. Dr. Beech, a semiactive community physician at this stage, was ambivalent about the future of the medical profession even with his daughter as a medical student: "It depends on your perspective. If you are a nine to five kind of guy, then you're more optimistic. But I'm turning into a curmudgeon. I think doctors are generally happier when they can work for themselves provided they could get through the bureaucratic BS. I could never be in the environment my daughter is going through. My son saw my career and said, 'No way in hell do I want to work as hard as you did, Dad.'"

More than ever, many predicted a major shift in the medical workforce, including a continuing move toward more salaried physicians, which doctors as diverse as Dr. Strelko, an academic physician, and Dr. Lynch, a community practitioner, seemed to accept, but not welcome. They also projected a continuation of the surge in midlevel practitioner nurses and physicians' assistants, which they deemed as necessary to help manage the advent of EMRs and hospitalists. (See chapter 5 on peer relationships and chapter 8 on disillusionment for more on hospitalists and EMRs.)

Looking to the future, given that all but one of the cohort were married with grown children, almost all mentioned wanting to spend more time with their spouses, whom many lamented they had neglected for years, and with grandchildren, who were often now in the picture. However, when thinking about a postretirement scenario, most could not imagine transitioning totally to a nonmedical role; instead, many foresaw volunteering at "free clinics," which Dr. Conley was already doing, and as Dr. Paul was doing at the time of his death (according to his obituary). Others saw themselves educating the new generation of physicians, perhaps similar to Drs. Allen and Cahn, who were already engaged in this endeavor.

Given the trend toward negativism or mixed reviews in the earlier entrenched period (1994–2004), the overall reversal toward more positive perspectives on their work with higher levels of satisfaction during this extended phase (2004–2011) was stark. It seems that what changed was their expectations, rather than reality. It was not so much that their compensation increased, but rather it seems that it did not get worse. And while most expressed similar dissatisfactions with the external environment, especially with the hospitalist and EMR developments, many seemed to assert that their intellectual stimulation, psychic satisfaction, and public recognition for themselves was satisfactory whether or not it had improved. In articulating these more positive views of their circumstances at this stage, some appeared to be reflecting over the previous five to ten years, while others seemed to be applying a retrospective lens to their whole career path over thirty-plus years.

All had survived to this point; and with hindsight, many felt they had thrived in spite of, not because of, the external environment. Notwithstanding their own predictions in 2004 or earlier, the vast majority were still working full time in 2011, and the rest, except for Dr. Conley, were semiactive. Most did not let go of their professional careers (at least not completely) and were now, once again, predicting some form of retirement at different time periods in the next five years, and for a few, even longer out.

The Ending Phase (2011–2016)

The Context

In 2016, five years after the prior interview cycle, the United States was in the midst of a slow economic recovery from the recent major recession, although President Obama maintained his personal popularity and was re-elected for a second term as President. The ACA was in full swing and had added 22 million Americans to the insured rolls either through new private insurance options or expanded Medicaid, in spite of continuing Republican opposition (Rawal, 2016). While more Americans were insured than ever before, the ACA remained somewhat unpopular, one reason being that a large number of Americans saw their insurance premiums raised. By early 2016, the presidential campaign was beginning to heat up, with the Republicans and then-candidate Donald Trump still threatening to repeal the ACA, and the political divide between liberals and conservatives widening and intensifying (Health Affairs, 2020). After winning a close election in 2016, President Trump continued for his almost four years in office to denounce and threaten to repeal the ACA. As this book in being completed at the end of 2020, Joe Biden has been declared the president-elect of the United States defeating President Trump, although the fate of the ACA is before the Supreme Court. (See a more detailed account of these physicians' views on the ACA and health care reform in chapter 7.)

At this stage, the institutionalization of both the in-hospital medical position of hospitalist and the EMR systems—both transformative trends affecting health care delivery and medical practice—were in full swing. Both of these developments in the way the American health system functioned that were identified spontaneously by many of the cohort in the extended phase (2004–2011) were magnified in this last ending phase in 2016. In this period the physicians were directly asked how they were affected by those two revolutionary features of the medical system. Their continued strongly negative and visceral responses to the EMR and hospitalist changes are presented next in this chapter. These factors are also described more in depth in chapter 8 on disillusionment, as both were among the reasons for the sense of despair conveyed at the end of their careers.

The Cohort

By 2016 it was expected that many more of the cohort would have been partially or fully retired given their predictions five and more years earlier. During this phase two more community practitioners, Drs. Jarvis and Melone, moved into retirement, joining the already retired Dr. Conley. Academic Dr. Finast, semiactive in the extended period (2004–2011), also moved into full retirement reluctantly because of illness, while Dr. Mahoney who remained in a non-internal medicine practice also retired a few years earlier than he had predicted, clearly disillusioned with the changes occurring in his setting. . Drs. Johnson, Allen, and

Beech cut back on their administrative and/or hospital responsibilities but were still practicing with identified end dates in sight, even though they noted that they still wanted to keep a foot in the "medical" door. They had moved over rather than entirely out. Additionally, Dr. Nolan had reconfigured his practice, giving up his long-term care investment and anticipating some volunteer medical work in the future.

The more surprising elements at this ending stage (2011–2016) were that several physicians had made significant professional moves laterally or vertically since the entrenched (1994–2004) or extended (2004–2011) periods. Drs. O'Brian, Lash, and Rosen moved up the academic administrative ladder in different institutions, and Dr. Lynch, who, after a stint of practicing medicine in another country, came back to his home city and obtained a part-time oncology position in his fourth new setting. The rest of the physicians (Drs. Strelko, Annas, Ross, Cahn, Polikoff, Finast, and Boswell) remained in their same settings.

Satisfaction Index

Moving from the extended (2004–2011) to the ending (2011–2016) phase, the satisfaction trend for the cohort was once again more mixed and less positive overall from just five years earlier. There were many more nuances and caveats to qualify their views of their career, regardless of their current working status. Had the interviews ended in 2011 when most were anticipating retirement in the next five years, a much more optimistic and content cohort would have been described. By 2016, however, that optimism had receded. This again confirms the proposition that career moves over time are not necessarily linear nor unidirectional (Saldana, 2003).

Applying the Satisfaction Index, twelve did not change from the extended period (2004–2011). But for those where there was some movement, it was in a less positive direction—e.g., from positive to mixed (Drs. Johnson, Allen, Lynch, and Jarvis) or mixed to negative (Mahoney). Drs. Melone and Beech, who moved from negative to mixed had either retired or were semiactive, respectively. Dr. Boswell, who was still in an academic position at SAMS, was classified as negative given his refusal once again to be interviewed with a one-word capitalized and bold **"NO!"** with an exclamation point in his emailed response to my request.

Satisfaction and Dissatisfaction Themes

There were multiple factors that seemed to account for a more toughened ending phase (2011–2016), including their self-described reality of getting older, being less in control of their setting, and in many cases, experiencing the acumen and observing the lifestyles of "the new generation." This is also discussed in more detail in chapter 5 on peer relationships, and in chapter 9 on the interactions between their personal and professional lives.

For the academic physicians, satisfaction continued to be the teaching and research aspects of their practice, and for some, their recognized leadership in their institution and beyond. As Dr. Rosen suggested, "The most satisfactory thing for me has always been teaching residents how to think through clinical problems so they will be better doctors. Also, it's really nice to be nationally known for your research and to be involved in big national organizations." Dr. O'Brian, who moved up the academic leadership ladder in the previous five years, reflected on the positive elements of overseeing a major medical division in a new institution: "I still like seeing patients and doing research." He reaffirmed, "I've enjoyed my career in academic medicine. My personality is such that I've always liked challenges and have dealt well with rejections. I still like coming to work. And I like the fun part of the job recruiting young interns who are energetic and enthusiastic." He then applied a macro lens as he turned to what was least satisfying: "The health care system is in trouble. Managing our patients, managing education of our students, and, managing a research operation—are all challenging in difficult financial times."

In his response to what was most satisfying, Dr. Strelko acknowledged the same quintessential academic perspective: "My answers are going to be the same as I gave you last time. I have no regrets. You're working in a field with a lot of smart, nice, and highly productive people."

Patient-care-related factors remained prominent for the community practitioners. Nevertheless, in the context of describing what is satisfying and not about his career, Dr. Nolan for example, brought in a negative theme echoed by him in the past and by so many others, sleep deprivation, which plagued him his whole career: "The most satisfying part is I don't have to do as much of the physically demanding part any more. The dirty dark secret of medicine has always been night call; now it is once or twice a month. Previously it was every third night for too many years. That took its toll."

Dr. Nolan and others, like Dr. Beech, voiced the existential, ever-stressful lack of sleep aspect of practice well into their career trajectory: "The least satisfying had been the nights and the weekends. You miss all kinds of stuff with your family. Many times, you have to begin your day with less than full REM sleep." A few of the doctors like Dr. Beech, semiactive, compensated for the dissatisfying aspects of their environment by taking more control over their practice and eliminating some of those elements: "Insurance companies are less of a negative to me now only because I don't go to the hospitals anymore. I'm just hired help. I show up, see patients, collect a paycheck. I don't run the practice or hire or fire anymore."

Dr. Allen responded first to the positive patient aspects of his thirty-five-plus years of cardiology practice as he did in each of the past stages: "Seeing patients in trouble and making them better has always been satisfying." Still, Dr. Allen, who had been positive his whole career, was now classified as mixed as he was planning to retire a few months after the final interview because the external pressures facing his group practice became too severe: "My new patient consults have always been ninety minutes long or longer. I can't see people every fifteen minutes, and that's what I'll have to do if I stay fighting with the hospital and lawyers. That's why I'm quitting. As the president of my group, I was engaged in a sixteen-month contract negotiation. I couldn't take it anymore. I gave up. I'm out of here in just six months."

Some put up with similar negative facets of practice, only because those were outweighed by the positives. Dr. Johnson, who also was classified as mixed in this final stage, revealed, "As a medical oncologist, it's the relationships with your patients that have been satisfying. You take care of people in difficult times; you make strong bonds. And it's great to have my daughter here practicing with me; that's fun. I would have probably walked out of here some five years ago if it wasn't for her and my ties to the patients in this practice."

Dr. Jarvis, who was already retired, noted his satisfaction from patient care and teaching, like others. But he continued without prompting to rant about the changes to GI practice that led him to leave medicine a few years earlier: "My subspecialty had become more about medical invasive procedures than medicine; I didn't want to become a 'surgeon-light.'" His dissatisfaction then morphed into a much longer diatribe about how his hospital system had swallowed other hospitals, which was making hospital practice harder: "It's a physical beating and that type of stress is for younger people, so I pulled out."

Dr. Polikoff, is an outlier as he remained the only community practitioner falling into the continuing positive subgroup. He continued to be overwhelmingly satisfied ever since he left academic medicine for an HMO practice after the early phase (1980–1984): "It's amazing that I've been working in the same place with the same doctors for as long as I have. Still I'm glad I did a fellowship in infectious disease because it was an additional two years to really get good in something. I say my career is one hundred percent satisfying." In spite of Dr. Polikoff's statement that he has been fully satisfied, he spent more than twice as much time during this final interview defining the problems rather than the positives of his practice: "Things we have to do to satisfy the demand of the insurance companies in order to get paid now are ridiculous. You've got to make sure you've considered all the different diagnoses and documented them. We are pushed by the insurance companies to meet certain benchmarks. That's not very satisfying." Dr. Polikoff wasn't finished; he added negative views about some colleagues, also echoed by many others: "My other pet peeve is that I double-book myself to see all the patients. Yet we have seventeen internists who won't. It upsets me that colleagues are not willing to see walk-ins; it's still aggravating."

Both academics and community practitioners frequently discussed the administrative and system-related hassles of their institutions over which they have little control. This caused dissatisfaction and even despair and cynicism (also discussed in chapter 8 on disillusionment). Whether driven internally by deans and CEOs, or externally driven by public or private insurance companies, the dictates from above had a negative impact on them to varying degrees. For the first time, Dr. Rosen added a stressful component to his description of his otherwise fully satisfying career: "Recently, there have been administrative hassles dealing with my dean. I've been in leadership positions and have very strong feelings about his micro-management style. He's a surgeon and acts like one! So that's been less fun."

Academic oncologist Dr. Strelko, who had moved three times in his career to different medical centers, took the opportunity of the interview at this stage to expound on changes over time and his overall mixed assessment of his academic leadership career. He addressed what is least satisfying first, although the question was asked in reverse: "It all comes down to turf, ego, and money. I did medical school when there was a never-ending supply of money. If the hospital wanted to build or start a program, they did. Times are different now. My institution is under financial pressures which create a lot of tension. But being a doctor is still a pretty good job. I could practice anywhere" (as he contemplates moving out west from the New England area after retirement).

Dr. Cahn, the always-negative community practitioner, had succinct harsh answers regarding his dissatisfaction with his work: "There's no art in medicine anymore. It's about filling out forms from the ACA and dealing with the absurdity of hospitalists. The quality stinks, although hospitalists take away the scut work of hospital admissions. And don't get me started on EMRs!"

Retired community nephrologist Dr. Melone balanced the positives and negatives after his career of more than thirty-five years: "Least satisfying has been the interaction with the payers, having to justify everything. Also, the EMR made me crazy." On the other hand, he touted all the components of satisfaction: intellectual, emotional, and personal recognition from his career: "What's satisfying is that once a patient is with a nephrologist like me, you become the primary care doctor since other doctors are too afraid of those patients. Second, most folks think nephrologists are good doctors; third, it's intellectually stimulating, It's fun."

Components of Satisfaction

The cohort was the most affirming of their *financial remuneration* at this stage, despite some disgruntlement, which was even more than at the end of the extended phase (2004–2011), five years earlier. Almost all expressed the views that they have received adequate or satisfactory financial compensation. Perhaps as they have achieved their life's comforts for themselves and their families, they did not aspire to acquiring more material wealth and did not need additional assets.

Even the academics expressed satisfaction with remuneration at the end. Dr. Annas reiterated that he always felt he was compensated well, while Dr. Lash responded, "It's exceeded my expectations." In the main, they seemed more affirmative at this stage. Dr. Strelko put himself in the role of an informant for the physician community by responding similarly to the way he did years earlier: "I once asked an orthopedic surgeon who made a lot of money, 'How much is enough?' His answer was, 'A little bit more than last year.' It's never enough for certain people."

Likewise, Dr. Finast also uses the term "embarrassed" as he, Dr. Strelko, and others took the opportunity to lash out at greedy physicians who they believe give the field a bad reputation. "I think the medical profession right now still produces so many doctors who are so rich. Salaries often exceed the value of the work. I'm embarrassed by some doctors' payments."

There were some variations on the income theme by the community practitioners. Dr. Melone, who retired a few years earlier, noted, "In the early years it was too much; now it's too little; so, I guess it averaged out." Dr. Jarvis began with, "I'm absolutely well remunerated," and then provided a much more complex assessment. He also served as an informant for his subspecialization: "Money was never my driving force. I just read a survey where half the current gastroenterologists feel like they're not getting paid enough, which is shocking. I've made more money than I ever needed. My pediatrician daughter gets paid much less." As with Dr. Jarvis, more often than not, these physicians adopted a relative, rather than absolute, sense of whether they felt they were adequately compensated.

Not surprisingly in this final phase, the topic of EMRs and related issues of corporate-driven expectations crept into several conversations about finances for the first time. As outliers, Drs. Nolan and O'Brian, in very different settings, spoke negatively about their finances in this regard. As Dr. Nolan noted, "It's getting harder and more complicated with the advent of EMRs to be compensated for the time you put in. EMRs raise the requirements for the standards of care, but decrease your productivity, so you get paid less." Dr. O'Brian commented, "I always groan because money is tight. My salary is performance-based, based on how the system is doing. There is a sense of loss of control. Unlike individual faculty, my productivity is based on whether hospital bills are justified and on patient satisfaction. I'm doing okay, but barely."

During this ending phase (2011–2016) of their careers, the physicians indicated that *intellectual stimulation* was strong, and their overall responses to the intellectual aspects of their careers remained very positive. It continued to be a raison d'être for the academics. Dr. Annas's response was typical: "I receive it 24/7 because of the teaching environment with bright, energetic people." Dr. O'Brian suggested that "this academic medical center [where I teach] still provides [intellectual stimulation] with smart students who ask dumb but provocative questions. It's stimulating."

Community practitioners, speaking positively, also noted their opportunities for intellectual stimulation, particularly from the scholarly and cerebral aspects of medicine which, unexpectedly, seemed to temper other negative components of their practice. Dr. Melone suggested, "As a nephrologist you've got to keep your brain awake!" And it was a motivating force for Dr. Beech to remain semiactive: "This is one of the reasons I agreed to work another year. I would hate to be sitting and watching TV. I get stimulation from seeing patients with unknown conditions—I go to the books. It's like trying to solve a puzzle." Dr. Johnson described his subspecialty as intellectually stimulating, more so than in earlier stages: "That's the great thing about oncology; there's just been an explosion of new drugs and new treatments. That's one of the reasons I chose oncology as opposed to primary care."

For the community physicians, one might assume that a sense of boredom would creep in because of doing similar tasks for so many years. Furthermore, the need to keep up with their subspecialization because of the fear of lawsuits and making mistakes could lead to stress rather than satisfaction. On the contrary, however, staying current prevented them from succumbing to routinization and complacency.

Dr. Nolan, however, was an outlier on the cerebral benefits: "I think the intellectual aspect has suffered. It's what I miss about the old system. There used to be a much better feeling in the medical community; you knew everybody. We used to have medical education meetings. County medical societies have withered away." Clearly Dr. Nolan appeared to be missing more than just intellectual stimulation; he, as do others, seemed to long for a sense of connection and camaraderie.

While the specific question about *psychic satisfaction* was omitted in the ending phase, it seems that that aspect of their careers was of great importance, given that their responses to receiving adequate *professional recognition as a physician* were the highest-ever in positivity. Most felt that they received sufficient appreciation, and in some cases, "more than enough."

Yet as an outlier, Dr. O'Brian, who moved up to run a large medical department, was one of the few who had a complicated answer to whether he received sufficient public acknowledgement, a comment that echoed Dr. Nolan's sentiment above. Dr. O'Brian missed the personal connections from colleagues who provided him with positive feedback: "In this job as a top medical administrator, you're not as intimately tied to the people you oversee because it's a larger group. It's 400 faculty around the state. It could be lonely up there!"

There were a few others who downplayed the importance of public recognition as they had back in the entrenched stage (1994–2004). For example, Dr. Beech commented, "I'm not interested in that," while Dr. Allen noted that public recognition had not made a difference except "being called 'doctor' instead of 'mister.'" Most had positive reactions, which ranged from a humble, "I get more than I deserve," by Dr. Rosen, to an expression of appreciation, as Dr. Mahoney recalled, "A physician who was treating my wife remembered me and said how they missed me since I retired. That was nice to know."

Others also qualified their affirmative perspectives in notable ways. For example, Dr. Lynch compared how he is viewed versus how the profession is seen by using "we" rather than "I": "We still have some esteem in the community, but I don't think it's what it was. Still, when I'm in a situation where I don't know anybody, and it comes out that I'm a physician, it's generally considered a positive." Dr. Jarvis, on the other hand, with wry humor, revealed his deep emotional feelings about no longer receiving that kind of attention now that he is retired: "It was very humbling to read all the cards people sent me when I retired. I also got a bunch of awards for being old, and for teaching. There were a lot of tearful goodbyes from patients." For him it appears that psychic satisfaction and personal recognition were related.

The cohort was also directly asked about their view of the *status of the medical profession*. The last time this question was directly asked was in 2004 in the entrenched phase, when virtually all had believed that medicine had dramatically fallen in status, whether justified or not. Now in the ending phase, specifically asked again twelve years later, their responses were much more complex and nuanced, although in the view of most, the downward trajectory they noted in 2004 had been only partially reversed. In a comment that was typical of the cohort's responses, Dr. Beech noted, "I don't think the status is what it once was. I think we're viewed as blue-collar workers now. We may be viewed better than insurance salesmen or lawyers, but still everyone second guesses you."

Although he had retired six years ago, Dr. Conley thought both he personally and the profession had weathered the storm, although not without costs: "It's better now, but I remember times when it felt like all the doctors were under siege. Every group comes under attack at one time or another, whether lawyers, teachers, doctors, or politicians. I think our status has pretty much stayed the same. It's not an easy lifestyle, but it's a satisfying one, and still prestigious."

Dr. Allen, speaking as an informant, referenced the difficult work arrangements that Dr. Conley had also noted: "Our status has gone down a little bit given all the lawyer ads on TV stating that 'this drug will kill you if you take it.'" Dr. Cahn was the most negative: "I don't think for a minute it is what it was," specifically referencing the system of hospitalists once again.

Dr. Lash was an outlier as the only physician who was fully positive about the profession: "Its status has gone up. Medicine still gives you a very secure life. There's an enormous amount of respect and prestige, and it's a satisfactory professional life. You're contributing to people's lives every day; it doesn't really get much better than that."

Anticipating the Future

Whether they would *recommend medicine to their children*, and whether they would recommend it more or less than in the prior ten years, has been one proxy for how the physicians view not only their own career but also the new generation of physicians and the medical profession more generally over time. Just five or six years earlier in the extended phase (2004–2011), the answers to the question of whether they would recommend medicine to their children were a resounding "yes," with and without provisos, doubling of the percentage of positive responses from the entrenched phase (1994–2004).

Yet once again, the path was not straightforward, and in the ending phase (2011–2016), a greater ambivalence on this issue returned. This time, a smaller majority endorsed the idea, but with added caveats and cons along with the pros. Full-throated positive testimonials were very few. Three clearly said they would not recommend it, including Dr. Jarvis, whose daughter became a pediatrician: "For sure I'm much less enthusiastic now."

Dr. Mahoney suggested he would recommend it only "because we need people to provide it if they have the aptitude and capacity to deal with what's involved with it," which is not exactly a resounding endorsement. Similarly, Dr. O'Brian would only recommend it "if they had a passion for it." Dr. Nolan may have been only half joking when he replied, "I didn't have to recommend it to my children. They saw my lifestyle and they both said, 'No thank you; never.'"

In spite of seeing a number of issues complicating their professional practice—including things they identified as encroaching on their autonomy, interfering with their decision-making, and external peer pressure—the physicians nevertheless tilted toward optimism when asked their feelings about *the future of medicine* at this final stage of their career. (Perhaps, hope springs eternal!) Nevertheless, there was a caveat; their optimism focused mostly on technological and clinical advances in medicine—similar to what was expressed in the entrenched phase (1994–2004)—and less on the practice or career aspects of professional life.

Not surprisingly, the academics overall were more optimistic than the community practitioners. They appear as a subcohort to be the most fulfilled in these later years. Dr. Lash's enthusiasm is palpable: "I think the explosion of genomics leading to new discoveries and changing lives is just extraordinary; hard to know what's going to happen next. I would say in the next ten to twenty years there will be lots of medical breakthroughs."

Nevertheless, even a few academics inserted a note of caution in their otherwise positive outlook related to mounting costs and consequences. Dr. Strelko proclaimed, "I am optimistic in the cancer world. Understanding molecular biology is translating into better treatments. In the next ten to fifteen years, there's going to be dramatic improvements. I am less optimistic about the corporatization of medicine."

Many community practitioners identified several downsides in contemplating the future of medicine, pointing to restrictions and rationing on health care, thus painting a complex picture of the direction of medicine. Here Dr. Beech qualified his answers, as did Dr. Strelko above, separating the science from its application in the practice world: "I would like to be optimistic because my daughter's a doctor. One of the allures of medicine in my time was that you would hang up your shingle and do things the way you thought they ought to be done. Now, you try to get hired by a big hospital group; that would be very stressful to me. I'm pessimistic about medicine, even though we're entering a phase where we can test your genome and know exactly what medicine to give. In that sense, I'm optimistic."

Two others in the community cohort were totally pessimistic, projecting no redeeming value as they neared the end of their careers. For example, Dr. Cahn, one of the two most negative physicians still actively engaged in a subspecialty area (the other being Dr. Ross), suggested, "I'm very pessimistic, but I view myself in my last chapter. I feel sorry for my younger partners. I see nothing optimistic. There's very little down the road for GI procedures with the continuing ridiculous rules, and insurance companies deciding medications and procedures." Dr. Ross expressed similar sentiments: "I'm pretty pessimistic because medicine has modest prestige and modest income now, with an onslaught of physicians' assistants and nurse practitioners. But it doesn't make a difference to me. I'll work a couple of more years and then get out."

To be sure, the prognosis articulated by most of the cohort was that the future in medicine would be different. *Change* was the operative word. This sentiment was accompanied by various laments and ambivalence as to the high-tech, low-touch future. As Dr. Melone, who was retired at this point, reflected, "I'm pessimistic because it's not going to be the calling that I thought it was when I began. They're not going to be doing it for the same reason we did." Perhaps not surprisingly, those still working felt more apprehension about the future of medicine compared to those who were retired or close to retirement, with the latter expressing more acceptance of what they saw as the inevitable future trends of the profession.

At the time of the interviews in 2016, while the nature of practice continued to change and the external factors affected the provision of medical care, a number of doctors were on their way into retirement. Current financial and administrative pressures leading to stress and discontent were strongly expressed as the most common reasons for those anticipating retirement by Drs. Allen, Johnson, and Beech. Dr. Beech, for example, practicing four days a week at this stage, conveyed a sense of excitement as well as relief about letting go: "At the end of this year I'm done completely, and looking forward to traveling and seeing my grandkids. Never, never will I return: Amen!"

Drs. Nolan, Ross, Lynch, and Cahn had decided to continue practicing medicine for the near future—happy or not. Dr. Nolan changed his views several times: "It's my game plan now to do this for another two years and then retire. My wife is shocked that I ever would think about retiring then. We have a farm in the county with a free clinic trying to recruit me, that's a plus."

Dr. Cahn, always a negatively classified physician despite a burgeoning and lucrative GI practice, seemed conflicted about his future as he reflected on the past, linking psychic satisfaction and professional recognition: "What's satisfying is first, my relationships with patients that I've cared for now, some for over thirty years; second, I'm very good at what I do, so the psychological, positive feedback from patients is what drives me to work every day. If I were retired, I could never get that. To sit at home and not be stimulated mentally and not receive that regular positive charge from patients that make your day, is unthinkable." On the other hand, the external pressures made him think about retirement, albeit reluctantly: "I've already told my wife that I will likely retire in six years. If it continues to go on the path of destruction, I don't know that I'll last till then. I'm tired of it."

Deep sentiments were revealed as they reflected on their current lives, both by those who had already retired and by those who tried to envision their lives once they made the move. Dr. Melone, who retired in 2013, served as an informant for his peers as he reflected upon his own retirement and compared it to others who are having or had more difficulty: "I'm doing as much of nothing as I can now, laughing at all the guys doing the work. But there is a large segment who believe that you are what you do; when you stop being a doctor, you're nobody. Those guys have trouble filling that big void. Other physicians who retire raise horses or something else that identifies them."

It's not clear what Dr. Melone felt in his heart. When he revealed what he had been doing since retirement from full-time nephrology, it is evident that he did not let go of his profession entirely; rather he chose a third path—working part time in another field of medicine where he feels valued. Seemingly he had not practiced what he preached earlier. "My idea of retiring is now working a half-day a week in a specialized clinic, not doing nephrology. I'm the only internist in this new setting, so I get some of the off-the-wall cases to play with. It also keeps my brain awake. I've also been goofing off, playing golf, keeping two condominiums, plus a little travel." He seemed to be following what he identified as essential earlier in his career, the need to keep alert and stimulated.

Nevertheless, Dr. Melone and others were struggling to find and maintain a happy balance, with health and well-being seemingly paramount. (This issue is further discussed in chapter 9 on the intersections of the personal and the professional.) Dr. Jarvis, who retired in 2013, praised the retirement path he took by presenting an undesirable view of the alternative process of cutting back rather than leaving completely. He chose the latter path. "I thought about my retirement process. Several of my partners went part time. None of them enjoyed it. In the office, you become a second-class citizen, not worth much because those working still need to cover afterhours and weekends. The full-time partners felt the part-timers were getting paid too much; the part- time guys felt they weren't getting paid enough. I decided to set a date and stop."

Although Dr. Jarvis did not miss the stress, he seemed to miss greatly the peer interaction and recognition from colleagues, which Drs. Melone, O'Brian, and Nolan all alluded to earlier. Dr. Jarvis conveyed an element of loneliness under the surface, although he denied it. One can also interpret a tinge of nostalgia and wistfulness: "You don't realize how much stress you are under when you're working. Now the time pressure is gone—it's just fantastic. I have plenty of time to take long bike rides, read like crazy, learn photography. I haven't defined myself as a doctor. But I admit it's a little different. Whereas before you'd have interns and residents taking down everything you said like it should be on stone tablets; you'd speak and people would jump; now, nothing. That was a big change."

For Dr. Polikoff, who had maintained his HMO practice, the external pressures affecting so many of his community practice cohort did not seem to disturb him. He appeared content with his rather stable professional life and could not imagine it another way. Hence, his trepidation about leaving was causing him anxiety: "I'm going to have to make a decision when I'm going to retire. It's something my wife and I talk about all the time. I'm not ready. I'm going to be cutting back so I can have Friday off. In five or six years, I'll have to decide, but I'm not sure how." Dr. Polikoff continued to describe many of the after-retirement activities he anticipated, not unlike what has come to pass for Dr. Jarvis. He also admitted to struggling with his wife: "I plan to ride my bike, play my guitar more, do photography, argue with my wife more. We have lots of grandkids and are active in our community. Should we stay in our big house or move? My wife is on me all the time, and it is not pleasant." He reflected the ambivalence that so many articulated or conveyed by their affect and tone if not their words.

Formerly positive, Dr. Allen seemed to be ending on a downward trajectory: "After sixteen months of negotiating hassles with the local hospital, I said, 'I quit.

I can't take it anymore.' I gave them a one-year notice. I'm quitting on April Fool's Day. I'm looking forward to playing golf, not getting up at six o'clock every morning. Having fun. I might do a little teaching. Sadly, in the negotiation, the hospital said I have to stay away from patients." It is clear how strongly he was affected by the restrictions placed on him. He was also counting the specific day two years after officially leaving when he said he can stop worrying about patient lawsuits. The sadness was palpable.

Dr. Johnson's perspective on his plans for retirement reinforced the narrative that the external climate for group-based community practice was becoming more restrictive: "I'm not sure yet about retiring. My contract is up September 2017. At sixty-five, I don't think I'm going to be seeing patients anymore. Maybe I'll remain a medical director, depends on how things go with the hospital. If I don't make progress, I'm out of here. I'm not going to miss the insurance companies and EMRs."

Dr. Lynch was approaching a future without medicine cautiously: "What I'll do when I retire in two years is unclear. Travel, enjoy my grandkids, take some classes. I don't have any compelling goals. I guess that's why I initially thought I would like being retired, quickly realized I was bored, so I'm back part time."

On the other hand, Dr. Lash, who was in a new administrative position, was an outlier. He discussed the future only in general terms; he really could not imagine a life without leadership and formal responsibility in a health care setting. He was frank about retirement: "I think it's a privilege to see how science might change clinical medicine. Now, I'm still committed to seeing how medicine will develop. I don't see myself retiring while I still have a capacity to contribute. I'm not looking forward to ending."

The questions about their futures brought up heretofore hidden aspects of their personal lives, health, and age, as well as heartfelt comments on the status of older physicians. Their own issues with health and aging came out slowly. I am not sure the doctors would have revealed them if I had not probed deeper on their plans for the future, or if they did not know me as well and trust me (discussed further in chapter 9 on the personal and professional)

As a few anticipate leaving and many have recently left professional life, their thoughts about the future of medicine seem even more profound. They have given so much to their profession since entering medical school and have seen it change profoundly, while it also changed them at the same time. Perhaps the "through put" that Saldana describes is adaptability and resilience (2003). For so many, the problems appeared to outweigh progress as they pondered their own prospects and that of the profession more generally at the end. Still, except for Dr. Paul, who died while still active, and Dr. Boswell, who appeared too pained to even discuss his life, they all found some redeeming features of their career choices (discussed further in chapter 10 on what they miss and regret).

5   *"Speaking of Their Own"*

RELATIONSHIPS WITH PEERS,
PARTNERS, AND PROTÉGÉS

These physicians' relationships with fellow physicians were complicated and changing throughout the course of their careers. This chapter examines the cohort's interactions with peers and colleagues in depth, including the way the terms *peer* and *colleague* take on different meanings at different times in their professional lives. While they were still in the SAMS residency program, the term *peers* was used for their fellow house officers at their same level, or one or two years ahead of, or behind them. As they moved through various phases of practice, the physicians began to make a distinction between peers who were their partners or close colleagues in their setting or referral network, and physicians who were either outside their network, or physicians more generally as a profession.

They were asked about their relationships with their subordinates, superiors, and contemporaries with a particular focus on the "new generation of physicians"; that is, how they experienced the younger cohorts who were still in training or who had recently emerged on the medical scene. Recurring questions included, "How does it feel now that the shoe is on the other foot? (for those who had left the academic environment)" "How do you relate to the current group of house staff, and how do those house staff view you as a physician?" "What is your relationship with other physicians inside and outside your setting?"

The chapter is divided into two areas: the first part looks at the physicians' perspectives on their peers and mentors when they were house staff, as well as how their perspectives on house staff evolved over career stages—both in terms of their views on the new generations of house staff coming up behind them as well as their evolving views on attending physician roles. It sheds light on some of the underlying professional dynamics that inform these physicians' views on their peers and professional networks. This section also provides an overview over time of a dilemma that the community physicians faced, that of being labeled as an *LMD* (a "local medical doctor")—a term that they had used pejoratively when they were house staff and later applied to many of their colleagues and even to themselves, once they had moved out of academia into their own community practices.

In the second part of the chapter, I focus more directly on providing the physicians' changing views on their own contemporaries, highlighting the way the physicians' views of their relationships with their colleagues and peers—both in their practices and outside their own settings—developed across career stages.

Physician Views on House Officers, "LMDs," and Attending Faculty across Career Phases

The Entry Phase (1979–1980)

Relationships with Fellow House Staff and Attending Faculty.

At the very beginning of their careers, right after they completed the SAMS residency program and most were moving into fellowships, the physicians described their house staff peers as being critical to their professional development (Mizrahi, 1986). In the first interview cycle in 1980, as ending house officers, I asked them to comment on their contemporaries (that is, reflect on their fellow house staff in the SAMS internal medicine residency program, including those who were a year or two in front of or behind them). I also asked them to comment on the attending faculty who supervised and taught them. Here I summarize and present their responses to these questions which are described more fully in my earlier book (Mizrahi, 1986).

On the whole, the cohort extolled the virtues of the SAMS program because they characterized it in their own words as a "house staff-run program." As SAMS house officers, while many had built bonds with individual faculty members, without question, the most memorable and positive aspects for almost all were their close relationships with their fellow house officers (Mizrahi, 1986). Time and again, they recounted that their peers were the ones they trusted the most, the ones they turned to for support, and even the ones from whom they learned the most. Their definition of *peer* was quite narrow; it was limited primarily to those fellow house officers within internal medicine. Near the time when they were ready to move to the next career phase (in 1980), they discussed with me the pros and cons of having had almost total autonomy and responsibility for patients, while under the tutelage of fellow house officers who were, for the most part, one or two years their senior (Mizrahi, 1986). Attending physicians who had the formal supervisory role were a distant second. Some of the cohort characterized the program as a "peer socialization" model (Hafferty, 1988).

The physicians in the cohort described most of the attending faculty (the term for the academic teaching physicians), with the exception of a few "role models" in their pending subspecialties, as unavailable, uninterested, or incapable of supervising them, particularly given the structure and culture of the residency program. From this cohort's perspective, those academic physician faculty could do no "right" by the house staff. If they were too "hands off," they were criticized as being derelict and detached. If they were too "hands on," the house staff resented their intrusion into their work as being duplicative or disruptive. They limited their accolades for the few faculty physicians who knew the latest research or practice techniques within their own subspecialty (Mizrahi, 1986).

Dr. Nolan's sentiments were typical: "The residents really make or break this program. If you had bad residents and good attendings, you're not going to have a good educational experience. If you have good residents and bad attendings, you'll still get a pretty good education." Dr. Jarvis's view of SAMS' attending faculty was more extreme: "Some of the faculty never talk to patients. All they do is write a note, and some don't even do that. As far as I'm concerned, they are totally useless to anybody." Dr. Lynch went so far as to perceive a role reversal between attendings and his fellow house officers: "You realize you probably know more about day-to-day patient management than do most faculty members. You feel as though you have something to teach them that they don't know."

The context of these interactions between house officers and attending faculty was one where the federal government was beginning to require additional supervision over residents, especially in relation to Medicare and Medicaid patients. This included examining patients upon hospital admission and writing daily notes on the patient's chart (Mizrahi, 1986). The residents questioned the appropriateness of this additional oversight responsibility as they discounted the importance of the attendings' role in contributing to patient outcomes. As Dr. Johnson conveyed, "In general, attendings rarely know the patients. I also think many of them are peeved that they have to write a note daily instead of co-signing the resident's notes, and now they must include a history and physical. Since it's a federal regulation now, many just paraphrase what the house officer wrote in his notes. I don't blame them."

By the time they completed their training, and most were beginning a subspecialty fellowship or practicing general internal medicine, the cohort overall believed that they had acquired both the competency and confidence to practice general internal medicine. Indeed, several commented that they were now "on top of their medical game" (Mizrahi, 1986, p. 120).

The LMD Paradox

Academic faculty were not the only ones disparaged by this cohort in this entry phase (1979–1980); the general perspective of house officers about physicians in community practice was even more contemptuous. Many house staff used the term *LMD*, which had a literal and figurative meaning, but generally had a negative connotation and colored the cohort's views of many "local" primary care physicians. An LMD was generally viewed as an incompetent or out-of-date doctor from outside the academic environment. They obtained this generalized and, no doubt, skewed view of community practitioners primarily from their peers in relation to the patient referrals to SAMS made by these community physicians from outside the university. In conversing about his view of these physicians, Dr. Beech offered, "I'm so tired of those LMDs dumping their patients on us through the SAMS emergency room or the ICU. It makes more work because I can't trust anything they report verbally or in writing." An additional source for these pejorative views came from observations of house officers who "moonlighted," meaning they held second jobs in local hospital emergency rooms or clinics outside of SAMS and could speak from their observations and interactions with local physicians.

The Early Phase (1980–1984)

Relationships with the New Generation of House Staff

As the physicians completed their subspecialty fellowships and were starting out in academic or community practice five years later, the external policy environment significantly affected peer and attending relationships. The federal rules and regulations for residency training programs were changing once again even more dramatically across the country at this time. A nationally publicized case critiquing medical training in the United States was brought to the fore by "60 Minutes" on CBS television in the mid-1980s as a result of the Bell Commission, which blew the whistle in New York state (Holzman and Barnett, 2000). It was known as the "Libby Zion case" (Robins, 1995) and was headlined because of the untimely overnight death of the twenty-one-year-old daughter of a *New York Times* editor, Sidney Zion, after she was admitted overnight to a major New York teaching hospital emergency room. Physicians at each level in that system blamed a physician at a lower level in the training structure, or blamed her outside private physicians, and also blamed her (Hinckle and Simon, 1995).

That case, and similar exposés, ultimately resulted in all state governments restricting the hours medical residents could work each week and requiring greater attending physician involvement in supervising house staff and overseeing patient care (Bloch, 1989; Holzman and Barnett, 2000). By and large, the latter regulatory change was not welcome by those new academics in the cohort, who now had responsibility for educating and overseeing medical residents and students.

Nine physicians (Drs. Annas, Rosen, Finast, O'Brian, Paul, Lash, Boswell, Strelko, and Polikoff) moved into full-time academic practice, six of whom remained at SAMS (Drs. Rosen, Paul, Polikoff, Boswell, Lash, and Finast) and were already familiar with that culture. A common refrain was their assertion that the residents as a cohort believed that their medical acumen as internists was at its highest, just as they and their fellow house officers did right after they completed their residency training five years earlier (Mizrahi, 1986). Now, as young academic attendings themselves, their challenge ironically was to demonstrate to the current house staff that they were better physicians with a few years of practice experience behind them.

The ability of these academic physicians to influence their respective house staff's perspectives and priorities was complicated by the fact that their own perspectives on what constituted internal medicine competencies had changed dramatically in just a few years. These now encompassed the doctor-patient relationship, or as some characterized it, a "reasoned approach to the patient." As Dr. Finast described, "I don't have as much impact as I would like on the current house staff. I give the residents lots of opportunities to develop a relationship with patients and ask them about those contacts, but all the house staff want to do more procedures—it's a different perspective now." Dr. Annas admitted that, in actuality, "I don't enjoy house staff when they are taking care of my patients. It's a lot easier to deal in the abstract, didactically, than to do battle with them over specifics of given patients, especially mine and my team's. That happens more than occasionally." Most confirmed the difficulty of penetrating the house staff culture, which ironically, they obstructed five years earlier when they were house staff at SAMS (Mizrahi, 1986).

Many had chosen an academic career path in part because of the ability to be surrounded and supported by peers with the latest knowledge and skill in their subspecialty areas (as described earlier in chapter 2). Yet it seems that their fear of becoming out of date and losing their acumen led many to change their view as to what it meant to be a competent internist—primarily from a more technical one to a more practical one. At the same time, those who chose a subspecialty also began to change their physician identity to be of that subspecialty, such as a nephrologist, cardiologist, or gastroenterologist. They no longer viewed themselves as internists per se as they admitted to losing their edge in general internal medicine interventions. As Dr. Ross admitted, "I couldn't even pass the internal medicine boards today."

As they compared themselves in this early phase (1980–1984) to the current house staff, many already recognized that the newer cohorts knew more as senior residents than they did about medical diagnosis and treatment of diseases not in their subspecialty. With this widely held revelation, their views about their role as attending physician shifted concomitantly with their perspectives on the role of the competent internist. Dr. Polikoff described, "I think our attending function is to guide the residents not to go too wild in their assessment of patients. They take everything too far. They keep up with the literature and they do all the fancy technical procedures to work up every problem. I may not know as much physiology and the fancy gadgets now, but I think I have a more practical approach to the patient. But if I was practicing internal medicine on the outside, I'd have to keep up with everything; that's scary."

Additional factors seemed to separate their cohort from the generation they were now in charge just five years later, that related in part to the changing structure of residency training. As a SAMS attending in general internal medicine, Dr. Rosen valued his teaching role while commenting on the difference he perceived between his own cohort when they were house staff just five years earlier and the newer ones: "The current senior residents at SAMS whine and complain more than I ever remembering doing. Even as a chief resident at SAMS, I found that they make excuses not to work at night. We sucked it up more. And boy, it sure is different being on the inside of the process now as a faculty."

As a SAMS academic generalist now serving as attending faculty, Dr. Paul acknowledged the tensions in trying to satisfy both house staff and patients who in his sphere of practice were primarily veterans: "I come up against the house staff when I admit a patient such as one being dumped from a nursing home. I am sure the residents grumble under their breath: 'I'm a sieve!' Yet, I used to be in the same situation. Although I'm acting in the patient's best interest, it's hard to convince the residents. This type of situation could destroy an evening for me. It takes four martinis to get over it; it's a schizophrenic kind of role."

As academic attendings, the amount of responsibility for patient care decision-making they held also affected their relationships with "the new generation." Dr. O'Brian, for example, believed he had ultimate control of his residents and fellows. Other physicians in their rather new attending teaching roles in different institutions seemed to be frustrated when they had to compete with or defer to a private attending in their medical center who also directed the tasks of some residents. Dr. Strelko admitted, "I'm not responsible for patient care, just teaching; so I can't ask, 'Why didn't you do that?' My comments to residents have no teeth. It's not my role to call up a private attending and say something; that would be bad politics." Still most enjoyed their teaching roles because, as Dr. O'Brian asserted, "It keeps you on your toes."

The community practitioners were a different breed. Since most of the community practitioners were removed from the rigors of teaching and administration, at this point they did not express missing the academic environment much, if at all, and therefore did not seem to care about influencing the behavior of those coming behind them. Of those who went into a subspecialized community practice, only a few had direct contact with the next generation of residents who were primarily family practice residents or nurse practitioners. Not one felt that these trainees were on par with the SAMS internal medicine residents. Still, Dr. Melone, a nephrology subspecialist, admitted, "It's fun to deal with family practitioner residents because you can teach at the hospital, but it's not the same thing as dealing with real medicine residents; they're not as sharp. But I have no illusion about being able to go down to SAMS today and do ward rounds on internal medicine anymore, only in nephrology." Dr. Nolan, in a community-based internal medicine referral practice, concurred: "We are the only private medical group that has patients on the teaching service at the nearly medical school. These residents are terrible. I would like to have an impact on them and I enjoy the intellectual stimulation, but I'm not sure they value my teaching."

The LMD Paradox Revisited

Earlier, during their fellowships and as they did as house staff, the cohort generally disparaged the LMDs that they encountered at SAMS. But during the early phase (1980–1984) of their careers in the years following their fellowships, as they began their community-based practices or academic positions, the physicians' unflattering views of the LMD starkly and surprisingly changed. One question I asked was, "Do LMDs exist?" And more specifically how they felt "now that the shoe is on the other foot." It was almost painful and ironic to hear their perspectives as they realized how they were probably viewed by current residents only a few years after completing their own graduate education. As Dr. O'Brian, an academic physician, said, "We used the term 'LMD' in training to kid around. It did have connotations that a patient was referred from someone who hadn't discovered penicillin yet. It's not the way I view them now." Dr. Conley concurred, "As a resident, you tended to think the LMD was out of touch with recent medical treatment, so we looked down our noses at them. Crazy! Still, I'm sure when I send a patient to our big teaching hospital, the residents use the term in reference to me. But now I know things can be done more than one way. There is an art not just a science to practicing medicine. An intervention that works is acceptable even if I wouldn't do it that way. They will learn that eventually."

Their view that the current crop of house staff think they have superior knowledge to practicing physicians like them, remained intact, as Dr. Conley continued in discussing his changing perspectives somewhat self-consciously: "The labeling still goes on. I recently went on rounds with SAMS residents who were talking about a complicated patient referred by somebody from my area. They used derogatory terms inferring the doctor didn't do what he should have. It's so easy to think that way, but in retrospect, I remember saying the same thing when I was there. In fact, I still use the term 'LMD' for someone who's not from my community."

Dr. Cahn, another community subspecialist, expressed frustration at the way he was treated at this stage: "Five years after SAMS, my view is very different because I occasionally refer patients to my city's big medical center. The house staff there complained that I didn't do a procedure or that I was defensive. I always write out my findings to counter those reasons. Probably they weren't listening anyway! The term 'LMD' may or may not be justified. When I send a patient to that medical center and get Joe Blow at the bottom of the totem pole who knows less than I do, it ticks me off. I've passed the boards and this resident is second guessing me!"

There were additional reasons for their overall contempt of independent practicing physicians when they were house staff besides their view that they were ignorant of current diagnostic and treatment protocols. These relate to structural and environmental factors governing payment for services. From their experience while residents, they were on the receiving end of the way many local physicians treated patients with no insurance. As Dr. Melone reflected, "At SAMS, when you were called at 3 A.M. to admit a patient, it was an imposition on you. Now I appreciate what those community docs are going through. When you are a resident you think LMDs are touring around in Cadillacs. But now I understand why they send patients to the ER. No one is going to cover the costs of care they are providing." From the perspective of house staff, it was easy to blame those physicians for not caring for an indigent patient. Rather it was the lack of coverage system-wide that created these dilemmas for them since neither the federal nor state government were paying physicians to treat uninsured patients.

The Established Phase (1984–1994)

Relationships with the New Generation of House Staff

As they moved into the next phase of their careers, the academic faculty continued to maintain close relationships with students, residents, and fellows as teaching attendings and in supervisory roles. They also persisted in reporting mixed reviews about their roles in helping the new generation acquire needed clinical skills and professional responsibilities fifteen years later. They also each commented on how much medical education and patient care had changed since they were house officers.

By this established phase (1984–1994), the physicians continued to distinguish themselves from the newer generations of house staff while remaining ambivalent at best as to the trade-offs involved in restricting house staff autonomy. Those in academic practice recognized the pluses and minuses of giving more responsibility to the residents for their patients; if they spent more time in teaching than research, they would have more opportunities to be role models. Those in community practice were surprisingly self-conscious about the lack of a relationship to house staff and to the academic community more generally.

These views reflect the tension between house staff culture and the world of academic and community practice, especially since the Libby Zion case and its aftermath: How did these physicians convey a message to younger peers about what it takes to practice good medicine, since virtually all of them at this point viewed medicine as being as much an art as a science? Dr. O'Brian was emphatic: "I have become more jaundiced about the precision of science and more appreciative of the art; I'm cognizant of the variations in practice styles from one physician to another. There would have to be an absolute mistake before I would take action against a peer."

Dr. Finast expressed a common sentiment that he and others had originally asserted ten years earlier; the house staff's perspective about what it takes to be a competent internist is too narrow: "There is no time in one's life as a physician when one is more heavily invested in medicine than as a resident. However, there's more to medicine than the mechanics of correcting a patient's serum potassium or ordering medications. Doctors need a lot of experience besides information. I am a better doctor now than I was then because I'm better at comforting patients than recognizing some esoteric facts."

Ten years since the end of the early phase (1980–1984), Dr. Finast was even more conscious of trying to bring a different perspective to house staff training against all odds: "Today there is a beginning understanding that medicine is more than science of cells and chemotherapeutic agents. Some residents will recognize that the ICU is an emotional time for patients and families, if I ask about it, but it's only given lip service from the dean." He and many other academics continued to describe themselves as "role models" as they try to impart a more holistic sense of medicine in this phase with increasing uncertainty as to how it is being received.

Like Dr. Finast, Dr. Strelko also described challenges he faced as an attending from house staff culture and the larger medical structure: "I have to work very hard to engage residents in such discussions." Dr. Boswell, as a supervisor and teacher of students and residents, looked back over his years at SAMS and asserted that his stress level as an academic attending had been raised significantly: "The house staff arrangement has changed a lot since I was a house officer and a chief resident. Many types of patients I admitted then are either not admitted now or only for a short period. There's a lot more pressure to get things done quickly and get rid of patients. That was the title of your book as I recall. Also, the increase in supervisory responsibility is stressful. They require us to be there for all work rounds, write detailed notes now; we are forced to be much more involved in decision-making. Ironically, as we take the stress off house staff and provide more support for them, there's less support and more pressure on us."

Dr. O'Brian also thought the pendulum was swinging too far in the opposite direction from when he was a chief resident, repeating his views of a decade ago: "As I told you before, at SAMS we had too much responsibility as house staff; now the fellows and attendings take more responsibility for patients. There should be a balance. At SAMS, no one held your hand. We were forced to grow up fast; the current crop isn't."

Dr. Rosen, formerly a SAMS faculty member, contrasted the relationships at SAMS with the internal medicine residency program he was running by this stage in another southern medical center: "One of the main reasons I left SAMS was because I could not convince the residents of the intellectual basis for patient care. Still, I love teaching medical students and influencing their decision to go into internal medicine." Drs. O'Brian and Rosen and many others in different academic environments continued to identify changes in the mentality of the house officers that affected their relationship with them generally.

Likewise, the few community practitioners who had some contact with other residency programs in the established phase (1984–1994) continued to remain unimpressed with those residents' attitudes or behavior for the most part. Dr. Melone interacted with family practice residents periodically and gave occasional talks to hospital staff and nurses. Since the early phase (1980–1984), he seemed to have soured on the teaching role. In blunt language, he described his changing views: "The guys are dumber than those you went to medical school with. I used to think house staff kept you awake by their questions, but now I think they are just idiots. The next generation is looking for how much pay for how many hours. They argue about your decisions based on a zero fund of knowledge."

Community practitioners like Dr. Jarvis had become disillusioned about the newer physicians entering the profession in the last ten to fifteen years. He made dire predictions: "Anyone who can leave will leave. The new generation will not be totally devoted or enslaved by medicine as we were. I'm not sure they will deliver quality care, and the quality of people going into medicine will be less."

On the other hand, Dr. Cahn, who did not have formal connections with house staff, confessed: "Every once in a while, I get pangs of missing academics only because the lifestyle is so much easier. I long for the days as an attending when my resident or fellow could take the trash calls at night instead of me!" Dr. Johnson, who admitted he did not have much to do with the local family practice residency program, presented a third, more ambivalent perspective on academic medicine: "At times I miss teaching. When you get a smart, energetic person, it was fun to teach them. But otherwise, it was frustrating." He confessed, "I don't miss 'medical center medicine.' You have to explain things to people with varying intellects. It is time consuming and inefficient."

The LMD Paradox Reframed

Many of the community physicians continued to have contacts with local hospitals that employ residents. Once again, they were asked, "Have your views changed about being perceived as an LMD by current house staff now that 'the shoe is on the other foot'? How do you think the current group of residents view and treat physicians in community practice?" Dr. Ross, in community practice, had a different response to the LMD question: he still accepted that acronym for certain groups of physicians but defended himself against such disparagement: "No, it doesn't bother me that they use it about me because I know as much as they do. But there is such a breed of LMDs here in my community as there were in the SAMS community. They are crude people who don't call ahead to the hospital. If I refer patients, I always make arrangements beforehand."

Dr. Melone, who practiced in the city where SAMS was located, confessed, "I am an LMD now. When I was a nephrology fellow, I used to enjoy writing sarcastic notes to the local LMDs in the charts. I am sure residents make fun of me now that many of my patients wind up at SAMS. I did the same."

Dr. Jarvis gave an example from fifteen years earlier and compared his views currently. He was "pissed off" then that the emergency response team brought an old man to the ER who had a stroke and could not eat or drink: "Some kind of country doctor dumped him on us, so I called him at 2:30 in the morning and screamed at him. I would never do that now. In answer to 'Are there LMDs?', he responded that "some of them are. We get patients from small hospitals whose doctors don't want to try high-tech, high-risk procedures. Also, some surgical residents treat me like an LMD. You can tell from the way they talk that they think I am brain dead. I slap them down pretty quickly."

Dr. Mahoney, in hospital-based practice, recalled his transition: "You get a feeling that these residents are not viewing you the way you view yourself, which is as the best doctor in the world. Yes, you are going to lose some of the basic science, but that's more than made up for by experience, judgment, and wisdom. I confess I was one of those who used the term 'LMD.' A few years ago, while I was at St. James Hospital, I had to transfer a patient to SAMS. I went over there to check on him. I looked at the chart and there it said, 'Patient was treated by LMD at a local hospital!' That hit me harder than a brick! I never used that phrase again."

Dr. Polikoff, who moved to a community HMO at this career phase, interacted with medical students. "I am the LMD admitting doctor. But these university hospital residents respect us, rather than seeing us as LMDs who send them 'trainwrecks' as happened at SAMS. We're not like the docs who send a patient and then never show up again. Still, there are cocky residents who act that way."

The Entrenched Phase (1994–2004)

Relationships with the New Generation of House Staff

During the next phase of their careers (1994–2004), physicians became increasingly discontent overall. Many of them described this phase as the age of managed care, consolidation, and corporatism. This trend toward discontent also affected the culture surrounding relationships with younger physicians. At the end of this phase in 2004, more than twenty-five years since their SAMS residency, the physicians presented themselves in a much more favorable light compared to subsequent generations. This further ratcheted up their negative critiques of younger physician cohorts and references to the newer generations of house staff and physicians disparagingly.

Dr. Strelko, for example, worried about the impact of the changing culture and structure on the attitudes and behavior of the newer physicians entering the field: "A lot of medical students are choosing careers that are lifestyle friendly. You worry about whether the doctors we are training now will go that extra mile late at night to take care of patients if they have problems, or are they just going to punch the clock? Sadly, maybe that's the way it's going to be."

A majority were pessimistic about the future of medicine in this era of managed care, and many, like Dr. Ross, predicted the medical field would get worse: "Most doctors make a wonderful living today, but there are some who make only borderline incomes because of malpractice rates and lower reimbursement. In twenty years, I predict fewer will go into medicine, and those who do, will have more debt. Everyone is out for themselves."

In reflecting on their relationships with the younger generation, several envisioned and predicted a changing "mindset" and speculated about physicians' incomes. The physicians often repeated something like: "They will be salaried, have debt to pay off, have less responsibility, and work strictly nine to five." Medicine was viewed through a new practice paradigm, and only in that sense did they think the next generation might be content with their career choice. Most believed that this new mentality would negatively affect the quality of peer to peer as well as doctor-patient relationships. A few lamented that young physicians did not care as much about forming bonds with patients or peers or needing practice autonomy. Some, like Dr. Johnson, were harsher: "The new generation of MDs are in it for the money and will adapt to the new environment. My generation wouldn't tolerate it. They'd gripe and retire before it got to that point." Camaraderie and a sense of community were going by the wayside.

All the academic physicians continued to refer to the mandates that had restricted the number of hours house staff could work per week. With even more passion than in prior stages, many still worried about whether the pendulum had swung too far toward constraining opportunities for house staff growth, experience, and autonomy. Dr. Annas, prefiguring the EMR, characterized the amount of required documentation in medical records and commented that "the manner in which documentation is being required is overkill. You become isolated as you sit at your computer instead of consulting with peers." Dr. O'Brian concurred, and, as he did in the past, suggested there would be negative consequences: "There is a tension here. Regulations result in shifting responsibility from the interns to attending faculty. There is too much burden on the attending, and the residents have lost some of the sense of autonomy. Thinking back, what I did as a resident was ridiculous; I shouldn't have shouldered that much. Now, house staff get less responsibility, attendings are doing busy work, and the patients get short-changed."

Dr. Paul pinpointed that this mandate to engage attending physicians more intensively was institutionalized in the early 2000s, citing the Accreditation Council for Graduate Medical Education (ACGME): "I agree with the ACGME in principle, but it requires my spending more time with regulations, enforcing their standards rather than worrying about the content of student learning. It's becoming more time consuming and unrewarding."

Dr. Strelko echoed some of the other physicians when he described how residents are treated by their superiors now: "They are being 'coddled' and 'pampered.'" Dr. Boswell, like Dr. O'Brian and others, also used expressions like "spoon fed" to characterize how attendings treated residents and fellows in this era: "The house staff of today don't feel pressure of the full responsibility like we did. They are just going to be clock punchers. A lot of us were workaholics. I'm not sure that was healthy for us or our families, but we made decisions and took charge."

Most of the community practitioners continued with only intermittent relationships with trainees in a supervisory capacity, and as in the past, mostly with family practice or non-physician (PA, NP) interns. Their overall perspective didn't change much in the last ten years; it remained one of disappointment in the quality of the novice professionals. Dr. Nolan predicted pessimistically, "I see continued worsening with eventual decline in quality of medical professionals." Nevertheless, those few who had teaching roles spoke of them positively from a self-interest perspective; it gave them intellectual stimulation. It "keeps me on my toes," Dr. Jarvis repeated from prior time frames: "You feed off the energy and enthusiasm of people doing things for the first time. Otherwise, I'd be just grinding it out in private practice."

The LMD Paradox Endures

In the interviews at this stage, the cohort was asked again to discuss relationships with current house staff: "How does it feel, now that the shoe is on the other foot?" For the community practitioners, the question "Are you considered an 'LMD'?" was also included.

In his response, Dr. Jarvis was emphatic: "I hope not. I think I'm a pretty good doc, and I have won a number of awards from interns and residents for being the best teaching attending." Other subspecialists who had a teaching role asserted that they were exceptions to the LMD phenomenon because they were valued for their expertise in their subspecialization. Dr. Ross, whose practice had evolved from oncology/hematology to general internal medicine, defended himself by saying, "Sure I'm an LMD, but I'm smarter than they are. I've gotten old and 'curmudgeoned' enough to think I know more than a lot of the young whippersnappers who are coming along today."

The Extended Phase (2004–2011)

Relationships with the New Generation of House Staff

In the interviews at the end of the extended phase in 2011, the cohort focused on looking back over their careers and on their relationship with the younger peers and colleagues. At this stage, more than thirty years since they completed SAMS training, their responses were more nuanced and balanced as to the dramatic changes that had occurred in residency training, especially from those who were closest to current residents. The question whether the novice cohorts coming up would go "the extra mile," remained a centerpiece of their concerns.

Six of the academic physicians were still in close contact with the current cohorts of trainees (which included medical students, interns and residents, and fellows) in teaching and supervisory roles (Drs. Annas, Rosen, Finast, O'Brian, Strelko, and Boswell). As a whole, their views were less critical than six years earlier; they seemed resigned to the changing structure and expectations of residency training. They appeared to be distancing themselves from expecting anything different from the attending-resident structure and relationship. Dr. Annas appeared reconciled if not acquiescent to the differences he saw in the current house staff but admits that it is in his self-interest to not get too worried about this: "Those coming into the profession now have a different knowledge set and are more well-rounded. Also, the ethnic makeup has changed dramatically with more female and non-Caucasian now. I've given up worrying or complaining about trade-offs—fewer hours the house staff have to work, for less continuity of patient care as a result. I think the current system is about right. At least there are fewer complaining house staff, and that's good for me."

Among the academic physicians, Dr. Finast, who had remained at SAMS, noted the value that the newer groups place on latest technical procedures. This was something he had mentioned in the past as well, believing that it had narrowed their expertise and vision: "I see some people who are extremely good at the things we never did before. And that's about all they do. It's so highly specialized now that I couldn't train in my subspecialty today." Furthermore, Dr. Finast also noted that these factors have negatively impacted collegial relationships: "It's fracturing the club of pulmonary physicians into sub-subspecializations, and that is a problem. It's not as much fun as it used to be, and the training is still deficient in the caring realm."

A few physicians asserted that the positives may outweigh the negatives for the system of patient care. Dr. Rosen whose career has been as an attending physician in general internal medicine, believes the critique of the new generation has been overblown: "Everybody talks about the different generations, yet what I see are students and residents who want to become good docs." Dr. Rosen validated the more intense attending faculty input, but presented it in a more favorable light: "The work hours and the involvement of faculty have drastically changed. I know what's going on with every one of my patients. The faculty had no clue what was going on with the patients back then at SAMS; we were cowboys. Now educationally and financially, we provide better house staff training."

While describing the new balance, one cannot help but read acquiescence into their acceptance of the changes, without necessarily approving. Dr. O'Brian, for example, wondered if the trade-off is worth it, and for whom? "The new trainees learn differently. The combination of technology and the expectation that attendings will provide them with information has changed things. I'm not trying to be judgmental here, but the system has changed—both the selection process and the people who go into medicine. The public view of us physicians has changed for the worse, and that has also influenced who goes into medicine, not as many of the best and the brightest. I don't think that the Nobel Prize winners of the future are coming into medicine."

By the extended phase (2004–2011) most of the physicians shifted their lens from merely condemning or denigrating the "new generation," to explaining their motivations, and even acknowledging the benefits for them, albeit at times reluctantly. Still, there was ambivalence, and even sarcasm and irony interspersed in their responses. As Dr. O'Brian further noted, "Again, at the risk of sounding like an old man, it's a different mentality. The house staff now have much less responsibility than when I was a house officer. The pendulum has swung, perhaps too far now the other way." Likewise, Dr. Mahoney chided, "I could put on my gravelly ninety-year-old voice and say, 'In our day, we had to be on call every other day and work for seventy-two hours in a row and not be tired by it. These young pups are just lazy.' We now have hospitalists in the hospitals so the young ones can get their beauty sleep! Boy the times have changed."

Physicians pointed to downsides they perceived among the younger generations, specifically in terms of omissions in the training programs, that is, what they believed was missing or undervalued. Ironically, this sentiment echoed what their own attending physicians had said about this cohort's training environment back in the entry phase (1979–1980). They occasionally conveyed to me that there was too much reliance on acquiring technical skills related to laboratory diagnosis rather than acquiring clinical judgment. For example, Dr. Rosen expressed sentiments that were strikingly similar to what the attendings commented privately to me when Dr. Rosen himself was a house officer more than thirty years earlier. As Dr. Rosen suggested, "Too often the attendings who are teaching omit the basics, so students and residents aren't learning them, such things as how to take a good history, how to do a good physical, etc. There's way too much reflexive ordering of lab tests or imaging studies. I also worry as do most of my colleagues about the fewer work hours. Are they seeing enough patients, are they getting enough clinical experience to recognize when they're in trouble?"

Dr. Strelko also critiqued a component of the learning environment that academic Drs. Boswell and Annas had identified back in the entrenched phase (1994–2004), the notion that students and residents expect to be "spoon-fed" material: "When I did my fellowship without computers, we learned the content primarily on our own. Those in my generation are all in agreement that the accreditation-imposed curriculum expectations are just nuts. Trainees ask now, 'Who's going to teach me? What do I need to know so I can pass boards?' That's sad."

From the community practice side, the physicians were also very critical of the younger generation at this stage of their careers. Although they identified a number of different reasons for this, it was nevertheless a consistent theme. Dr. Lynch, for example, contemplating the similarities and differences between his cohort and the newer generations, expressed a clear sense of disappointment at what he felt was being lost in the approach of the younger physicians: "I've had this talk with many doctors of my age group. We think that younger physicians, meaning the current thirty- to forty-year-old docs are not as committed and are a little less compassionate than our generation was. They're probably better at using technology. I just don't think they provide it in quite the committed way; they are less likely to go the extra mile," echoing the sentiment of many of his cohort.

Dr. Cahn, even more than Dr. Lynch, disparaged the new generation's commitment: "The doctors we hire now in our practice are totally different from us. Their work ethic is less; they are much more mired in their wives' and family's needs. We were basically married to medicine. Medicine was a priesthood. Now it's 'I want to be home by six, latest seven, and I want my free time.'"

As in earlier career stages, most of the community practitioners had only intermittent contact with physicians-in-training, but all had interactions with younger, more recently trained colleagues who joined their practice, settled in their community, or assumed the role of "hospitalist" in the institutions where their patients were admitted. But even among those who had more regular contact, a similar critique of the younger generations was present. Dr. Allen, one of the few who was working with family practice and physician assistant residents, suggested, "They're all idealistic, of course, but they are pampered. Maybe it goes back to in medical school since they passed that rule that you are not allowed to work more than eighty hours to one hundred hours per week. I would have given anything to only work one hundred hours per week my first five years of practice. They want high salaries instantly, don't want to be on call very much, want weeks off. Our generation wasn't pampered like that."

Dr. Johnson depicted the trade-offs with the training climate and culture: "The big difference with residents here is that they seem to want better control over their hours; they don't want to be on call all the time. They are not averse to being employees like I would have been. The problems with set hours and multiple caregivers is there's too much fragmentation. But the problem with my old system was that it wore people out."

Across both academic and community practice settings, almost all the physicians seemed to analyze the differences between generations through rose-colored glasses. They saw themselves as having sacrificed—justifying the grueling SAMS training over time and comparing themselves favorably to the newer cohort in the aggregate.

The Ending Phase (2011–2016)

Relationships with the New Generation of House Staff

By the ending phase in 2016, many of the physicians had retired or were contemplating retiring in the next few years. The topic about relationships with peers—contemporaries or younger cohorts—arose in a number of discussions about their sense of satisfaction, strains, disillusionment, along with discussions about their relationships in general with the new generation of physicians. In this stage, their perspectives had not changed significantly. However, for the first time, many expressed relief that they were leaving the field, particularly as transformative changes affecting their practice and the medical delivery system as a whole were taking place.

In comparing their cohort to the new generation at this late stage in their careers, so many referred to their becoming a physician as a professional "calling." That was a familiar refrain from some in earlier time periods, while several others characterized it that way for the first time. Nevertheless, the meaning of "calling" may be relative and "in the eyes of the beholder," as it appears embedded in the context of the times in which these physicians were trained. From their vantage point, the investment in their careers was paramount in their lives; their dedication was unquestioned. In that sense, they seemed to want that same or comparable commitment from others, while deprecating that very commitment: "Maybe I was crazy to be so invested!" was a common phrase.

At best, in characterizing the new generation, there was a grudging respect for the new norms, and at worst, there was resentment and a bit of jealousy aimed at the different work ethic and priorities outside medicine for the younger crop. Dr. Cahn's stark comment at an earlier phase comes to mind: "We were married to medicine," was not far from the mark. He continued his tirade from the prior extended phase (2004–2011) by chastising the hospitalist physician as emblematic of the new breed of physician. Then he generalized about the subsequent generations: "They have no overhead expenses and they want to be home after a work shift like laborers. The calling as a profession has changed drastically; actually they have no work ethic."

Dr. Melone went even further, repeating a mantra from earlier time frames to validate distinctions between generations: "I'm embarrassed to say, I think they're lousy. When I became a fellow, I thought my residency group was brighter. The younger guys are never as smart as us older farts, but the actual answer is that the calling is different. They're signing up for an interesting, well-paying job, and us old farts signed up to be God."

Still, several recognized that the younger cohorts had exercised their privilege to gain concessions related to their working conditions, which this cohort admitted they tolerated. Virtually all acknowledged that the profession has been profoundly altered. The differences within the cohort revolved around whether they believed the trade-offs were worth it and for whom these worked best: physicians, patients, payers? Dr. Lynch, serving as an informant, reflected openly,

"They're more focused on their personal life. I don't think they're quite the workaholics as my generation was, and that's probably a good thing. My generation was trying to be successful and make a lot of money and have a big house. I think those are good differences."

Ironically, harking back to the entry phase (1979–1980), I recall conversations with the faculty attendings about how the SAMS residents (this cohort) did not have the commitment that the former generation had. The theme was usually, "What are they complaining about? We were on-call more nights per week than they were!" A common refrain was, "They complain now, but the intensive experience will make them tougher for it." In weighing the positives and negatives of the younger cohorts, Dr. Lynch, after making the remark above about the positive system changes, went on to state almost exactly what the attending physicians I met told me almost four decades earlier: "The thirty-, forty-, even the fifty-year-olds are very knowledgeable about technology, but they're less likely to take the time to do a good history or physical examination and more likely to order tests. They tend to not be as good with interpersonal skills. They see the world differently. I'm sure I was different to the people who preceded me." Others, like Dr. Beech in community practice, once again labeled the newcomers, including his now physician daughter, as "shift workers," a dismissive term he used in earlier stages as well.

Dr. O'Brian provided a personal anecdote to emphasize how both he and the profession have changed, which he recalled telling me almost four decades earlier: "When you interviewed me at SAMS in my second week of internship, my sister got married. I didn't go to her wedding because I was so committed to my career; that was a mistake in hindsight. But I think it's gone too far in the opposite direction now. There are some individuals who are not as committed; things outside of medicine are as much as, if not more, important." He continued to ponder both sides of the changed milieu, repeating almost verbatim his words from the earlier extended phase (2004–2011) that the medical profession was losing status, even though his personal career trajectory had been satisfactory: "Seeing the newer generation who are energetic and enthusiastic brightens your day. On the other hand, with the bad rap that medicine has received from the public, I'm not sure that we're getting the best and the brightest as we did years ago." Even Dr. Lash, one of the most optimistic academic physicians, projected a downward spiral for internal medicine: "When we were coming through, internal medicine was the most competitive specialty. There's been a shift to those specializations that offer an easier lifestyle and monetary rewards often because of mounting debt—fields like dermatology, anesthesiology, etc."

Drs. Nolan and Conley, as community practitioners, both felt that the issue of stability was having a notable influence on the profession. "When I came out of SAMS," Dr. Nolan said, "It was anticipated that you were going to take a financial risk. Now you're almost guaranteed a good salary if you are a reasonable individual." Dr. Conley put it this way: "My perception is that they want more predictable hours and are willing to sacrifice some reimbursement."

While their perceptions of changes were typically related to generational differences, structural changes were also identified that limit the newer cohorts' opportunities to forge out independently, including an increase in hospital conglomerates and networked group practices.

These physicians who went into community practice in the early 1980s started with one partner or a small group; now they are leaving or have left large group practices or corporate entities that have taken them over.

Moreover, there also appeared to be changing cultural and societal norms related to the importance of marriage and family; seeking a more equitable balance between family and work is clearly the new norm for younger peers, especially male physicians as will be discussed in more detail in chapter 9. There are also changing racial and gender demographics in the profession with more women and ethnic diversity, all of which many of this cohort viewed with ambivalence. Even when welcoming these changes (which a few did), they all implied, if not stated outright, that there was no closely knit peer community anymore, and sadly, from their perspective, such a community did not seem to be missed or valued.

The LMD Tension Reconsidered

During this final stage of interviews, the cohort was asked one last time to reflect on the connotation of the "LMD" as they knew of or experienced the phenomenon during their career trajectory. In the entry phase (1979–1980), almost forty years earlier, this concept was part of a cultural "town-gown" divide. In 2016 this question was asked again in an effort to determine whether this view was still held, or how it had changed.

Dr. Johnson, a community practitioner, and others distanced themselves to varying degrees from the exaggerated caricature of patients and physicians that house staff projected in earlier time frames. Nevertheless, they still provided examples of "LMD patient dumping," still defined as physicians who abdicated their professional responsibility by getting rid of problem patients through the ER, which was run by house staff at that time. Dr. Johnson reflected that definition by distancing himself from that description: "I don't know if house staff use the term *LMD* anymore. I know I did. But now I don't refer patients to any teaching institutions." He then defended himself against an extremely sarcastic and harsh image of the LMD all these years later: "I don't send residents the bodies of patients with a note tied to their toe, which is the still probably the LMD image. I send them a well-described patient with a specific question."

Other physicians distanced themselves from the term like they never had previously. A few said that the term they used at this point was *PCP* (primary care provider). Dr. Nolan went so far as to praise the PCP/LMD types: "They're the ones that everybody really likes; they are held in high esteem in the community. It is the hospital physicians who are viewed as individuals that haven't quite finished their training yet. Maybe that's why everyone has switched to using PCP; it sounds better." Dr. Allen seemed embarrassed about the pejorative meaning of the term as he also used the newer one PCP. The tables had turned. He explained

"I think the titles have changed. But around my community, it's hard to know who's out there doing primary care now. We try to nurture those collegial relationships to make sure PCPs get proper feedback from us in order to keep their referrals coming. We need them." Rather than eschewing them, Dr. Allen and others with community-based referral practices apparently needed the "LMDs/PCPs" for their economic and professional survival.

In an interesting shift, Dr. Melone reversed the implication of the label itself: "For me it's like a badge of honor. I claim that I am an LMD because I take care of my patients. 'I am Mrs. Magilly's doctor,' I say. 'You were taking care of her while she was in the hospital, but I'm her damn doctor.' I have always been quite proud of that ever since I was a fellow. I used to sign my notes in the chart, 'LMD Melone!'" Still, Dr. Melone acknowledged and explained as an informant that "there are still zillions of LMDs out there. They're guys that are just way too overworked either by greed or just because no one is paying them enough to keep the lights on. We did use the term then for guys who were not paying any attention, as they were seeing fifty patients a day."

At the same time as the community-based physicians dismissed the house staff's attitude and treatment toward them, almost everyone was defensive about the pains they took with patient admissions to "prove" they were not LMDs as did Dr. Johnson and Dr. Melone. Still, by the ending phase (2011–2016), some of the indignancy toward these neophytes had dissipated. But only some. The dynamics remained as part of their ethos always. This seemingly ongoing phenomenon, rarely described in the literature, deserves further scrutiny because it affects peer and patient relationships.

Relationships with Colleagues Near and Far

The relationships the physicians had with colleagues were an integral part of their professional life and culture. Certain aspects of peer contacts were sustained over their career trajectory, while others changed profoundly, depending on their institution and setting. Vast distinctions were made between those who were formally connected to a university department or group practice and those more distantly connected through referral systems or like specialty. There were also differences in their views between those colleagues they had direct contact with or knowledge about versus physicians they had heard about by reputation or rumor. They all had strong opinions about peers generally, meaning the medical profession as a whole (see also chapters 3 and 4, which include their perceptions about the status of the medical profession, and more about how peers figured into their satisfaction or dissatisfaction assessment).

In chapter 6, where the focus is on mistakes and malpractice, I discuss the physicians' views on and experiences with colleagues as it relates to peer review and issues of accountability. Following here, I discuss the physicians' relationships at each career phase with colleagues in everyday practice. Since I already discussed earlier in the chapter their relationships with fellow house staff during the entry phase (1979–1980), this section focuses on the physicians' relationships with colleagues during the career phases after that initial entry phase. Some of the questions posed included, "What kind of peer support did you receive as you established yourself in community practice or academic positions years out of training? Did you have a need to discuss your uncertainties, doubts, vulnerabilities, as well as successes with other physicians? If yes, were they willing and able to do so?" Considering the stresses and pressures they revealed in different time frames, it was important to determine whether they believed that their environments were open and collegial or competitive and isolating. Given the norm of self-reliance and autonomy acquired as part of their socialization to "physicianhood" (Mizrahi, 1986), I explore what kind of collegial relationships were experienced and/or sought after in each phase.

The Early Phase (1980–1984)

As discussed at the beginning of this chapter, peer relationships were primarily limited to their fellow house officers during the entry phase (1979–1980). These were of singular importance individually and collectively. The peer culture was an extremely close and closed one, providing camaraderie and comfort as recalled with nostalgia throughout the stages of their career. After completing residency, and entering what I label as the early phase (1980–1984), they went on to new positions, predominantly to subspecialty fellowships inside and beyond SAMS, and in three instances they moved into general internal medicine (Drs. Nolan, Paul, Rosen) or left internal medicine (Dr. Mahoney). For the nine leaving SAMS (Drs. Rosen, Conley, Nolan, Lynch, O'Brian, Ross, Lash, Strelko, and Jarvis), they had to build new sets of partners and peers connections. Those remaining at SAMS moved into new positions with colleagues they generally knew in their subspecialty department or general medicine division.

For most of the academics, their first reaction to a question about peer support in the early phase was affirmative; there was a collegial environment and so they did not feel isolated in the main. Indeed, that camaraderie was one of the virtues of choosing an academic career. Academics recognized that their positions could still be stressful but sought to find a remedy. As Dr. Strelko, who had moved into a New England oncology program, commented, "At my institution we discuss cases a lot. One of the keys to not feeling isolated and too stressed is to share decision-making; there was no reason not to do that there." While Dr. Paul saw some flaws in the SAMS system, he was satisfied in the early years with his primarily administrative and teaching relationships: "At SAMS, there is quite a bit of interaction here because of my administrative position, and my seniority and experience. Second, we are in close proximity with each other, so it's easy to talk about cases." But when asked who he conferred with about professional situations that might affect him adversely, he painted a different picture, testifying to his internalization of the norm of self-reliance: "There is nobody. That's one area of isolation. I have never had a mentor. There are a few colleagues here I could turn to if I am in serious distress, but I'm very much a loner. It's a product of my tendency and the medical profession's to be independent. I am the only one in my position."

Most of the community practitioners were building or joining a subspecialty partner or practice and working long and strenuous hours to build a patient base. In terms of contemporary peer relationships outside their practice, they indicated that they spent a fair amount of time introducing themselves to physicians in the community. For the most part, they presented these interactions as satisfactory if not satisfying. Most of the community practitioners did not feel particularly isolated professionally in these early years as they discussed their ability to consult with these close colleagues about patient concerns.

However, when asked about support for themselves given the stresses and responsibilities they had enumerated during the prior entry phase, most of them turned to someone outside the professional realm or to no one, as in the case of Dr. Paul. Several indicated that they primarily received support from their wives and occasionally from a close friend if they needed it. They minimized the need and were reluctant to reveal vulnerabilities, fears of failure, and self-doubts to their peers although they shared those with me. (These sentiments are discussed more in chapter 8.)

Beyond their immediate orbit and in more formal settings, a few physicians were already serving on hospital review committees, and as a result, got a glimpse into the way a range of physicians practiced and adhered to professional norms and procedures. For example, Dr. Lynch, a community oncologist had already become disillusioned about his fellow practitioners after he became involved in those review processes. "Problems are coming up with many physicians," he said, "because rules are not enforced in my hospital, for example, incomplete records. I get sick of it. Some of the culprits are my friends, but unfortunately the whole hospital gets into trouble because of these few people who are known as 'the good old boys' and not reprimanded enough."

The Established Phase (1984–1994)

By the established phase, the physicians had many more experiences consulting or observing other physicians beyond their close department or group practice and included more distant colleagues outside their practice sphere. Their perspectives on the latter were less positive; in several instances, they seemed to become more jaundiced. As the corporate sector became more dominant in shaping the health care system, there did not seem to be the sense of camaraderie and community so many expressed ten years earlier.

Dr. Strelko, who had moved to a Midwest medical center by this career phase, is typical of many of the academics as he discussed his complex relationships with peers at both his current and former academic medical center: "Here at [this Midwest medical center], I don't really feel isolated. That's one of the advantages of teaching residents. Even if you don't get along with somebody, that person might still ask you to discuss a case. It's a pretty healthy environment."

However, when he discussed his prior academic position, speaking both personally and as an informant, he revised his former views: "When I felt depressed at [the northeastern medical center] where I used to work, I talked to a lot of people, including my boss and my colleagues. But it turned out all the people I talked to were either as distraught as I was, or they were the problem! Your family is a major support, but that also has its pluses and minuses. I don't think there is much emotional support in medicine, and that goes all the way back to residency. Even if you were stressed enough to ask for help, I don't think there was a benign mechanism for you to get it." He seems to contradict himself in relation to obtaining needed support and whether and from whom he receives it.

Overall, the academic cohort emphatically stated that they received adequate intellectual stimulation from their community. But at this established phase (1984–1994), interpersonal relationships among colleagues in different positions and settings were still complicated. Dr. Rosen, for example, focused on some of the complexity of his internal professional relationships. "As far as my academic colleagues, I have lots of contact and that's what keeps me going! I turn to my colleagues and my boss and it is adequate. If I'm not sure what to do, I will ask somebody. It doesn't have to be a peer. There is no place for ego." It is worth noting that, ten years earlier, Dr. Rosen held a contrary perspective and had replied that faculty, including himself, were isolated from one another with only fragile bridges linking them. Now in his response to isolation, he admitted, "There's still a little remoteness, but not as much as in the past. I can see how people could be eaten alive in my position. I often talk with the leader of my organization. I consult with a few department chairmen whom I battled with formerly, once I realized that I needed them."

The physicians were also asked about whether they viewed peers as competitors or colleagues. In response, Dr. Rosen also served as an informant by making some astute observations about the relationship between academic and community institutions at SAMS: "As faculty who also maintain a patient practice, we compete with those outside. Everybody in medicine is competing with everybody, especially for private patients with insurance. Those in nonacademic settings resent us. Internal medicine programs trained too many specialists; they trained their own competition and trained themselves out of business. We are exceptions as generalists; they don't have enough of us."

Dr. Paul, who had spent much of the prior ten years teaching residents at SAMS among other administrative responsibilities, had just become a dean of medical education by this phase. Just as he was in the early phase (1980–1984), he remained conflicted about his peer relationships. He noted, "Lots of people approach me for advice," and "Many of my colleagues were former supervisees. We are also in close proximity; that makes a difference." Nevertheless, similar to other physicians like Drs. Strelko and Rosen, Dr. Paul offered contradictory perspectives on the more emotional aspects of his interactions. First, he emphatically stated that he "never" feels isolated in his work, but then later in the interview replied, "There is nobody to talk to about personal professional issues; that's an area I feel alone. I never had a mentor and there are only a couple of people I would talk to if I am in great distress." He separated his formal leadership role from his role as a colleague, asserting that he could talk about the pressures of being an internist in an intellectual capacity (as did Dr. Rosen), but less so in an emotional one.

Community practitioners focused on different sets of relationships depending on their roles and regularity of contact with fellow physicians. Dr. Melone, for example, noted, "We have four doctors in our nephrology practice, and we negotiate complex relationships financially as a corporation with the hospitals in town. Since we are one of the only renal practices in SAMS City, it's not that difficult to have cordial peer interactions." Dr. Melone also noted that he had generally good relationships with local primary care doctors, something that Dr. Beech, another community practitioner working in nephrology, agreed with: "I have a good relationship with primary care docs. They respect me as a nephrologist. As a renal specialist, most docs get rid of their patients to me, not the other way."

Dr. Cahn, a GI subspecialist, has had a changing perspective on peers over the time, and he suggested that his views on them depend on their position in the community and his relationship to them: "There have been dramatic changes with local internists. Up to ten years ago, I had a lot of respect for them. Now there is a flood of foreign physicians, and the caliber has deteriorated. Insurance companies hire them as gatekeepers, and regardless of their nationality, they are tools of the insurance industry. The competition has gotten worse." Beyond competition with colleagues, Dr. Cahn gave two reasons for his increasing isolation from peers—near and far: "I don't have enough time for intellectual exchanges given family and children pressures. Additionally, there is also an incredible grapevine and you can't trust anybody. I feel terribly isolated since I am often here late at night alone. My wife is supportive, but it's not enough."

Other physicians felt that their relationships with peers might be influenced by their subspecialty. Dr. Johnson, for example, contrasted his peer situation in oncology with other subspecialists: "Oncology can be a bit isolating. Other subspecialists don't know a lot about cancer and refer to us as promoting poisons and deaths, so I talk mostly to other oncologists. My wife will also listen a fair amount about my disasters." He then made a gender-related complaint and an unusual suggestion, which countered the view of physicians as self-reliant: "To the extent I need support I talk to other doctors in my group about problems. The fact that we don't have any kind of support groups for ourselves like patients and nurses have, is a problem, but men aren't into that kind of stuff." Several mentioned their wives as a support, but as Drs. Strelko and Cahn noted, that did not appear to be a substitute for more open and intense peer interaction.

The Entrenched Phase (1994–2004)

With another ten years behind them, most continued to make even greater distinctions between those peers with whom they interacted every day in their academic or community practice and those physicians in the wider geographic or professional community. For the most part, their association with peers within their setting remained close. Dr. Polikoff, who worked in a primary care HMO practice, was the most positive: "It's a great group of doctors here who support each other. It's a lot of fun coming to work."

Academics overall remained pleased with their collegial relationships in their medical centers, regardless of subspecialty at this career phase. However, a few identified physicians from community hospitals or from office-based community practice as competitors, some noting ironically that they had trained their competition. This continued a theme that Drs. Rosen and Paul both made in an earlier phase in describing the competition between the SAMS hospital system and local community hospitals in SAMS city.

For the community practitioners, positive internal peer interaction in their own setting was the norm, but that stood in sharp contrast with how they perceived physicians' external to their immediate practice. Those on the outside were for the most part viewed as competitors or as inferior ethically, and/or educationally and culturally by their standards of care. It was in this phase when, for the first time, the phenomenon of a new type of physician, "the hospitalist," was identified by title.

Dr. Cahn, who had previously been critical of his GI referral network, was even harsher at this stage: "Your referral base now is from hospitalists who are for the most part, third-world individuals who are not as well trained as we were. You have to wade through the bullshit of their inadequate patient care. Each partnership is its own fiefdom. There is no interaction." Dr. Allen accepted the trade-offs involved with the advent of the hospitalist but came to the same conclusion as Dr. Cahn: "Hospitalists allow me to get more sleep at night instead of getting called at 2 A.M., but these 'rent-a-docs' are not really great, as nine out of ten are foreign trained." The xenophobia was hard not to miss, but the reality of the training and roles of these hospitalists complicated an outsider's assessment of their perceived bias.

Dr. Ross predicted more and more dissatisfaction for the profession and connected it to problematic relationships with peers: "Reimbursement and malpractice and medical school debt will all cause a shortage of physicians as people leave settings because they are so oppressed they can't bear practicing. Unhappy physicians don't make good colleagues in the community." And finally Dr. Mahoney, in a non-internal medicine setting, experienced issues within his own practice setting: "The greatest dissatisfaction was with my partners at the hospital. There was no loyalty. They were one reason along with the hospital administration for my considering early retirement."

The Extended Phase (2004–2011)

Five years later in the beginning of President Obama's ACA era, differences emerged more starkly within the cohort as to whether there was more cooperation or competition among medical peers, with a lot depending on how they defined "peer." The division did not just break down between academic and community physicians but more on context, including colleagues' proximity and distance from the physician's practice. Dr. Johnson reported on the affirmative side from a small community rural practice perspective: "We oncologists have cordial relationships with most of the primary doctors in town. One nice thing about this community is that it is not very competitive; everyone has enough to do."

The physicians in community practice identified the transformative change in the relationship between hospital and community-based practitioners resulting from the introduction of the "hospitalist" as first mentioned seven years earlier by Drs. Cahn and Allen. In this extended phase in 2011, almost half of the cohort mentioned or alluded to that physician role without prompting. Almost all concurred that it had dramatically affected peer interaction and collegiality.

Dr. Jarvis acknowledged and even lamented the worsening collegial relationships for which he (and others) blame hospitalists, at least in part: "I spent my entire career establishing referral lines, building and nurturing relationships between family docs and internists, and now when they are put in the hospital it's up to the discretion of the hospitalist who doesn't know Doctor A from Doctor B." As Dr. Jarvis and others made clear, they mainly approved and identified with those whom they consider to be dedicated and devoted to their careers in the way they perceived themselves to be.

The Ending Phase (2011–2016)

At the final stage of interviews, when the physicians in the cohort were at or near the end their careers, many of them offered mixed reviews of their peers, sentiments that were not unlike what they had expressed several years earlier at the extended phase (2004–2011). For the most part, the physicians respected other physicians they worked closely with. However, as I discuss mistakes and malpractice and peer review in chapter 6, the scrutiny of their partners' practice behavior was not very deep. At the same time, those physicians who were far from them—whether in their own or another specialty—were looked on with a bit more caution and occasional concern. And as they discussed their colleagues, whether from an academic or community vantage point, many continued to make distinctions among the generations regarding their scope of practice and attitudes toward the collective. Dr. Strelko summed up his peer relationships realistically and on balance: "Along with the interesting and smart people you work with, there are a lot of folks who can be difficult. They don't play well with others. Still I do like coming to work and working with most of my physician colleagues and administrators. The pluses far outweigh the minuses. As a chair of a department, I treat my faculty like adults; they're a bit older group, they're old school, highly committed, and they get the job done. You're going to have to give other incentives, many more carrots, to younger people. That's part of the newer-generation ethos; it's not mine and I don't like it."

As they anticipated the future, many distinguished between the peers in their practice or setting they were leaving or left behind, and the field of medicine more generally. Dr. Allen described his experience: "I've been in a town and in a practice where there's only one group of cardiologists, so we don't have to fight with another group for patients. And the guys I work with have been mostly fantastic. They're all just smart, wonderful, pleasant people. I fuss at them when necessary. Knock on wood, my partners don't make a lot of mistakes." He then shifted to the physicians in his community. "With other doctors in town, I can tell which ones maybe less detailed. All I can do is write them a note and tell them, 'This is what I would do.' I don't see many jerks, fortunately."

He then presented his dejected views of the future for his practice and the profession. He is much less sanguine because of corporate takeovers: "The hospital took away our employees. They own them now, they run the show; they took away our office. I know that in two and half years, the hammer comes down and it will be all over then for our independent group practice. I'm very pessimistic, but it doesn't matter to me, because I am in my last chapter. I feel sorry for my younger partners because if I am not here to run the practice, they'll never be able to do it."

Dr. Johnson also ended with an existential note of pessimism for himself and his peers and fellow physicians in community settings: "With all these changes with mandated EMRs [electronic medical records] and other government regulations, my private practice oncologist colleagues are disappearing. Physicians in practice are going out of business and they're not coming back; they're a vanishing breed. Loyalty and camaraderie are sadly gone."

In summing up his practice in relationship to his peers, Dr. Jarvis, retired, identified the major demographic cultural, technological, and structural shifts occurring in community settings pervasively across American medicine: "I went into GI field in 1980 to practice as a general gastroenterologist. Now we hire people with sub-subspecialties within GI; for example, people with just an interest in the esophagus, or just who do endoscopies. We hired a lot more women and a number of Indian partners now, so I've learned a lot about different cultures. The other big changes that you see is hospitals which have grown bigger and are swallowing up specialty practices like crazy. We're one of the last standing independent, self-employed GI practices." Dr. Jarvis ended on a similar pessimistic note as did Dr. Allen and Dr. Johnson in spite of his personal sense of career satisfaction: "I'm very happy. It couldn't have been a better choice, a better city to live in, a better practice to have, better partners until now. I miss seeing my partners every day and I miss teaching the interns and residents. Unfortunately, I'm not as gung-ho positive about medicine as I was at one time. There's a lot of negative things coming in, which include a loss of control and independence. I'm glad I'm gone."

Conclusion

The changing structure and culture of house staff training remained as a core theme throughout their careers. Most of those in community practice became more and more distant from academic medical centers as time went on but still had their views of the current group of house staff in internal medicine, which was not generally favorable. Those in academic practice had continuing contact with medical students, residents, and fellows, and had a body of evidence about the newer group's attitudes and behavior over many years that were different from their own generation's. The community practitioners did not expect to have much influence on physicians-in-training; however, the academics with presumably more influence over neophytes surprisingly acknowledged the limits of their authority. While still extolling the virtues of younger cohorts' intellectual ability, they worried about the lack of compassion and concern for the patients, their overemphasis on technology, and the narrowing of their expertise. Even when the physicians acknowledged the different set of values the new generation placed on things outside medicine—and professed envy of them—it was not hard to detect a certain self-righteousness in the way they perceived their own generation's devotion to, and even sacrifice in order to, practice medicine.

Regardless of their setting, most of the cohort compared their own generation's work ethic each decade to the lack of passion they perceived in the younger cohorts from near (inside the hospital) and far (as referral or consulting physicians). Almost all weighed the pros and cons of a lifelong commitment to their craft versus the job-like proficiency of a "nine-to-five" mentality. Reading between the lines and listening to the emotional tone in their voices as they discuss contemporary and younger colleagues, there remains a palpable dissonance between their hearts and their minds, and between their own professional satisfaction and that of the medical profession as a whole. In terms of the future, most of the cohort lamented those changes that profoundly affected virtues of collegiality and loyalty among peers, but were not able or interested in participating in the organizations working to change policies and procedures.

6   *Mistakes and Malpractice*

THE BANE OF PHYSICIANS

The ability of the physicians to define, learn from, and prevent mistakes has been at the core of their professional being since they started on their career journey in the late 1970s. Over the course of their careers, the issue of physician errors also became a strongly held public issue, and the risk of malpractice lawsuits became a critical concern that physicians must navigate in their practice (Gawande, 1999; Kohn, Corrigan, et al., 1999). The first section of this chapter analyzes the ways these physicians acquired their attitudes and behavior toward mistakes when they were house staff at SAMS. It examines their understanding and explanation of theirs and others' mistakes and how they defend them when they are made, from the entry phase (1979–1980) until the ending phase (2011–2016). Additionally, this section also focuses on the consequences of their beliefs and actions for themselves and for the system of medical training and service delivery at the different stages of their career trajectory. It includes their perspectives on who should adjudicate perceived or actual errors in the diagnosis and treatment of patients, and their solutions for sanctioning different types of identified mistakes.

Closely intertwined with and complicating the issue of mistakes is the important issue of malpractice, including threats and actual lawsuits brought against them and their close colleagues at the various stages in their careers. These are discussed in depth in the second section of this chapter, followed by an analysis of how the physicians cope with potential and actual malpractice claims and the relationship of those claims to their potential and actual mistakes. The chapter ends with an examination of the major mechanisms used to maintain physician accountability and responsibility and prevent or address untoward events. These include the practice of defensive medicine and the use of peer review, the latter of which has been identified as the hallmark of professionalism in the medical field, despite the significant levels of discontent among physicians regarding the value and efficacy of such processes and norms (Al-Lamki, 2009; Hershey, 1972; Vyas and Hozain, 2014).

Defining and Defending Mistakes

A medical mistake has been defined in a variety of ways. These include a negative consequence of a decision and intervention by a physician or an adverse event that causes an injury or death; however, there never has been a universally accepted definition (Grober and Bohnen, 2005; Makary and Daniel, 2016). Medical interventions include making a diagnosis, conducting invasive and noninvasive procedures, prescribing specific drugs, or consciously deciding not to do any of those things (Grober and Bohnen, 2005; Reference MD, n.d.). As a result of a physician's diagnostic or therapeutic decision, an adverse outcome can occur, which includes prolonged morbidity or mortality.

My research on how residents at SAMS handled mistakes uncovered that when these unfortunate events occurred, house staff, by their own admission, used a variety of coping mechanisms and normative group practices for defining and defending them (Mizrahi, 1984b). Drawing on analogies to criminal justice, I characterized these strategies as the "3 Ds of Defense": denial, discounting, or distancing. *Denial* consisted of three components: (1) the negation of the concept of error by defining the practice of medicine as an art with gray areas; (2) repressing by not remembering an actual event (which they recalled at a later stage); and/or (3) redefining a described mishap as a nonmistake by explaining, "There is no right or wrong in medicine," or "We caught it in time." *Discounting* included a series of defenses that externalized the blame. They admitted to a mistake but rationalized that it was due to circumstances beyond their control. These discounting techniques included blaming the bureaucratic system, superiors or subordinates within internal medicine, the disease, and/or even the patient. It was common to hear "The patient would have died anyway," or "The patient's symptoms presented abnormally." When they could no longer deny or discount a mistake because of its magnitude or consequences, they used *distancing* techniques. These included resorting to the fallibility of human beings and the inevitability of something going wrong given the existing uncertainty in medical knowledge or inconsistencies in medical practice. Building on my earlier research and publication, I track these issues below throughout their six career phases.

The Entry Phase (1979–1980)

By their own admission in real time, at least half this cohort had been involved in serious patient errors while at SAMS, many of which caused serious complications or death or were characterized as "potential disasters" or "near misses" that were caught "just in time." Some described in great detail one or more grave errors that they committed as house officers or were committed by colleagues that they witnessed firsthand (Mizrahi, 1984b).

As house staff, using denial, the physicians overwhelmingly believed that beyond an obviously egregious situation, there is no right or wrong, no black or white. There are only differences of opinion or at best, there is a preferred, but no exclusive, way of addressing a medical problem. Using denial, the house staff did not identify many major patient-related problems that arose as errors. Many rejected such a notion by commonly commenting, "Everybody does things differently." This was often offered many times as a "defense" to junior house staff by both faculty and senior house staff when something untoward happened to a patient.

As a result, many situations that might have been labeled as a mistake were often redefined as nonmistakes, as this statement by Dr. Cahn demonstrated: "When you present a case to different people, you get many conflicting views.

Some people would have done what you had; some people would have done less. You come to realize that it is just the nature of the business. Things don't always go well. There is no right or wrong way to do it. It's unfortunate, but you can't let that overwhelm you."

A second type of "denial" exhibited was presumed repression. Several house officers admitted openly to blocking mistakes from their consciousness. Still, they insisted that they had probably committed errors but just could not remember any specific ones at the time asked.

Discounting occurred on many levels. Several admitted making a mistake but then were quick to blame others, including their superiors, other staff, the system more generally, and even patients. Blaming their supervisors as a discounting mechanism raised questions about levels of responsibility and authority, which have serious consequences for both patient care and house staff relationships. ("The senior physician should have caught it," argued Dr. O'Brian when he was a junior resident.) Occasionally, senior house staff pointed the finger at subordinates one or two years behind them. These subordinates did not easily accept the blame, as Dr. O'Brian recalled when he was a chief resident: "Last year, during an emergency situation, I told an intern to give a certain medicine. He gave the wrong dose, which eventually killed the patient. He blamed it on the nurse and me. The next day he was really hassled by the attending superiors and constantly told me it was my fault. I should have intervened."

By blaming the disease or the limitations of the science of medicine, house staffers attempted to absolve themselves of responsibility for a mistake. They resigned themselves to the fact that certain disease processes are irreversible or unknown. As Dr. Finast said, "I think I probably have been responsible for some gross errors. The youngest patient I ever had died because I didn't understand what was happening with her electrolytes. But she would have died within the year anyway given her type of disease progression."

A patient may be blamed because the presentation of his or her symptoms did not follow the classic course or what house officers often refer to as "cookbook" medicine. In other words, a mistake is made because the unexpected or unusual occurs, and the physician is either caught off guard or steered off course because there are more commonly accepted explanations. As noted here by Dr. Melone, "I made a serious error the last day of my internship. I gave eight units of insulin and the patient died. I learned later that some people would have done what I did, but the faculty at the time crucified me. They were upset since normally hypoglycemics are handled another way. But that patient had an abnormal response."

Patients are also blamed in more direct ways as well. They are blamed for not revealing sufficient information about their current problem or their past medical history, which the house officer Dr. Paul concluded impeded him from making a correct diagnosis or prescribing an appropriate treatment. Their overall view was that patients in the SAMS system are not trustworthy, as Dr. Rosen described, "Sometimes you feel like a detective, trying to find out if your patient is really taking his medicines. What we're really dealing in is honesty. I was duped more than once by a patient not telling the truth, with dire consequences." The SAMS house staff believed that many patients do not communicate the truth because either they forget or lie, an all-pervasive perspective when applied to certain patient types described as alcoholics, drug abusers, and other socially degraded categories.

When these young physicians could not deny or discount a serious and obvious mistake because of the magnitude of the outcome, distancing processes were used. These included a variety of shared beliefs, which allowed for a direct admission of guilt with justifications: "Everyone makes mistakes," "It couldn't be helped," and "I did the best I could."

These mechanisms are all ways of dealing with the imperfectability of human beings as well as the inevitability of errors. These were found in almost every discussion as to reasons why mistakes are made. The following comment by Dr. Strelko was typical: "So you make a therapeutic decision, and it turns out to be wrong. It's not usually regarded as a mistake. You don't expect to get to the right answer every time." Similarly, as Dr. Lash described, "You begin to realize during internship the limitations of everyone in medicine more and more. The problem is that you can't know everything."

The whole process of managing mistakes appeared to be an ambiguous one at best. Still, using any of the "3 Ds of defense" did not necessarily exonerate house officers from blame, either from themselves or from others. Peer and self-assessment after a potential or actual harmful situation was still fraught with confusion and uncertainty. As house staffers, they were continuously reshaping their perspective on their own and others' errors and redefining levels of culpability.

Overall there was increasing toleration and leniency for their errors, which they agreed with as they were socialized into the house staff culture and structure. As Dr. Nolan, who served as a chief resident at SAMS, admitted, "There are no black and whites, just shades of grey. What somebody might consider gross mismanagement, someone else might call an understandable error. You become more lenient, particularly when you see someone doing something that didn't work, but that you've done at least once yourself."

In addition to the 3 Ds of denial, discounting and distancing, there was also a sentiment that I uncovered and labeled a fourth D—*doubt*. These physicians accepted the transformation of their practice reality in which sharp black-and-white judgments were blended and shaded. Concomitant with, and perhaps as a consequence of, this "graying" process, nagging and lingering doubt emerged in their descriptions of their and their peers' errors made during this entry phase (1979–1980). These troublesome feelings neither easily nor automatically resolved themselves over time. Interspersed among their defenses were significant and fundamental questions about culpability and responsibility. These continued to disturb many house officers as they shifted from the entry (1979–1980) to early phase (1980–1984) of their career track regardless of whether they were entering community or academic practice. Dr. Beech's confessed doubt is palpable: "There's always a thought in the back of my mind that there's something I didn't do or something I did that caused the patient to die. I ruptured a spleen with a needle. That's probably the biggest mistake that stands out. It's the one I think about still at least two or three times a week even several years later."

As Dr. Lash entered a nontraditional academic fellowship, he vacillated between discounting, distancing, and doubt about this untoward event: "My most serious error? I sent a patient out of the ER who was probably having angina. However, she was a chronic complainer and came in very angry two days later with a heart attack [discounting]. Had I been a little more objective, I could have taken control of the situation [doubt]. I made a mistake, but I'm not sure it would have made a difference [distancing]. Still, I did a lot of thinking about it. I should have asked for a second opinion [doubt]. The attending physician commiserated, 'We all have been in your shoes' [distancing]. The house staff backed me up one hundred percent."

For many, "the case was never closed," as they moved into academic or community practice. Little in their three-year residency training seemed to allow them to work through the attendant vulnerability and ambiguity accompanying mistakes, especially given the variety of interpretations. The result appeared to be the collective acquisition of maladaptive defense mechanisms that remained with them in the early phase.

Although they expressed confidence in their abilities by the end of training, these residents had not fully come to grips with their own actual or anticipated errors while they were in a position to provide junior colleagues with defenses for theirs and others' mistakes. Senior residents provided the junior ones with these denial, discounting, and distancing mechanisms, they simultaneously conveyed a second or "double" message of doubt, which kept alive the question of guilt and responsibility (Mizrahi, 1984b).

What was starkly revealed during this entry phase (1979–1980) was how the house staff perceived their treatment for mishaps by their peers and superiors. Rather than being reprimanded, they indicated almost always that the situation was handled with consolation, commiseration, or humor. And for the most part, they believed that this seemingly lenient orientation—no reprimand, no repercussions—was both necessary and sufficient. They strongly asserted that this was the only appropriate and justifiable approach to managing most errors. There were only occasional reported rebukes from superiors, and most of those were either discounted or condemned outright as not fair.

They justified their defensive reactions and leniency because of their expressed willingness to be self-critical, that is, to "self-sentence." As Dr. Jarvis asserted, "I am my own worst and ultimately only critic." While they maintained great camaraderie and respect for their fellow house officers, ultimately they came to believe that no one else could or should hold them accountable. Instead, they owed their allegiance primarily or exclusively to themselves, as Dr. Jarvis noted above and Dr. Melone here conveyed, "I can't say I have a whole lot of allegiance to anyone. I feel accountable to myself and I feel accountable to try to do the best I can for the people I'm taking care of." After describing a negative event, Dr. Johnson professed, "I personally am conscientious enough to punish myself for that error I made, so I don't need to be punished by anyone else."

Since cues from outside groups were indeed ambiguous, contradictory, or unavailable, the physicians appeared to discount the importance of external and even formal internal evaluation and accountability mechanisms such as peer review (discussed at the end of this chapter). As many moved into positions of relative high prestige and privilege as physicians with the power to make life and death decisions, they see themselves as singularly responsible for their actions and disparage any attempts by others to insert themselves into the process of accountability.

Early Phase (1980–1984)
and Established Phase (1984–1994)

During the interviews for both the early phase (five years after completing their house staff training), and the established phase (fifteen years after completing house staff training), at a time when they had much more responsibility for others (patients, medical students, residents, nurses, etc.), the cohort was asked to again recollect mistakes they had made back during house staff training. Over the course of the first three career time frames (entry, early, and established phases), a total of fifty different mistakes were remembered by the physicians as having taken place. During the first round of interviews in 1980 at the end of their house staff training, the cohort identified twenty-one different mistakes they had made. When they were asked again later at the end of the early and established phases about mistakes made as house staff, they disclosed an additional twenty-nine mistakes. Overall, they revealed a total of sixty-six mistakes that had occurred during their time as house staff—twenty-one revealed as training ended; twenty-eight, five years later; and seventeen, fifteen years afterward. Some specific instances were repeated in all three time frames, while others were recalled only once or twice. More were recalled over time than forgotten or omitted.

Nine of these twenty physicians remembered at least one mistake made in training at one or both subsequent time periods. For example, Dr. Beech noted in each interview his error of having ruptured a patient's spleen, resulting in the patient's death. Other physicians remembered different mistakes at different time points or recalled one or more in later phases that they had not revealed closer to the time it occurred during their residency. For example, Dr. Annas recalled a different mistake made during his house staff training at each of the first three interview cycles, none of which was repeated in the other interviews. At the entry phase (1979–1980), he revealed, "A patient at the VA during my internship had kidney disease, was jaundiced and developed a low temperature that I dismissed. An attending caught it three to four hours later, or it would have been catastrophic." Although he did not recall that error later during the interviews at the early phase (1980–1984), he did recall a different one: "In the ER I was getting ready to send somebody out after a seizure, when he was stable. Then he stood up, seized again, and cracked his head open." Similarly, at the established phase

(1984–1994), he recalled a new one but did not mention the ones he revealed earlier: "There was a patient with pneumonia that I didn't take seriously. He came in debilitated with a malignancy. I should have intubated him and put him in the ICU. Instead, I put him on the ward. While I tended to other patients, he died."

On the other hand, some doctors revealed mistakes in different ways. For instance, Dr. Melone described an incident in the entry phase; yet five years later in the early phase in 1984, he denied having made any mistakes. Then, twenty years later in the entrenched phase in 2004, he actually recalled what appeared to be a version of that same incident in great detail early on. (Entry phase): "The biggest one was an error with a GI bleeder. He came in with necrotic cirrhosis and had his third massive GI bleed. He had a tube down, but we wanted another type, so I took the first one out and he bled massively. We never got another tube down, and he died." (Entrenched phase): "It was my last night. I took out a tube that I didn't intend to. The kid had bad hepatitis, so I put a tube down so he wouldn't bleed. He pulled it out. We spent the next 8 hours trying to keep him alive in vain."

Given the variations in recollection, did their definitions of mistakes change over time as their positions and experiences did? In 1994, at the end of the established phase (1984–1994), they were asked this question and were asked to "distinguish between an error and something that can't be helped." At this time, fifteen years after serving as house staff at SAMS, their responses remained inexact, confusing, and contradictory. Many stumbled, hesitated, and vacillated. Neither time nor experience clarified nor simplified the complexity of their thinking about this serious subject for themselves, their patients, and society.

The majority continued to use distancing techniques to discuss mistakes, including concepts of inevitability ("The patient would have died anyway") and fallibility ("Everyone makes them"). They continued to point to the lack of certainty in medicine, in essence blaming the "science" of medicine for not being more precise. Almost all continued to cite "gray areas" and declared that "medicine is more of an art than a science." Many commented, "It's a judgment call," or "It's a fine line." Dr. Finast went as far as saying that he never saw a medical judgment that he could not justify.

The term *adverse outcome* was not in their vocabulary during training, but it began to emerge in their language in later time periods as they contrasted certain patient-related negative events from actual mistakes. At the same time, it appeared in the medical literature, and its use indicated a change in the way physicians, including this cohort, separated themselves from possibility of culpability (AHRQ, 2019). In looking back, many of the cohort asserted that their views on mistakes and medical errors had not changed since training; that is, they always erred on the side of being tolerant or forgiving. Dr. Rosen stated, "I don't think my view of mistakes has changed over time. I tend to give physicians the benefit of the doubt. There are very few things that are really clear errors."

For those who said their perspectives had changed, it was always in the direction of a more lenient interpretation of adverse outcomes, which were not often defined as mistakes. As Dr. Paul asserted, "It's almost impossible to distinguish a mistake from a mishap. Since training, I've become more jaundiced about the precision of science. I've become more cognizant of the inexactness and the variations in practice from one physician to the next."

The context for understanding and assessing mistakes had become more visible to the public over time (Furrow, 1998; Kohn, Corrigan, et al., 1999), while the unfairness of linking bad outcomes and mistakes was more prevalent within the cohort. As a whole, the physicians asserted that they had become more lenient, while most of them viewed the external climate and culture surrounding mistakes as less tolerant. Dr. Johnson commented, "Our culture is much too quick to describe bad outcomes as errors, and that is a real tough thing to deal with. In oncology, the name of the game is to try to get people to understand what a reasonable likelihood of an outcome is."

Entrenched Phase (1994–2004), Extended Phase (2004–2011), and Ending Phase (2011–2016)

By the beginning of the twenty-first century, there were increasingly powerful external factors complicating the mistakes phenomena: that of malpractice, the role of lawyers, and lawsuits, real and threatened (Carrier, Reschovsky, et al., 2013; Grober and Bohnen, 2005). As these physicians advanced in their careers, the question of mistakes remained intriguing: Did their definitions of mistakes change? As years passed, how did they remember their own and others' mistakes in residency, and would they admit to making mistakes in practice?

In these later phases, the cohort was even more vague about the definition of mistakes than in earlier periods. With additional years of experience, they were more likely to discuss bad outcomes and the inevitability that "things go wrong," whether the circumstances were based on medical acts of commission or omission. They continued to distance themselves from problematic events that occurred, continuing to assert the "gray areas" involved, and/or that there were alternative courses of action that could almost always be defended.

In spite of the lack of clarity in defining mistakes, three-quarters of the cohort directly acknowledged making them when directly asked. On display was the vicariousness of professional life and their vulnerability as physicians at the hands of distrusting patients and aggressive attorneys, especially for those in community practice. The reluctance to "Monday morning quarterbacking" was an expression commonly used. "It's complicated," offered Dr. O'Brian, while others gave confusing responses with lots of hesitation. Dr. Melone responded, "Gosh, I don't know what constitutes a mistake. In our practice I guess it's not making a diagnosis in a timely fashion." Dr. Annas declared, "Cutting off the wrong leg in the operating room is a mistake. Treating someone who had an MI according to standard care and then he has a complication is not a mistake; it's a bad outcome. There are no guarantees."

Denial, discounting, and distancing themselves from mistakes when adverse outcomes or even a lawsuit occurred, were prevalent. Looking back over his professional lifetime, Dr. Strelko admitted to mistakes generically, and still, all these years later, he continues to discount them. Here recalling an error when he was an intern, he blamed the senior residents: "We made mistakes all the time. Our mentors were residents who were one or two years ahead of us. They were responsible. You know, even as I say we made mistakes, we don't always know what mistakes we made." How much responsibility should they bear still weighs on them, even as they continue to discount negative circumstances by often blaming patients. Dr. Jarvis asserted, "Everybody has made mistakes. We do lots of endoscopic procedures. So doing thousands, there will be patients, no matter how hard you try, who always have complications. I've had a few and I feel absolutely awful about them, but it's a fact of life."

In the extended phase (2004–2011), the comment that "Everybody makes mistakes" was similarly commonly heard. Although they would undoubtedly define themselves as scientifically minded professionals if asked, so many made comments and gestures in discussing mistakes and lawsuits, such as, "It's all luck"; "Knock on wood"; "Don't jinx me"; and "I'm keeping my fingers crossed." They did not appear to be reluctant to talk about this topic; on the contrary, they were seemingly forthcoming and candid. Here Dr. Lynch contemplated his past mistakes: "I've probably erred in judgments on how aggressive to be. I've pushed chemotherapy or radiation and had two people die from treatment. I guess I believed I still had done the right thing, and they just had an adverse reaction, but it was hard." Given the sensitivity of the subject, one might assume that their worst errors were not revealed to me, making the precariousness of medical practice even more problematic.

When their recollections of mistakes in these later periods are compared with those from earlier times, their trajectories were not consistent. Four different patterns emerged. First, there were those who, in the ending phase (2011–2016), omitted mistakes they had described during the entry phase (1979–1980), early phase (1980–1984), or the established phase (1984–1994). Second, there was a subgroup who omitted mistakes earlier and then introduced new ones not acknowledged or previously described. A third pattern could be discerned among a subgroup who reidentified incidents from the entry phase (1979–1980) in the extended phase (2004–2011) or ending phase (2011–2016) that they had omitted in the middle phases. And there is a fourth small group who continued to recall with emotion devastating feelings surrounding the same mistake they made at least thirty or more years earlier.

Remembrances Over Time

What accounted for the differences in remembrances of mistakes or bad patient outcomes under their watch? No external factors appear to be associated with the variations in their recollections of these serious matters in different career phases. Neither their subspecialty, nor type of practice, nor an actual malpractice suit seemed to account sufficiently for the different patterns. However, there was one key factor that, perhaps not surprisingly, played an important role in determining whether they remembered a mistake over the course of their careers—the nature of the mistake. Of all the mistakes that the physicians recalled from their time as house staff, there were two types of mistakes that seemed to stay in their minds the most and that were mentioned the most over the course of the career phases: the death of a patient and/or a serious rebuke by a senior house officer or attending faculty physician.

Of the fifty different mistakes recalled at least once, twenty had resulted in a patient's death. In the initial recollections at the end of training, nine of the twenty-one mistakes resulted in a death. Five years after training, the total number of recalled mistakes rose to twenty-eight, ten of which had resulted in a patient death. And, during the remaining interview cycles (fifteen years or more after the end of residency), while the total number of mistakes remembered declined to seventeen, eleven of those had resulted in a patient death. Additionally, of the nine mistakes recalled in the established phase (1984–1994) that were also recalled in the earlier time frames, death was the patient outcome for seven of them. This suggests that death of a patient, regardless of whether they felt it was justified or inevitable, was, not surprisingly, a profoundly critical variable in enhancing their recollection of reported mistakes.

This revelation sets a truly high standard for accepting responsibility—death. Hence, if mortality was averted, an incident may not be defined as a mistake needing additional repercussions, regardless of the pain and suffering it may have caused. Dr. Melone reflected in the early phase "There are a couple of things I would have done differently, but I don't think I killed anybody. I certainly made it tough on the guy with the GI bleed I discussed earlier when we couldn't get a tube back down, but not sure that would have saved him. That's the closest I came to a mistake."

Secondly, the perceived consequences of having made a mistake seem to have positively affected their recollection. At the entry phase (1979–1980), these physicians recalled almost no repercussions for their reported mistakes; even reprimands were rare. In fact, answers to the question then about how their mistakes were handled yielded contradictory responses ranging from "It wasn't [handled]" (i.e., there were no repercussions), to "[These were handled] with understanding." Fifteen years later, more of the physicians recalled mistakes for which they said there were some repercussions, even if informally situated, namely, such as being "called on the carpet." No one recalled a formal rebuke at any phase. For example, no one mentioned that they were subject to a morbidity and mortality conference or were asked to account for their actions in a structured setting. On the contrary, most were satisfied and even grateful, at least on the surface, for their peer or departmental responses even when there were negative patient outcomes including complications, longer hospital stays, and death. Dr. Conley noted at the end of residency that a patient of his had an "MI" and died because he took a poor history. He was then asked about repercussions: "There was some discussion then or a little later on with other people, particularly the residents— that was worse than any formal discipline, just having them judge me." He did not describe the incident five years later but did remember it again with specificity and emotion fifteen years later.

However, even with continuing defenses, many seem to endure lingering doubt about whether they should have been held responsible. They may suffer in silence. For example, in this poignant illustration, Dr. Paul recalled a situation from when he was house staff: "I don't think anybody knew about it but me. I think about the incident from time to time. The patient died; I felt bad for a while." Then, five years later, he raises the event again as doubt persisted: "I wish someone would have called me on the carpet. It might have made me feel a little better, but nobody did. Nothing happened; I was a resident."

Not being held publicly accountable may have resulted in the lingering question about how to reconcile these complex and clearly painful situations, owning up to their roles in the mishap, claiming responsibility, moving on, putting it past them using a norm of "forgive and remember" (Bosk, 2003). At the very least, none of the cohort remembered any of those higher up in the SAMS system providing any teaching or discussions collectively as a community to assist in recognizing and resolving these difficult but inevitable situations. For sure, out of sight was not out of mind.

Unforgivable Mistakes

In spite of the ambiguity and lack of precision in defining mistakes, and the various ways they defended their actions, these physicians had strong feelings about certain types of mistakes for which there should be consequences. They articulated distinctions between "forgivable" and "unforgivable" errors, which were almost always based on attribution, largely divorced from actual physician interventions that may have caused or exacerbated adverse patient outcomes. There was remarkable consensus that intolerable mistakes were almost always based on values, character, and/or moral standards, normative ones, as also found by Bosk in his study of surgical residents (2003). These included lack of compulsiveness, arrogance, systemic errors, and impairment.

These categories emanated primarily from strong norms they acquired during their internal medicine training (Mizrahi, 1986) and which were repeated by so many over multiple time periods. The most prevalent reason given for an "unforgivable mistake" was the violation of the norm of compulsiveness, which they believed to be the hallmark of a competent internist. Acquired during their graduate training, being compulsive encompassed not letting any symptom go past them and applying the process differential diagnosis in making judgments. At the extreme, it meant eliminating all possible reasons for a symptom, as Dr. Cahn explained, "Some of us are more compulsive than others, and those who aren't could get into trouble. Some fellow residents' personality types are more cavalier; it scares me." Several specifically reiterated that it was not a lack of knowledge or incompetence that was unacceptable except in the extreme, but rather it was the failure to pay attention to details. They believed overwhelmingly that it was being sloppy and careless that caused major problems for physicians.

This pervasive norm was often accompanied by the articulation of another norm acquired during house staff training: the norm of humility. It was frequently described in the entry phase as "knowing what you don't know," and "knowing when you're in over your head." Violations of these two norms were the most frequent reasons given to admonish a peer. Overconfidence, which could lead to arrogance, was cited as a cardinal "sin," as Dr. Rosen commented: "You can become overconfident. You think you know what's going on all the time; you think the patients are less sick than they are, so you worry less. You become less compulsive. That's the main cause of mistakes."

In this cohort's collective view, several factors, including the two norms, could combine to cause physicians to make mistakes. Dr. Allen explained, "There's a combination of reasons why mistakes are made: poor training; they bite off more than they can chew; they're not meticulous enough; or they're too tired. I don't judge them too harshly." Overall, there was little blame by these physicians attached to an adverse outcome based on competency; rather repercussions were affirmed primarily for the breaking of the norms of compulsivity and humility.

Contradictions between Mistakes and Malpractice

Beginning in the 1970s, malpractice issues were regularly raised in the media and in some policy debates (Chen and Yang, 2014; Renkema, Broekhuis, et al., 2014). However, the visibility of lawsuits and malpractice in the public discourse escalated in the early phase (1980–1984) of their careers, just when they were finishing their time as house staff and beginning their practices (Charles, Wilbert, et al., 1985; Hershey, 1972).

Over the course of their careers, more than half of the cohort would be sued and/or be close to a partner who had been. These experiences had a profound effect on their psyches as well as their practice. Almost nothing brought out the emotions and ire of physicians like the term *malpractice*. Yet, they did not view most of threatened or real lawsuits, theirs or others, as mistakes. Mistakes were still viewed as a matter of judgment with few external repercussions received or needed. The physicians continued to assert that the self-blame and criticism were severe and sufficient. Not so with being sued. From early on in their careers, the threat of or actual beginning of a lawsuit took an emotional toll on them and on their relationships with patients and their peers. The specter and outcomes of malpractice lawsuits weighed especially heavily on those in community practice, whether experienced or directly witnessed.

The Early Phase (1980–1984)

In their first years out of training as they began their academic or community careers, the uncertainty of medicine became real as their responsibilities for decisions about patient care increased (Mizrahi, 1986). They felt the weight of decisions about their own patients and, for the academics, patients under the care of less experienced trainees they now supervised. The pressure of being in charge and hence responsible and accountable for their actions was a revelation unanticipated until they began to practice. As Dr. Nolan asserted, "The buck stops with me now."

From the time they entered practice, the impact of malpractice was rearing its ugly head, whereas during their residency years, they had been largely able to ignore it. During their training at SAMS, there was little concern expressed for preventing lawsuits using the method of ordering tests, whether considered excessive or not or treating diseases aggressively. When they were house officers, intervention appeared to be better than nonintervention. It was important to "rule any possibility out" given the norm of compulsivity. Dr. Annas, as a young attending, acknowledged, "As a training institution, care is going to be more expensive since we are training doctors to make decisions. They are going to make mistakes when they order redundant tests, but they should be given the liberty to make them to satisfy their academic curiosity."

New academic practitioners like Dr. Paul were aware of greater public and government scrutiny on their practice behavior, and in particular holding the specter of malpractice over them: "I am constantly thinking about malpractice. I almost quit in December! When I moonlighted in a small hospital, I was constantly obsessed by it. I wonder if this is the way it is in private practice. I can't be sued here personally, but this VA facility could be sued with me implicated, so it is important that I defend what I do."

Those in community practice like Dr. Nolan felt they were in greater jeopardy than their academic colleagues: "People in academia don't have primary responsibility for patients. They don't have to get up in the middle of the night. They have residents and interns, and they can say, 'Call me in the morning.' I can't because something could go wrong. I'm in charge."

Even just a few years into their professional careers, several already had been sued or named in a suit. And this experience affected them profoundly, as Dr. Lynch confirmed: "I was named in a suit merely because I saw the patient once. It is still in litigation. I think about it a lot." As they entered the world of practice, they were aware of the impingement on their autonomy and the increased scrutiny by outside regulators, insurance companies, patients, and trial lawyers, without much justification in their view (Carrier, Reschovsky, et al., 2013; Tyssen, Palmer, et al., 2013). This worried them greatly.

The Established Phase (1984–1994)

When questioned about mistakes and malpractice ten years later—fifteen years into their careers—these physicians were immersed in the era of managed care, something that had exploded after the failure of Congress to pass President Clinton's health insurance legislation. Dr. Ross commented with some resentment on how he was treated by external regulators, and how he learned to play the system: "I got killed by the PRO (an outside professional regulator) a few years ago. I went through a period of being reviewed one hundred percent of the time before I learned how to play the chart game. I even went so far as to become a reviewer, so now I know what they are looking for. It's absolutely ludicrous. These committees have nothing to do with quality."

At the same time malpractice was getting increasing attention in the media (Renkema, Broekhuis, et al., 2014). Many more had been sued personally or witnessed a close colleague going through what they considered a painful even agonizing ordeal. The term "risk management" became part of their vocabulary (Kraman and Hamm, 1999; Wiener, 1998). Dr. Polikoff, practicing in an HMO setting by this phase, recalled misdiagnosing an abscess, and as a result, the patient left the practice. Although Dr. Polikoff did not define the incident as a mistake, he, like so many physicians, harbored many ongoing fears and doubts that seemed seared into his consciousness in spite of institutional supports: "It's been many years since it happened. I underestimated how sick he was, but my diagnosis and treatment were appropriate. I always feel guilty, I don't think it was a mistake, but I always wonder if I had been there rounding instead of my partner, whether I would have caught it?" Dr. Polikoff also revealed how much he and others are influenced by what happens to a peer: "Several people in our practice have been sued. One colleague was really devastated even though the case was eventually thrown out of court. The patient died, but the family kept pursuing it. It left its mark on all of us."

Attending academic physicians got into the malpractice mix by the established time frame as they became increasingly aware of the impact of malpractice on their own performance. Both Drs. Annas and Strelko, respectively, found themselves directly and indirectly a target of malpractice lawsuits. Dr. Annas recalled, "I was sued for predicting someone would die. It never got to court. Yet for three years every time you apply for something, you have to check, 'There is a malpractice pending.' We have a good risk management team. The minute there is a hint of trouble we call them."

During this established phase (1984–1994), the cohort was learning how to adjust and respond to lawsuits that were the result of, at the very least, questionable decision-making outcomes (Ghalandarpoorattar, Kaviani, et al., 2012). In so many instances, like in the examples above, the physicians' rationales for the process and results continue to include a vacillation among the three Ds of defense—denial, discounting, or distancing—first identified during their residency years (Mizrahi, 1984b).

The Entrenched Phase (1994–2004)

By the end of the entrenched phase, the physicians had practiced in one or more settings for twenty-five or more years. Their disgruntlement about outside interference, especially by insurance companies and attorneys, abounded, and the continuing enmity toward lawyers was palpable. Dr. Rosen referred to it as "that evil tort system," while Dr. Ross lamented, "The business side of medicine is more painful than ever. I hate lawyers more than I ever thought I could. I got sued ten years ago. I'm over it, but it's crippling medicine and America."

Others anticipated at this entrenched phase that the number of lawsuits would be going up along with skyrocketing costs. The impact on their and their peers' practice styles and future behavior was stark. As noted by Dr. Jarvis, "It's pure greed on the part of attorneys. I see doctors retiring every day. The risks of staying in practice are so high that they don't want to expose their financial well-being to some malpractice suit. I feel that way. I'm taking precautions."

Most continued to blame the greed of lawyers and the huge profits realized by the private health care system for the number of lawsuits and the increasingly higher costs of insurance (Seabury, Chandra, et al., 2013). Rarely did they think that physicians were at fault. Many of the physicians went so far as to assert the contrary: that most lawsuits were not founded on mistakes and, ironically, that actual mistakes (meaning blatant omission or commission) rarely resulted in lawsuits (Sohn, 2013). Dr. Jarvis described the problem for the profession: "Our malpractice premiums have gone up. We've had trouble getting insurance because of the number of claims against us, although all were subsequently dismissed. The future of medicine is very much in jeopardy unless this malpractice thing gets resolved. Insurance companies and lawyers are sucking all the profit from medicine with their lobbies."

The Extended Phase (2004–2011)

At the extended phase of their careers, actual and potential lawsuits continued to loom large in their psyches. The major development in this phase was the passage of the Patient Protection and Affordable Care Act (ACA) by Congress in 2010 championed by President Obama. However, the ACA did not address malpractice and tort reform, which disappointed many of the physicians, both in academia and the community (Chirba and Noble, 2013). By this phase, ten of the cohort had been sued and another three were adversely impacted based on the experience of a partner or close colleague. Many of these untoward events had occurred in the last ten years, while others were recalled from the earlier time. Moreover, a few revealed these negative experiences at this point for the first time, although they had occurred at earlier stages.

Nevertheless, for the first time, many of the cohort began to articulate solutions along with causes of the culture of litigation. Several physicians who had been involved in lawsuits disputed the relationship between bad medical practice and legal proceedings. Dr. Annas, for example, suggested it is a bad relationship with patients that leads to lawsuits. "Unless it is something incredibly stupid, no one gets sued for medical decision-making. If you did the right thing ninety percent of the time, and ten percent was off the beaten path, it's not really malpractice, even if the patient died. If you start screaming at a family member blaming the patient who died that he needed to lose weight, you will be sued. It's that bad relationship that triggers the lawsuit."

This disconnect between getting sued and making a mistake continued to resonate with many of the physicians years after these controversial and consequential events occurred. They asserted the randomness of the circumstances that contributed to their potential or real tribulations. Here Dr. Beech admitted, "There were medical things that happened that made me wonder if I would get sued. I didn't, but I probably could have. Maybe it was my good communication.

Sometimes these were mistakes and sometimes bad things just happened. There's a lot of gray areas."

Two community practitioners, Drs. Lynch and Cahn, who had not been sued at this point, still answered the question with concern about the risk, both suggesting they had been lucky so far. Dr. Conley, who was retired at this point, recalled the effects of that risk: "I was always very fearful of lawsuits just because they could occur randomly. In the 1980s and 1990s there was negativity in the air about doctors when managed care entered the market. I had a bunker mentality and always worried." The use of superstitious terms by many of the cohort continued to be common, despite being otherwise out of character.

Many of these physicians also commented on the plight of colleagues with great empathy; no one distanced themselves from the risks involved: "It could have been me in similar circumstances," acknowledged Dr. Lynch. He also spoke for and identified with the plight of the community of physicians as a whole: "It's been quite depressing for my colleagues. There is a physician mental health group that I could avail myself of if something bad happened, God forbid! The medical community tries to take care of its own." It is noteworthy that Dr. Lynch was the only physician to identify that collective peer support was available to discuss sensitive and even disturbing matters. They otherwise seemed very alone with their fears and vulnerability.

The Ending Phase (2011–2016)

As their careers ended or were on the verge of terminating, the physicians' experiences with malpractice lawsuits for themselves or a close peer remained a blight on their perceptions of the medical profession. Many recalled with precision what were clearly traumatic events from years past.

These incidents or prolonged processes more than almost anything else seem to have contributed to their cynicism, disillusionment, and even self-doubt, regardless of whether a lawsuit was threatened, settled, or dismissed (also see chapter 8 on disillusionment for a more in-depth exploration).

Dr. Mahoney was impacted by two such events that affected him and his decision-making about his career trajectory profoundly: "Being sued affected how I did things, and it contributed to my decision to retire early. One dragged out for five years before it was finally settled. I was wrapped up first in worrying about a suit, then the suit occurred, and then I went through the process of lawyers, testimony, and depositions. Lawyers on either side played the game."

The impact of malpractice suits continued to bring many strong critiques of lawyers and the tort system at this late stage in their careers. Anger abounded, even for those who had not been directly sued. As expressed by Dr. Cahn, "Malpractice is grossly unfair. There are some doctor outliers that fuck up, but that's not the majority of lawsuits. The majority are those where lawyers can make money. We need tort reform to screen out those bullshit cases. Like Shakespeare, I say, 'Kill all the lawyers.'"

Dr. Allen recalled at every phase of his practice, a malpractice suit against his partner all the way back in 1982 that continued to have a deep impact on him. Although after three and a half years, his partner was eventually found not guilty, Dr. Allen described how he regularly attended the court hearings and met with lawyers. For Dr. Allen, it was clear that experience was indelibly branded on his psyche, since he repeated that story spontaneously at every phase, including at this one: "I can't think of anything that changed my life forever more. I can't imagine what it would be like if I'd been sued." He had even marked on his calendar the date two years after the day he will quit, because, as he said, "You can be sued up to then."

Moreover, the impact of malpractice suits extended to their perceptions of its impact on certain specialties and on the profession as a whole. According to Dr. Strelko, "There needs to be some rational plan for the whole malpractice business. There shouldn't be a whole industry of lawyers making millions."

Prospective and Retrospective Solutions to Medical Mistakes and Malpractice

In the final section of this chapter, I look at two issues connected to medical mistakes and malpractice—the practice of defensive medicine and the use of peer review as an accountability measure. First, I provide a general summary of these physicians' commonly held views of defensive medicine: namely, that it is a method that physicians use to protect themselves from a malpractice suit. Then I present a deeper examination of peer review. Because some type of peer review process was in place when the physicians were house staff, I track their perspectives on this issue more systematically as they progressed through their career phases.

The Practice of Defensive Medicine

The practice of defensive medicine was used extensively by the cohort with varying degrees of justification. Defined as medical protocols done to avoid malpractice lawsuits, it includes practices that may not be standard but may help avoid being accused of negligence, such as ordering additional tests, prescribing certain medicine or procedures, avoiding high risk specialties, or cherry-picking certain patient types to include or exclude in their practice (Sekhar and Vyas, 2013). Such behavior has been attributed to increasing health care costs and ultimately even harming patients in the long run. Yet it is part of the vocabulary of health care policy-makers, critics, and physicians themselves for more than a few decades (Carrier, Reschovsky, et al., 2013; Chen & Yang, 2014; Renkema, Broekhuis, et al., 2014), although it has also been condemned in the public and policy sphere (Sekhar and Vyas, 2013).

Almost every physician identified one or more of the components of defensive medicine that they used when asked how they protected themselves from lawsuits. Over time they admitted to doing so with more impunity. Even in the early phase (1980–1984), Dr. Lynch asserted, "I sure do practice defensive medicine like charting, with pages of documentation." Real and perceived threats were on their minds if you scratched the surface. Dr. Cahn, for example, also during the early phase, served as an informant for his peers who were clearly on guard: "All doctors in my state are worried about malpractice. Anybody who says they don't practice defensive medicine here is lying. For sure, I practice it for certain patients, reflective of their personalities more than because of DRGs (a government reimbursement system)."

As the physicians progressed in their careers, and the risks and realities of being sued continued, they maintained a clear willingness to practice defensive medicine. For example, after having been sued twice, Dr. Polikoff admitted, somewhat facetiously, at the end of the established phase (1984–1994) that his behavior, not just his attitude about practice, had changed: "I think when you are in practice, you have to practice defensively. Defensive medicine is to imagine every possibility, even if infinitesimal, to be sure you don't get screwed; for example I do lots of PSA screening in case a patient might develop prostate cancer in three or four years."

Dr. Allen, like many others, admitted that he practiced a cautionary type of defensive medicine, including a snide side note like Dr. Polikoff: "When I see somebody in the hospital, I always list all twenty-seven diagnoses that person carries. I see a lot of other doctors make mistakes because they don't do that. My practice is more compulsive. You know, a guy comes in with his heart beating fast, you better get a thyroid panel because he has a one in 200 chance of having thyroid cancer!"

Even the academic physicians were actively approaching their practice through a defensive lens. For example, Dr. Lash, discussing the role of defensive medicine and risk management in his faculty practice midway in his career, confessed to the difficulty in deciding which medical interventions are necessary or not, while Dr. Paul reacts strongly to its role in a malpractice: "It is something I obsess about. It is always a scary thought. I'm compulsive and I attend lectures on avoiding risks. My practice style has become all about risk management."

As their careers progressed, the physicians seemed to grow more open about the fact they practiced defensive medicine. In the entrenched phase (1994–2004), for instance, Dr. Ross felt no need to hold back and defiantly bellowed, "Hell yeah, I do!" Dr. Lynch admitted for the first time, "Every time you meet a new patient, you want to make sure you cover your ass. Good medicine is defensive medicine absolutely." This attitude was widespread among the cohort at this stage, and with a few exceptions, like Dr. Rosen, who claimed not to do it, defensive medicine appeared to be generally accepted as part of a risk management strategy against the threat of malpractice suits.

Because of the cost and waste that is known to be associated with the practice of defensive medicine, many of the physicians spent time at the later stages of their careers describing ways that the practice of defensive medicine might be reduced, although the solutions, not surprisingly, were overwhelmingly the need to get rid of malpractice suits, eliminate private lawyers, and minimize physician blame. For example, in the extended phase (2004–2011) and ending phase (2011–2016), the cohort identified a range of solutions they could imagine for this quandary of practicing defensive medicine.

Dr. Lynch, who had practiced for a year in another country, suggested several professional and cultural reforms: "I've been very lucky not to have been sued because in everything I do, there's always some risk. In other countries there is no suing. They have a compensation system when somebody has a bad outcome. There's a system for counseling the physician and making changes. It's a nonconfrontational, non-punitive approach and works well."

Overall, the practice of defensive medicine clearly continued from the very beginnings of their careers until the end. As the risks and realities associated with malpractice became more prevalent, so too did their openness about the need to practice defensively, despite the documented costs associated with it, and even the harm to patients in the long run because of iatrogenic effects (i.e., harm coming from interaction with physician and medical care intervention).

Peer Review

Traditionally, the mainstay of professional accountability for all recognized professions has been their Codes of Ethics, which articulate principles of obligation and responsibility to protect the patient/client and society writ large (American Medical Association, 2001; Ochsner, 2003). Unlike in the marketplace, where "caveat emptor" ("let the buyer beware") applies, the professional model has been "credet emptor" ("let the buyer trust") (Freidson, 1970, 1995). Traditionally, the mechanism articulated for enforcing these codes has been a collegial, nonpunitive peer process within each profession. Indeed, self-regulation is one of the principal hallmarks of a recognized profession in the public sphere (Freidson, 1970). These ethical processes had been codified into standards overseen by various professional associations (AMA, 2001; CFA Institute, 2014). The enforcement of these standards and the obligations that professionals have to adhere to them have been handled in the past internally through accreditation processes and other non-governmental peer review organizations and quality care systems. Ultimately, over time these processes were reinforced by externally sanctioned methods through licensing laws and public state regulatory agencies, which have the responsibility for oversight including the revocation of a physician's license. If the public at large as well as individual patients are to trust their physicians, they need to know that their interests and rights are being protected by public and private agencies. To the extent that physicians believe they should be held accountable for acceptable practices using "reasonable and customary care" standards and the "do no harm" tenet of the Hippocratic Oath, then the best and least intrusive means of achieving those ends is the development of a peer review-based system (Deyo-Svendsen, Phillips, et al., 2016; Vyas and Hozain, 2014).

Over the course of their careers, the physicians were questioned about their perspectives on peer review as a mechanism for physician accountability. Most of them, surprisingly or not, stated that peer review was either not working or was only minimally effective. Furthermore, many ultimately believed that it could not work. Some felt it was not necessary because they believed that they were able and willing to self-regulate; their progression on these views across the career stages is presented next.

The Entry Phase (1979–1980)

When these physicians completed their residency in the entry phase, they did not believe that they needed to be accountable to others outside medicine nor to those inside their profession (Mizrahi, 1984a). Regardless of whether they were entering academic or community practice, beginning a subspecialty fellowship, or moving into general internal medicine, almost every physician believed that there should be no inference by outsiders, even physicians, in their medical practice decision-making.

The Early Phase (1980–1984)

As newly minted community or academic practitioners, the physicians held perspectives on peer review that remained similar to how they felt at the end of their training. Hardly anyone thought peer review actually worked, nor could it work philosophically or pragmatically. "It's a joke!" noted Dr. Strelko, while Dr. Beech pondered, "There's always a nagging doubt in any physician's mind, if we come down too hard on this guy, who's to say that he may catch us when we make an error in judgment and screw up." Dr. Mahoney resorted back to one of the tenets of professionalism—trust—in refuting the value of what he believed to be these contrived systems: "I think physicians have to be trusted. We are well motivated and honest. Yes, we have to make sure that the bad apple is cleaned out, but I think it's up to physicians, not to an outside agency to do that. Peer review doesn't work as well."

Since these physicians all believed they were well intended and that most adverse outcomes were not mistakes, many resented outside interference. As Dr. Melone reflected, "When an outside review organization comments about a hospital admission, they don't know what they are talking about. The problem is most doctors don't need a quality review system, and those who need it won't put up with it." Or, as Dr. Rosen asserted, "It doesn't work putting yourself in someone else's shoes. All physicians are very reticent about criticizing another physician unless we really see gross negligence. There's no good way to do peer review."

Even in the early phase (1980–1984), some of the community physicians like Dr. Nolan had already been both the subject and object of peer-related inquiry processes. Neither he nor others believed the benefits outweighed the costs. As he stated, "The problem is establishing criteria for appropriate medical care. What happens when you find someone has screwed up? I've been in a situation of having to write reprimand letters to physicians and got several incensed responses back. Hospital quality review may be of some benefit, but I don't want someone standing over my shoulder."

Although in the later career phases, the physicians would offer more thoughts on alternative collective systematic solutions to accountability, at this stage no one articulated an alternative. Instead, they seemed to focus more on the complexities of reviewing another person's medical practice at all. In the five years since they had begun practicing in their career settings, almost all the physicians had come to increasingly believe that there is more than one way to practice medicine and that other physicians may know and do things differently. The "gray areas" in medicine had become wider and more nuanced. Thus they were not only more lenient in their own evaluation of themselves but also more understanding and flexible when assessing medical care provided by colleagues (Mizrahi, 1984b).

The Established Phase (1984–1994)

As they entered the established phase fifteen years after their SAMS residency, the cohort's overall perspective on the value of peer review remained largely negative like in the earlier phases. However, it became increasingly couched in terms of the larger environment of managed care and competition. Many continued to emphasize that their wrath toward peer mechanisms was limited to structured regulatory entities they believed were intruding on their practice. Moreover, so many believed that these were staffed by incompetent outsiders (whether people with an MD, RN, or some other degree).

In attempting to be dispassionate, a few of the academics tried to imagine a fair and workable peer-driven solution. Dr. Strelko, for example, who had moved to a new academic center, suggested, "We need more time for things like patient-oriented conferences and tumor boards, which should be done for both quality review reasons and for physician education. There isn't much support for peer review except for the extreme 'impaired' physician."

Most of the physicians continued to assert that formal peer review to assess competency was inadequate. The term *impaired physician* was first acknowledged as a systemic problem for the profession in the 1970s (Furrow, 1998; Ross, 2003). However, the programs put into place to address it focused on the severe aberrant behavior of an individual physician and rarely addressed a needed cultural shift in collective peer accountability. It was only mentioned by a few of the cohort in these later years in this context. Since the cohort viewed those damaged doctors as rare outliers, no one thought the problem was severe or widespread enough to introduce more formal structures of accountability. Typical is Dr. Ross's view from a community perspective: "We do have relapses among community physicians. Our State Board of Medicine puts out a bulletin every year. I am amazed at the number of repeat offenders, year after year, who are put on probation. But we have to admit there are a few impaired physicians."

Moreover, they continued to distinguish between what was happening in their own practice setting versus what they assumed was happening more generally, as Dr. Johnson, a community oncologist, did: "I don't think continuous quality improvement (CQI) picks that up on the subtler things like giving a double dose of chemotherapy. There is no good process for doing that. In my own practice I can judge my peers because I cross-cover for them. I can look at their charts and see if a complication was expected or was something out of the ordinary. The only way to do it would be case reviews in physicians' offices, and most doctors would be very uncomfortable with that."

The Entrenched Phase (1994–2004)

By the first decade of the twenty-first century, in practice more than twenty years, these physicians continued to comment skeptically on the major changes in accountability, self-regulation, and external review structures that were being imposed on them and physicians everywhere by government regulators, hospitals, and insurance companies. Even those in academic medicine with responsibilities for assessment of residents and fellows as well as their own performance were generally dissatisfied with what they perceived as excesses of constant review. Dr. Annas, typical of many, commented that he does not consider those who carry out the formal mandates as credible: "Documentation is good, but the manner in which it is being done is overkill, and in some instances irrational, like including a family history even if I am seeing a patient three times a year. But if I don't include it, my encounter is downgraded a level."

Still, many of the academic physicians who were involved in the process of establishing standards for their peers accepted both the need for peer review and the resistance to it among physicians. As Dr. Rosen expressed, "I'm helping to develop practice guidelines through the state medical society to get doctors to adhere to more than they do now, for example, with patients who have heart attacks or diabetes. It's a challenge; we're trying to understand the problems for practicing physicians, and make these standards an aid rather than an imposition."

The Ending Phase (2011–2016)

Twelve years after discussing their views on peer review in 2004, the physicians were asked again one more time about their views on peer review in 2016. (They were not specifically asked about peer review during interviews at the end of the extended phase [2004–2011].) Interestingly, at this phase, while not embracing it, many were resigned to trying to make it a more effective tool for accountability and mutual responsibility, although it was clear they viewed that as a complex task and difficult to attain. There was a more balanced view, especially looking back over forty or more years since they were in medical school. As they matured, they became more measured in their responses. Nevertheless, they continued to make a distinction between a formal/structural peer mechanism that they rejected for the most part and the informal/cultural norms and practices that many of the cohort felt had worked, at least at the micro level.

There did not seem to be a major difference in perspective between academic and community practitioners, or between those who had been involved in an actual lawsuit and those who had not. Many remained ambivalent, even dubious. Some pointed to the need for a system of oversight and compensation for physician behavior but suggested any intersection with the courts was a problem.

Others noted its potential but suggested the way peer-review systems were implemented was not effective. As Dr. Annas, an academic physician, described, "It can be made to work, but I don't know any place where it's actually being done. There's frequently retrospective peer review, but nothing prospective that would truly modify behavior. Here at my academic medical center, there's a peer-to-peer assessment of everybody once a year, but I don't know how much good it does."

On the other hand, at this ending stage, others believed with some caution that a peer system could work with fair-minded and knowledgeable professionals. Dr. O'Brian, who served in an oversight and administrative position in this last phase of his career, identified in detail how he felt his institution's peer system has been successful: "I think peer review works to hold physicians accountable, at least at my former institutions. We raised red flags early on, put people on notice that their behavior had to change using outcomes such as infection rates, death rates, etc. If they treated patients or staff poorly, they were put in an improvement program. You don't want to ruin someone's career, but you can't put patients in jeopardy. There's a fine line, but there's a professional responsibility to report them." Some doctors felt that an alternative approach, favoring arbitration, would be better. For example, Dr. Lash suggested, "I would put in a system of mediation to eliminate frivolous litigations, some kind of tort reform. The current situation is traumatizing to those who've been sued."

At this last phase, a minority of community practitioners, especially those who had been hurt by these external review systems, weighed in about the absurdities of a system that tries to codify practice behavior and norms. As Dr. Melone asserted, "An insurance company defines a peer as anybody that has an MD from anywhere. When they denied one of my orders for my patient in the ICU, I asked who decided that, and they said, 'One of your peers.' I responded, 'I'm a board-certified nephrologist. The only person that has this credential is my partner. He's not the one you used.' It turns out it was a gynecologist from Iowa; that's not peer review."

Even Dr. Polikoff, who considered himself to be in a very collegial setting, was cynical about their HMO's structured peer review system, even in his setting: "I have a review with our chief physician once a year, but it's a bunch of BS. She gives me graphs of how I'm doing, benchmarks, etc., I take those papers and throw them out! But there is a less formal way. I discuss my patients with other doctors. Sometimes we make comments about what we should have done. That's how you get good peer review. Still it's wrought with tension and suspicion by us."

Dr. Beech described a system that has gone too far: "Now they are going to publish how many infections or how many deaths your cardiac surgeon has had. To me, that's a bunch of BS. Because if the cardiac surgeon looks at you and says, 'You're too high risk, I'm not going to operate on you,' he's going to have pretty good statistics. Do you want someone willing to try to save your life or do you want somebody to say, 'You're too far gone'?"

At this stage of their professional life, most of the cohort had enough peer review experiences on both sides of the equation and so were in a better position to carefully balance the pros and cons. Dr. Lynch as an informant generalizes for his generation about reasons for the resistance: "For those of us who came into the practice in the '70s and '80s, it wasn't part of the culture, so it was very threatening. But over time, it's become more expected. I think a lot of doctors never really learned how to behave such as not belittling other staff members, which can spill over to patients. But you can learn how to behave. And we can review each other's charts collegially."

The Other Side of the Coin:
The Role of Expert Witness in Peer Review

Although the physicians complained about peer review more or less throughout their careers, many of the cohort had been involved in malpractice cases as "expert witnesses." While I did not pose a question to them directly about this role, many physicians spontaneously raised it a number of times at different phases. Despite their general disapproval of the official peer review systems in place, their comments pertaining to their experiences as "expert witnesses" made it clear that serving in this role gave them a new appreciation of the complexity of such lawsuits. They commented on the difficulty in reaching a decision, often painful and difficult, regardless of the side that hired them. This topic, with a specific focus on physician's personal experiences, is rarely discussed in the literature (Kass and Rose, 2016; Kassirer and Cecil, 2002).

Dr. Mahoney (1994) described several cases where he served in that role in great detail and then concluded, "I do some legal consulting work, and in two of the cases I supported the patient and they settled in the plaintiffs' favor. And there is one now where I support the patient because the physician made an error. But it isn't easy." Ironically, Dr. Mahoney was sued himself with an adverse impact on his career.

Dr. Rosen commented on the other side, "With mistakes, I tend to give physicians the benefit of the doubt. There are few things that are really clear that you could call errors. I have testified on behalf of a doctor, but I would testify against one if I saw something that is blatantly wrong. When I was asked to review the case we just discussed, I told them I didn't think they could make the case for the patient. Physicians get sued way too much and mostly for the wrong things, but juries have given them huge rewards." Dr. Annas described his experiences: "I have been asked to review eight cases. Boy it's difficult. Two of the doctors blew it; no question. For another two, there was no basis for suing; and four were questionable." He provided a detailed example of one case of a young aggressive surgeon and then concluded, "I told them to open their checkbooks." Dr. O'Brian concluded: "These were agonizing situations. I decided not to do it anymore; it was too painful."

It seemed that happenstance found some of these physicians in that role of judge rather than being judged. There were at least eight who revealed having served in this capacity. Their own personal history as to whether they had or had not been the subject of a malpractice lawsuit did not seem to determine whether and how they reacted to this opportunity. Overall, their experiences in this "expert" role seemed only to reinforce their views about the difficulty in deciding whether or not an adverse outcome was a mistake worthy of a legal rebuke and penalty, especially when considering the severe emotional and professional toll that decision would have on all the litigants.

Conclusion

It should not be surprising that these physicians struggled with these serious conditions of professional life—self and system regulation, balancing accountability and autonomy, and addressing mistakes and malpractice before and after the fact—issues that profoundly affected their professional and personal lives as well as those of their patients and their families and the greater community (Chimonas, DeVito, et al., 2017; Seys, Wu, et al., 2013). Both the medical profession and public policymakers have been grappling with the relationship between adverse outcomes and errors with the goal of improving systems and minimizing their numbers and consequences (Schleiter, 2009; Sohn, 2013). For the physicians in this cohort who felt these issues up close and personal, the whole field of defining and adjudicating errors still has a long way to go (Grober and Bohnen, 2005; Newman, 1996). Consensus seems elusive. "There must be a better way" was a repeated refrain. But, individually, the physicians seemed to feel powerless and only on occasion identified solutions beyond their own practice or department.

The term "honest mistake" was used to distinguish those from "unforgivable" ones. Imbedded in the latter category were judgments about motivation (intentionality), concealment (not confessing/admitting), recidivism (repetition), as well as mistakes made as a result of character traits (carelessness, laziness, and arrogance). When they apply those four criteria over time to their peers and to physicians generally, the cohort concluded that no one intentionally commits a mistake; most physicians are conscientious if not compulsive; most are smart and learn from their mistakes in order not to repeat them; and rarely do they hide them. With these explanations and caveats, and despite their occasional work as "expert witnesses," their overall conclusion is that physicians should be exonerated from most medical mistakes. Indeed, from their collective perspective, there are no such things as mistakes in the way the public or the legal system defines them. And they find for themselves and for most of their colleagues that the whole system of malpractice and formal external peer review is inappropriate, unfair, and onerous. They return in spirit if not in words to the sentiment expressed aptly by one of the doctors early on: "I am my own worst and therefore should be my only critic."

In 1999, the Institute of Medicine (IOM) published a report (Kohn, Corrigan, et al., 1999) that included a discussion of errors while demonstrating the complexity and diversity of definitions in its lengthy literature review. It surfaced the issue of medical errors nationwide, urging the need for a comprehensive approach. In addition to the external environment creating enough pressure to make errors costly to organizations and providers, they suggested enhancing the knowledge tools to break down legal and cultural barriers that impede safety improvements:

The committee believes that a major force for improving patient safety is the intrinsic motivation of health care providers, shaped by professional ethics, norms, and expectations. But the interaction between factors in the external environment and factors inside health care organizations can also prompt the changes needed to improve patient safety. . . . Factors inside health care organizations include strong leadership for safety, an organizational culture that encourages recognition and learning from errors, and an effective patient safety program. . . . The committee seeks to strike a balance between regulatory and market-based initiatives, and between the roles of professionals and organizations. (p. 5)

Since this report from almost twenty years ago and subsequent data and public pronouncements criticizing the whole system about litigation and errors, there has yet to be major tort reform on a national level to change the litigious nature of the malpractice system (Boothman, Imhoff, et al., 2012; Sohn, 2013). Although there is no specific mandate or certainty with respect to defining and adjudicating medical errors, the possibility for any agreement among concerned parties will depend on incoming President Biden and his administration (Chassin, 2019).

7   The Physicians on Health Regulations, Reimbursement, and Reform

In the first four decades of the physicians' careers, from the 1980s until the 2010s, the health care system changed in both subtle and dramatic ways as has been documented in the previous chapters. These changes had a significant impact on the way they cared for patients and the way they experienced their life and work as physicians within the larger health care system. This chapter presents, first, a brief historical overview of the health care system reform debate that took place over the course of these physicians' careers (Beckers Hospital Review, 2014). This provides some background for understanding the financing and organizational context shaping their experiences and perspectives. It is followed by a discussion of their views about the attempted and actualized structural health care reforms made by the government and private insurance sector in each of the six stages of their careers. Clearly, these proposed and implemented public health policies had a major impact on the cohort's attitudes and behavior over time.

As they all completed their SAMS residency with many leaving the SAMS environment in the entry phase, neither I nor the cohort was focused on the costs, payments, and financing of health care, but rather I emphasized their relationship with patients in the context of the SAMS training and patient care environment (Mizrahi, 1986). Although rising health care costs and proposals for cost containment had been part of public health policy discussions since the early twentieth century. As the physicians moved into practice in the early 1980s, major health care reform was not on the national political agenda, nor on theirs (Brill, 2015; Gorin and Mizrahi, 2013).

But there was one element of health care that was a growing issue within the government—cost. By the mid-1970s, when the cohort was first beginning their SAMS residency, the rising costs of Medicare and Medicaid, the first public national health insurance program established in 1965, had emerged as a key issue on the agenda of President Carter. Seeking to manage the expenses of the program, he sought a hospital cost-containment bill, which did not pass Congress. After the Carter administration's failed attempt, the Reagan administration created a prospective payment system (PPS) under Medicare regulation based on diagnostic related groups (DRGs) (Bushnell, 2013) as a different type of proposal to address cost factors. It was designed to control Medicare reimbursement payments to hospitals by imposing a cap on spending for a patient's care based on an assigned disease classification. The DRGs coded the services a patient received and then determined how much Medicare would pay a hospital, rather than paying for the cost the hospital charged the patient. This was a major shift from a fee-for-service system, moving away from a system in which hospitals were retroactively paid for hospital-based patient care, and toward a prospective payment method where the amount to be paid was determined in advance, based on these DRG categories.

This shift fundamentally changed the way hospitals and medical centers operated. It directly contributed to the phenomenon that I referred to in my earlier book on these physicians as "getting rid of patients"—where hospitals sought to shorten the length of hospital stays for patients; one of the reasons was that they were no longer being paid per diem (Mizrahi, 1986). As a result, attending physicians were incentivized to discharge their patients as early as possible, although among the medical students and house staff at SAMS, the cost of diagnosing and treating a patient was not the motivating factor for shortening lengths of hospital stays and, therefore, was rarely raised on rounds.

However, beginning in the early phase (1980–1984), as they began their academic- or community-based practice, they were faced with intrusion by public and private insurance regulatory and payment systems. These became a thorn in their side, which was reflected in their levels of dissatisfaction during this time as were discussed in detail earlier in chapters 3 and 4.

It took about ten years before substantive health care reform measures appeared on the national scene. This occurred when President Clinton campaigned and won on a major health care reform agenda, a time period corresponding to the physicians' established phase (1984–1994). It was a period that began approximately fifteen years after they had finished as house staff at SAMS. Clinton's election in 1992 led to great anticipation for major health reform legislation that would substantially increase the role of government and the private sector in health care financial management and ultimately move in the direction of universal health insurance (Brill, 2015; Taylor, 2014). These projected changes would set the amount and type of payment reimbursement for hospitals and all health providers and impose additional accountability measures. President Clinton's proposal was generally viewed as impinging on the autonomy of physicians and opposed by the American Medical Association and other physician organizations. These organizations specifically opposed the Clinton proposal to create large conglomerates known as "managed competition" that were a combination of public and private insurance (Hinko, 2012).

The Clinton administration attempted to gain consensus on a compromise health reform bill under the policy leadership of First Lady Hillary Rodham Clinton, but ultimately failed to convince Congress to pass any legislation. This collapse helped contribute to Republican landslide victories in the 1994 midterm elections (Johnson and Broder, 1996) and led to an increasingly conservative legislative agenda for the remainder of Clinton's two terms. Corporate entities gained greater control over health care decision-making, through avenues including the passing of Medicare + Choice, which introduced private insurance into the Medicare program (Jasso-Aguilar, Waitzkin, et al., 2004; Light, 2005).

In what was labeled as the "era of managed care," insurance companies became prominent players in determining which health plans patients would receive, mostly through their place of employment. These included restrictions on how many office visits and procedures would be authorized. The corporate sector also became gatekeepers for access to specialized care (Starr, 2013). Continuing in the spirit of the DRGs of the 1980s, further limitations were imposed differentially on physicians' clinical judgment. These trends, combined with continued reductions in Medicare payments to academic medical centers, were the context for both the academic and community practice world of these physicians by the established phase (1984–1994) and beyond (Sturm, 2002; Tyrance, Sims, et al., 1999).

President George W. Bush, who took office in 2001, did not focus in a major way on health care reform, with the exception of the bipartisan passage of a complicated and costly prescription drugs benefit added to the Medicare program (known as Medicare Part D). His administration also added Medicare Advantage (an expansion to Medicare Part C), which expanded the private health insurance option in an effort to privatize Medicare.

Access to specialty care was loosening, but concerns about the rising cost of health care and the proliferation of internet-based information in the hands of patients combined yet again to alter the relationship between physicians, patients, and payers. In the view of these physicians as a whole, it was a turn for the worse. Steering away from government intervention, attempts to bring so-called "efficiencies" to the system were based on business models to health care and resulted in the emphasis on pay for performance, evidence-based medicine, and treatment protocols (Domagalski, 2005; Light, 2005).

At the end of the first decade of the twenty-first century, during the physicians' extended phase (2004–2011), there were new major policy shifts, particularly after the historic election of Barak Obama to the presidency. The election of Obama in 2008 created the potential for monumental changes in the health care system, fifteen years after the failed Clinton attempt. President Obama promised and delivered on his pledge to reform health care and move toward universal coverage. The process, however, was fraught with contention and opposition before and after the passage in 2010 of his signature legislation—the Patient Protection and Affordable Care Act (ACA), or "Obamacare" as it was pejoratively labeled by its opponents (Kirsch, 2011). The fact that it became law with only Democratic Congressional support continued to be a problem (Brill, 2015; Starr, 2013) in the years following. This transformative change to health coverage that has been constantly challenged by Republican leadership corresponded with the physicians' extended phase (2004–2011) and ending phase (2011–2016). Since President Trump took office in early 2017, the ACA has never been accepted as the law of the land by Republicans and their conservative allies, even as a final vote to repeal and replace the ACA by President Trump failed in the Congress in 2018 by one vote. Nevertheless, Trump and Republican opposition has continued with court challenges heard by the Supreme Court at the end of 2020, to be decided in 2021 (RAND, 2020).

The ACA made significant changes in Medicare and Medicaid rates and regulations and other accountability mechanisms (Rawal, 2016). These protocols affected this physician community in differing, but significant, ways. The physicians railed against the many changes that were occurring concomitantly during the extended phase (2004–2011) and ending phase (2011–2016), namely, the mandated electronic medical record (EMR) system and the advent of the position of the "hospitalist" (a full-time physician hired by a hospital to handle inpatient services). These major structural changes had a profound impact on these physicians both directly and indirectly as their careers were winding down, just as DRG laws and related regulatory changes had affected their early practice years. (These two phenomena are discussed in more detail in the next chapter, as major sources of physician disillusionment.)

In the following sections, I present these physicians' responses to the many structural changes to the health care financing and insurance system that occurred during their years of practice, beginning back in the years just after they completed their work as house staff at SAMS in 1980, until they were at or near retirement in 2016.

The Early Phase (1980–1984)

Rules, Regulations, and the DRGs

During both the entry phase (1979–1980), as the physicians were completing their SAMS residency, and the early phase (1980–1984), as they moved into academic or community practice, health care coverage was not yet on the national agenda in a major way. Neither were these issues prominent topics of conversation among the physicians. By the end of the early phase, I asked them about their views more generally of the impact of external rules and regulations on patient care and on their practice. And, as described in chapter 3, those in early practice situations already reported that their clinical judgment in decision-making was being questioned by outsiders. Several discussed their dubious feelings about the changes in the medical profession with a heavy emphasis on cost containment, the encroachment of rules and regulations on their practice, and compensation for their services.

Most were not prepared for the impact of government policies on their practice. At this stage, the doctors were worried less about which patients were covered, but rather how they were getting paid. The Reagan administration had shifted to PPSs through DRGs and the promotion of Health Maintenance Organizations (HMOs), as part of attempts to curtail the fee-for-service paradigm. As an area of dissatisfaction, the physicians were unhappy about the way a managed-type system was beginning to encroach on their medical decision-making and other aspects of their practice environment. Many were beginning to speculate about the public policy proposals to control the cost of medicine, with varying perspectives on the extent of the market's or the government's role in solving this issue. Dr. Jarvis, a community practitioner, noted, "The future of health insurance depends on whether Teddy Kennedy's bill passes." (Edward Kennedy was a prominent Democratic Senate leader in health care reform legislation at that phase and until his death in 2009.) "If yes, medicine will go to hell on the bandwagon. Yet, some changes under Reagan are overdue—the cost of medicine is enormous." Dr. Annas, an academic, asserted, "Proposals to increase competition should drive costs down in theory."

The physicians in community settings, although only in practice for few years, already understood the shift in emphasis away from fee-for-service medicine that was beginning to take hold. As Dr. Cahn facetiously noted, "I was just offered to join an HMO, but I turned it down because, if I am here at 11 P.M., I will get paid as much money as if I was only here until 6 P.M. My partners keep saying they can't wait for socialized medicine to become a reality because then we can close at 5 P.M." Dr. Cahn also saw the handwriting on the wall: "Hospitals will decide which doctors are part of HMOs, and this will divide the physician community here in town even more."

Others expressed concern that either market or corporate control of medicine or both would impinge on quality of care in favor of profit and efficiency. Dr. Conley, a community practitioner, commented decisively, "Overutilization of resources and reimbursement needed correction. There isn't a lot of equity, but neither government nor market forces are the answer. If they treat medicine like a business, then patients will be treated like merchandise. Personal aspects will be left out. The public doesn't realize or give a damn. The public wants quality care, but at a low cost."

Some attributed the increased cost of health care to the lack of patient responsibility. As Dr. Ross commented, "This is what I have against public health insurance—if I made you pay the bills, you'd be much healthier. Medicaid patients abuse the system because they don't have to pay."

Academic practitioners were also beginning to express concerns that the new inducements towards HMOs and controlled care shifted incentives toward medical procedures and away from research, and that it would also diminish the loyalty of patients to their doctors. By Dr. Strelko's standards, "The HMO idea contradicts clinical research which is not cheap or cost-effective; it provides incentives to earn $1,000 a pop for procedures, to slide tubes in certain orifices, but not for careful clinical examination." Then Dr. Strelko commented on both how his academic practice and, acting as an informant, how the whole medical system has been affected: "I see the spread of corporate medicine as akin to the VA system, where docs are on high salary, essentially technicians, losing their ability to be all-around docs. Corporate medicine may be cost-effective, but the result is that patients will stop looking at their doctor as a friend or advisor. The image of the doctor will change for the worse. That's not a good thing for patient care and medicine."

Overall, many were worried personally about how they would be compensated for their services in the future, although in early years most were satisfied with their financial reimbursement. Dr. Mahoney, who left internal medicine, was already pessimistic: "It's called 'free enterprise,' but it doesn't exist. I resent it. Third-party billers are responsible as much as hospital administrators; they are promoting sweeping changes from paying for everything, to drawing back; not covering important things. It's a mess already."

Attempts made to control costs through the beginnings of managed care meant an increase in rules and regulations that dictated what doctors could do—for example, what tests they could run, and whom they could refer patients to, and more. Most of them reacted negatively to this control, emphasizing this impingement on their autonomy repeatedly and on its impact on their relationships with patients and even peers.

The Established Phase (1984–1994)
The Promise and Problems with the Clinton Health Care Reform

During the established phase, the physicians were specifically asked about their views on health care reform during contentious debates about President Clinton's proposed health legislation, whose failure in 1994 would later usher in the era of managed care and the dominance of the business sector (Skocpol, 1995; Starr, 2013). The cohort also responded to specific questions about managed care and its impact on their practice. Furthermore, they were queried about their perspectives on a single-payer system, which generally meant a universal government funded and regulated health insurance system for all Americans.

Those who specifically mentioned Clinton's proposal were mostly negative about it, as Dr. Annas suggested, "I think what is being proposed by the Clintons is an inappropriately aggressive attempt to solve problems that may or may not exist. Yes, there are people without insurance, and there should be a mechanism for providing that. Whether it should be from cradle to grave is a big question." Or, as Dr. Johnson noted, "It's hard to know how the Clinton plan will play out without a crystal ball. I'm not optimistic. I have conservative political views."

The doctors continued to criticize managed care almost universally on several grounds: for increasing their patient load; creating perverse incentives not to provide care; reducing physician autonomy, prestige, and fees; diminishing quality of doctor-patient relationship; and making the practice of medicine overall less pleasurable. Dr. Strelko complained, "The volume of patients seen in HMOs by individual physicians is extraordinary by my standards. 'How many patients can you see?' The job they do is not bad, but it's an assembly line kind of thing. The business of HMOs will change now, so patients won't have a choice. They can get second opinions but then they have to go back and get prescriptions from the original doctor."

The new rules and regulations hindered physicians' ability to refer patients to specialists, which, in an effort to cut costs, were controlled by the HMOs. Dr. Rosen identified his concerns: "It's affecting the quality of medicine. Physicians are not doing as much referral: they're becoming isolated." Similarly, Dr. Boswell also saw it affecting quality of care: "For patients with rheumatoid arthritis, some of the family physicians in an effort to cut costs, won't refer the patient to a rheumatologist who really knows that illness. It ends up with the patient having a big flare up. I am better off seeing a patient when they are doing well. Quality of care is getting short changed."

Alongside their complaints about incentives not to provide care, almost all the doctors mentioned the system of capitation, which means that a specific group of patients are assigned to them in advance. In a capitation system, hospitals or physicians receive a lump sum each month or annually for a certain specified group of patients regardless of how many times they treat those patients. Dr. Boswell continued, "You get so many dollars to take care of a patient a year. You can see that the wrong motivation is built in." Dr. Conley, speaking as an informant, was even more critical: "With capitation, people get less care rather than appropriate care; yet the country wants cheaper medicine; it doesn't care about the quality."

Not surprisingly, limits imposed by managed care companies resulted in most of the cohort resenting the impact it had on their decision-making capacity. As Dr. Cahn, a community practitioner, described, "With more and more managed care, we are absolutely captives of the insurance companies. You can't do a procedure on a patient without prior approval. Managed care absolutely affects us clinically because we're dependent on the primary care physician. I have to jump through a series of new hoops to get something done." Similarly, Dr. Paul, an academic physician, noted, "There needs to be a more balanced negotiating stance between managed care and physicians. Physicians need a sense of autonomy. Now we are more and more like employees of insurance or HMO companies."

To some academic doctors, a managed care system meant decreased institutional support for educational opportunities and research first mentioned in the early phase. It became much more prominent in this established phase as typified by Dr. Finast's admission: "Scrutinizing the cost of care brings dilemmas for educational institutions. Some procedures are done by trainees for education purposes and may not specifically enhance patient care. Managed care makes a university setting less attractive." Other academic practitioners projected somewhat pessimistically about what life would be for a private practitioner under managed care, as did Dr. Rosen: "I feel bad for private practitioners because government, private insurers, and lawyers are making life miserable for them. We need real health reform, to allow doctors to be doctors."

Despite the broader negativity during the established phase (1984–1994), there were a few positive remarks about managed care and the changing system. Dr. Allen commented with some sarcasm that it might be better for getting patients home earlier from the hospital: "Patients get treated quicker; you get things done out of the hospital, in home and office—if you call that good." Although Dr. Cahn and Dr. Boswell complained bitterly about its impact on their practice, they could also understand its rationale when they served as informants. Dr. Cahn was positive about its impact on outpatient care: "I think managed care has done wonders for medicine in general. When I first started, some of the stuff we used to do in the hospital seemed absurd, such as a preprocedure hospitalization." Dr. Boswell also noted a positive impact on care: "It means that everyone has a primary care physician. That is good in that no one expects me, a rheumatology specialist, to be a primary care physician."

Prospects for a Single-Payer System

In addition to the discussion of managed care described above, during the established phase (1984–1994) many of the physicians also weighed in on the possibility of a single-payer system, in responding to a question about health care reform proposals. Many spontaneously referred to a single-payer system as a positive and/ or as an inevitable direction for the future. While their views on its desirability differed, the single-payer option was a common theme raised for the first time by most of the physicians, regardless of political affiliation in this phase. Although not specifically defined, it was generally inferred that the federal government would become the insurer or payer in one form or another (i.e., a "Medicare for All" for patients of all ages) (Antiel, James, et al., 2013; Jacobs and Skocpol, 2010).

Three main themes emerged from the discussion of a single-payer system: the choice between the "external forces" of government and private sector insurance companies in regulation and medical decision-making; the inevitability of a single-payer system given the current perceived crisis in health care; and the discrepancy for some of the cohort, between their conservative political views and their support for a liberal to radical single-payer health care model.

Many of those in favor of a more socialized approach to medicine praised the single-payer system as an answer to the micromanagement they were experiencing through a corporate privatized managed care system. They were becoming aware of health care systems in Canada and in northern European countries and were not adverse to the prospect of a larger role for government, unlike many of the professional medical associations. Dr. Strelko who defined himself as a liberal politically (which means he accepts a proactive role for the public sector in meeting human needs), commented, "I think it is somewhat sinful that we don't have universal coverage like most civilized Europeans. Health reform here is controlled by only a few insurance companies. Market forces are creating a system of profits; entrepreneurism is out of control."

Surprisingly, several of the physicians in community settings who defined themselves as politically conservative also made a number of favorable comments about a more socialized universal health care system. For example, as Dr. Beech, noted, "I'd pass a law that says the health insurance industry has to give everyone insurance. I'm for universal care. Have a no-fault system like auto insurance. It's better to deal with one carrier than twelve to thirteen insurance companies." Dr. Jarvis felt similarly: "I would prefer a government-run single-payer system to this managed care that I see developing. That's a 180-degree change for me. I think in ten years there will be a national health one-payer, socialized system. I would trade lower income for less meddling in my practice." A number of other community practitioners expressed a similar willingness to move toward a single-payer system. Several viewed a single-payer system as a solution to the monopolistic power of insurance companies and the corporatization of medicine and sided with government.

There were still a few doctors who opposed a single-payer system. However, those physicians, such as Dr. Mahoney and Dr. Cahn, tended to only do so because they were afraid of a complicated public bureaucratic system: "I predict health care will become more corporate," said Dr. Mahoney, "But I don't like single-payer; more is spent on bureaucracy than on service." Dr. Cahn concurred: "I would never agree to any program run by a government agency. I support a compromise, like a preferred provider organization with a good quality assurance."

But during the established phase (1984–1994), the physicians were also overwhelmingly frustrated with the status quo and the complexity of the system, summed up by Dr. Lash: "The hassle factor is intolerable; prior reviews, administrative frustrations, charting, the duplicative and contradictory forms are all unnecessary." More than in the entry phase (1979–1980) and early phase (1980–1984), they had become acutely aware of the system's impact on them and on the profession, and they were now more invested in identifying solutions, even radical ones by American standards, like single payer.

The Entrenched Phase (1994–2004)

A Decade of Managed Care with More Bark than Bite

From 1994 to 2004, after the failure of Congress to pass Clinton's health care reform, changes in health care reform were less dramatic than anticipated. Without government taking a proactive role, the marketplace reigned supreme. After the attacks on September 11, 2001, the national agenda turned away from health policy and toward the two wars in Afghanistan and Iraq initiated by the administration of George W. Bush. As a result there was less focus on any major domestic reforms.

By the entrenched phase, the physicians had experienced a decade of working within or alongside the changes posed by the implementation of a managed care system. Most of the physicians continued to feel embittered by corporate dominated managed care and critical of it as a system. Many once again discussed health care reform within the context of a single-payer-type universal health care system, with several looking forward to that possibility.

The cohort's perspectives on why they disliked the managed care system remained mostly the same as ten years earlier, with almost half continuing to complain about intrusion on their autonomy, poor or perverse system incentives, lack of access to specialists, and difficulties with how much reimbursement they received and how they received it. Doctors like Dr. O'Brian stated managed care meant that they were forced to live with "many more obstacles than there used to be." This included the lack of insurance company reimbursement for subspecialists, referrals, prescriptions, and procedures. The list was long and familiar as per Dr. Beech's blunt sentiments: "Managed care is a pain in the butt. You write a prescription, and some moron in the managed care department sends a note: 'We don't think the patient should have this drug.' Makes me cynical."

For several doctors, the intrusion of managed care resulted in their viewing their overall practice as being dictated by external entities—from pharmaceutical companies to insurance companies to lawyers. Dr. Ross complained, "It's the continued intrusion. [He then refers to me during my in-person interview as he continues]: I am reading you a letter telling me I should have admitted this patient to the hospital. There's always someone looking over your shoulder telling you what to do. It's getting worse and worse. I just throw those letters away." Dr. Melone identified the consequences of such "degradation": "You have people who aren't doctors making medical decisions. Their assertion that the tests being done are not medically necessary is because they're not inclined to pay for them which I consider as the erosion of medical prestige."

Several doctors continued to express the view that managed care was creating poor incentive structures by pushing doctors to treat more people quickly rather than provide quality care. Dr. Conley's comment was typical: "Basically, I have a negative view of insurance companies as they have thrown roadblocks into providing health care. There may be some positives in promoting prevention, but capitation was a particularly bad idea; it's dangerous to pay doctors more to provide less care." Dr. O'Brian, who moved into an administrative system in this phase, made this analysis: "It's an incredibly complicated health coverage system. There are a number of different operating systems; it's a quagmire, and if you amplify the problems of one patient times one hundred systems, it's a nightmare."

At this entrenched phase (1994–2004), the physicians expressed a stronger emphasis on their frustrations with how financial payment and reimbursement systems adversely affected them because of managed care. Many expressed with passion that doctors were making less money while having to see more patients. They continued to speak about shortages of specialists, which related to both the intrusion of business in medicine and bad decisions. In Dr. Mahoney's estimation, "The corporate middlemen came in and got rich, while we physicians earn less, and patients don't even receive better care." Dr. Allen made a similar assessment: "We've spent way too much money and ordered too many tests, so managed care got in, got the fat out of the system, and now they take their fifteen percent cut and patients get less care. Doctors get less money. Everybody's grouchy again. Capitation was a good idea that ran amuck." As Dr. Cahn commented, "We have to run faster on the treadmill just to keep up."

The resentment felt by many of the physicians about the abuses and mismanagement by the corporate sector were palpable, as Dr. Lynch complained, "HMOs and PPOs have heavily penetrated the market in my western state. They've been extraordinarily aggressive and poorly capitalized, so there have been many bankruptcies and much confusion." Dr. Ross exposed the darker consequences: "The way to make money is to have a gimmick: own your own nursing home or an MRI machine or a physical therapy practice. The business side of medicine is here; forget about the conflicts of interest."

While Dr. Strelko personally had a positive experience with managed care, he still commented on the negative experience of others: "Managed care is different everywhere. Here at my institution, everyone is a part of an HMO, but not micromanaged like elsewhere. It's managed financially, but not the doctor. I don't get hounded about what I can and can't do."

Dr. Polikoff, not surprisingly was the exception as he had moved into an HMO practice and believed the incentive structure was actually a good thing: "I think managed care is great. Capitation forces you to practice medicine wisely and can produce a more streamlined, more efficient, cost-effective system."

Prospects for a Single-Payer System

In this entrenched phase (1994–2004), the physicians began talking more explicitly about their perspectives on the direction of health care reform. Many spontaneously mentioned a single-payer system ten years after President Clinton's failed proposal in 1994, having lived through the complexity of a managed care system. Overall, almost all the cohort favored some form of health care access for all. For some, a single-payer system continued to be or became a positive option, while for others it was an inevitability. Several outrightly supported a shift to a single-payer system promoted by progressive Democrats and others with and without caveats (McCormick, Himmelstein, and Woolhandler, 2004; Serafini, 2018).

Some of those who supported such a system with caveats focused on concerns about quality of care. As Dr. Polikoff cautioned, "I support a national health care program as long as it's run in a way that doesn't impede medical care. You hear in Canada you have to wait a year to have your gallbladder out or get an MRI. I don't want to be in a situation where the government says there's only going to be so many MRIs per 1,000,000 people."

Others, however, even if they didn't necessarily see a single-payer system as good policy, saw it as inevitable. As Dr. Conley concluded, "I don't think that a national health system is going to be good, but it's probably going to happen sooner or later." Or as Dr. Melone noted, "I think the only solution is a single payer system. I just don't want to be here when it hits."

For several doctors, the mix of government and market forces in administering health care made them uncertain and ambivalent about viable health care reform. As Dr. Beech reflected, "I'm in favor of some reform, but I have no confidence in government. I don't see how we could do a Canadian style policy—you'd have a two-class system. Anything more than the basics you would have to pay for yourself. Congress doesn't have the courage to make the necessary changes. You don't have enough money to do everything for everyone; someone has to draw the line." Dr. O'Brian concluded, "I've got mixed feelings. Some principles are good—everyone is entitled to good health care, on one hand; on the other hand, the question is how to pay for it. It requires expertise and a sophisticated group of people." Dr. Allen concluded, "I'm not in favor of national health insurance. Best solution is a two-tier system, Medicaid and you wait for the doctor they choose, or if you have money, you see your own doctor tomorrow. Everyone gets a Ford; you pay for a Mercedes. I'm afraid we're going to give everyone the lowest and only the basic services."

Drs. Rosen and Johnson, from very different settings, both felt it was important for the market to continue to play a role in creating competition to ensure
quality of care. As Dr. Rosen, an academic, noted, "I just read last week a study
that showed that people in a socialized system have worse outcomes than people
in the free market system, I'm not in favor of national health care." Dr. Johnson,
in community practice, also expressed strong reservations: "I don't think that it
would work. You get bureaucrats who want to impose idiotic mandates. You have
to have competition, but now people are competing to screw doctors to make
more money. I'm not optimistic."

Overall, while many were still idealistic about the concept, there was a pre-
vailing attitude of negativity and pessimism about whether real health care
reform would benefit them personally and the profession as a whole. But in the
coming years, as discussed later, with the election of President Obama, who ran
on universal health coverage, the politics and possibility of health reform would
change drastically, leading to a renewed scrutiny of health care reform plans.

The Extended Phase (2004–2011)

The Coming of the Affordable Care Act

The passage of President Obama's ACA in 2010 resulted in a transformative shift
in health care coverage and regulatory changes. The ACA legislation promised
affordable health care coverage for millions of uninsured Americans among
other priorities to improve the quality of and access to health care. The cohort
was interviewed just a year or so after the law's passage, so the effects of the ACA
had not been fully implemented, and therefore had not yet impacted their practice.
To be sure, they still had their opinions.

For the most part, the physicians were apprehensive and unsure about what
the ACA would produce, regardless of their general sentiments about health care
reform. When faced with the actual legislation going into effect, there was both
praise and criticism of "Obamacare," as it was increasingly and disparagingly
called by Republicans. A primary critique from the liberal faction in the country
was that the ACA did not go far enough in simplifying the current medical system and making coverage more universal. The more conservative faction voiced
pessimism about the cost as well as government's ability to administer this huge
reform even with all the political concessions that had to be made by the Obama
Administration.

Notwithstanding their views, the health care climate in which these physicians practiced had definitely changed once again. While they were still concerned with how they were getting paid, they were much less concerned with
managed care transforming their practice. When specifically asked about managed care in this time frame, many physicians reported a shift in their perspectives on the system from outwardly disliking managed care in 2004 to a majority
expressing that it had had little to no impact on their practice whether in an academic or community setting seven years later in 2011.

From an institutional perspective, Dr. Finast noted, "Managed care was just another way of paying for health care. It doesn't affect me much one way or another. I think there are a lot of things that are good about trying to manage the whole system rather than just trying to respond to problems as they pop up. Trying to be proactive makes a lot of sense." From a community practice setting, Dr. Cahn commented, "Managed care doesn't really affect us, only in the sense that certain plans will only allow you to use a certain panel of physicians or a certain hospital, so you're handcuffed in that regard. But other than that, not a big deal." Dr. Melone echoed Dr. Cahn's assessment: "There's been a lot less impact than I thought. The only thing that managed care did was to make everybody callused. I don't get as pissed off as easily anymore."

Physicians expressed mixed feelings when specifically asked about the ACA. In line with their own concerns about reimbursement in their practices, they were also concerned with how the ACA system itself would be paid for generally. Dr. Annas revealed his preferences: "I'm not sure about forcing everyone to get insurance and fining people who don't get it. But is it the right thing to do? I would have much preferred to see a public option and getting the government into the direct financing of health care business (meaning a "Medicare for all" approach)." Dr. Conley, the first physician in the cohort to retire by the extended phase, is representative of those who worried about costs and who bore them: "I think the concept of covering more people is certainly desirable. I feel like that may be a big burden for the economy and some individuals are going to get hit with tax increases."

Others, like Drs. Lynch and Jarvis, voiced ambivalence about the ACA related to their lack of belief in the efficacy government resulting from partisan and corporate interests. As Dr. Lynch noted, "I was all for health care, I just wanted it to go further. But you get what you can, that's the political reality. Any kind of reform has to be an improvement. I don't feel optimistic because the health care industry lobby is just too powerful. We're probably never going to see any kind of meaningful reform." Dr. Jarvis had a different critique: "I'm very unhappy that the ACA didn't address malpractice."

As Dr. Cahn suggested, "I am very much in favor of the ACA. I'm also very much in favor of paying higher taxes, when it is fair; that's how I grew up." Or, as Dr. Lash suggested, "It's hard to argue with a law that covers 32 million people. Morally it resonates with me. The reason I went into medicine was to take care of people."

Those against the ACA took issue with the complexity of the new system and what they believed would be uncontrollable cost increases, a topic that rarely resonated with them in earlier stages. Dr. Johnson was among a minority who were cynical: "I think the ACA is unlikely to help much and will probably make things worse. I don't think it's going to control costs. They really need to look at something that would create efficiencies as opposed to just adding more regulation."

Toward a Single-Payer System

During the extended phase (2004–2011), many of the physicians on both sides of the political spectrum still favored a single-payer system given its seeming simplicity, compared to the financing complexities in the era of managed care. This time, the sense of inevitability of a single-payer system, after years of increasingly corporatized medical practice, was even more prominent among the doctors. As Dr. Conley, on the conservative end of the political spectrum, predicted, "I would support universal care. I think we're going in that direction. In fact, I thought twenty-five years ago it would already be here by now. Now at least we're moving in that direction. Our current system has gotten so distorted that it's unsustainable." Dr. Finast, on the liberal end, moralized, "Everybody should get medical care. It's important to the health of the country to have a healthy population. People who aren't well taken care of in the first place will likely have more expensive health problems later."

For some of the political moderate physicians, their practice experience with Medicaid and Medicare, as well as knowledge of single-payer systems in other countries, contributed to their belief in the need for universal coverage. Dr. Nolan concluded, "I've been living with a single-payer-like system for a considerable period since my practice is almost all Medicare. I find it actually pretty good. At least I know what the rules are. It's not different rules for different patients or patient classes by different insurance companies. Also, Medicare is a political system, so it can be politically accountable to voters. Insurance companies are not politically accountable."

Consistent with their sentiments during the prior entrenched phase (1994–2004), those who remained opposed to a single-payer system continued to express greater trust in the market than in government. As Dr. Mahoney reflected, "I think everybody should have health insurance but kept in the private sector with private insurance companies running it and forced to do so across the state lines so there is fair competition." Or, as Dr. Rosen succinctly concluded once again, "I'm strongly against a single-payer system because the government has screwed up everything else."

A few conservatives like Dr. Beech were not convinced that either sector was the solution but continued to believe in individual choice: "I think individuals should make the best decisions for themselves in terms of their own health care. They should negotiate with insurance companies, and they should negotiate with their doctors how much they're going to pay for certain services."

At the start of the biggest and most comprehensive national health policy change since the passage of Medicare and Medicaid in 1965, they were at the same time cautiously optimistic and ambivalent about the ACA. Still, almost all the physicians had strong opinions with a range of suggested solutions for both government and market forces in transforming health care. None of the cohort revealed any professional or political activism on the subject; however, they were open to sharing without reservation their strong views about the health system and its potential reforms with someone who listened nonjudgmentally.

The Ending Phase (2011–2016)

Assessing "Obamacare" and Beyond

By the ending phase, the physicians had spent five or more years experiencing the effects of the ACA, both on them personally as a physician, on the profession systemwide, and on the country as a whole. As with their reactions in 2011, there was a variation in their perspectives. But at this stage, as they reached the end of their professional careers, a larger majority expressed overall support, and only a few expressed outright disapproval. For those in academia, the ACA still had very little direct impact on their work and practice. Still, the fact that more people were getting health care was considered an overriding positive factor of the ACA, even if it did not directly affect them or their own small group of patients. Dr. Lash, looking at the system more broadly, concluded, "The ACA has been very positive, at least until now. It's expanded coverage so that people are seen mostly now in ambulatory care, not like before going to the ER. Access overall is much improved." Dr. Polikoff, who has worked in a managed, primary care HMO environment for many years, also remarked, "From my standpoint, I have several patients who I had been treating with no charge. Now, I can actually run tests on them; they are getting the care they need."

Many were able to get behind the ACA, even if it did not include all of the changes they wanted. It is worth mentioning, however, how their different geographic locations impacted their perspectives. Some states were better in providing health care benefits to their residents before the ACA; the Southern states, however, the locations where many of the cohort practiced (in SAMS state and three others) had rejected the Medicaid expansion aspect of the ACA. The physicians noted this and pointed out how this adversely affected the working poor whose incomes were too high by standard Medicaid limits, but too low to afford quality health care, some of whom were their patients.

A few physicians expressed their praise of the ACA while criticizing the oppositional political forces. As liberal Dr. Strelko commented, "There are 22 million people who have insurance now that did not have insurance before. Why the Republicans feel that that's a bad thing is beyond me. It's too bad that a big part of the country feels that health care is a privilege, not a right."

On the other end of the spectrum, a few community physicians were more uncertain about the ACA, although they recognized that such legislative reform was inevitable. Still this small group doubted its positive impact as they planned to retire. As Dr. Beech noted, "If I had to make a guess now, I would probably say the ACA is not going to make any difference. Is it better or worse than what we had before? I don't really think so. It's just different."

Those who opposed the ACA because of their conservative ideology still acknowledged some potential benefits of the reform compared to their past experience with managed care. For example, Dr. Jarvis stated, "I have subjective feelings because I don't care for Mr. Obama's approach, but in the great scheme of things it's more positive than negative; a better direction than before."

Nevertheless, the complexity of the ACA led to an overall distaste from a few who had been in favor of health care reform in general. Dr. Cahn, for example, now noted, "I was one of the physicians in my town who supported the ACA originally. The concept was originally sound. I think the evil of the system is the mandate for the EMR. You can't possibly understand what it's like to practice in this system now. It's a nightmare."

The ACA affected the administering of residency programs differently in different states. For Dr. Rosen, practicing in another southern state, the ACA had a positive effect: "One huge impact was it made the money available for us to start a residency. The ACA had a priority for which states could apply for those funds. And our state numbered high among underserved areas, so that's how we got our residency funding." Dr. O'Brian, on the other hand, who chaired a major department in a state whose government did not pass Medicaid reform, reflected, "We're a red state that hasn't bought into the ACA and state funding for medical care, especially for indigent care. With the initial Obama administration there was an influx of money to the National Institutes of Health that we benefited from. After a few years there was no money to sustain that effort, which has made funding for research more difficult. We're getting squeezed."

The physicians, like Dr. Cahn above, continued to note what many saw as the negative effects of the mandated use of EMRs, now highlighting how the ACA intersected with that system. (The broader complaints about the EMR across career stages is discussed more in the next chapter.) The physicians also complained about reduced reimbursements and the necessity of hiring new personnel. As Dr. Cahn, working in a community setting, continued to complain, "We had to install a second EMR system at the price of half a million dollars. Washington is not reimbursing us for even close to that. It has forced us to hire 'medical scribes' and additional nurse practitioners. Plus Obamacare made GI specialists take a nineteen percent cut in reimbursement for endoscopies. I'm no longer a fan."

Single-Payer and Alternative Proposals

Overall perspectives on passing a more universal and comprehensive health care reform were somewhat jaded unlike in earlier phases. With many of the physicians approaching retirement or having retired, their feelings about reform were expressed in the context of knowing that they would not be around to experience it. Some even expressed gratitude that they wouldn't be in practice to be part of or witness the changes they predicted coming down the line.

Still, in the twilight of their careers, a few had soundly thought out alternatives to the current ACA from both ends of the political spectrum. Some remained steadfast in their support of a single-payer system for the future regardless of their political and social views, unlike found in other studies (Antiel, James, et al., 2013). This was exemplified by Dr. Conley: "If we are going to tinker with the system, it should just be one single-payer system." Dr. Nolan stated, "The reason I went into geriatrics partly was because I realized that I only had to know one system—Medicare, not Blue Cross or Humana and dozens of others. I could make that system work for me well. And a single-payer system to some degree does that."

While most physicians spoke favorably about a single-payer system, a few outliers remained opposed to universal health care. Dr. Allen for many decades was against it and had not changed his views. He noted with some irony, "I think America has the best health care in the whole world. Everybody needs health care, but some people just aren't going to pay for it. Still, if you need your appendix taken out, and you don't have any money and you're homeless, we take your appendix out for free, thank you very much." Dr. Cahn, who philosophically and practically supported that approach, was convinced over time that Obamacare was the wrong framework. "My problem with single-payer situations is we have tons of people who come from Canada or England who tell horrible stories about in their home country, for example, in my GI practice it would be waiting for a colonoscopy, up to three years. You could be dead by then."

Conclusion

Experiencing the ebb and flow of health care reform over the last several decades led to a feeling of hope or inevitability about universal coverage from a philosophical if not a pragmatic view for most of the cohort (Pearl, 2014a). Their experience over their careers working with both private insurance companies and government entities left many more of them in support of a simplified system that would be financially neutral and not tied to the number of patients they saw. These thoughts ran counter to a few other studies (Harris and Puskarz, 2017; Tilburt, Wynia, et al., 2013) in which physicians were less sanguine (Mostashari, Sanghavi, et al., 2014). In this very late stage of their careers, however, with a few exceptions, they could let their imaginations run wild because they also acknowledged that they had one or both feet out the professional door.

As this book is being completed at the end of 2020, the ACA is under attack by the Trump administration. Its legal fate is being decided by the U.S. Supreme Court (Thompson, 2020). Moving forward in the future, it is most likely that the ACA or some version of health insurance will remain in place with the new Biden-Harris administration, given that 22 million people are covered by it and that it has gained popularity among the majority of Americans (Crowley and Bornstein, 2019).

Vulnerability from Within

How has the changing climate of medicine over the last several decades, along with the myriad criticisms of the health care system, affected these physicians emotionally? In this chapter, the cohort reveals their vulnerability that is deeper and more personal than elements of satisfaction or dissatisfaction presented in the earlier chapters. This chapter explores the meanings of these physicians' experiences, which are not typically captured or expressed in physician surveys. The chapter looks closely at their more private feelings, presenting their responses to questions about cynicism, disillusionment, fear of failure, and self-doubt. They were asked whether they have experienced those sentiments and, if so, the reasons they felt them at different stages of their careers. Each question was presented as open ended; I did not provide any definitions when referring to these sentiments in the questions. One of the issues I sought to explore with these questions was whether the physicians experienced these sentiments (to the extent they occurred) in ways that were context driven, or whether they felt one or more of them regardless of situational factors and the changing external environment.

In their responses to experiencing disillusionment and vulnerability, which were often quite personal, the physicians spoke openly and candidly. No one refused to answer a question nor said the questions were inappropriate or intrusive. It is not likely that they would describe incidents that were not their true sentiments, but it is possible that they may have withheld the most embarrassing or intimate ones. Hence, the disclosures here err no doubt on the conservative side.

Earlier, in chapters 3 and 4, in which the progression of the physicians' satisfactions and strains in their careers were presented, I attempted to capture the impact of historical, political, economic, and social changes on their career trajectory and medical practice. This included a question about whether they received enough emotional/psychic satisfaction, which was one of the components used in evaluating whether a physician was positive, negative, or mixed at each career phase. This chapter goes further with an emphasis on the hidden dimensions of their emotional and psychic lives, including their private thoughts, worries, and anxieties, even in the face of what they (or others) considered successful or positive careers.

In some instances, the feelings these physicians express reinforce prevalent themes of dissatisfaction in their professional careers, especially in relation to two fundamental shifts in the later years: the emerging role of hospitalist physicians and the advent of electronic medical records (EMRs). (The impact of these factors is presented in detail in the final sections of this chapter.) In other instances, the physicians expose certain vulnerabilities and uncertainties that are rarely described in the literature, such as fear of failure and self-doubt. Moreover, since this area of inquiry was directly posed in different phases of their careers, both consistencies and changes over time for individual physicians as well as for the cohort as a whole are uncovered.

In the first two-thirds of the chapter, I present examples of the myriad physicians' expressions of cynicism and disillusionment across the various stages of their careers. These are different but overlapping concepts, which generally focus on external factors—systems or situations—that have profoundly affected their personal experiences and perspectives on their careers and those of the medical profession more generally (Domagalski, 2005; Jauhar, 2014). Alongside that discussion of cynicism and disillusionment, there is a robust and deep discussion of these physicians' fears of failure and self-doubt across those same career stages. Whereas cynicism and disillusionment focus on external factors, these fear of failure and self-doubt concepts relate more to internal processes—their vulnerabilities and uncertainties (Kuhlmann, 2006; Zhao and Wichman, 2015). In the final third of the chapter, I discuss the two specific changes mentioned above that profoundly affected them both psychically and practically—the advent of hospitalists and the EMRs.

Background

During the last decades of the twentieth century and early twenty-first century, an increasing percentage of physicians in the United States and elsewhere have seen their professional lives deteriorate. The extent of deterioration has been associated with a number of factors, such as practice setting, age, practice arrangements, payment method, geographical location, and subspecialty (Arnetz, 2001; Bury, 2004; Chehab, Panicker, et al., 2001; Dunstone and Reames, 2001; Jovic, Wallace, et al., 2006; Linzer, Gerrity, et al., 2002; Murray, Montgomery, et al., 2001; Ofri, 2013a, 2013b; Zuger, 2004).

Policymakers, scholars, and critics of medicine in many countries are increasingly associating a relationship between the subjective feelings of physicians and objective outcomes such as choice of specialty and setting among others (Cole and Carlin, 2009; Linzer, Gerrity, et al., 2002; Williams and Skinner, 2003; Zuger, 2004). Yet there are only a few studies besides this one that have used in-depth interviews, journals, and narrative approaches to uncover the way physicians find meaning in their work and work context (Dunstone and Reames, 2001; Elliot, 2006; Horowitz, Suchman, et al., 2003; Jauhar, 2014; O'Rourke, 2014).

In 2006 Carl Elliot, a physician and a contemporary of these physicians, commented on his and others' increasing disillusionment and cynicism since his U.S. medical school years in the mid-1980s. Elliot asserted that medical educators fail to take into account the realities of contemporary medical practice. "They [physicians] are treated as skilled technicians trading services in the marketplace. . . . As a result there is likely to be even more disillusionment" (p. 96). Ironically, he concluded that those who seem happiest practicing medicine are the people for whom it was never more than a job. "If doctors go into medicine without illusions, they will not become disillusioned . . ." (p. 97).[1]

The Entry Phase (1979–1980)

When they entered internal medicine residency training at SAMS, the physicians were already certified as MDs. As a cohort, they served as doctors to thousands of mostly poor and uninsured patients while they were simultaneously learning to become internists. In my earlier book, *Getting Rid of Patients*, I described the physicians' emotional state during this entry phase in detail, so I will only highlight and summarize some of those key findings and responses here (Mizrahi, 1986).

During the entry phase, the physicians demonstrated a pervasive cynicism regarding the medical educational process and culture, which they transmitted to subsequent generations through peer socialization, or what other scholars have labeled "intergenerational transmission" (Testerman, Morton, et al., 1996). A survival mentality dominated the house staff culture at SAMS. Peer socialization was the method by which they acquired their perspectives on patients, peers, and attending physicians and well as on service delivery. This type of socialization led to a cynicism among most of the physicians about the SAMS patients and their needs. As a result, the physicians developed approaches that sought to prevent many patients from being admitted to the hospital and/or that sought to transfer or discharge them as quickly as possible, an approach which, at the time, I named a "GROP" ("getting rid of patients") mentality.

Typical of most large hospital-based urban residency programs, that socialization included learning to adapt to a series of short-term relationships with faculty attendings, peers, and patients as they rotated monthly among different medical services. Of necessity, this resulted in superficial and instrumentally focused interactions. Nevertheless, many of these interactions included traumatic situations with very sick patients and their families, and despite the emotional stress of such encounters, the cohort lamented that they did not receive any visible support from their superiors. They also experienced myriad frustrations from short-term relationships and superficial interactions with patients, something that further led to varying degrees of doubt about the organization and their own impact on the social determinants of health evidenced by SAMS patients.

In my year conducting the ethnographic portion of this initial study (1979–1980), I never observed a senior physician asking a resident how he felt about a particularly difficult situation, neither publicly nor behind the scenes in conference rooms, nor on daily medical rounds. These physicians admitted to me that revealing heartfelt emotions and personal feelings was not encouraged. Commiseration and emotional support were seemingly not part of the culture. Yet, they highly valued the camaraderie among their house staff colleagues, which, to the contrary, was described and observed as primarily one of bantering and ridiculing outsiders, patients, and their families, generally using locker room or military-like metaphors. Those who revealed some vulnerability said they received support from their spouses or a few close friends inside or outside SAMS as discussed in chapter 5; others were reluctant to admit needs in this whole emotional realm.

Moreover, the "norm of self-reliance" uncovered in the SAMS culture, which promoted professional autonomy and a measure of self-confidence, at the same time seemed to result in their reticence to admit their vulnerability, disillusionment, self-doubt, and fear of failure. Yet all four sentiments were uncovered to varying degrees during the SAMS residency, even at the end of their three-year training. One might have expected a less disparaging view of their circumstances, given their perceived autonomy over their education. However, many expressed sentiments to the contrary, sometimes stating that they would be carrying forward those feelings with them into the next stage of their professional development.

During that entry phase (1979–1980), I talked with the residents about a then-popular satirical novel, *The House of God* (Shem, 1978), which described a disillusioned intern's experiences in a disguised northeastern urban hospital. For many of the physicians, as discussed in chapter 3, this book—which was full of irony and what they and the field identify as "gallows humor" (Hafferty, 1988)—validated their cynicism and disillusionment. A typical and frequent comment to me was, "Do you want to know what our lives are like, read *The House of God*." After reading the book, however, I did not observe a clear parallel between the extent of chaos and disregard for patients described by the fictitious physicians in the book and this cohort at SAMS. Nevertheless, that reaction to the book was communicated multiple times to me, and years later it is still viewed as a book that resonates with house staff, particularly those whose residencies took place in urban settings (Markel, 2009). As a result, questions about *The House of God* and the use of pejorative slang terms were incorporated into interviews in subsequent time frames.

Whether they anticipated having more or less intense feelings of self-doubt, cynicism, fear of failure, or disillusionment moving forward depended in large measure on their selected career path for either further training or a practice setting. Some were cautiously optimistic that a different patient population (read: White, middle class) and/or a different setting and role (read: middle class communities or academic institutions) would lessen their pessimistic feelings, while others anticipated that patients and the external environment would be as, if not more, problematic and demanding, regardless of the class or color of their projected patient cohort. This was especially true for the seven who remained at or came back to SAMS for a fellowship or faculty position (Drs. Cahn, Beech, Boswell, Polikoff, Rosen, Paul, and Finast).

Pursuing a career trajectory in a generalist internal medicine academic track, Dr. Paul commented, "After finishing three years here at SAMS, depending on how frustrated I am with general medicine, I may subspecialize. I think it is going to be more of being pushed away from general medicine because of the hassles with patients and the system." In discussing his cynicism, Dr. Jarvis, heading toward a subspecialty community practice in gastroenterology (GI), reflected on whether the intensive training experience was both toll-taking and necessary: "I didn't appreciate the amount of time and fatigue involved. But house staff training is a necessary indoctrination. You've been a student all your life, and you've got to get shoved into making decisions, getting up in middle of the night and doing all the crap things. It's not pleasant. Still I thought it was a reasonable trade-off for my long-term goal of going into GI."

For so many of the physicians, the disillusionment and cynicism they felt about aspects of their experience at SAMS would have an impact on them right at the time when they were beginning their careers as practicing physicians. It affected their practices and lives no matter which subspecialty or setting they pursued. Moreover, their fear of failure and self-doubt, which they kept largely hidden from the outside world and even from their peers, nevertheless continued to stay with them, often emerging when they reflected on perceived mistake as demonstrated in chapter 6.

The Early Phase (1980–1984)

By the time the cohort was interviewed in 1984, five years after finishing their work as house staff at SAMS, sixteen had completed their subspecialty fellowships, and all had found a place in an academic or community setting (including Dr. Mahoney, who left internal medicine). I revisited the questions that had been posed earlier about their experiences as house staff.[2] In this early phase, more than half stated that the SAMS program had taken a great toll on them personally, but surprisingly at this stage, fewer physicians expressed disillusionment than they did when their residency had just ended. Only a minority still felt the program had made unrealistic demands on them. Most stated that the amount they learned at SAMS compensated for the stress and strain they experienced, and so they considered the trade-off worth it looking back. Much of the cynicism and disillusionment expressed during their residency were submerged in their focus and for some, enthusiasm in assuming new roles and settings.

As they faced the new world as academic or community practitioners, both new and recurring deep emotional sentiments about their career tracks emerged. For example, Dr. Nolan's typical comments, looking back over his first few years in general internal medicine practice, compared it to his residency: "I think the hours you put in at SAMS are only long in retrospect. I was on call in my internship every third night; now starting practice I'm on call again every third night. I am my own intern now! What do those guys think they are going to say to their patients when they get called at 3 A.M.? 'Clutch your chest until 8 A.M., then come to my office'? It was a rude awakening. I do have some self-doubt now."

Disillusionment and Cynicism

In the questions during this early phase (1980–1984), the physicians were asked to look back over their last eight years or more, to assess where they were currently, and to assess what they were looking forward to and not looking forward to. Almost all the physicians expressed some cynicism and/or disillusionment at the beginning of their careers, some of which was carried forward from their days as house staff, where negative views of the patients and the environment were rampant (Mizrahi, 1986). Sometimes similar answers were given to both sets of posed questions; one physician's disillusionment was another's cynicism. For example, competition from colleagues was a source for both.

For the first time, unsatisfactory relationships with peers and other medical personnel postresidency resulted in a large number of disheartened physicians in their early years. This was not anticipated given their close peer bonds during training. Some of the academics expressed more generalized negative expressions about the impact of the organization of medicine on relationships with colleagues and superiors. As Dr. Finast commented, "I'm not very optimistic about physicians doing social good because I'm a cynic. Physicians respond to their wallets, and now their wallets are being threatened by different practice styles. HMOs are causing competition and greed. It's not good."

Several of the new medical academics were also disillusioned about not getting grants or support from their department early on. Dr. Paul, a consistently dissatisfied academic practitioner, expressed his disillusionment and cynicism about the whole gamut of medicine—patients, academic politics, colleagues, and external conditions in the larger community: "People I respected in the field are getting worse over time. The forces are not rational or honorable. So-called researchers grind out papers, but they can't take care of and even hate patients. The quality of research is garbage. I'm cynical about the VA and patients who come looking for a 'free lunch.' It's a socialistic system, and that bothers me."

Similarly, many of the community practitioners, almost all of whom were subspecialists, were already expressing some disillusionment about the workload attached to private practice as did Dr. Nolan above. Dr. Allen, in a community cardiology subspecialty, commented at this stage, five years into his practice, "I've been disillusioned on a few occasions when everything seemed to be piling up. I thought it would be nice doing something else. It's self-imposed pressure, but it's happening more since the fellowship, so I wonder how long I can keep it up."

Although patients gave them satisfaction overall, some physicians described a variety of styles and behaviors that made them disillusioned and/or cynical about some types of patients or patients more generally. For example, Drs. Ross and Jarvis, also in community practice, expressly described futile aggressive interventions demanded by patients and family members. Others, like Dr. Johnson, an oncologist in community practice, expressed disillusionment about the treatments available to patients, upset at the lack of impact of science and technology on diagnostic and therapeutic remedies that affected his subspecialization. Cynicism abounded.

Self-Doubt and Fear of Failure

At this early phase (1980–1984) of their career, the academic physicians felt pressure from the external environment acutely. They had doubts and fears about choosing a research trajectory when they failed to obtain funds for their research. As Dr. O'Brian expressed, "I'm trying to establish an independent lab, but I haven't been able to so far. I don't know what I'll do if I'm turned down. I'm at a crossroads, and the outside and internal pressure is growing. I never thought of alternatives to academic medicine, but now it's not good to be so dependent on outside funding."

Self-doubt expressed by other academics was attributed to the downsides of holding a diverse portfolio with multiple responsibilities. As Dr. Boswell noted, "Yes, [I feel] fears of failure in relationship to whether I can do everything on this job well, being able to keep up with medicine, do research, teach, and take care of patients. I'm doubtful."

The community practitioners were now worried about something going wrong or making the wrong diagnosis. Several expressed what was characterized as "the norm of humility"—that is, to know when to consult with peers about a patient's situation without appearing indecisive (Mizrahi, 1986). While I was interviewing Dr. Beech in his office, he pointed to his desk and complained, "Look at this stack of unread medical journals on my desk; it's getting bigger and bigger. I wonder what kind of doctor I'll be twenty to thirty years from now, when young 'whipper-snappers' come to town. I worry about when to call a specialist if I'm in over my head. There's always a sense of pending doom."

At the same time, not to seek the advice of others when uncertain could foster arrogance and ultimately lead to a mistake, as described in chapter 6. Those tensions about decision-making could be characterized as tensions between over-confidence and self-doubt. However, this apprehension of doing something wrong in these early years was usually because of the fear that they would acquire a "bad" reputation among their peers rather than because of negative consequences for patients or the threat of a lawsuit.

Very few of the self-doubts expressed by community practitioners at this early phase (1980–1984) related to the external environment. They were not as concerned about how they would be viewed by regulators or payers, but rather how they would appear to peers and the public in general. Some provided qualifiers to their affirmative responses about feeling self-doubt, such as, "not for long" or "only momentarily." While there were many private worries, a few physicians, regardless of practice setting, indicated paradoxically that self-doubt and fear of failure had its positive aspects. Dr. Finast confessed, "That's probably one of my biggest strengths: I may outwardly appear 'cocky,' but I'm always asking myself internally if I am doing a good job."

The Established Phase (1984–1994)

Disillusionment and Cynicism

In 1994, ten years after the last set of interviews, the cohort continued to cite many areas of disillusionment and cynicism, but this time in greater numbers and intensity. Almost all of them identified similar areas of disenchantment or disparagement, and many expressed increasing cynicism over time with harsher tones. Almost half of the participants had changed settings or switched career tracks presumably to find more success or contentment by this stage.

For the community practitioners, much of their cynicism continued to be focused both on patients and patient care management. Some also expressed cynicism related to ethical dilemmas with harsh comments for what they felt was the medical profession succumbing to public pressure to favor longevity over quality of life. As Dr. Ross, a GI practitioner, lamented, "The ethics of keeping certain patients alive is getting to me. Why do we do CPR in a nursing home? It happens more often now, and I'm running out of empathy." Dr. Johnson and others also questioned the motives of those in control of technology more fervently than he did a decade earlier: "I'm frustrated with the lack of medical advances in oncology. I suspect the motives of insurance companies. They tell lies and will leave you to die."

Additionally, skepticism about the profession's financing system was common as typified by Dr. Jarvis: "I am disgusted with the legal system, with malpractice, with hospital administration—it's a disgrace. Look at the $120 million expansion at this medical center. Hospitals are managed poorly; there's too much focus on self-advancement. With shrinking revenues, the hospital is advertising, 'Come, get your cataracts taken out here.' Imagine!"

Self-Doubt and Fear of Failure

Almost every academic practitioner's doubts continued to revolve around being successful in their institutional setting with respect to building research agenda and/or climbing the administrative ladder. All of them recognized that they were not autonomous practitioners; they were dependent upon those higher up in the hierarchy and on outside funders and on other physicians for referrals for their research endeavors. And some of them had indeed experienced disappointment at a past or current institution. As noted, a few had changed institutions to find more success, like Dr. Strelko: "I fear getting in over my head. There were times at (my prior institution) when I felt responsible for the whole institution, until I realized it was screwed up, not me. Politically, I'm both more savvy and more cynical now." But like many of the academics leading comfortable academic lifestyles doing research, teaching, and running clinical projects, Dr. Strelko's overall expectations for the profession appear to have been lowered substantially: "I don't expect as much from colleagues or superiors anymore."

For the community practitioners, now fifteen or more years after completing their residency, disillusionment with patient outcomes appeared connected to even greater feelings of self-doubt. As Dr. Conley expressed, "I worry, 'Did I do the right thing? Did I do anybody any good?'" Several continued to comment on the need to maintain their humility and avoid overconfidence. Dr. Melone repeated his sentiments from a decade earlier: "If I am not the best nephrologist in the SAMS city, something's wrong. As a patient, I should always want to go to me. Self-doubt is part of the job. The most intellectually honest doctors always have self-doubt; they always think they could have done something better."

The Entrenched Phase (1994–2004)

Disillusionment and Cynicism

Although a large majority of the cohort was still disgruntled ten years later in the entrenched period fifteen years postresidency, fewer expressed the intensity of disenchantment that they had in the earlier established phase (1984–1994). It appears that these physicians had either matured or had set lower expectations for themselves by then. They "weathered the storm," as Dr. Jarvis put it. For the first time, a few respondents stated philosophically that it was their nature to be cynical. This could be interpreted as an expression of a certain tiredness and resignation as they are closer to the end than the beginning of their careers. Yes, they are surviving, but at a cost.

For community practitioners, external factors were the predominant focus of their disillusionment, even disgust. Repeatedly and much more intensely than in the past, lawyers and insurance companies were blamed for their cynicism, while unrealistic patient expectations continued to dishearten some. One exception highlights this point. Dr. Allen had the satisfaction of seeing his large group practice beat back the demands of a managed care insurance company, a rare victory for their organization (or for any that I heard about), although it left him drained: "A few years ago, a managed care company came to town and tried to push us around. For about ten to twelve percent of our patient group, they wanted us to take a cut of forty percent. We said 'no,' and those patients had to drive forty miles further for nine months. Then they (the MC company) came back to us, and we negotiated a more reasonable rate." Still Dr. Allen expressed his growing disappointment, if not disdain about the profession: "Medicine seems tougher now, but I was probably more idealistic when I went into it. We didn't have all this managed care. You can't pick up a paper here without doctor bashing going on. The politicians are hammering doctors for political gain. This is the first time I started to feel so negative about the whole deal."

While the community practitioners were most cynical about lawyers and lawsuits, many academic practitioners were disillusioned by other physicians, some even expressing shame about many of their medical colleagues. As Dr. Strelko revealed, "It's money, money, money. I see a cohort driven by money. They feel entitled to unfettered profits." At the very least, those who did not express their disaffection seem to have reconciled, albeit with some disillusionment, to being part of a less than ideal profession.

Self-Doubt and Fear of Failure

Even though almost all the physicians were embedded in their community practice or specialty department for a quarter of a century or so, a large majority still expressed deep fears and doubts when asked whether they were disillusioned overall.

Academic physicians like Drs. Strelko and Dr. Paul revealed some profound vulnerabilities. Dr. Strelko, who objectively had achieved a fair amount of prominence, still questioned himself, even at this stage: "As you grow older, you realize you're not going to accomplish everything you wanted. I assume that's a product of aging. I had an individual patient failure in clinic just yesterday, so I can't imagine doing this five to six days a week for the long haul; burnout would set in." Dr. Paul, a less successful academic general internist by traditional scholarship criteria, tried to depersonalize his limitations: "There was a time when I felt inferior because I wasn't a researcher. Clinicians are vulnerable at times in academic settings, and we are approaching one of those times. The incentive programs offered to researchers discriminate against clinicians like me. I am disillusioned and cynical."

Similar fears were present at this career phase among the community practitioners. Dr. Allen confessed, "I feel more now than ever this fear of failure and self-doubt, because in the last couple of years I don't care about practicing medicine as much as I used to. It's a hassle, harder to get things done. I've taken the path of least resistance and don't complain if I don't think it's right or being done the right way. I know deep inside that your chance of making errors or something going wrong goes up a bit."

Some community practitioners expressed the need to maintain a work ethic that included vigilance and the norm of humility. As Dr. Melone noted, "The fear of failure is always a significant driving force for me. It's more of the negative than getting positive feedback that keeps me on my toes. You don't want to be stupid and have somebody die because you were dumb." Then Dr. Melone repeated what he had said almost verbatim in both past early and established phases about the usefulness of self-doubt: "I've never had the problem of asking another doctor for help. The last thing I want to do is think I know everything."

(Specific questions about these issues were not directly posed at the end of the intervening extended phase [2004–2011].)

The Ending Phase (2011–2016)

Disillusionment and Cynicism

Interestingly, in this latest phase in their career, the doctors expressed less rancor overall and more qualifiers than in the entrenched phase (1994–2004) with a sense of resignation. Overall, as a cohort, their revelations were poignant. Many were still focused on disillusionment with specific physician groups, while others concentrated on the medical profession more broadly. For Dr. Finast, the cynicism noted in his early career around the theme of greedy doctors surfaced once again: "I'm always uncomfortable when people are talking salaries. 'I can get this much, or I got that much.' They were missing the point of being a doctor in the first place. They were just going into it to see how much money they could get. It's disillusioning to think that some of your colleagues have such bad attitudes."

Still, fewer of the academic physicians felt the brunt of the environmental pressures impinging on them than their community counterparts. In general, the academics were less cynical and plagued with less self-doubt overall, with the exception of Dr. Boswell. A few of the always positive academic physicians were even dismissive of the question about cynicism and self-doubt. Dr. Annas succinctly responded, "Nope! Never!" And Dr. Lash expressed his view in general terms: "No, medicine is a great profession. It's just an amazing opportunity to see the application of science, an extraordinary privilege." However, even perpetually optimistic Dr. Rosen qualified his answer for the first time, as he reflected on his professional lifetime: "You've been interviewing me for forty years. You know self-doubt doesn't fit my personality. I love doctoring, but I admit that I'm a bit cynical about the administrative stuff and this 'deaning' role I took on in the last year."

During this late stage in their careers, the community practitioners notably expressed disillusionment with colleagues, specifically aimed at greedy doctors who they felt were focused on the bottom line rather than on patients. Dr. Jarvis railed extensively about a core theme affecting the actual patient-centered clinical medicine: "I'm cynical about the practice of medicine; we've completely eliminated the doctor-patient relationship. Basically, you can examine the patient and tell what he has, but that is not officially what he's got until you do the lab test. Imagine, I just read an article stating that stethoscopes were extinct. Everyone wants doctors to use an echo ultrasound instead of listening to the heart. Maybe that's better, but using stethoscope, while talking to patients, getting their histories, contributes a lot to patients getting better." Dr. Mahoney, who had already retired at this point, also expressed cynicism about relationships with patients and corporations, similar to what he expressed back in the early phase (1980–1984): "My sense of cynicism says there's not a whole lot I take as truthful coming from patients. I think human beings have hidden agendas. And the corporate climate of this country toward medicine also adds to my cynicism."

Self-Doubt and Fear of Failure

The responsibilities for life and death still weighed heavily on the community practitioners all the way until their professional ending. It is quite telling that after all these years, fear of making mistakes still loomed large in their psyches, resulting in varying degrees of disillusionment and self-doubt, regardless of their sense of accomplishment and whether they had actually been sued. Some of the physicians continued to express self-doubt about making the wrong diagnosis, pointing to recent clients who had a fatal illness, for example, and wondering if they could have caught it sooner, would it have made a difference? Consider Dr. Polikoff, who had a successful career in primary care (by his own assessment), yet self-doubt about patient outcomes still plagued him: "In the last three years I've had at least six patients who died of pancreatic cancer. And in every instance, I wonder if I could have done something different."

Others pointed to perennial issues such as sleep deprivation as being sources of their anxiety related to fears of getting the diagnosis wrong and generally feeling depressed related to their work. Dr. Beech, who clearly felt worn down at this point in his career, after pointing to a couple of painful lawsuits, reflected on his life's work: "On balance, it's been an interesting experience being a physician. Still, I don't know if I had my choice to do it all over again, I would do the same thing."

Nevertheless, many of the other physicians responded to the questions at this phase by contemplating the entirety of their career challenges, and many seemed to do so through a more positive filter. Looking back on their whole careers, they appeared willing to let go of a lot of the "trees" and focus on the "forest"; that is, to reflect on their professional career as a whole, which many felt had been ultimately rewarding, despite its challenges.

Delving Deeper: Revelations on Facets
of Disillusionment and Despair

Two transformative changes in the structure of medicine occurred within the extended phase (2004–2011) and ending phase (2011–2016) of the physicians' careers: the advent of the hospitalist and the electronic medical record. Hospitalists are salaried hospital-based physicians who first came on the inpatient medical scene in the 1990s (Gunderman, 2016; Pantilat, 2006). EMRs also became a prominent feature in the practice of medicine in that same time period, although computerization had begun a decade earlier (Greenhalgh, Potts, et al., 2009). Both of these issues notably contributed to disillusionment and self-doubt among the physicians. A few of the physicians identified both systemic phenomena as early as the entrenched phase (1994–2004). However, their commentary and complaints became more detailed and pronounced in the extended phase (2004–2011) in responding to questions about major changes affecting their practice, as well as to questions about satisfaction and dissatisfaction.

Because of the way EMRs and hospitalists had emerged so pervasively into the physicians' responses during the extended phase (2004–2011), I asked the physicians in the ending phase (2011–2016) specific questions about the impact of these two phenomena on their work, if they did not bring it up themselves. To be sure, one or both of these themes were major contributors to their disillusionment and, for some, factored in their decisions about when and why to retire. The majority of the physicians' responses provided below were made at the time of the final interviews in 2016.

Hospitalists

The shift to the new hospital-based, salaried position was consistently disparaged by the physicians. Almost universally, the physicians highlighted what they perceived as downsides to this phenomenon. Many of their comments were focused on what they saw as a diminishment in patient care. As Dr. Jarvis, already retired, commented, "A downside to quality patient care is that too many doctors have decided that they'll just let the hospitalists take care of their patients. So, for example, most surgeons don't write notes anymore; they let the hospitalists do it. That's not good." Additionally, the primary care generalist physicians worried about their deteriorating relationship with patients specifically, and the doctor-patient relationship generally. Some questioned the competency of most hospitalists or thought that the position exacerbated the dehumanization of the medical service system. As Dr. Nolan lamented, "People are becoming patients of the corporate hospital, not of a physician." Dr. Johnson asserted that hospitalists created fragmentation in care, which he felt introduced a higher risk of error as patients might fall through the cracks. He also felt that the hospitalists were causing physicians to shift away from dedication to patients as they moved into a hospital career. "This new generation won't do what we used to do; the hospitalist will do those things now," he said. "Physicians in private practice are going out of business and not coming back. We're a vanishing breed." Dr. Beech also pointed to the adverse impact he sees of hospitalists on the system: "I have two criticisms from an office-based perspective. The hospitalist doesn't have to be concerned with what happens to patients when they leave the hospital. Nobody follows up. And from the system impact side, these hospitalists are looked upon as shift workers, not doctors; just breathing bodies."

Their condemnation of hospitalists is part of their collective belief in the de-professionalization of physicians, as Dr. Beech observed. Dr. Rosen provided a cogent and detailed analysis of what he saw as the cultural and informal aspects of the hospitalists' presence, which he believed adversely affect both a physician's practice in hospitals and in office-based care: "The negative externalities are that it's made the traditional internist role almost obsolete. In the 1970s, you'd make hospital rounds. You'd run into subspecialists and you'd ask them a question like, 'Would you give me an opinion about something?' Almost no office-based doctor goes to the hospital anymore. They're isolated and miss both social and intellectual aspects with their colleagues." Ironically, Dr. Rosen suggested, on the contrary, that hospitalists have increased costs and inefficiencies: "In the old days, your doc would know you and admit you to the hospital. They didn't have to re-take the entire history as hospitalists now do."

As a cohort, many agreed on only two positive aspects of this full-time hospital physician position: the first being relief for office-based community practitioners of having to admit and visit their hospitalized patients, especially at night and on weekends. They labeled this trade-off as the "shift-to-sleep ratio," my term for having multiple rotating physicians caring for a hospital patient over time versus the longer hours that one resident or attending physician would have to devote to a patient's care in order to achieve continuity.

For example, Dr. Allen, a cardiologist, noted that the new system could be useful to physicians working in a subspecialty who did want to take care of their patients' health problems outside their area of expertise: "Hospitalists have made it easier for us. First, it used to be anytime anybody had a chest pain, they called me in. Now, the hospitalists admit even heart attacks to the hospital. So, I can sleep in and see that patient tomorrow. Second, there's somebody who can take care of diabetes and sprained ankles my cardiac patients have. Not me. Yay!"

The second positive aspect reflected a shift in these physicians' perspectives about the "new generation of physicians," whom many criticized for the latter group's lack of devotion to the profession (as discussed earlier in chapter 5). Some acknowledged that the hospitalist is an acceptable career track for those trained as general internists or family practitioners because for this newer generation it was a lifestyle issue. They all said that it is a job, no longer a profession and for some, no longer a "calling." It provides a fairer balance between family and work than they had—predictable hours, relatively good pay, and better working conditions. Dr. Nolan cautioned about the trade-off from the perspective of hospitalists themselves; they can move around easier, but "they are giving up their commitment to patients and a location. They are trading stability for mobility." Ironically, he admits that if he were finishing his residency now, he might have considered that career path.

Although nearly all of the cohort held broadly negative views of the hospitalists, there was one outlier: Dr. Lynch, a community practitioner specializing in oncology. He cited his positive experience working with a stable group of hospitalists over the last decade, although he also acknowledged trade-offs with this new position. He was the only physician who praised the greater level of expertise hospitalists have in diagnosing and treating inpatient manifestations of diseases, which he concluded he and others who practice mostly outside the hospital do not have. He also admitted that they have negatively affected the career track for generalist community internists because "if you go into practice you don't make as much income. Plus, you still take night calls. Hospitalists work seven days on, seven days off." Ironically of all the community practitioners, Dr. Lynch had the least stable career, having changed settings and practice styles multiple times. As a result, perhaps his perspective reflected having less loyalty himself to a specific group of patients or peers.

Within the physicians' strong critiques of hospitalists, there appears to be an undercurrent of nostalgia however, as they recall an earlier era with rose-colored glasses. Many cite their own caring role and long hours in the hospital as residents that they no longer observe in the present scene. However, looking back on their reported experiences as house staff in their own words in the entry phase (1979–1980), they were not happy with the former arrangements. The "good old days," to the extent that they existed, were generally only "good" for middle-class and well-insured patients. Millions of poor, uninsured people and underserved communities received care in clinics around the country from house staff who characterized their experience in a negative light, as I observed almost forty years earlier (Mizrahi, 1984a; 1986). Nevertheless, the physicians' sincere and deep objections to the hospitalists demonstrate how the introduction of them to the health care system created a profound structural change in their professional relationships and for the profession as a whole.

Electronic Medical Records (EMRs)

The other profound change that the physicians described near the end of their careers related to the way medical information was being documented and shared, the EMR. The EMR was a prime target for extraordinarily negative intellectual and emotional reactions from almost all of the cohort, in spite of their belief in its irrevocability. Moreover, they did not link their resistance to the EMR to their age or generation, but rather it was aimed at the core of what quality medicine meant to them. Many identified enormous inefficiencies associated with EMRs, which was viewed as a contradiction, because the system was presumably designed for the opposite result.

For example, Dr. Johnson spoke at length about his disillusionment with the EMR, specifically complaining about the impact EMRs have had on him as a senior managerial physician ready to retire: "I have to deal with EMRs because of my administrative role, but it affects every physician adversely. We just went through an ICD (a disease classification system) conversion, so every patient had to get a new diagnosis. I'm not going to miss any of that when I retire." He saw the shift to a hospitalist-based, inpatient hospital system and the advent of the EMR as ominous trends—away from community-based autonomous practice.

Other physicians focused on the inefficiencies they experienced as they tried to adapt to the changing systems. As Dr. Lynch stated, "We converted about a year ago, and I was very disappointed in the lack of functionality. I finally figured it out, just in time to convert to another system next year. The computer software business was supposed to be sophisticated; instead, it slows me down."

Additional critiques emerged that appear to undermine the internal medicine ethos, that is, the anti-intellectual and dehumanizing element of the EMR. According to Dr. Beech, "What suffers is that the EMR leaves out what you are really thinking is going on with that patient. I used to hand-write that in the chart. The other thing is that instead of talking face-to-face with the patient, I'm staring at a computer screen. It puts a barrier between the patient and me and slows everything up." Several other doctors also pointed to the ways that the EMR hinders doctor-patient communication and ultimately could impede clinical outcomes. As Dr. Allen described it, "The EMR drives me crazy. When I see a patient, I'll dictate a complete note that's one and a half pages. When I get a patient referred from another doctor now, I get a fourteen-page note. It's cut-and-paste junk." During the final phone interview, he sought to demonstrate the absurdity of the EMR by reading a note from a referral MD that was in front of him: "Here's what it says: 'This note was completed using a medical speech recognition software. Grammatical errors, random word insertions, and incomplete sentences are occasional consequences of this technology due to software limitations. If you have any questions about the content of this note, they should be addressed with the physician for clarification.' Is that unbelievable or what?"

Their view of how hospitalists depersonalize the doctor-patient relationship was consistent with their view of how the EMR distorts and dehumanizes that relationship. However, there is some irony in their responses, since when they were house staff, I observed dozens of instances where the residents paid closer attention to the paper medical charts in front of them than to the patient in clinical encounters (Mizrahi, 1986). At that time, as house staff, they frequently focused on the often thick and messy paper records of their patients, frustrated as they tried to catch up with their patient's data at the expense of concentrating on the patient in the room. It seems like a similar dynamic is being reported years later with the digital substituting for the paper record.

But there were also notable sources of frustration that the physicians pointed to with the EMRs that were directly related to the technology. For example, Dr. Melone described in detail some real-time transactions that had happened between a patient and a physician, raising some ethical concerns for him and underscoring that the EMR experience had significantly influenced his levels of cynicism: "EMRs are making doctors into liars. For example, the computer generates a note that says that you listened to the patient's heart and that it was regular when you didn't check it on that visit. You find yourself questioning what's on a patient chart. Forget about the ethics."

The academic physicians were no less inclined to disparage the EMR. For instance, Dr. O'Brian, who had recently moved into a new administrative academic position and supervised hundreds of physicians, did not believe the EMR system helps with medical decision-making: "We have an EMR system, but physicians don't know how to use it. They've just adapted what they did in written form to the EMR, like we treated the paper charts. We have to educate our residents and faculty to provide just enough information to get a message across but not regurgitate all information." Dr. O'Brian also graphically described how accountability measures may be compromised: "The EMR has shifted the workflow. Before, in making rounds, most physicians would see the patient and write a note in the chart at the time. Now you see the patient and leave. The fellow or resident will write a note later on in the day. They wait until the night to get their notes into the EMR. That's less efficient. If the attending doesn't agree with the resident, he needs to chase him down." In the final analysis, Dr. Annas, an always-positive academic physician, summed up with resignation his acceptance of the EMR technology: "It's a real pain in the butt and caused some disruption, but it's the new fact of life at this point, and we have had to adapt to it."

Conclusion

It is clear that the introduction of hospitalists and EMRs has profoundly affected this cohort and their colleagues, transforming their practice and their sense of control and fulfillment. At best, these phenomena have been tolerated by a few at the end of their career, and at worst, have frustrated and confounded many. Both EMRs and hospitalists contributed to or exacerbated their sense of disillusionment and cynicism as well as self-doubt, perhaps propelling retirement. For some in community practice, these occurrences these last years were the proverbial "straws that broke the camel's back."

The experiences of this cohort of physicians suggest that their generation of physicians has faced much greater struggles than has been described in the professional and popular literature. While dissatisfactions are found in surveys, disillusionment and fear of failure remain largely hidden. Indeed, the public media and medical scholars have historically portrayed physicians as confident, powerful, and even arrogant political actors (Light, 2005; Rodwin, 1993). At the same time, increasing critiques of the elitism of the medical profession have negatively affected their public influence and trust over the past forty and more years (Mechanic, 1996; Schlesinger, 2002). While organized medicine has been on both offense and defense at the macro level, the quality, quantity, and impact of physician disillusionment and vulnerability at the micro level have been only occasionally revealed (Bailie, Sibthorpe, et al., 1998; Kuhlman, 2006; Zuger, 2004). The depth and breadth of despair found in this cohort was unexpected. These sentiments existed side by side with expressions of satisfaction and happiness, as described more fully in chapter 9.

These inner worries of physicians came to the surface primarily when probing questions were posed in a trusting environment. It is understandable that professionals do not want to openly feature expressions of fears of failure and self-doubt. However, ignoring those inner feelings in training and practice may have done a disservice to the medical profession and to the practitioners, and perhaps to their patients as well (Coulehan and Williams, 2001; Kenny and Shelton, 2006). These more private feelings seem to take their toll even among those who are satisfied overall and may be endemic to professional life today (Cole and Carlin, 2009; Evett, 2003). But in the case of medicine, the negative aspects may be exacerbated by silence and/or defensiveness among many of its professional leaders (O'Rourke, 2014).

Community practitioners were dealing with threats of and actual lawsuits, which heightened their own self-doubts and fear of failure. There were indeed many externally driven intrusions into practice. Malpractice threats, lawsuits, and state-based proposals for tort reform loomed larger over time. These added to financial stress, fears of loss of reputation and referrals, and competition between practitioners (Linzer, Gerrity, et al., 2002; Zuger, 2004). Most of them did not believe that politicians nor the public at large had their backs.

Concomitantly, academics have been largely ignored in research on physicians' careers related to dissatisfaction and disillusionment (Cole, Goodrich, et al., 2009). Yet, many struggled with issues of promotion, and several of them had experienced disappointments with funding at varying points in their careers. Moreover, they also were dealing with external environmental factors that affected their research and clinical responsibilities, including competition, cutbacks, and constraints on research. Moreover, fewer training dollars with more regulations affected the size and quality of residency programs (Edwards, Kornaki, et al., 2002), which may have also affected their teaching responsibilities.

Most efforts in the last few decades to address these deleterious effects among physicians have been limited to the micro or individual level, focusing on the individual physicians. The term "impaired physician" first came into the vernacular of medicine with a few different programs in the 1970s (Johnson, 1988). However, these were primarily confined to assisting at the personal rather than at the system macro level (Boisaubin and Levine, 2001; Boyd, 2015). Horowitz and colleagues (2003) present ways to help physicians "recognize and reconnect with what is most meaningful about practice [which] may be re-moralizing to doctors and may help them advocate for their needs more clearly" (p. 772). Likewise, Diane Meier, Anthony Back, and Sean Morrison offer a program for preventing and adjusting adverse physician behaviors, which includes recognizing high-risk clinical situations and risk factors, monitoring signs and symptoms, developing a differential diagnosis, and determining a practical means of responding to these emotions (2001). Bengt Arnetz reported in 2001 on a prospective intervention study to enhance physician well-being that was successfully implemented in Sweden at three levels—structural, organizational, and individual. The author concluded that there is a need for individual coping mechanisms as well as positive work environments including participatory management and social supports, connecting the micro to the macro level. As this cohort demonstrates, for U.S.-trained and practicing physicians imbued with the norm of self-reliance, there is a powerful need for effective collegial and collective interventions at the macro level as well.

9   *The Personal and the Professional*

THE INTERACTION BETWEEN PRIVATE
LIVES AND PUBLIC POSTURES

Building on the prior chapter's discussion of the emotional and psychological stresses physicians face in their professional lives, this chapter turns to look more closely at the intimate aspects of the physicians' personal lives: in particular, whether and how their private struggles affected their professional careers, and vice versa. Documenting their responses to specific questions about their personal life over the course of their entire career, this chapter highlights the ways the physicians attempted to balance work and family life, and their relationships with specific family members, particularly their spouses and children (for all but Dr. Paul, who did not marry nor have children). This chapter also uncovers the status of the cohort's health and well-being, especially in their later years. And finally, the chapter reveals their private feelings about aging and retirement (Dellinger, Pellegrini, et al., 2017; Merritt Hawkins, 2015).

From the early phase (1980–1984) of their careers, each interview cycle included a question about the impact of their personal lives on their professional development and the contrary. In the previous chapter, I discussed the physicians' vulnerabilities, inner doubts, and insecurities related to their work life. This chapter continues to probe their emotional experiences as physicians, looking beyond their work situation to their family and personal lives to explore key issues in work-life balance, especially relating to burnout and personal satisfaction (Shanafelt, Hasan, et al., 2015). Finally, the chapter presents some additional comments the physicians made during interviews spontaneously. These were not in response to a specific question but shed additional light on a number of related issues, including the physicians' struggles resulting from illness, disability, aging, spirituality, and sexuality, also discussed by Hunter (1993), Klitzman (2008), and Weiner (2017).

During the ending phase (2011–2016), the physicians were also asked directly about their perspectives on their wives' attitudes and behavior relating to their careers. Although I had asked questions about their personal lives from the beginning, it wasn't until the final career stage that I asked specifically about this topic. Over the nearly four decades of interviewing these physicians, I had become increasingly attuned to women's issues, particularly regarding the tensions women faced between their work and home life (Hagar, 2012). I also became more concerned about the inequality that women faced in the domestic arena (a topic that has emerged more stridently in professional and public literature in the twenty-first century [see Perlman, Ross, et al., 2014; Rodsky, 2019]). During this final phase, with more self-awareness, I probed more deeply these physicians' sense of their wives' perspectives on their husband's careers. It was a line of questioning that, as I discuss below, revealed a great deal about the larger personal aspects of what it meant to be a White male physician at this time in American society.[1]

Balancing Work and Family Life

Not surprisingly, at each career stage, the physicians pointed to a number of common issues that affected them, including time constraints and conflicts between needs of work and family. These concerns have become increasingly relevant in the professional and public sphere for all careers (Croner, 2015; Kelly, Moen, et al., 2014), but especially for physicians (Pololi, Krupat, et al., 2012; Witzig and Smith, 2019). When asked about how they did or did not balance their work and home life, most acknowledged that the balance tipped toward their careers, at least in their early years, when the demands of getting established at an institution or new practice were very high.

By the early phase (1980–1984), all but two of the doctors had married and had small children. Did the combination of adding the role of father to that of a spouse while becoming a practicing physician have an impact on their professional lives and choices? How much stress, if any, did it place on them? Did any tensions that arose during this time cause temporary or permanent rifts in their domestic relationships from their perspective, and if these did, how did the physicians cope?

There were some differences in how the physicians spoke about the intimate details of their home life. The complexity of medical practice and the need to keep up with both family and personal matters overwhelmed many of them in the early years, with a greater pressure, for the most part, on the community practitioners than on the academics. In the paragraphs below, I focus on the trajectories of six individual physicians—three community practitioners (Drs. Cahn, Ross, and Beech) and three academic practitioners (Drs. Finast, O'Brian, and Boswell). The experiences of these physicians reflect a spectrum that is largely representative of the cohort more broadly. For each doctor, I present the general arc of the tensions they faced as they sought to balance their personal and professional lives across career phases and the impact this struggle had on their careers.

Dr. Cahn's experience represents one end of the spectrum, where the intersection of the personal with the professional resulted in profound tensions for him throughout his career. From the very beginning of his time as a practicing community practitioner with a subspecialty in gastroenterology, the professional responsibilities took a toll on him and his family, ultimately leading to his first divorce. Although he did not alter his professional priorities, he noted that the effects of the tension between work and personal life during the early phase (1980–1984) were significant: "It took a tremendous toll on my family. I've got a two-year-old and a four-year-old. My wife got her master's degree in the health professions. She was offered a job to head the local university professional program. However, without a caretaker she resigned and now is looking to go back when my son starts school. Between helping me and being a mom at home, it is a full-time job. I'm building my practice and hiring an associate. I'm on the go and away almost all the time." (Please note: The types and particulars of all the wives' careers discussed in this chapter have been altered for the purpose of anonymity.)

The situation Dr. Cahn described would lead to additional problems for him in the coming years. By the end of the established phase (1984–1994), he and his wife had gone through an acrimonious divorce that he discussed with me confidentially in great detail. He remarried another professional woman, also in the health care field, who he reported was "not practicing anymore. She worked for me a short time, but that didn't work. But she understands medicine and is extremely helpful. The crisis I am going through now are with my fifteen- and thirteen-year-old children." During this period, he continued to build a lucrative practice, working seven days a week, while upheavals apparently continued.

During the interview ten years later, at the end of the entrenched phase (1994–2004), he reported new major personal and family stressors. These included another divorce and a third marriage, which he revealed had made him happy: "About six years ago, I found a wonderful woman, who I married, and my life and perspective have changed. When you're personally happy, you interact with people totally differently. And when you're miserable, you really can't devote yourself to people." Seven years later, in 2011, as Dr. Cahn looked back to earlier times, he reported being less happy with his career, although his work habits appear not to have altered: "Fifteen years ago, I met a marvelous woman, who I happily married. That's been critical to me, because the practice of medicine is less appealing to me as it goes on. My relationship with my children remains complicated." For the first time, he questioned whether he struck the right balance. "The way my personal life and career are connected is that the practice impinges on my personal life, timewise, which is a burden on my family. As I get older, I come to realize that a little more time with my family is more important than my practice." And yet, despite this, his practice style remained unchanged. In 2016, closer to the end of his career, he expressed a sense of disillusionment and anger as a physician: "My practice is becoming less and less desirable. In order to meet overhead with less reimbursement, you have to work more hours. I'm sixty-four years of age. I went to work at 3:30 A.M. this morning, and I just walked in five minutes ago, and it's 9 P.M." Nevertheless, as he contemplated the possibility of retirement, Dr. Cahn was clearly conflicted: "It is the feedback from patients that drives me to work every day. If I retire, I could never get that. I have a wife who's younger than me. She's an executive who works every day, so to sit at home and not be stimulated mentally from that charge of patients loving you, is scary."

Dr. Ross, a community practitioner specializing in a combination of oncology and general internal medicine, is at the other end of the spectrum from Dr. Cahn. Dr. Ross went through his residency and fellowship and into practice with a family, but that circumstance did not seem to have complicated his perspective. His responses suggest that he accepted the tensions of any impact of his family life on his professional life and vice versa, and he readily discusses them. During his interview in 1984 at the end of the early phase (1980–1984), he pointed to his expectation of struggle: "I didn't neglect my personal life in residency or now. I have four kids. It's rough because I have to finish rounds in the evening, go home and help feed, bathe, and put them to bed, and then go back and finish up. I hope it gets better. But I anticipate less time at home because my practice has gotten me dizzy; still I'll need to go home and bathe and feed the herd." Indeed, unlike Dr. Cahn, Dr. Ross seemed to take his home life in stride, if not for granted: "Stresses and strains on me were time and lack of sleep, and that mostly occurred during internship. Then it eased up. I think those factors are overplayed."

Despite the expected struggles of his professional life throughout his career until the end, Dr. Ross suggested that the effort to balance his personal life with work was straightforward. In the entrenched phase in 1994, and then again in the extended phase in 2004, when asked about the impact of personal life on his professional life, he succinctly reiterated the same response: "No problem." In 2016, at the ending phase (2011–2016), he repeated that sentiment tersely in no uncertain terms: "No divorce, have four children, moved into a different house. All is good."

Despite Dr. Ross's ability to find a sense of equilibrium between his personal and professional life from his perspective, he nevertheless noted that his personal life infringed on his professional one, particularly his ability to keep up with new research in his field. Although he presented it as a choice he had made, he noted the impact this had on his work over time. For example, in the early phase (1980–1984), he pointed out that he was determined to keep up with the literature: "I try to read all the time and spend a lot of time on continuing medical education." Ten years later, however, by the end of the established phase (1984–1994), he admitted, "As I come home more beat up and then want to spend time with the kids, I spend less time reading medical stuff. It has dropped off dramatically. There is no way I can work twelve hours a day and then go home and read." In 2004, another ten years later at the end of the entrenched phase (1994–2004), he admitted once again, "As I get older, I get too physically fatigued to do as much reading. It takes a much greater effort."

Dr. Beech, another community practitioner, tended to change his views over time. In the early phase (1980–1984), he expressed feeling a sense of balance: "I don't think the demands are that great. I have adequate time for personal life. I'm getting better about not bringing work home; still being called at 3 A.M. is hell." But ten years later, in the established phase, he began to complain about a lack of balance: "I don't like the hours as I get older. As I get woken up two to three times a night, less and less can I function well the next day. I shortchange my family; time away causes stress. It's gotten worse; I'm at the pre-burnout stage. I antici-pate more in the future; but the money helps me put up with the crap." By the ending phase, however, having gone through many ups and downs in his per-sonal life, including the death of his wife after a long illness and subsequent remarriage, Dr. Beech found a number of things to express frustration about, looking back on the same existential theme: "I think the least satisfying aspect of my practice has been the nights and the weekends. You miss all kinds of stuff with your family."

Drs. Cahn, Ross, and Beech portray three different perspectives on the impact of physicians' personal lives on their professional lives. The demands of their work as doctors clearly intersected with their family life, particularly in terms of time constraints, and it forced them to make decisions about which part of their life they would devote themselves more to. Dr. Cahn chose his career over his home life more intensely than did Dr. Ross, while Dr. Beech, once he'd moved past the early parts of his career, struggled to find a balance that worked for him.

Among the academic practitioners, the overall story was similar, although the specifics of the tensions, levels of devotion to work or family, and time constraints varied primarily because of their practice setting. But their stories clearly demonstrate that it was not just the community practitioners who faced difficulties in finding the right balance. The academic practitioners, who were also building and maintaining their practices and careers, faced tensions in work-life balance as they navigated the pressures to practice clinically and in the laboratory, as well as teach and supervise medical students, residents, and fellows (Borges, Navarro, et al., 2010; Strong, De Castro, et al., 2013). Here are the experiences of three academics: Dr. Finast, pulmonary specialist, Dr. O'Brian, a nephrologist, and Dr. Boswell, a rheumatologist.

Dr. Finast was one of the physicians who seemed to find more balance between his home life and work, a perspective that may have also come from a somewhat different level of respect for his family, and possibly a different dynamic with his wife, who appeared, as he described it, to be more vocal about her needs than many of the other physicians' wives. At the early phase (1980–1984) he noted that choosing the SAMS city was a joint decision with his wife because she was studying for her own professional degree in another institution in the SAMS city. Still he highlighted tensions between personal life and his medical practice: "The biggest stress is multiple demands on my time between the hospital and family. You feel like you need to stay in the hospital to take care of patients, but you also have a life outside the hospital. Kids growing up, a spouse that needs you—the lack of quality time was the biggest stress, trying to balance the demands. My wife is not one to suffer quietly, so it didn't make it pleasant at home. She'd complain, 'Where the hell were you?' I think we've reached some reasonable balance now."

For the next twenty-five years, Dr. Finast and his family stayed at SAMS, where he built his academic practice. But he acknowledged that doing so was more about his focus on his family than his career. As he reflected in 2011 at the end of the extended phase (2004–2011), when he was already semiretired, "When we moved to the SAMS city, the plan was to be here to finish my training and then to go somewhere else. But we're still here. That's all about personal decisions; where the kids are in school, and a good home and neighborhood, affected the decisions. Now we are having that discussion again." By the time Dr. Finast was interviewed five years later at the end of the ending phase (2011–2016), he was fully retired, still lived in SAMS city, and was suffering a major illness.

Like so many of the others, Dr. O'Brian, an academic physician in nephrology, was candid from the outset about the stresses that medicine put on his relationship with his wife and children. He described it openly at almost every point in his academic career, beginning in the early phase (1980–1984): "I was devoted to the work, and in that sense, it took its toll. My family life suffered. I got married when I was in medical school, and we had a child my last month there. That's when we separated for about two years. We got back together and that's where we are now. I'm sure medicine was the major part of the problem."

Nevertheless, his family circumstances affected his career mobility. He reflected twenty years later, in 2004, "I've looked at a number of jobs over the past five years in other cities, and it just hasn't worked out. One of the issues is my daughter's in high school so that impacts on life's decisions as well. There had been issues with my wife's jobs over the years as to whether she could move or not. So, all of those things impact us."

Dr. O'Brian's wife's career presumably impacted their family life, although his focus on his career still led him to move his practice several times. In 2016, by the ending phase (2011–2016), he looked back after having moved to three different academic centers in three different cites: "I think I was too tied up in my career early on, and my personal life suffered a bit. While my wife is still my wife, my family could have been a little better. Although, I did manage to coach my son and my daughter, I wish I had spent a little more time with them."

From the early phase (1980–1984), Dr. Boswell seemed overwhelmed with demands of job and home: "I need to do a lot of research and attending responsibilities. That means lots of time in the lab, including weekends, plus lots of reading and teaching on rounds. I have two young children, who take a lot of time. When I come home, my wife's been taking care of them all day, so nothing's done. The house isn't cleaned; supper is not ready. It's stressful. I try to understand, but it is frustrating."

Ten years later, in the established phase (1984–1994), Dr. Boswell reported still facing the same kind of tensions: "The kind of parent that I want to be takes a lot of time. You have to make sure kids get the right kind of direction. Working these long hours, it's hard. When I get home, I do a bit of paperwork at night and on weekends, after the kids are taken care of. There is not much time for anything else. We go to church on weekends for an hour, but I don't do other church activities that I want to."

It is possible that Dr. Boswell's struggles to find a good balance between life and work and family, which continued over the years, may have also led him to neglect his career and his personal psychological health. During the entrenched phase (1994–2004) and extended phase (2004–2011), his negativity about his career became extreme (this was presented more fully in chapters 3 and 4 on satisfaction/dissatisfaction, and in chapter 8 on disillusionment). By the ending phase (2011–2016), he even refused an interview, replying with an emphatic "NO! It's too painful."

Wives in Their Lives: Multiple, Complex, and Contradictory Roles

The physicians in this cohort and their wives came of age during the second femi-nist wave, as it is called by some—the women's movement of the late 1960s and 1970s (Heriot, 2017; Maxwell and Shields, 2017). Their generation saw many more women seeking careers along with marriage. Yet, while conducting the research for this book over the decades, I found that in the literature on doctors and their careers, there was a paucity of studies related to the impact of spouses and family on career decision-making, especially in medicine and other high-stress, high-status, traditionally male professions. The only book located specifically written on the topic at the time was *Married to Medicine*, a study about male physicians and their wives in the United Kingdom in the early 1980s (Gerber, 1983). Recently a few works on these dilemmas have appeared (Shanafelt, Boone, et al., 2013); however, more often than not these are advice-giving publications geared to the spouses, predominantly wives, of physicians (Croner, 2015; Hagar, 2012; Read and Addington, 2011) and occasionally to couples (Sotile and Sotile, 2011).

During the interviews with these physicians, however, they made many ref-erences to the impact of their professional lives on their home lives and on the relationship with their spouses, especially in the earlier stages: in particular, the difficulties in balancing work and family as noted above. In 2016, at the end of their careers, I asked the physicians in greater depth for the first time about the impact of their career choices on their wives. In this section, I present their reac-tions to this question, including their reflections on whether they thought their wives were satisfied with their status and whether they had sacrificed their careers whether that included raising children while working part or full time, or staying at home.

About half of their wives did not work, before or after having children, while the other half had a career or worked in a job outside the home mostly part time or intermittently. With only a few exceptions, their wives' careers never seemed to be of primary consideration for these physicians. A quarter of the cohort married women in a health profession (Drs. Nolan, Rosen, Cahn, Johnson, and Melone), a seemingly commonly accepted occurrence among physicians, although with few hard data to confirm that assertion. Over their professional lifetime, three of the twenty divorced (Drs. Cahn [twice], Lynch, and Annas) at different phases and for different reasons. Data show that physicians marry and stay married more than most other professions with only twenty-five percent divorced (McGreevey, 2015), and this is more than borne out with this cohort's fifteen percent rate of divorce.

Overall, these physicians believed that their wives have been content with their lives and have had little to no regrets. As Dr. Conley conjectured, "I think my wife's been happy with her life and her family life. I don't have any specific regrets. I feel like we've both been pretty satisfied. If we had to do it all over again the same way, I'd be perfectly fine with that." Although the question asked him to speculate about his wife's "sacrifice, if any," Dr. Conley continued, from his own perspective, "I really haven't sacrificed a whole lot on the personal side. If I'd had more free time, I'd have done the same things. I think my wife has been very satisfied with staying at home. She's never showed any interest other than being a mother and a housewife, and that was okay by me."

Dr. Allen, a community practitioner, was among those like Dr. Conley, who did not think his wife sacrificed her career for family. On balance, he asserted that she was satisfied with her lifestyle. He repeated the same story in both the extended phase (2004–2011) and ending phase (2011–2016), acknowledging that his wife was an anomaly in their community: "My wife put me through medical school and quit teaching six months before our daughter was born. She never went back, which I was thrilled about. She knows it was the exact right thing to do; but nonworking females are so often looked down on by everyone else. She gets all the time asked, 'Could you volunteer for this because you don't have a job?' It was the best thing ever for our kids. Still my wife was accused of being a single mom because I was never there" (laughing). And five years later, at the ending phase, he lauded her: "She was a trooper. She did the job and I wasn't there. She even got called a single mom because no one ever saw me. She raised our kids. We've been married forty-five years."

Dr. Annas, whose marriage ended in divorce during the extended phase (2004–2011) after their children were grown, recalled in 2016 the reasons for his wife's unhappiness—which were the opposite of Dr. Allen's assertion about his wife. Dr. Annas believes his wife was unhappy after they moved to a Midwest university community because all the married women worked full time. He asserted that she was the anomaly: "I would not say that my wife did not fulfill her own career. I'd say that she never had any ambition to have a definite career. For her being married to somebody who provided good support was a benefit. I don't think my ex-wife sacrificed." As noted earlier in the chapter and elsewhere, Dr. Annas remained fully satisfied in his career and proclaimed that the reasons for his divorce had nothing with his career. Regardless of their wives' choices, both Drs. Allen and Annas emphasized, with different domestic outcomes, that their wives had not sacrificed.

Dr. Melone repeated throughout his career that his wife as a health professional understood what doctors did, which was a major factor in why he considered his marriage a successful one. "Her background gave her the sense that I am important and have a worthwhile profession. Then when we had children, she stepped back from her career and did the important job of getting my kids raised, which was what she always was supposed to be doing. I think that she always understood that medicine from time to time would screw up the routine."

Looking back from the ending phase (2011–2016) on his early years, Dr. Melone justified his wife's satisfaction again and why it was acceptable to give up a full-time health-related professional career: "I think she would say that she did fine. She was always the most important in a global sense, but minute to minute it was, 'I've got to go the hospital.' There was never a question that medicine was more important to me than she was in the general sense. That's why she was willing to put up with so many trips I made to the ER." From my perspective, it is not clear whether so many multiple absences over the years may have added up to a major problem in the way his wife may have assessed the quality of their marriage. Without having interviewed her, there is no way to tell.

Dr. Johnson's spouse had trained in a health-related career and worked part time in that field throughout their whole marriage. He, like Drs. Allen, Rosen, and Melone praised her decision to put children first: "We had four children. One of my sons is a health professional here in town now, and my wife still helps me and also goes in to help him one day a week. I think she's satisfied with the extent of her career, but she would tell you that her primary career has been raising four children. I think she really liked children more than her health career."

Drs. Strelko and Jarvis, on the other hand, admitted that there were sacrifices involved regardless of how they interpreted their wives' perspective. Looking back from the entrenched phase (1994–2004), Dr. Strelko commented, "Raising family is stressful. The major difference between residency and now is that I have to carve out time for my family. I missed a lot of suppers, weekends—how quickly time goes. On the other hand, the added dimensions of having a family has been a very big help. I know a lot of doctors who do nothing but work."

Ten years later, in 2011, he praised his spouse and also served as an informant in comparing himself to his peers: "My wife was supportive, but not always happy. She didn't want to go to the Midwest, but it turned out well. I see so many doctors where their work and home don't mesh. I feel pretty fortunate." But then, expressing a shifting or fluctuation in his views, at the ending phase (2016), he acknowledged, "Yes, absolutely I neglected my personal life, but then I made the conscious decision to have family and not take a job that would prevent me from spending time with them, hence an academic career." In that sense, Dr. Strelko seems to be one of the few to admit to making major career decisions because of the primacy of family factors. But, as his comments across career stages indicate, Dr. Strelko had conflicting views at different phases about the impact of his wife's input into his career-related decisions.

Dr. Jarvis was perhaps the most candid in the early phase, in depicting with humor the sacrifices to his sexual life with his wife and admitting which came first. "There's nothing that kills your libido more than being dead tired. I'm glad I slept with my wife before I started my internship. I think my wife is still resentful of the amount of time I put into my medicine residency because to be very honest, medicine comes before family."

In 2011, however, twenty years later, Dr. Jarvis expressed more sentiments of gratitude to his wife than in earlier phases: "I'm more appreciative of the sacrifices that people did to make me successful, mainly my wife. She raised the four kids and does an extensive amount of volunteering. She's the main reason why I was able to succeed." And five years later, Dr. Jarvis, already retired, again reflected, "I think that I was very self-focused for a good long time, longer than I should have been. I would like to think my wife doesn't hold that too much against me since we've been married forty-one years. Still, I could have been a better dad and a better husband."

Wives and the Milestone Measures

During our interviews, I asked the physicians about milestones in their lives so that they could reflect on life-changing events that transformed them, particularly in a professional context. (Those milestones were introduced earlier in chapter 2 in their self-narratives on career choices.) While discussing these milestones, several of the physicians spontaneously mentioned their wives in some capacity, often in relation to decision-making about career factors. In a few instances, their spouse (specifically) or their family (more broadly) was identified as part of a milestone, as a determining factor on where they settled or whether they changed settings.

The extensiveness of bringing in the personal to the professional varied, but more than half of the physicians mentioned their spouses and/or children in responding to milestones without prompting, whether as a positive or negative factor (Drs. Lash, Finast, Strelko, Cahn, Nolan, Mahoney, Allen, Lynch, Jarvis, Beech, and Johnson). Dr. Cahn commented, "A milestone was my wife dragging me into taking the SAMS residency reluctantly." Dr. Beech rather casually replied, "Well, your usual things: You get married. You have children. Those were milestones I guess."

Drs. Nolan, Jarvis, and Mahoney met their wives during house staff training, which they assert affected their and their wives' futures. Said Dr. Nolan, "A milestone during my OB-GYN rotation was meeting my wife. She worked as a health practitioner before the kids, and then stopped." Dr. Mahoney elaborated on significant life-changing personal events: "I wouldn't have met my wife and had my kids if I went anywhere other than SAMS. And there were considerations of my wife who was working and wanted to stay in the SAMS city." Dr. Allen was emphatic: "Fatherhood was more life changing than becoming a doctor. My girl was born in 1979 in my residency, and my boy three years later at the beginning of my practice." Dr. Johnson noted, "In the last ten years, milestones included my practice taking off and having kids."

Many of the cohort were specific in continuing to describe the role their wives played in choosing the city or community and/or the setting where they practiced. In some cases, it clearly caused tension and even conflict whether or not it was a determinative factor on where they finally settled. For Dr. Johnson, as Drs. Finast and Cahn discussed earlier, it was decisive in his residency and fellowship decisions: "I decided to stay in [the SAMS city] because my wife was a health student and two years behind in school there. So, the reasons for choosing SAMS were personal and financial, nothing else."

For sure, almost all the cohort expressed appreciation for their wives' presumed willingness to put their own careers on a back burner or play second fiddle to their primary role as homemaker and mother, even if they worked part time outside the home. For the most part, these doctors seemed content to let their wives "do their own thing" or have their own space, as long as it did not interfere with that domestic role, as Dr. Rosen recalled at the ending phase (2011–2016): "We're happily married for forty-two years now. Maybe it's because I was in academics, or maybe it's my personality. My wife worked half time for most of my career. She's a health professional and very happy with her career. She is pleased that I can afford the quality of lifestyle so she was able to only work half time. She's been extremely supportive. I made a really good decision."

As an exception, however, Dr. Polikoff presented his wife's truncated career path at the ending phase (2011–2016) in great detail. Ironically, as he was fully satisfied with his career since he left academia at the end of the early phase (1984–1994), he was also blunt in his characterization of her disappointed or resentful feelings: "She always wishes she had done something different. She was teaching in a health professional program at SAMS. She stopped when we had our four kids and went back to work when the youngest was fourteen. After other jobs, she retired about three years ago. She always wishes she had done something else."

There were very few exceptions to their assertion that their wives were content with taking a back seat. Besides Dr. Polikoff, the two clearest exceptions were the two wives who were more than a decade younger than their husbands. Age disparity was a factor for Dr. Cahn's third spouse and for Dr. Lash, who acknowledged that he married his wife "later in life." Those two women were described as having full professional careers before they were married and continued doing so and were depicted as partners intellectually and professionally. Their wives' support for them appeared to mean more than just providing emotional understanding. Dr. Lash said proudly, "My personal life always impacts decision making. There's no doubt that I wouldn't be an executive leader without her. She's a great asset. I get good counseling from a fully educated professional."

At the ending phase (2011–2016), spouses also came into play in responses to questions about decision-making in relation to retirement plans and conjectures about how they would be spending their time after departing from their medical positions. Not surprisingly, almost everyone mentioned spending more time with their grandchildren along with engaging in sports and recreational activities, reading, and travel, presumably with their wives.

Overall, the physicians' relationships with their wives seems typical of the gender disparities in work and family life in the United States for their generation regardless of the career or background of the man. The physicians may have downplayed the tensions that emerged at different phases, especially during the first half of their career, when most admitted that their work came first. Others may not have experienced tensions because their wives accepted a more traditional female role in domestic life. Nevertheless, their families, if not their wives specifically, loomed large in their reflections on their careers as evidenced by how often domestic life or life outside of medicine was raised by them spontaneously, particularly in the question about milestones. I regret not being more intentional in focusing on such a critical aspect of the changing gender roles and relationships in work and family life in the last several decades. Given what was offered, I can only speculate that the imbalance was larger than they were aware of or assumed.

Personal Struggles

In addition to exploring how the physicians viewed their spouses within the context of their professional and personal lives, I also sought to document other areas of the physicians' personal lives that might have had a significant impact on their careers, or vice versa, particularly relating to any personal struggles they encountered.

Up until the ending phase (2011–2016), seven of the physicians had revealed personal struggles at some point that had impacted their professional lives, including spousal separation or divorce, drug addiction, heavy drinking, and their own physical illnesses and/or those of their wives. One doctor also revealed that he struggled to accept and eventually come out as homosexual. Almost all those physicians with significant personal issues were classified as mixed or negative at many career stages, whether or not they specifically described their personal struggles as adversely affecting their professional circumstances directly. Dr. Annas, however, whose divorce occurred before the ending phase, was one exception since he was satisfied professionally throughout his career. By 2016, eleven of the cohort revealed personal or private issues from either earlier times or at this final phase.

Dr. Lynch, "came out" about his sexuality between the early phase (1980–1984) and established phase (1984–1994), raising it for the first time with me in the established phase. He asserted that his transformative personal change did not directly affect his view of his work in spite of a couple of failed professional partnerships and changing settings by then. During the entry phase (1979–1980), Dr. Lynch had been married to a woman, which apparently lasted through his SAMS residency and fellowship completed in a western state, where he remained. As he explained five years later in the established phase in 1994, he was extremely unhappy while married, although he did not explain whether his private struggle with his sexuality was the source of that unhappiness. But he did discuss how being "closeted" while married and having children negatively affected their lives: "I am divorced. I came out of the closet two years ago as a gay man, and I'm comfortable with it. I'm functioning as a single parent of two (ages nine and twelve). My kids suffered some, for sure." Although he asserted that his sexual orientation did not affect his professional practice before he came out, he described difficulties in that prior period: "That was a time when I was depressed. I was on Prozac, but I was careful to make sure I continued to do a good job. I worried about coming out since most gay physicians are closeted. This western city [where he moved after the residency at SAMS to pursue an oncology fellowship] is an open community. I don't hang my sexuality on my door, but I'm not hiding it anymore. My children know and now are comfortable with my life."

In addition to Dr. Lynch, Dr. Paul was the other physician who I am aware of who lived in what appeared to be a same-sex relationship, although he never disclosed it to me. Dr. Paul passed away in 2012 but left SAMS sometime before the extended interview cycle in 2011. An obituary about Dr. Paul located in 2012 noted he was survived by a male-named partner. I assume but cannot confirm that he was in a same-sex relationship at the time of his death, which may have been hidden while at SAMS for many years prior. I wrongly assumed over time that he was single since unlike his peers, he never discussed having a domestic relationship with either gender, and in response to a question about "recommending medicine to your children" indicated that he did not have children.

Looking back, I found that Dr. Paul revealed that "I go home every night and drink too much," in responding to a question about handling stress in the established phase. It's not clear whether his admitted excessive drinking may have been related to other personal or professional struggles at the time, which resulted in his unhappiness about his career. He also revealed that he had an illness that occurred during that same established time frame: "In the last ten years, I had a disease which affected control of my muscles. It's gone now, but I was thirty-five years old. I took drugs, saw a psychiatrist. It was a bad time, but then I got better spontaneously. It changed my view of patients with disabilities and AIDS. I gave up going out, driving, sports. I learned what it was like to live with a disability." Unfortunately, I uncovered his leaving SAMS and his subsequent death several years after the entrenched phase (2004), so I never had additional in-depth conversation with him about the later phases of his professional and personal life.

Dr. Mahoney, who faced more challenges than most of the cohort, admitted that his personal life affected his professional life. These struggles included helping his wife who suffered from a long-term illness resulting in a chronic disability, as well as a long-term illness of his own. In 1994, at the end of the established phase (1984–1994), he was most candid about the difficult circumstances of family life, describing serious surgeries that his wife had undergone in years past: "Over the last two years there was significant stress because my wife has had three serious surgeries from symptoms which first occurred seven years ago. She has been gradually recovering, but with some permanent disability." Ten years later, in 2004, he disclosed that he had an addiction to pain-killing drugs connected with major surgery he had undergone a few years earlier: "It was my own realization that led me to say, 'This has got to stop. I need some help.'" He sought treatment and, according to him, had been "sober" from then on.

At the end of the extended phase in 2011, in addition to revealing that he remained under supervision, he described how the addiction and recovery affected his practice: "My approach is a little different when I'm talking to an active addict or alcoholic who is wheeling, dealing, conniving, and trying to get a prescription for drugs. I have no patience. But when somebody comes who's hit rock bottom, seeking help, not unlike where I was at one point, I feel immense compassion. Not infrequently I give up my own anonymity to tell them there is a way out."

Dr. Cahn revealed a major change in his health status in the established phase (1984–1994), something he concluded that would impact his empathy for patients. "I had major incident which almost ended my career. I was frightened to death.

I had emergency surgery a day later and was out of work for six to eight weeks. That was a major life-altering event because it allowed me to be a patient and see things that I would never have seen. I don't look at patients or nurses the same way anymore." Dr. Cahn also described ways that this injury, along with other chronic illnesses that he revealed in the extended phase (2004–2011), would impact his motivation for maintaining his health. However, by his own admission, these disabilities did not change his work habits.

Dr. Cahn's revelation that becoming a patient himself profoundly changed his attitude, if not behavior, toward his patients is a revelation that several other physicians made as well, including Drs. Paul and Mahoney. It is worth noting that this role reversal was one of the few conditions that physicians highlighted as having notably changed their behavior toward patients (Klitzman, 2008; Pearl, 2014b; Weiner, 2017).

The Decision to Stop Practicing: Confronting Aging and Illness Later in Life

Although several of the physicians discussed their personal and/or family health issues before or during the extended phase (2004–2011), these topics escalated in the latest stage of their careers. Perhaps all professionals would answer questions about health and well-being the same way at this similar age (mostly in their mid- to late sixties), but the aging of medical professionals is also a public and professional issue (Dellinger, Pellegrini, et al., 2017; Merritt Hawkins, 2015). As the health of some of cohort declined in their later years, several of them tied their health status directly to their ability or desire to continue practicing as a physician.

For example, in 2011 Dr. Conley, the first of the cohort to retire, described moving on from illness into retirement: "I don't think I'll be going back to work. I had some health issues over the last two years with some internal problems and that set me back physically." He added, "I'm looking forward to some more grandchildren and playing more golf. I'm looking forward to finally getting all that behind me and getting my energy level back. I don't have anything else in mind for now other than getting healthy." He described a postretirement life that includes active leadership in a health organization and volunteering in a community clinic.

Dr. Finast, who was still semiactive in 2011, is another physician who decided to leave practice because of the impact of health issues. Almost eerily, he revealed after a few minutes into the ending phase phone interview in 2016: "My kids said to my wife several years ago, 'Dad doesn't seem as smart as he used to.' So I went through a battery of tests. It was confirmed that I have a mild cognitive impairment. That was one of the signals that it was time for me to get out. I didn't want to fully retire because I liked being a doctor. Finally, it was clear that I needed to get out. The department chairman made a plan to distribute my patients to others. I said a lot of goodbyes and retired in 2013." He described needing to make plans for the future, continuing to take some trips with family, and do some more traveling. "I'm trying to keep up with our kids." In spite of describing future days with hobbies, gym and family, his lament about his fate and future was clear and sad, since he seemed to sorely miss his professional connections more than anything.

Other physicians, however, despite confronting serious health issues at later stages of their life, maintained that those issues would not necessarily be a determining factor for their retirement. Dr. Nolan, for example, who apparently was a serious runner his whole life, revealed, "Let me tell you one thing that did happen to me. I noticed in 2011 [apparently right after my interview with him that year] I was not physically capable of doing things as well as I used to. I used to run marathons. I got really bad pains in my chest. It turns out I have a congenitally abnormal heart, and six months ago I underwent cardiac surgery with a valve replacement. The surgeon said with alarm, 'We're scheduling you tomorrow!' I had the operation. Scary, but now I feel better than I have in ten years." Dr. Nolan was quick to point out that he is planning to leave practice in two years not as much because of his health but because "it is not so much 'fun' anymore." Once again, the operative word "fun" appears again as a way to judge whether someone remains in practice.

In the ending phase (2016), Dr. Mahoney also confronted another significant health issue later in his career that had occurred in 2013, which he clearly wanted to reveal to me: "I don't know if your question will include, 'How's my health these days?' The answer is I have developed a neurological condition, and how quickly that will progress in the next five years I don't know. My plan is to continue doing what I've been doing until I can't. It's in the early stages." Although Dr. Mahoney retired that same year in 2013, he expressed a similar sentiment as did Dr. Nolan, emphasizing that it was not the illness that caused him to retire, but rather the frustrating pressure and loss of control over his practice: "I was working at a private hospital until I retired in 2013. It had been my plan to retire some years before, but the economy in 2008 didn't allow me. It was factors such as the EMR as well as changes in the administration of the hospital that all contributed to my leaving. The hospital administration came down hard on waiting times and cut back in personnel. We got visits down to thirty minutes, and then they said twenty minutes, and then it was fifteen minutes. At sixty-two, I said, 'Some folks have to adapt to this new reality, but not me.' I left."

Dr. Mahoney, who seemed to have struggled more than others in the cohort over his career with personal and family issues, noted that he was still contemplating an avocational future in spite of this deteriorating physical condition: "I would continue to travel; I just got my daughter married. I have toyed with relaxing in my wood shop. I've had the opportunity to read more. My wife and I might decide it's time to move after thirty years raising two girls."

At this late stage in their careers, however, whether or not they faced serious illness, all of the physicians were in some ways confronting the question of their age, health, and retirement. Dr. Rosen, for example, who planned to stay in academia for several more years, nevertheless for the first time mentioned in this ending phase (2016) that he was paying careful attention to his health: "I'm not looking forward to arthritis and not being in the health I am now, although I'm in much better shape than the last time we talked. I lost about thirty-five pounds. I became a runner. I hope I can maintain that for the next five to ten years at least." Always positive and still healthy, he nevertheless had retirement on his mind as he used a sports analogy to contemplate his future: "Everybody wants me to continue teaching for at least five years given good health. I'm turning sixty-seven. I have friends who are supposed to tell me if I'm starting to flip intellectually, because as I phrase it, 'I don't want to be Willie Mays.' He played a year too long. I don't want to have people saying, 'Rosen was really great one time.' I look forward to good golf games and continuing my research and teaching. My passion is trying to figure out how to reduce a common illness."

Dr. Strelko presented the complexities of his health and retirement issue for himself and then for his wife, and then serving as an informant, for physicians more generally: "I just turned sixty-six. I'm at an age right now where in the next year or so I have to decide whether I want to work part or full time. The stress of relocating is something I'm not looking forward to. My wife has been spectacular for thirty-five years. It's her time. She's only in fair health since she had surgery last year. My health is good. I enjoy work unlike some who are counting the days until they retire."

But as he continued, Dr. Strelko contradicted himself. The pressure he felt related to his health appeared to be generated internally as well as by his peer culture. "I can tell you in the last five years, I'm starting to feel my age. If I sprain or twist something, it doesn't bounce back the way it used to. Yeah, getting older sucks! But, I'm not being pushed out."

He then presented a very personal concern related to aging and discrimination that was never acknowledged by the cohort, as he moved back and forth among first, second, and third person: "There's a lot of age issues. When I moved out here, it was my third major move, at fifty-eight. That's getting to an age where there's discrimination. I see it all the time. You get up into your early sixties and you want to switch to a new job; the opportunities are fewer for leadership-type ones. I did make that move and it turned out well. One of the things that we doctors are not good at—you've probably seen this in all your interviews—they become so defined by their being a doctor that doing something else is hard to imagine. You're at risk for stopping being who you have been for the last thirty-plus years. So that's intimidating. It's a little scary to leave."

In discussing transitions and termination, Dr. Strelko moved from those personal circumstances to the professional realm in raising the critical issue of aging and ageism: "Some of us have talked with a national organization of clinical oncologists recently about older docs and how most institutions don't know what to do with them. They have tremendous experience to teach younger people. Transitioning older docs into semiretirement is poorly done at most medical institutions, including my past and current one." Dr. Annas, an academic cardiologist, raised a similar issue for the profession as did Dr. Strelko. In discussing his future, Dr. Annas thought aging is handled well at his institution, while recognizing that his department is not the norm: "In the next five years, I plan to continue working full time, then drop down to fifty to sixty percent. Here, we have a long history of keeping senior clinicians, but their cutting hours and responsibilities. They do more patient care and teaching. We hire older clinicians in their mid-sixties from competing institutions who don't value them. We want our younger people to build their research careers."

In his relatively new position as an academic administrator at the ending phase (2016), Dr. O'Brian discussed prospects for his future, hinting at some of the underlying subtle pressures he was facing: "I'll continue working the next three to five years here if they'll have me. But I am getting old. My wife and I have talked about retirement and how to transition. I haven't done it yet. Old department chairs don't necessarily die; they get involved in other activities! I could teach on a part-time basis." I struck a sensitive cord inadvertently when I probed further about his retirement: "You sound like my wife! 'What are you going to do when you grow up?' Those are questions I haven't sorted out. My dean is asking me the same thing: 'What are you going to do? We're not throwing you out now, but when do you want to retire?'"

At this same time, Dr. Lynch was also trying to figure out his future career trajectory. He too was not looking forward to "getting old and sick." He added, "But I'm not ready to retire." Dr. Jarvis succinctly summed up the general feelings about himself and his cohort as he stated what he is not looking forward to: "Getting old! Getting older is a bummer." Clearly, failing health and aging are on these physicians' minds for themselves and for their peers of comparable age. These profound issues resonated whether they were still practicing or not (Dellinger, Pellegrini, et al., 2017).

Hidden Issues of Spirituality

Beyond a personal or family illness, other revelations of a personal nature were uncovered in the ending phase (2011–2016), including those related to spirituality, which ended up reframing comments made by some physicians in earlier phases. I did not probe issues relating to religion and spirituality directly over the course of this project (which is an example of how a researcher's interests and biases may affect what an interviewee reveals or not). Dr. Johnson made an unprompted comment during the final interview about how religion had impacted his career, although occasional studies have appeared about physicians and their religious beliefs and practices (Curlin, Chin, et al., 2006; Robinson, Cheng, et al., 2017). It is a pertinent issue I missed. Dr. Johnson suggested that my omission of these matters could also be construed as an implicit criticism: "You asked about whether my political views affected my medical practice, but you never asked and you need to ask people about their religious beliefs." He then expounded on its role in his life and work as an oncologist: "If you have faith in God, and you pray and you look for guidance, that helps you through a whole lot of things. You're more at peace with life and with your direction. I have one patient a week die. I personally think it's impossible to do this job if you don't have some faith."

In response, I asked him to offer some thoughts on how he thought other physicians might view this issue: "Do you think that the spiritual or psychosocial component in medicine is becoming more important?" Dr. Johnson replied, "I think there are a lot of doctors who are people of faith. I see them all the time at church. We have different conferences on the topic. The idea that you can understand as much complexity as there is in the world, in biology, in life and assume that that's random is crazy." In response to whether he raises it with patients, he commented, "My job is to function as a physician, but if people are open to that, I think you can incorporate that into the conversation."

At the end of the established phase (1984–1994), Dr. Boswell had also mentioned that he went to church every Sunday but did not have time for other church activities given his frenetic schedule. When I reread that passage, it became clear to me that he lamented not being able to do more with this religious aspect of his life. Dr. Polikoff, a practicing member of the Jewish faith, had identified to me early on that locating himself in a Jewish community was important to him and his wife, but I never asked him about how his religious practices affected his professional realm. Besides these examples, no other physicians spontaneously offered comments regarding their spiritual side. Unfortunately, without any direct questions on this topic, the issue was neither raised nor explored more fully, which is a limitation of the study.

Conclusion

The impact of personal circumstances outside of medicine on components of their medical career revealed some expected as well as unanticipated responses and self-reflection. As important, it brought to the surface some of my hidden biases and blind spots. The impact of the researcher on their research project is in recent years gaining more attention, especially when related to qualitative studies and narrative methods (Charon, 2008; Muhammad, Wallerstein, et al., 2014; Murphy, 2018).

Asking about their personal lives resulted in many of these physicians focusing on their relationship with me, asking me questions as well as commenting on a particular question I asked or the absence of one as noted by Dr. Johnson. Indeed, in some critical instances they provided the prompts that led to more intimate and deeper revelations such as life-altering illnesses and disabilities. What often began as a more traditional qualitative interview at times turned into a deep narrative reflection by these physicians, in large measure because of their trust in and relationship with me over time. They opened up about their pain, struggles, uncertainties, and even sadness.

*Physicians' Happiest and
Unhappiest Times, and Their
Wishes and Misses throughout
Their Careers*

The focus of this chapter is on the factors contributing to the happiness (and unhappiness) of these physicians. In earlier chapters, the components of satisfaction and dissatisfaction in their careers were presented at each phase, based on patient, peers, and practice themes. This chapter presents the physicians' responses at each phase to the open-ended existential questions, "When were you most happy?" and "When were you least happy?" These questions speak to a deeper, more personal meaning given to their lives in retrospect and in real time. While the query was not specifically tied to their professional life, most focused on their career given the context, but some did not.

Additionally, this chapter presents the cohort's reflections from each phase on what they "miss" and what they "wish." And during the final ending phase (2011–2016), the physicians were also asked a significant question about whether they had any regrets. Similar to the questions discussed in prior chapters, these general queries were used in an attempt to elicit from the physicians a more profound reflection on their sense of self, often hidden from others. It should be noted that the whole cohort provided deep and heartfelt responses to these subjects and that their reflections were sometimes consonant with, and in some instances separate from, how they were classified on the Satisfaction Index. Their recollections on when they were happiest—and why they felt that way—provide additional insight into their feelings about their lives that often go beyond their work.

As they moved through their careers and their lives became more complex because of both professional and personal factors (e.g., family and personal growth, external encroachment on their practice, illnesses), a number of the physicians' perspectives on when they felt most happy or unhappy changed. Others, however, despite numerous changes to their personal and professional lives, tended to describe the same memories over time as they reflected on these questions about happiness, unhappiness, longing, and regret. In the following section, I present the different ways that these physicians addressed these particular issues, first discussing those who continued to identify the same period as happiest or unhappiest over most or all career phases, followed by those who had different or fluctuating responses at each phase. After that, I present a third group, who seemed to live more in the moment, as their responses to when they were happiest included

"Now." In the second part of the chapter, I highlight their responses to what they "missed" and "wished," and if they had any regrets at the end of their careers.

"When Were You Most Happy?"

Physicians Responding Similarly across Career Phases

Most of the physicians whose answers focused on the same phase throughout their career maintained that their happiest times were experienced during medical school and/or at the beginning of their practice years, that is, during the entry (or even pre-entry, medical school years) and the early phases of their career. Looking back, they perceived lower stress levels and a more manageable work/life balance as contributing to the happiness factor. Several added—half seriously and half in jest—that their ability to play sports or engage in recreational pursuits contributed to the happiness equation. The stereotype of doctors playing golf rang true since most of the cohort mentioned it.

Dr. Ross, for example, a community practitioner, identified his time just after medical school and early career as his happiest times. It was a perspective that he maintained throughout his career. At the end of the early phase (1980–1984), he suggested, "Happiest is a good golf game now. Also, when I was in med school that was a very happy time. I had a sailboat; nothing like being in med school with your wife. Then, after a few years in practice here, it got easy and you could mess around more." Later, during the established phase (1984–1994), and then again at the entrenched phase (1994–2004), he continued to cite those early stages of his career as the time when he was most happy. When he was asked this question at the ending phase (2011–2016), however, his recollection of when he was most happy shifted slightly forward away from med school to emphasize his happiest time as being when he completed his residency and began to practice: "When I started to practice, we had a nice little house, two children, young and healthy—really happy." It is worth pointing out that, at each stage, Dr. Ross included his spouse and family life in his happiest times.

Similar to Dr. Ross, Dr. Strelko also identified his personal happiness with contexts outside of medicine. And like Dr. Ross, he maintained throughout his career that his happiest time was when he was still in the early phases of his career, and his children were young, particularly the early phase (1980–1984) and established phase (1984–1994). Several years later, at the end of the entrenched phase (1994–2004), he made the association with his family again as he recalled his happiest time being in the early phase, "when I was in my fellowship and married and having kids." In 2016, at the end of his career, he continued to highlight that period as the happiest time: "The happiest time was probably when our kids were young, at home. Plus, that was a good stretch there when work was really good."

Like Drs. Ross and Strelko, the other physicians who consistently reflected that their happiest times took place during the early phases of their careers spoke about a youthful enthusiasm, family life, and an emphasis on the excitement of learning. Dr. Annas, an academic practitioner, described, "I was happiest in my early career days in [Mid-Central Medical Center] during the second and third year of my cardiology fellowship. Things shifted away from direct fatiguing responsibility to thinking and decision-making type work. I was a relatively new father, buying our first home, starting out—new things I'd never done before. Exciting."

Feelings of having "made it," without the impending burden of the economic or legal factors that would affect so many in their middle and late careers, were common. Dr. Paul, for example, reflected in his early phase (1980–1984): "My fourth year of medical school was so easy. So relaxed, lots of reading. You mastered your discipline and there was no night call." Years later at the established phase (1984–1994) and entrenched phase (1994–2004), Dr. Paul again recalled his training years at SAMS, this time "as chief resident I was the happiest. The combination of endless enthusiasm, energy, youth, and the mix of responsibilities including patient care and administration. That's how I found out what I wanted to do."

Dr. Melone, a community practitioner, also reiterated throughout his career that his happiest time was during medical school and his senior residency. During the early phase (1980–1984), he noted, "In my senior year in medical school, hours were reasonable, you could read everything. As a senior resident, people started leaving you alone and you were running the show. I was comfortable with my job and making money more than before because I moonlighted and my wife was working at that time." Later, in 2004, twenty-five years after his time at SAMS, he recalled once again, "Happiest was probably medical school. I had just been married. I always wanted to be a doctor and here I was going to be one; that was kind of cool. Maybe a close second was when I first started practice for the same reason. I could say, 'Wow, I've made it.'"

As the physicians reflected on their happiest moments, their perceptions of their years at SAMS often drastically improved the further removed they were from their residency period. It may be hard to pinpoint the full impact of this on the physicians' decisions about when they were most happy, but many of the physicians who remembered those early years as their happiest highlighted the pleasure they recalled when looking forward to their future careers. Dr. Conley, for example, who would identify throughout his career that his residency years were his happiest, suggested at the extended phase (2004–2011), "At the end of residency, you still had this view that your career was ahead of you and there was a lot you were going to accomplish, there was a lot to look forward to. The best is yet to be." And in the entrenched period ten years later he recalled that same sense of accomplishment: "I was happiest in residency. There's a lot of satisfaction because you felt like you were learning; you knew a lot and you had all this ability that you didn't have three or five years earlier." At the ending phase (2011–2016), still highlighting those years as his happiest, he described how much "fun" they were: "A great time was when I was a senior resident. That was fun because you reached the top of the heap at that phase. You were too dumb to know you didn't know everything, because you thought you did."[1]

Physicians Responding Differently across Career Phases

In contrast to those physicians who continued to highlight the same time period throughout their careers as being their happiest time, there were also a number of physicians who did not identify one single time period as being their happiest but instead shifted their perspectives on this feeling over time. For these individuals, developments in their professional lives, personal milestones, and manageable work environments all came to define their greatest happiness at different phases of their careers. The amount of variation in these physicians' responses speaks to the dynamism of medical practice and the complexity of their experiences across all phases.

Among the physicians who did not continue to identify a single moment as their happiest, many—particularly the community physicians—defined periods of greatest happiness based on when they felt lower stress levels and increased capacity for self-care, specifically in the form of sleep and time off. These criteria were particularly prominent in responses during later career phases after they had experienced decades of long nights and weekends on call no matter how financially successful they were.

Dr. Allen, for example, when reflecting at the early phase (1980–1984), named his fourth year in medical school as his happiest because "there were no nights and weekends. Married with no kids. It was carefree if there ever were such a thing." But later, at the end of the established phase (1984–1994), ten years into his community practice, he identified that current phase as his happiest, while similarly emphasizing less stress and rest as key rationales: "I stopped having to work every other night, so I was happiest in these last ten years." In the entrenched phase (1994–2004), he again mentioned the time in medical school, using a similar reason as he did twenty years earlier: "Happiest when I was first married, working my fanny off with no money and no kids." But he also suggested the current (entrenched) phrase could be considered similarly: "Now is also wonderful. Kids out of the house, making lots of money and doing what I like to do every day." And once again, it was the easier workload that he highlighted. Finally, at the ending phase (2011–2016), he noted that his happiest time was in current time period, again using sleep and less stress as the criteria: "Probably from six years ago until three years ago was the best. I was on call every eighth night instead of every second, third, or fourth night; and every eighth weekend. That made all the difference."

Similar to Dr. Allen, Dr. Lynch, another community practitioner, identified different time periods as being his "happiest" including the current period, whichever it was. He too frequently focused on the issues of stress and rest. During the ending phase (2011–2016), for example, he highlighted that current time period as his happiest because of the freedom and lack of stress (at the time, he was working part time with no administrative responsibilities). In earlier career phases, he had also identified work/life balance as a major contributor to happiness, something that became increasingly pronounced as his attachment to his identity as a practicing physician began to wane toward the end of his career. As he reflected in 2016,

"I think now is my happiest. My life is good. I feel healthy and I feel mentally well. I'm enjoying the work. I don't feel overly pressured. I'm not exhausted."

In addition to the issues of stress and rest, professional milestones and status were also a consistent theme driving many physicians' perspectives on their levels of happiness. Dr. Mahoney, for example, was focused on his professional status at both the early phase (1980–1984) and ending phase (2011–2016). In the former, he noted that it was his first year after residency: "I had passed my internal medicine boards. I felt like I was getting on with real life for the first time after so many years in school—so to be really independent was the best." Then, forty years later in 2016, having retired three years before, he again pointed at career accomplishments as key criteria for answering this question: "Happiest was probably in the early 90s after I had gotten the feather in my cap for passing my (non-internal medicine) specialty boards, and before that horrible lawsuit against me."

Besides to professional milestones, another major theme in the physicians' rationales for identifying different time periods as their happiest was the importance of personal milestones in their family life and home environment. Some described a mix of personal and professional criteria. For example, early in his career, Dr. Cahn noted the arrival of his children: "I was happiest when my kids were born. Having kids gave me something to take the edge off—but it was difficult being away from them." By the end of his career, however, Dr. Cahn, identified a different time frame as his happiest, and his rationale for doing so was different. It was based on a lack of professional frustration. In 2016, when he was closer to retirement, he noted, "[I was most happy] probably about ten to fifteen years ago before electronic medical records, before reimbursement fell, and before the politics of medicine took over."

Always Happiest in the Present

Among those who changed their opinion regarding when they felt most happy, there was an additional subgroup of doctors who answered consistently that their happiest time was the current period in which they were interviewed. "Now," they would say, or simply claim that they were always happy at each phase of their career. Dr. Lynch, for example, reports consistently that his happiness is rooted in the present moment—for reasons related to both professional and personal factors discussed above. In the early phase (1980–1984), he responded, "Happiest now. My personal life is fine. I'm comfortable with my sexuality, have two kids, comfortable with my practice." (Dr. Lynch "came out" as gay during that phase.) In the entrenched phase (1994–2004) he noted, "I think I've gotten happier as I've gone along." And finally, during the ending (2016) phase he said, "I think now is my happiest time."

Dr. Annas, an academic, also consistently claimed that each phase was his happiest. In the early phase (1980–1984), he said gleefully, "I don't know what I would do or how I would get to happier. I'm perfectly happy now." After moving to North Central Medical Center, he commented similarly about that setting in the extended phase (2004–2011). "I'm happier now than I've ever been." Five years later, in 2016, he concluded, "There's been no one time that's profoundly happier than another." (Dr. Annas who had divorced in that time period is one of the academics who has no set time to retire.)

Dr. Beech, a community practitioner who always rooted his happiness in the present moment, suggested at the end of his career that he wanted to identify two periods as happiest: the current and the early years. "The happiest parts, I would say, if you give me consent to have two times, would be the first few years in practice because it was kind of cool to assert, 'I'm a real doctor now.' Second happiest would be where I am now."

There were also a few doctors who may be defined as outliers because they name a situation or function rather than a stage as to when they were happiest. Dr. Rosen, an academic, said he was always happiest as an educator in his teaching role. In the final phase, he reflected on his happiest times in this way: "It's usually when I'm teaching. It's when I see the lightbulb going off in the students' or the residents' eyes. Those are my happiest moments."

Dr. O'Brian, also an academic, described his happiness during the early phase (1980–1984) in relation to his job being "fun"—patient care and teaching—more so than accomplishing any particular career mobility. Many years later, at the ending phase (2011–16), he still defined his happiness as a function of comfort within his work environment: "In terms of what I've been doing independent of what my rank or title or who I'm supervising, I still have fun taking care of patients, fun running my lab, which is relatively small, and fun teaching students."

As mentioned above, the fondness of many of the cohort for the early years of their careers grew as they progressed in their life and careers. Based on the fact that many of them did not identify those phases as being their happiest times during those earlier stages, this tendency to "forget the bad" seems notable. Increasingly locating their happiness in the entry (or pre-entry) phases as they grew older meant that many were necessarily forgetting or at least omitting many of the negative aspects that they raised in other areas of their interviews or in earlier periods (Mizrahi, 1986). Some of the physicians appeared aware of this. For example, Dr. Beech acknowledged it directly in his responses at the end of the established phase (1984–1994). He reflected, "Time has a way of blurring how bad it was back then." Dr. Nolan, at the ending phase (2011–2016), answered with humor, "The problem is you've got to be careful when you look back because you forget the pain. What's the adage? 'If you forget pain, that explains second children!'"

Dr. Ross, a community practitioner with a combined oncology and general internal medicine practice, called his medical school years his happiest time during the established phase (1984–1994). At the same time, he identified a common rationale for forgetting the bad: "As you think over your life, you forget about all the miserable things; all you remember is the good stuff. My internship was great fun and adventure, but torture while I was doing it. Residency was just a ball; life was fun. Forget the torture!"

There is some commonality in their answers to when they were happiest, regardless of whether the period remained the same across career phases or varied at different points. Their responses illustrate many aspects of medical practice that helped to sustain these physicians throughout the longevity of their careers. Given the depth of personal and professional challenge that these physicians faced during their practice years—and the associated unhappiness that these experiences incited (discussed below)—their reflections on what brought them joy provide a window into the possible motivation to continue on in spite of long hours, sleepless nights, and perceived interference from governmental and legal entities.

"When Were You Most Unhappy?"

Physicians Responding Similarly across Career Phases

Many of the cohort identified their happiest times as being when they were medical students, residents, and/or early practitioners by highlighting low stress, time to focus on learning and discovery, and higher status of their professional lives. However, a different group of physicians cited the same factors but in reverse (i.e., high stress, lack of opportunity to focus on learning and discovery) as the times when they were most unhappy.

As described in detail in my earlier book on these physicians, stress, lack of sleep, and disconnect from patient interaction were the major sources of unhappiness in their training years at SAMS (Mizrahi, 1986). The physicians who cited these entry and pre-entry years as unhappy described them as grueling and barely tolerable, resulting in a "survival mentality" reigning supreme. The "black hole" of medical school, internship, and residency was described by some physicians throughout their careers in terms of the physical and mental demands it placed on them. Five years beyond his house staff experiences, for example, Dr. Melone reflected, "Least happy was my second year of medical school. Hard to adjust. Nobody should ever be that tired. My head fell into a plate of spaghetti every evening when I made it home." Decades later in the entrenched phase (1994–2004) he recalled that same period with the same resentment: "The most aggravating period was the second year of medical school. It was physically demanding as opposed to intellectually demanding." And again, at the ending phase (2011–2016) with continued specificity, he said, "The second year of medical school was dreadful because the guys who were teaching were different than the guys giving the exams. It didn't matter how much effort you put in. In my internship I remember being too tired to spit. I swore I was never going to be that tired again."

These same physicians who continually recalled elements of the internship and residency periods with emotion noted the deep self-doubt and insecurity they experienced about managing an unreasonable workload. As Dr. Lynch at the entrenched phase (2004) reflected poignantly, "Internship was really the worst. Because you're physically exhausted and mentally exhausted, you didn't have the confidence you needed, and the support systems were terrible." In 2016, in the ending phase of practice, he once again recalled, "My residency was pretty unhappy. I think I was completely overwhelmed and stressed out. And then with my fellowship, there were pros and cons. I was still physically tired and still stressed out."

Interestingly, and similar to their responses about when they were happiest, when asked about their unhappiest times, some of the doctors' answers remained consistent throughout each phase, while some added an additional unhappiness factor once they reached the ending period (2011–2016). During the early phase (1980–1984), Dr. Ross spoke about his unhappiness related to stressors then: "Least happy was third month of internship—I wondered what I was doing. There was no relief; that period ties with the first six months of practice. You see things you never saw before and can't refer out. It was so stressful trying to figure out what you can and cannot do." In his mid-career, at the entrenched phase (1994–2004), he again spoke of stress related to his lack of competence and confidence at the time: "I was unhappiest in my internship for sure. You're not comfortable with what you're doing. You hadn't seen enough to know what's going on." But at the ending phase (2011–2016), like several other physicians, he went on to incorporate an additional major contributor to his unhappiness—namely, external intrusion: "Every time that boards of medical examiners or lawyers bother me, I am profoundly unhappy. It happens just often enough to become too much, and it really bugs the crap out of me." It should be noted however, that those externally related themes were not often mentioned in response to the unhappiest time question, even for those who have been sued once or more.

Dr. Rosen continued to be an outlier as well in his unhappiness responses. His unhappiness was experienced as a disconnectedness from the real world of patient care. After answering similarly at each phase, he once again recalled almost verbatim the same two unhappiest times during the ending phase (2011–2016): "I would say that the two times that I was least happy; one was my second year of medical school. I hated sitting in the classroom. And second was the year that I spent doing renal research. I missed patients so much that those months were miserable."

Physicians Responding Differently over Time

Most physicians' answers to the question of when they were unhappiest varied during their career. Some of the themes they cited when describing their unhappiest time mirrored themes the doctors cited for happiness. To the same extent that low stress levels and greater work/life balance are referenced as contributing to their happiest times, perceived stress and inability to meet professional and personal needs simultaneously were revealed by the cohort as primary sources of unhappiness.

At the early phase (1980–1984), for example, Dr. Conley first complained about the physical ramifications of his work: "You are so tired so when you get home, you can't do anything; it is awful. I didn't like being tired all the time." Later in 1994, once he became more established in his career, he related some of this stress to what he has internalized as professional expectations for his role as a physician: "Long days, demanding patients, compulsive feelings you had to get everything done, get all these charts off your desk before you go home; answer every message—because that's what a good doctor was supposed to do. This makes me so unhappy." As Dr. Conley continued his career into the entrenched phase (1994–2004), his unhappiness focus shifted yet again; this time he voiced his unhappiness with the "business part of medicine" and expressed "uncertainty about the future of health care in the next five to ten years." By the time we talked again, he had been retired for six years, the first of the physicians to do so. He identified his unhappiest time as "when we had all that managed care scare; there was a lot of stress, and it wasn't fun" (probably referring to the years from 1994 to 2004 when, as discussed in chapter 8, many of the physicians faced significant disillusionment).

Among the physicians whose perspectives on their unhappiest times changed, many cited a lack of peer support as a significant factor. At each career phase, a group of physicians expressed extremely unhappy feelings about being alone or isolated in their practice even when they presumably were surrounded by professional and support staff (see separate chapter 5 on peer relationships). For some, this manifested as insecurity about their roles and responsibilities. Dr. Lynch recounted his entry years at SAMS during the established phase (1984–1994): "Worst was the ER in my first month as a senior resident. No one was around. I was in charge. I think I did a good job, but I always felt vulnerable." At other career stages, he focused more on stress (in the early phase [1980–1984]) and unrealistic patient and peer expectations (in the entrenched phase [1994–2004]).

Dr. Nolan's response during the early phase (1980–1984) also shed light on the commonality of this feeling during the cohort's transition from medical training to licensed practitioner: "They can't prepare you for every type of practice. In internship you had a whole lot of peer support. Around here in my group practice, you're still on your own. No one cares." Dr. Beech expressed a similar sentiment about inadequate peer support in the beginning of his practice from the established phase (1984–1994): "I was least happy in my internship and then in my first two years of practice—managing your first challenging patient; you're all alone."

In the latter part of their careers, lack of peer support became more associated with office politics and social dynamics, rather than practice insecurity. Dr. Paul, whose unhappiness was rooted in the pressures of his career development at the early phase (1980–1984), came to resent the interpersonal strife he experienced in the workplace over time. In 2004, at the entrenched phase (1994–2004), he lamented, again highlighting the word *fun* as a key criterion: "This past year I was truly unhappy, knowing I had to come in to work every day with people in charge who I felt were at odds with me. There was no collaboration; there was no fun."

Beyond the hostile work cultures that many of the cohort identified, another unhappiness theme emerged unexpectedly: negative perceptions of medical reform. For most this feeling was expressed in later career phases, but for some of the cohort a connection was made between major public policies and their daily lives early on. For example, Dr. Conley, a community practitioner in gastroenterology, noted feeling this in the early phase (1980–1984), as he remarked, "Changes coming are negative and are making me unhappy, the infringement on the practice of medicine. There are more and more rules and regulations. Government is dictating what to do and how, and how much to charge." During the ending phase (2011–2016), he broadened the scope of the type of infringement that caused him unhappiness in his practice: "I remember when we had all that managed care scare. There was a lot of stress back then, including the business part in constructing our offices and assuming more debt, plus the accreditation process. These were all giant hassles and created profound unhappiness. And now add the uncertainty about future of health care in next five to ten years."

With all these demands and stresses at work, a few of the physicians recalled the effects of their schedules on their home lives, which caused them particular unhappiness. (This dimension on the intersection between their personal and professional lives is also discussed further in chapter 9.) At the early phase (1980–1984), Dr. Finast named when he was most unhappy: "Internship was really bad. My wife was unhappy, and there were two small kids. I didn't get to see them very much. My vacation was gone, and I was depressed." Dr. Nolan expressed a similar sentiment looking back from the established phase (1984–1994): "Least happy was during my first year of practice. I was spending a lot of time in the office and hospital. I was working my buns off. During that first year or two, I didn't have any time at home." In subsequent interviews, Dr. Finast did not speak again about family sources of unhappiness. And Dr. Nolan trends with the rest of the cohort in focusing more on work than on his personal life.

While the achievement of status defined many physicians' happiness throughout their careers, a contrary theme emerged as contributing toward their unhappiness. For several physicians, anxiety about upward and forward mobility in their careers stirred deep angst from the very beginning of their careers. Dr. Paul spoke during the established phase (1984–1994) of a time in his early years where he was deeply shaken by a professional setback: "I was least happy in 1992. I was let go and humiliated; my self-esteem was destroyed. After my leadership failure, I was directionless and left in dishonor."

In the ending phase (2011–2016), professional status was discussed more in relation to professional identity. Dr. Finast expressed these sentiments when he was already retired: "I was not happy to leave. It was so much of what I did and who I was." At this final phase, he discussed other unhappiness factors that emerged later in his career: "Toward the end, the last maybe two years I was probably most unhappy as I became more cynical about the pay issues. So many physicians are making unreasonable financial demands." Most of the doctors expressed dissatisfaction about both the financial side of medicine that affected their own income adversely and the lowered the status of the profession in the public's eye toward the middle and end of their careers. But it was only Dr. Finast who identified it as a major cause of unhappiness.

Unhappiness about professional mobility and development during early phases of their careers was remembered again at the end of their careers for both academics and those in community practice as typified by Dr. Ross: "There were some times toward the end of my time in the Midwest when I felt stressed because I couldn't picture what I was going to be doing there for the next five years, and

I was profoundly unhappy." Dr. O'Brian also shared his anxiety about a lack of forward direction at various phases. During the established phase (1984–1994), looking back ten or more years, he said, "When I didn't move up here a couple of times, I was very unhappy." Later in 2016 he reflected, "I guess I've been unhappy, mainly over upward mobility especially when I was younger. I was much more anxious about career development then."

A few doctors focused on more intangible and existential angst as the source of their unhappiness. Dr. Melone spoke about the transition from training to practice during the established (1994) phase: "By the time you got out of your training, you have big choices. How are you going to end up with your life? The big challenges for me have been, what areas to work in. Now, the idea about what you are going to do in the next five years is a bigger challenge. There is more fear and worry. You have to figure out how to solve problems alone."

Finally, another notable factor cited as a source of unhappiness among those who changed their perspective on when they were most unhappy related to personal struggles and tragedy outside a medical context. Dr. Cahn described, "The worst time was in medical school. I hated the grind. I had a roommate who tried to commit suicide, although thank goodness he's now the chief of a service at a major teaching hospital. I was going through personal things—my father had just died. It was just a horrible time."

Interestingly, there were only two physicians, both in community practice, who asserted that "now" in the ending phase was their unhappiest time. Dr. Cahn, who always had a negative attitude was one: "The least happy is now. Just the burden of work. Just to keep up. You feel like you are on a rotating gerbil cage!" The other was Dr. Allen. In 2016 in referring to the takeover of his group practice by the local hospital, he decried, "It was the last sixteen months [that I was most unhappy]." He continued in response to the unhappiest time question in a paradoxical way. He asserted that the intensity of the weekly grind may have contributed to other physicians' unhappiness, but not to his: "Maybe I should be saying that my unhappiest times were when I was working one hundred hours a week. This may sound funny, but I enjoyed working, so it wasn't that awful, although I was getting very little sleep. So I had one hundred hours a week of fun!"

Missing and Wishing

From the early phase of this study on, I asked the cohort specifically, "What do you wish?" and "What do you miss?" to probe more personally about their work and life as physicians. My goal was to give the physicians an opportunity to contemplate their professional lives more philosophically—to move from a glaring light focused on their hard-hitting world of practice to their ruminations about the essence of their professional being.

(These "miss/wish" questions were asked in most but not at every career phase. In a couple of timeframes, only one or the other question was posed, so in those phases in which a question was not posed, there is no entry provided in the discussion below.)

The Early Phase (1980–1984)

What They Missed

As most (seventy-five percent) of the cohort had just completed subspecialty training when first asked, the common themes around what they missed were primarily related to their prior settings and roles in their fellowships, and for the rest, related to establishing their practice in either a community or academic setting. Some physicians, like Dr. Conley, focused on the loss of social interactions: "I miss having others around in my field to interact with." Others, like Dr. Jarvis, focused on schedule and work constraints: "(I miss) time. I'm too pressed. I don't have enough outside interests because in medicine now I can't drop anything." A number of physicians in academic settings who were assuming responsibility for teaching, patient care, and research projects lamented about not having more time for study. As Dr. Finast put it bluntly: "I miss having more time to read." Others noted having less opportunities to focus on career development like Dr. Annas: "I miss not having the administrative duties needed to get ahead. I need more of a blend than I have now."

Although almost all were married, and several had small children during the early phase (1980–1984), their focus was overwhelmingly on their new professional lives. There were many expressions of contentment as to where they were in their career pursuits. Dr. Rosen suggested there was nothing he missed: "I told you that I was one of the luckiest people in the world. I hope I can continue to be in a position to influence medical education." Or, as Dr. Lynch put it: "Nothing [missed]. I have an enriching job and a comfortable busy practice." Dr. Allen commented that he missed "nothing except time. I never wanted much. I don't have a big house by choice." He, like others, implied that his income is adequate, certainly more than anticipated, and that he was stimulated intellectually and emotionally. These physicians suggested they want for nothing except for the elusive quality of time.

What They Wished For

Similar to the way many noted they missed time for certain people or things, many of the physicians also directly expressed a wish for more time. Some answered the same for both questions. However, in general, the way most physicians expressed their wish, perhaps surprisingly, was not related to wishing they were spending more time with their families or devoting more time to a personal life outside medicine; rather it was a wish to become a more competent, well-rounded, and in some situations, more secure physician. Some wished for more support in their workplace. For example, Dr. Finast, who reflected on the limits of the academic medical culture to carry out research responsibilities at the expense of patient care, commented, "I spend a lot more time than I should trying to provide support for patients. I wish I knew better how to unload some of that, but these dying patients expect me to be there, and that limits my time for research."

The Established Phase (1984–1994)

What They Missed

In 1994, ten or more years after entering their practice setting, the physicians were again asked the question about what they missed. This time, for the cohort as a whole, their responses emphasized different things and were expressed in more complex terms. While the most prevalent "misses" at this stage continued to be related to their professional being, personal "time" was introduced as a concept into the equation more consistently than in the past. They missed "time without," "time away," "free time," and "time with family." As Dr. Allen, a community practitioner, stated, "I miss time off. I think I did a pretty good job seeing my kids grow up, but I still missed piano recitals and baseball games." Or, as Dr. Ross, expressed, "I miss playing God and my vacations. As a type A personality, there is never enough time."

More of the cohort than in the past began to lament some downsides or drawbacks to their career choices, as did Dr. Beech, a community-based nephrologist: "I wish I had time to do the feel-good things in medicine—teaching a bit, keeping up with the literature better, and more intellectual stimulation." Dr. Conley, in his community GI practice setting, felt the continuing workload pressure: "I've missed something by spending too much time working. That's the regret. It would be nice to work nine hours a day and have a regular schedule without as much call. If the hospital would hire doctors to handle the ER assignments and to admit patients at night, that job would be good for my life and for many guys right out of training." (He actually anticipated the role of hospitalists that emerged more than a decade later, which is discussed in depth in chapter 8 on disillusionment.) Ironically, for the community physicians who were working from sixty to seventy hours a week on the average, cutting back to nine hours a day seems to be, as he puts it, "wishful thinking." Here Dr. Paul reminisces about his residency, which for him included that fourth year as chief resident, compared to the current times: "I miss the excitement and enthusiasm in my work—the thrill is gone. There was something romantic about what I did as a house staff; I was learning and growing."

The Entrenched Phase (1994–2004)

What They Wished For

In this stage, twenty-five years since the completion of their residency, there were deeper and more extensive contemplations of wishes beyond their work, revolving around their personal circumstances and for the first time, perhaps surprisingly, the world more broadly. A few wished, after all these years, that they could maintain or achieve a balance in their lives. Dr. Lash, an academic physician who chose an administrative career track, asserted, "I wish that my contributions will make a difference. I want a productive life and then die. I want to stay healthy and see my daughter grow up. I don't care if I don't have 200 publications or become an incredible investigator. My only wish is to maximize my talents, and to have a healthy balance between professional and personal life."

A poignant comment by Dr. Lynch, who had moved into a solo oncology practice at this point in his career, not surprisingly, included once again, his isolation from his peers. This was similar to what Dr. Finast and others wished or missed earlier in their careers: "I wish that I had been a better friend to my peers, supported them; let them support me. But I was too independent, and real lonely. When you ask me years from now, I wish I could say I read, worked hard, spent time with friends, and traveled. I wish I had a colleague available to feel a lump or listen to a heartbeat; that's the downside of independent practice."

Here Dr. Allen, a community cardiologist, expressed a wish that also points to some profound struggles for himself and his peers: "I wish some of the anxiety I see in myself and others could be taken away. But stress is something we give ourselves." Without prompting, he then moved on to discuss what he, like many others, wished for the profession and the health care system: "I wish the field of medicine in the country decides to have a health plan that the public would be willing to pay for. Everyone should agree on universal coverage and health care as a right." (Health care reform is discussed more in depth in chapter 7.)

The Extended Phase (2004–2011)

What They Missed

In 2011, more than thirty years after completing residency at SAMS, the physicians continued to reflect on these questions in complex ways. Many of their responses were wistful, poignant, and at times, ironic. For example, as Dr. Mahoney commented, "I miss the strikes when I bowl. I miss hitting a ball when I swing a bat. Wouldn't it be nice if one could be naive and innocent, and yet wise? But it takes the abolition of naiveté and innocence to gain wisdom." Dr. Jarvis conveyed both practical and philosophical sentiments: "I wish I had more time to do a little more reading. I miss lots—having my children around every day. I miss my memory, not quite like it used to be. I have less energy. I'd love to have a couple of do-overs. I would have done some personal things better."

Only a few of the cohort unconditionally continued to express contentment—not missing anything. They were more likely to be in academic practice. Dr. Polikoff was the only community practitioner who concluded that he did not miss anything: "I've been blessed by working with an amazing group of doctors and a system that supports clinicians, plus I have plenty of personal time."

While most of the physicians identified specific misses and wishes, they still ended up assessing their careers at this stage as more positive than negative. Dr. Conley, the only one who was retired by this phase, ironically lamented, "I miss the most the interaction with patients and the feedback I got from helping them. I miss some of the people I worked with; that was a positive. I'm glad I went into medicine and gastroenterology. I'm proud I got through it." (Yet in discussing his dissatisfactions with his career, he described with some bitterness, the stresses that drove him, the first of his cohort, to retire.)

Dr. Lynch, who at this extended stage had moved once again to a new oncology group practice, weighed the positives and the negatives: "I miss free time and get frustrated that I don't have enough personal time. Not much else. I have a good life. It's very rewarding and busy." Perhaps because he was once again in a new setting, he no longer focused on the drama of his former group practices and contentious peer relationships that he had described in earlier phases.

"Fun" or the absence thereof, as consistent theme, loomed large once again in the reminiscences by several of the cohort in their answers. As Dr. O'Brian reflected, "I missed the fun of doing outpatient care especially early on. I missed my family. I feel my career has gotten in the way of my family life a bit. Still, I've been pretty happy." Dr. Cahn also used this concept to frame his reminiscences: "I miss the fun of medicine. It's a business now. I desperately miss the collegiality with a group of doctors talking about patients. We don't have fun anymore; the hospitalists killed it."

At this stage (2011), one year after the passing of President Obama's Affordable Care Act, many looked beyond themselves to incorporate a national health agenda into their miss/wish musings to a greater degree than they did in earlier phases. Dr. Conley responded first by offering: "I wish we could stop bickering about health care and get some kind of solution." Then he, as did Dr. Strelko and many others, took the opportunity to criticize their own profession in considering what is missing: "We can make reforms without a lot of money. Doctors don't need to make as much money, although they work hard with long hours and tremendous responsibilities, with serious consequences. I wish we could change that. The problems have gone on too long." Dr. Jarvis also contemplated the system dilemma for medicine: "There's going to have to be big structural changes in health care costs, but I wish the government (with the ACA) doesn't drive the brightest and most talented people away from medicine." This sentiment was also expressed elsewhere by several of the cohort in commenting about the quality of the latest generation of physicians. (This is discussed more in chapter 5).

What They Wished For

At this phase, there were detailed ruminations about what they wished for themselves and others. Family and personal time themes were often conveyed with humor and wistfulness: "To catch a world record red drum fish," wished Dr. Beech. Others joined the national health agenda to their own wishes like academic Dr. Rosen: "I wish I can continue to help improve health care by improving internal medicine. And I have the opportunity to do so because of my involvement in important national organizations."

Nevertheless, with a more serious tone, a few others reflected on core beliefs about what it means to be a physician by bemoaning the problems they predict for the future. Here Dr. Melone, whose son was studying to be a physician, reflected, "I wish my son gets what he wants out of medicine, as opposed to what I think he should be signing up for. I wish we could make medicine more about the doctor-patient relationship—that's what it has always been about, and we lost that along the way, focusing too much on costs." Nostalgia was evident in the way so many viewed the massive changes that had occurred in thirty-plus years as moving away from "the golden years."

The Ending Phase (2011–2016)

What They Missed

In 2016, thirty-five years since beginning their careers, more than half of the physicians were still in active practice. The rest had retired within the prior few years. (Dr. Paul died a few years earlier.) They were asked once again to look back over their lives—with an emphasis on what they missed and whether they had any regrets. These questions gave them an opportunity to express their feelings in both philosophical and pragmatic terms at or near the end of their careers.

For the first time, Dr. Strelko brought personal elements of his life into discussions about what he missed during his career: "I've always wanted to have a vacation home; maybe someday I will. I miss not taking more time off. My wife and I talked about doing a sabbatical, but it never worked out. Still we have been pretty fortunate in not having any major tragedy in our family. We feel pretty lucky."

Dr. Jarvis, already retired for three years, commented with ambivalence on the choices he made in the context of what he missed and regretted, "I'm very happy. Internal medicine with hem-onc (hematology/oncology) couldn't have been a better choice, no better city to live in, no better practice to have, no better partners. Still I miss seeing my partners every day. I also miss teaching interns and residents. They would love for me to come back, but now, I want time for myself for the first time in my life." Dr. Conley, who had already been retired for six years at this point, also focused on his prior office life and similarly commented on freedom as a paramount priority after so many years of sixty-plus-hour work weeks: "I miss the patients and I miss the people in my office. But, after about two or three years, I don't miss it as much now. I love the freedom of my schedule."

Earlier, in the extended phase (2004–2011), a theme emerged among some of the community practitioners regarding missing the teaching component of an academic career path, a path that they had rejected early on. At this ending phase, several returned to that theme, contemplating what the academic life could have offered, while they also identified different reasons for not missing a university environment. Their conclusion was that the costs outweighed the benefits. Dr. Nolan assessed his choice of community practice: "Being in academia is like being part of a family, part of the community. So why did I ever leave without regrets? Because there comes a time when you have to leave the nest." Dr. Melone admitted that an academic career was on his mind during his time as house staff, although he provided at least a partial rationale for turning outside: "I dodged the bullet. For a long time, I thought I would have enjoyed academic medicine, but the pressure to modernize medical education would have made me crazy. The stress of learning how to intubate a mannequin instead of learning how to intubate a real patient is only one example of what I don't miss. Working on dummies as they do now, would have turned me into an old fart a lot earlier."

Dr. Cahn, like Dr. Melone, in reflecting on what he missed, admitted that a medical center career held sway, even as he railed against the community system he chose: "Professionally, I've always had a piece of my brain tell me I should have stayed in academic medicine, but the problem is I'd be a pauper, and terribly unhappy. So, the thrill of academia had to be balanced with missing the profitability of private practice. Teaching is becoming less desirable because to meet expenses with less reimbursement you have to work more hours. And it's getting worse."

Dr. Johnson was one of the few community practitioners who missed the research rather than teaching aspects of academia but fell short of regretting his career choice because "the same reason why I don't do well in the hospital system is the same reason why I wouldn't do well in academics. Just too many meetings, too much nonsense; it's just too difficult to get something done." Then he focused on the current community-based medical system, and like Dr. Cahn, acknowledged that he would not bemoan leaving his current practice; indeed, he became more negative in the last phases of his career: "I regret that it's going to be more and more a bureaucratic and centralized system. But I don't regret that I'm not going to be here to have to deal with it."

On the other hand, those who remained in academia did not miss the alternative; no one wished they had pursued community practice. Indeed, academic leaders in the ending phrase like Dr. Strelko criticized aspects of oncology private practice as he reflected on what he would not miss: "Private practice is not doing well, at least in my specialty of oncology. Many doctors are not making a go of it and are trying to get hospitals to buy their practices. And then there was the selling of chemotherapy. Many doctors made tons of money. I could never understand how you could get through that conflict of interest where your salary is influenced so much by whether you give someone chemotherapy or not."

Regrets at the End

In 2016, at the end of their careers, in addition to what they missed, the physicians were also asked about whether they had any regrets. When asked about this directly, most of the physicians suggested they had little to none, or that on balance, the positives outweighed the negatives. Nevertheless, many still described negative occurrences and unhappy periods throughout their careers, including in the final phases. Dr. O'Brian, for example, repeated almost verbatim the same regrets he had noted much earlier in his career: "I was too tied up in my career early on. I think my personal life suffered a bit. My relationship with my wife, although she's still my wife, and my family could have been a little better. I did manage to coach my kids; still I wish I had spent a little more time with them."

Others like Dr. Beech, however, presented a conditional happy ending with caveats: "I've had a couple of lawsuits which have been painful; but on balance, it's been an interesting experience and also a privilege. I don't know if I had my choice to do it all over again, I would become a doctor. I'm not sure, but since you've got to do something, it's not too bad a thing to do."

Sadly, Dr. Mahoney left practice with regrets at the end of his career. "The first regret goes to the malpractice case against me; if I had to do that one over, I'd do it differently if it would have prevented the lawsuit. It would have prevented five years of worry, and the question of trust and fear that I experienced years after." (Dr. Mahoney contracted a debilitating disease around the time period he left his [non-internal medicine] practice, and he confessed that that circumstance may have also affected his professional attitude and behavior leading to a premature retirement.)

Dr. Jarvis identified a number of regrets, particularly relating to the work/life balance tinged with envy toward those physician colleagues who were now in the earlier phases in their careers. He commented in the ending phase: "I guess, looking back, I regret the lack of time; the lost time that I'll never get back with the kids when they were growing up. I'm jealous of my young partners because when I look back at the things that made me profoundly unhappy, I remember the first year of practice. I got zero weeks of vacation. Now, we hire people who start out with six weeks' vacation and work only every eighth weekend, and they want more!"

Dr. Finast, who also retired a few years earlier primarily because of a serious illness, was one of the few academics who gave up the research component of academia early on, and mentioned it again as he pondered regrets: "In fantasy land it would be nice if I had discovered something to make all who have serious lung disease better. But I was trying to be the best I could in patient care. I think I did a good job and so do my colleagues. As a teacher, I was pretty successful. It's been hard to turn it off. Being a doctor is a good thing."

Several focused on a combination of personal and professional factors that affected their career regrets—positively and negatively—although the bottom line was undeniable; almost all would take the same path again as physicians. As Dr. Allen conveyed, "The regrets that I have are that I worked way too hard the first ten years. I shouldn't have done that when my kids were growing up. But other than that, I don't have any regrets. It's been a great run. I've loved doing what I do." Still, elsewhere in the final interview, Dr. Allen described in vitriolic terms that he was leaving his cardiology group defeated by the local hospital system; he was not a happy camper at the end and even worried about the possibility of being sued for two years postretirement.

Dr. Lynch, who was an unusual community practitioner in that he made several moves to different oncology settings, assessed his career: "No regrets that I live with every day. I certainly have regrets in my personal life. But, in my professional side, I've made some silly decisions in terms of my practice with some situations where I probably should have left quicker. I put up with stress for too long. But you can always second guess yourself. I think everything has led to my being where I am now; that's what's most important."

For Dr. Nolan the positives outweighed the negatives—but he noted the new generation, including his children, do not see it that way: "I couldn't imagine doing anything else. I think I made the right choice. You don't have to worry about anybody laying you off in private practice. You get rewards because some people get better. It's a good career if you can manage the bad parts. Still, that's what kept my kids from going into it. I was on call too much, or I always had to go to work. They didn't want that for themselves."

Implications

Clearly there were mixed sentiments about the wishes, misses, and regrets, with some laments and some nostalgia. Not surprisingly, there was no one pattern or direction for the cohort; rather, there were themes that emerged at various phases, accentuating other aspects of their professional lives such as demands from different external actors as far apart as regulators and spouses. Complexity was evident as they attempted to balance competing facets twenty-four hours a day, seven days a week, three hundred sixty-five days a year—some more successfully by their own account than others.

In examination of their reflections on these issues, happiness and unhappiness themes emerge across all career stages—from the woes of impossible workloads to the joys of intellectual stimulation, from the burden of intrusive reform to the nourishment of collegial kinship. Each of these themes evoke a multidimensional resonance. Tracking happiness/unhappiness themes and their relationship to intervening circumstances and other emotional tones across physicians' careers illustrates consistencies within the cohort. At each career stage, academic practitioners cited positive peer relationships to varying degrees, while community practitioners cited positive patient interactions as the main source of happiness, for the most part, regardless of subspecialty.

At the same time, almost every physician described deep unhappiness early in their careers related to the intensity of medical school, internship, and residency; most came to recontextualize that unhappiness later in their careers, even if it was still identified as a primary unhappiness source. Government reform, the rise of insurance companies, lobbying by trial lawyers, and new medical technology dramatically shifted physicians' practice experiences. The vast majority of the cohort described negative or deeply ambivalent feelings about these external factors, regardless of whether particular stages or a full career was steeped more in happiness than unhappiness. What emerges is a trait of resilience that appears to allow them to cope if not adapt to changing circumstances using informal networks and supports, although neither consistently nor uniformly. There was a certain grit and determination to plod along that is prevalent, with attempts by many of the cohort to seek fulfillment by changing settings or practice emphases well into their career trajectory.

As increasingly expressed by these physicians in the later stages of their careers, this cohort saw itself as the last generation of autonomous medical practitioners, even though they faced encroachments on their professional autonomy from the early phase (1980–1984). The shifts and changes that defined the landscape of their professional lives distinguish this cohort presumably from the generations of physicians that follow. The physicians' responses were rarely uniform and unidirectional. Their narratives were wrought with inconsistencies and contradictions across and within career phases, as suggested by Saldana (2003). At the same time, these showcased cohort trends and patterns, more similar than different in pursuit of happy and satisfying medical careers.

11   *Conclusion*

Policymakers and people at the top of public and private health organizations are often accused of not knowing what the people "at the bottom"—meaning clients, patients, and recipients of services and benefits—are thinking and feeling. Those with power are also criticized more generally for not knowing how the targets of their policies and programs are directly and indirectly (advertently and inadvertently) affected by their decisions. This long-term study over forty years presents a chance to learn directly about the "view from below"—that is, the informed opinions and lived experiences of a cohort of twenty physicians who have been on the front lines while myriad major public and private regulatory changes affecting them have been enacted in the American health system.

Over the course of this study's time frame, physicians have been considered a high-status professional class. But their individual and collective experiences have not been exposed in depth or in a sustained way over such a long period of time as this study has done. Most of these physicians were not active in their professional organizations, and many admitted to me that "no one ever asked me these questions about my opinions and circumstances." Yet these physicians' experiences provide critical insight into the larger health care system and point to dilemmas and opportunities for improving both physicians' satisfaction in the future and the outcomes for medical practice more generally. Given our continued communication over these years, I feel confident that the information they shared with me has been trustworthy and credible. To be sure, there may have been some omissions about the darker sides of their forty years' worth of encounters with patients and peers. But the best of their world is on full display.

The twenty doctors who remained in this study represent a sample (albeit not statistically arrived at) of physicians who, for close to a half century, have been acutely and dramatically affected by profound changes in the structure and culture of medical training and practice. When considering their own experiences, these physicians would no doubt say they are typical of White male physicians who went through an American medical residency program forty or so years ago and are now leaving the medical field with varying degrees of fulfillment tempered by a range of disappointments for themselves and especially for their profession. In my interviews with them over the decades, they provided rich perspectives on how they got to where they are and why, the choices they made, and the choices made for them by family or fellow physicians or external forces.

In a number of ways, these doctors' stories mirror what scholarly literature has found regarding the sources and levels of physician satisfaction and dissatisfaction with their medical careers. But there were also many things that affected these individual physicians that were unexpected and surprising, which have rarely been revealed before in the public discourse on health policy and graduate medical education. Within this physician cohort, there were certainly trends and tendencies—but rarely one hundred percent in one direction. There were almost always a few outliers with minority and even unusual perspectives. There were also many inconsistencies and contradictions revealed by different physicians over time, and even within the same time frame. Frequently, the trends or outlying opinions would come more into view as the doctors offered themselves as "informants," speaking for a larger group (e.g., their subspecialty, their setting, or for physicians as a professional group).

Close to four decades have passed since these physicians were first interviewed (1979–1980) and close to a half century since they first began medical school in the mid-1970s. When they embarked on their career paths, it was the beginning of a turbulent time in the health care system as the political climate was shifting toward more conservative, free-market economic policies of the Reagan era. In both the United States and some western European countries, support for corporate medicine (insurance companies; managed care plans) dominated the health care agenda. As presented in the chapters in this book, these changes had a powerful impact on their medical practices and on their professional and personal lives.

As these changes in the medical system took root, and the physicians moved into the later part of their careers, they continued to witness or were directly affected by these major adjustments to medical practice, instigated by both the government and/or the marketplace. These included structural changes that had a significant impact on models of reimbursement, including the contentious passage in 2010 of President Obama's Affordable Health Care Act and its implementation over the next several years. Many of these changes intersected with the advent of hospitalists and electronic medical records, both of which, as the physicians described at length, had a transformative, mainly negative, impact on their experience of what it meant to practice medicine and more profoundly, to be a physician.

At the very end of or close to the end of their careers, many left or were planning to leave medicine disillusioned with the profession and the trends in the health care system in spite of some cautiously optimistic views about the technological advancements in medicine. Nevertheless, many endured with perseverance and fortitude, motivated to make a difference in people's lives and to continue to find ways to value their work and achieve satisfaction. Indeed, looking at the long arc of their experiences and conversations, it is clear that this desire to make a difference, and the sense of satisfaction they drew from this, sustained most them over the course of their professional lifetime through difficult and uncertain times.

By 2016, more than half (twelve out of twenty) had one foot out the door toward retirement or had already left their practice. Some left with ambivalence or reluctance, while others left or were on the brink of leaving with disappointment, even those who had a positive overall sense of their career. There were, however, a few among the academics (and the one HMO community practitioner) who expressed a largely positive and happy experience as a physician over the full course of their careers, despite the regular and significant shifts affecting the practice of medicine. Nevertheless, considering the challenges that so many faced, the fact that almost all endured the deep fluctuations of their field speaks to their resilience and fortitude. Overall, as a cohort, they struggled over the course of their careers with how to find meaning in their professional lives amidst uncertainty, public scrutiny, government oversight, and corporate control.

Their core specialty, internal medicine, has radically changed over the past four decades. The average length of stay for patients in hospitals across the country today is dramatically less than it was in the early 1980s. The population of hospitalized patients has become older and sicker, and those patients who, twenty years ago, would have remained in hospital, are now getting care in nursing homes (such as patients who were ventilator dependent, in dialysis, or in need of infusion therapy), or at home with assistance. For those training in internal medicine, the introduction of the hospitalist in the last twenty years has fundamentally shifted how community practitioners understand their responsibilities and obligations, and it has also led to substantial changes in the way academic practitioners interact with medical students, residents, and fellows.

Additionally, significant advances in technology have transformed the field. Procedures that used to be the domain of surgeons have become simpler and are used by medical subspecialists, particularly in cardiology, pulmonology, and gastroenterology. Over the course of their forty-year careers, these technological changes presented unique challenges for the physicians to remain current. But many, particularly those in those subspecialties noted above, were also excited by these changes that contributed to their intellectual stimulation. These were likely critical for maintaining a sense of satisfaction as they worked hard to keep up with new technologies and with their younger colleagues well versed in them.

Alongside the rapidly evolving clinical and surgical technologies, administrative technology profoundly altered the practice of medicine for these physicians, particularly relating to record-keeping and accountability requirements. These latest changes included the advent of the electronic medical record, a system that was viewed almost unanimously by the entire cohort as the bane of their existence. They described it, at best, as a necessary evil, while at worst, inefficient and injurious to their abilities to thrive both intellectually and in caring for their patients. The emergence of EMR and the hospitalist also led the physicians to worry about the changing role of primary care doctors and the community-based general internist. Many of the physicians expressed concern that the government and commercial insurers had not shifted the reimbursement rates for counseling, educating, and caring for patients. The disappearance of the clinical internist was among their greatest fears. Many expressed great anxiety at the idea of being replaced by lesser-trained medical personnel, and also becoming isolated further from peers outside their practice intellectually and emotionally.

Many studies have identified the way time factors and conflicts between family needs and their practice are prevalent throughout physicians' lives. The physicians whom I followed reinforce these findings. Community practitioners are often thought to be the ones who face the most difficulty in finding the right balance working more than sixty hours a week on the average. But many of the academic physicians also faced notable struggles in finding this similar balance. They often experienced disappointments with promotions and funding at varying points in their careers, while the need for building and maintaining their academic status inflicted significant time pressures to produce, both clinically and in the laboratory. Additionally, some felt pressure in the middle and ending phases to contribute financially to their medical center's bottom line.

Although the academic physicians in this study generally expressed more satisfaction with their professional lives than most of the community practitioners did, the academic physicians' responses over the decades made it clear that there was less stability in the academic pathway than I would have anticipated. Indeed, half of the academics had changed settings during the first twenty-five years of their careers because of disappointments or conflicts with colleagues and superiors. Even as they neared retirement, almost half of the remaining academics were still contemplating making changes to their practice and position, looking for ways to move upward in the academic hierarchy at their own institution, or even at another institution. It was surprising to me that, in the latest stage in their careers (the ending phase 2011–2016), three attending physicians would be focused on shifting to new settings or making notable changes to their own practice, while two community practitioners in those last few years had moved to new settings, and one shifted his office-base and hospital practice in geriatrics to long-term care only.

The community practitioners felt tremendous pressure to establish their reputations and practices, to see patients in the office and in one or more hospitals, to stay up to date with and utilize new technology, while also dealing with the well-documented dilemmas of arguing or negotiating with patients' many insurance plans. Considering the frequent uncertainties and structural changes in the American health care system over their careers, these issues posed severe difficulties as these physicians sought to effectively find a balance between the needs of their personal and family life, while also managing a successful community practice. These challenges were only further compounded by the risk and reality of malpractice lawsuits, as at least half of the cohort had experienced one or more lawsuits themselves and/or watched a close colleague deal with malpractice. In these later years, many physicians cut back on administrative or hospital responsibilities and/or cut their hours to four days a week with fewer on-call nights and weekends (something that might still seem like a fairly full workload to us non-physicians, considering that many were already in their sixties). Yet it is notable how the physicians generally remained committed to professional development and patient care until the very end of their careers.

Components of Career Satisfaction

Many of the key career satisfaction components that this study examined (financial, psychic, intellectual, and public—for self and the profession) match the components that have been the focus in other studies. However, it is not clear that all the outcomes for these physicians could have been predicted based on existing research, and it is also the case that this study revealed important new insights into the way physicians experienced these components of their professional lives. In this final chapter, it is worth briefly highlighting a few of the key take-aways from these findings that also have relevance for other health professionals and policymakers.

Regarding these physicians' financial satisfaction, one of the key findings was that the physicians determined their level of satisfaction in different ways depending on whether they judged their financial position in relative or absolute terms. They frequently discussed this issue by comparing themselves to other MDs, to the average American worker, or to what they were making earlier in their careers for the hours they put in. Relatedly, the way their levels of financial satisfaction progressed over the years is also worth noting, although their answers tended to be nuanced. For the cohort overall, their levels of satisfaction on this issue went up over time, even as they complained that they were working longer and harder to keep pace out of fears that their income might stagnate or decline.

The issue of these physicians' psychic/emotional satisfaction remained a complex and important component in their professional lives, and their responses vacillated to a notable degree over the phases of their careers. While a majority of the cohort remained satisfied with this affective component across their careers, there were periods where their satisfaction decreased. It may be reflective of the issues the cohort struggled with as described earlier in the book: the complexity of their relationships with patients and colleagues over time; the increasing pressures to keep up and be competitive; external scrutiny of their practice by lawyers, insurance companies, the media, and even certain types of patients; and the lessening of clinical autonomy. All these challenges contributed to a substantial amount of cynicism and disillusionment, as well as to deep fears and profound doubts that they kept hidden from public view, even for those who were classified as satisfied overall.

While financial and psychic/emotional satisfaction remained significant factors in determining the quality of their professional lives, intellectual stimulation was also a significant component, with scholarly and cerebral elements increasing in importance over time. For those in academic practice, it was about "being on the cutting edge." They received intellectual stimulation from their interaction with their peers, from their teaching new generations of novice physicians, and, for some, from their research. They liked being kept sharp and on their toes. While many lamented the less intense practice styles, the less-committed work ethic, and the increasing career-related expectations about hours and working conditions, most of the cohort were impressed with the new generation of physicians' depth of knowledge and facility with technology. For the community practitioners, intellectual stimulation was very important; something they obtained from their interactions with peers in their practice, by taking on small teaching and supervising positions, and/or by assuming a challenging administrative position. Surprisingly, so many of the community practitioners pointed to the teaching aspect of their work as being a component they would most miss after retirement. Given their academic backgrounds, years of study, and the mandate for continuing education, it is understandable that all physicians would highly value the scholarly aspect of their practice, but its staying power as an important factor of satisfaction over the lifetime of their careers is noteworthy, especially for the community practitioners.

The area with the greatest discrepancy among the physicians' perceptions of satisfaction was between the way they described the high levels of recognition they received personally from their community (however they defined it), and the way they believed the medical profession was viewed by the public overall. Their sense of satisfaction with the former increased across the phases of their careers, while in response to the latter, regardless of their setting or specialty, these physicians held an almost universally consistent belief that the medical profession was held in low regard or was decreasing in professional status over time. It remains to be seen whether the 2020 pandemic increases doctors' status over time, given their prominent role as clinicians and health career leaders.

These findings have important implications for medical scholars, professional health organizations, public policy makers and reformers, medical career proponents, and community health advocates. Understanding components of and ensuring physician satisfaction are relevant for patients and the broader society since the provision of health care is so essential to societal as well as to individual well-being.

Analytical and Methodological Considerations

While the trend toward negativism was greater than the trend toward positive satisfaction over the phases of their careers collectively, there were inconsistencies and contradictions in both directions as the framework for longitudinal analysis by Saldana (2003) suggests. It is also essential to examine the individual variations among the cohort at each career stage.

Fundamentally, Saldana's methodology is about understanding the impact of time on change. Longitudinal data collection is about treating time as an integral aspect of the data itself. In analyzing the interview transcripts of the doctors, the question of time has often been in the foreground—what is it about a particular period of time, characterized in this study as one of six career phases, that contributes to the conditions, experiences, and perspectives the doctors have about their careers? How have these conditions, experiences, and perspectives changed or remained firm from the beginning of their career (entry and early phases), to the middle (established and entrenched phases), to the end (the extended and ending phases)? Essentially, when analyzing longitudinal data, Saldana (2003) argues that the researcher must consider the ways time may be felt, interpreted, or understood differently by different subjects, which has been demonstrated in this study.

As time is considered contextually, so is change as another unique variable. While it is important to define in a longitudinal study what constitutes a change (e.g., an increase or decrease in career satisfaction from one phase to the next), Saldana emphasizes that researchers may not know from the beginning how to define the change they are looking for. Building on a grounded theory approach, as Saldana suggests, this study sought to push for more complexity and nuance in its longitudinal analysis by acknowledging multiple theories of change and allowing for increased flexibility in the process of interpreting the data emanating from the perspectives of these twenty physicians at each time frame and over time.

For Saldana, what is most useful in grounded theory is the task of coming up with a "through-line," which explains an overarching theory or narrative of the participants' experiences or of the data. However, one narrative or through-line is often not enough given the complexity and quantity of data in a longitudinal study—as is the case here. One of the study's central goals was to examine what sustains the doctors through time as they attempt to control or adjust to major, even transformative, external forces impinging on their professional lives. In examining the doctors' experiences, my analysis focused on trying to understand the complexity of what it means to be a doctor, whether and when it goes beyond a job and becomes an all-encompassing identity. Ultimately, it was critical to demonstrate how changes have affected their identity, their perceptions (attitudes), and their practice (behavior) in each time frame, most especially at the end of their career, and how they assess their experiences over a professional lifetime.

A Comment about *The House of God*

The House of God, as I discussed earlier in this book, was a compelling satire of the medical internship experience that became a symbolic and actual reference point for me during the early years of this study (Shem, 1978). The novel's absurdist, catch-22 view of medical training resonated with most physicians in the cohort. During my early interviews, so many physicians made a point of recommending the book to me spontaneously as a window into their world. Reflecting a remarkable staying power as a satiric portrayal of life among novice physicians, the book has continued to be popular among house staff more than thirty years later (Markel, 2009), and also continues to create controversy among older physicians and social critics (Pearson, 2019). As a result, when the physicians were near retirement, I decided to ask them again about the book's portrayal of residency training, to see how they might reexamine this book and the residency culture, and whether it was viewed as exaggerated or not. Their responses provide another layer of insight into which circumstances of their profession had changed over time, and which had not.

Almost all the physicians recalled the book in 2016. However, with their own internships more than thirty-five years in the past, many more distanced themselves and/or disapproved of the farcical and dark behavior carried on by the fictional interns. When I asked them how the fictional portrayal compared with house staff culture today, the cohort was divided. Some suggested the condescending, dismissive attitude toward patients among house staff that the book described might still be present in some types of residencies. But they differed in the way they thought it would be received by those in training today (in medical school or residency), and, more generally, whether the house staff comportment would be tolerated by the attending physicians or medical managers. Most thought the caricature would be viewed with amusement as "by-gone days," although no longer acceptable. Some even went on to say such behavior would be grounds for dismissal—referencing government HIPAA privacy rules as one reason for the cultural shift, touting that the medical training climate now is one with more respect for the patient. As Dr. Lash told me, "Then, we could have written the book; today it would be seen as a parody." All of them recognized a sea change in the structure and culture of medical residencies from when they were first entering the profession, referencing the cut in work hours and on-call schedules. Still, there were a few who were wistful for the camaraderie and fun portrayed in the satire: "Those were memorable times" said Dr. Melone, while Dr. Ross hoped that "we haven't gotten so sensitive that they would be offended or not recognize the spoof." A few even went further, expressing that things had not changed all that much for certain types of residency programs.

Ultimately, their reflections on this book corroborated insights that had been offered into the way academic physicians dealt with their trainees. Attendings were portrayed as if they, begrudgingly or not, accepted the seriousness of their roles as medical educators. But many also expressed that current medical students and trainees were missing "the fun." Many suggested that the pendulum had shifted too far in the other direction, with house staff given too little autonomy, and attending physicians taking their oversight role too far, willingly or not. One of the academic physicians specifically mentioned that he had given my book (Mizrahi, 1986) to many residents over the years and felt that the mentality had not changed. He suggested there still was an emphasis by house staff on reducing the number of patients on their shift. Some community practitioners also thought that the G.R.O.P. phenomenon I described, remained. There were still overworked residents struggling to maintain control of their educational and patient care responsibilities, which could adversely affect patients under their care.

The Impact of Gender Balance

While I regret not asking specific questions about the impact of the SAMS female physicians on the SAMS house staff culture, several of the cohort suggested that greater gender balance had affected the profession. Many of them claimed that when it came to dedication to the profession among the newer generation of physicians, the trends were "gender neutral." But they also noted that greater gender balance had made a specific difference in the field because of female physicians wanting more of a balance between work and family life. Most also described how this represented a paradigm shift in perspective held by novice physicians in general: it was no longer a "calling." Drawing contrast to the type of life/work balance sought among newer physicians (of either gender), Dr. Cahn suggested there was no comparison: "We were married to medicine," as he put it.

All of the cohort recognized the way the changing gender balance were one of the factors that had dramatically affected medical education, including reducing residency training hours because of the phenomenon of sleep deprivation. The physicians did not specifically identify the Bell Commission as the pivotal report that led state governments to limit residency hours in the hospital per week and require a more direct hands-on role for the attending physicians. However, there was unanimous sentiment that dramatic changes had occurred for both academic attending faculty and for the new generations of current residents.[1]

These changes also had their impact on community practitioners when hiring new physicians. Many asserted that the new generations following them demanded fewer hours and better incomes and working conditions than they ever did. Underscoring the way the field of medicine had transformed around them, some of the physicians defined themselves as from the old guard and increasingly becoming obsolete. At the same time, they expressed a degree of resentment at these changes, and disparaged the younger cohorts' lack of humanity and commitment. Others paid begrudging respect to these new generations who had more limited career expectations than they ever had or could imagine when they were starting out so many years ago.

Looking Ahead

Scholarship of the past forty years has emphasized the decline of the medical profession imbued with self-interest, together with associated theories of organizational conflict (Starr, 2004). These increasing critiques of the elitism of the medical profession have negatively affected physicians' influence in the public arena and have eroded patient trust over the past forty years. While organized medicine in the United States has responded defensively to these sentiments at the macro level, the quality, quantity, and impact of physician disillusionment and vulnerability at the micro level have been largely hidden from public view. The outcomes of this longitudinal study provide an important correction to that by revealing that this cohort was willing to adapt and change to maintain an overall level of satisfaction, although it was not without cost—periods of dissatisfaction, doubts, and, for a few, deep despair.

As this book is being completed, the world is in the midst of the worst pandemic in over 100 years. Millions of people have become ill and more than one million have died worldwide, including millions of Americans, with the numbers of deaths and severe illness climbing at the end of 2020. This tragic situation is a result of the viral COVID-19 attack in the beginning of 2020 on individuals, their families, and the economy. It has caused a systemic crisis for the U.S. health care system, placing enormous stress on the health care workforce, including physicians. Ironically, as the media has extensively and continuously covered these frontline "essential providers," the status of physicians in particular seems to have risen as so many have demonstrated courage and even sacrifice. It remains to be seen whether these positive assessments of physicians in this crisis period will permanently raise their stature in the eyes of the public and policymakers and on themselves (Cooch, 2020; Fargen, Leslie-Mazwi, et al., 2020; Funk and Gramlich, 2020).

Looking ahead, with new concepts and language, a different version of organized medicine from that of the past might be invented for the future—one that draws on multiple medical organizations, and encourages more effective cooperation and collaboration with other health care professions and with patient and health advocacy organizations (Evett, 2003; Light, 2004; Stevens, 2001). It seems important to emphasize the need to maintain an independent professional sector separate from government and the corporate sector (Freidson, 2001). Nevertheless, there was little evidence among this cohort of the collective professionalism and collegiality called for by many health policy analysts and academics (Hafferty, 2006; Kuhlmann, 2006).

The results of this longitudinal study of physicians contribute to the need to develop a different version of the sociology of medicine that goes beyond the old language of dominance and submission between professionals and their constituents. Instead it should examine the factors that have had a serious impact on professional practice and career satisfaction. Both this cohort and many critics of American medicine (Conover, 2014; Emanuel, 2020) agree that there must be a focus on structural, cultural, and behavioral factors if this country wants to continue to attract "the best and the brightest"—as well as the most committed—to a career in medicine.

Acknowledgments

Where do I begin with appreciating and articulating the support I received along the way?

This book would never have come to fruition were it not for Peter Mickulas, executive editor at Rutgers University Press, who had patience that went beyond that of a proverbial saint. He believed in the importance and uniqueness of my study and was ever supportive as the years passed after I was awarded a contract. Providence won the day, because his allowing me to delay the final product resulted in another phase of deep interviews which extended and enriched the analysis of the doctors' careers in 2016.

This project has been more than a forty-year journey from the birth of my question: How do doctors learn the doctor-patient relationship, to the presentation of the professional career tracks of twenty prototypical American physicians from "residency to retirement," the title of this book.

This book comes thirty years after my *Getting Rid of Patients: Contradictions in the Socialization of Physicians* was published by Rutgers (1986). It presented my observations and interpretation of their training world as they simultaneously provided medical services to a predominantly low income and disproportionately Black urban population in the south while continuing their graduate medical education toward becoming internists.

I express (albeit belatedly) my profound gratitude to the late Dr. Florence Vigilante, a colleague of mine as I continued my teaching career at the Hunter College of the School of Social Work in New York City. One day after I completed my PhD dissertation study of the house staff in the early 1980s, she asked me over lunch: "What happened to those novice doctors you intensely observed for a whole year?" I credit her for igniting the light bulb that went off for me at that point—"Why not follow up?" Needless to say, her question was the unintentional start of what became the major study of my career for the next three plus decades.

There were so many colleagues who shared their reactions, challenged my analyses, and provided insights at various critical junctures in this ongoing research that started me on the road to writing *Getting Rid of Patients* and *From Residency to Retirement*. Early on, Professors Diana Scully and the late Jeffrey Hadden, the chair and member respectively of my dissertation committee, scrutinized my ethnographic analysis of the house staff. They gave me "tough love" when I needed it, making my work a better one. Then, as I began the analysis of these physicians in their early career stages, I sought out and received the insights of Professors Stanley Aronowitz, David Rosner, Rob Burlage, Ralph Larkin, and most especially my former dean, the late Harold Lewis. Later on in this journey, Professor Howard Waitzkin,

Robin Elliott, Dr. Oliver Fein, and Carolyn Clancy offered their emotional as well as intellectual support. Thanks go to one of my oldest and dearest friends, Dr. Ira Mehlman, who followed the doctors' careers with me along the way. And through the years, there was always deep friendship and bonding with Sylvia Leonard Wolf and Victor Alicea. It is hard to overestimate how their questions and comments challenged me to understand these doctors' responses more critically and compassionately.

Over the years, a group of Hunter colleagues encouraged me to keep the project going, in spite of a busy professional and demanding personal life—Andrea Savage, Paul Kurzman, Mimi Abramowitz, Steve Burghardt, Michael Fabricant, Darrell Wheeler, among many others. And thanks go to my research partners on other projects through many years: Yossi Korazim, Martha Garcia, Julie Abramson, Beth Rosenthal, Darlyne Bailey, and the late Barbara Joseph and Marcia Bayne-Smith, both of whom we lost too early. They were all immense sources of intellectual stimulation and close camaraderie. Our outcomes were always better for the synergy and respectful process.

The book would not have the comprehensive analysis and framework without my two research collaborators at various stages—Stuart Kaufer and Jennifer Zelnick. We waded through hundreds of pages of transcripts of the cohort, developed our Satisfaction Index, coded and classified the data in the best tradition of qualitative research. Our colleagueship grew to friendship in the process for which I am most grateful. Stuart has been an intellectual and emotional support since he was first my student in the late 1980s.

A special thanks to my several research assistants at various points, who kept the documents and databases and over time became sounding boards, adding their own interpretations and rich insights—Nora Moran, Julia Sick, and Julian Goldhagen. Julian moved to become a research partner with his unique perspectives on the language used in characterizing sensitive topics and his deep dives into health policy.

I want to acknowledge the importance of the small grants I received along the way from the Research Fund of Professional Staff Congress of City University of New York (CUNY) and internally in the last several years from the Silberman School of Social Work at Hunter College, thanks in part to Dean Gary Mallon and the wonderful tech and administrative support from Jim Agolli, Jacob Gutter and Irene Stater. In the mid-1990s I was also awarded a substantial grant from the Agency for Healthcare Research and Quality (AHRQ) of the U.S. Department of Health and Human Services. That funding allowed me to travel to SAMS city and the other places throughout the US where the doctors had settled, and to meet most of them once again in person. A special shout out to Robert Buckley, Research Administrator at Hunter College, for shepherding me through the grant process, and without whose patience and technical expertise I would have not succeeded.

Finding Chris Lura, my developmental editor, was one of the most important occurrences, enabling me to bring a rough manuscript to completion. He helped alter, add, subtract, and streamline my ideas and words with finesse and respect for my years of investment. And much appreciation for the essential finishing touches put on the manuscript by an anonymous copy editor, Alissa Zarro, production manager at Rutgers, and Sherry Gerstein, my production editor at Westchester Publishing Services, Linda Hallinger who indexed the book, and Sangeun Isabel Lee.

This book is the culmination of decades of intimate and robust conversations with a group of internal medicine trained house staff beginning in 1979. In spite of their busy schedules and daily stresses they found the time to tolerate my intrusions and even welcome the interludes at times. They revealed their successes and struggles as practicing physicians in academia and community practice for almost four decades. I can't thank these determined physicians enough who stuck with me as they endured transformative changes in the American health care system and in their own lives and relationships.

While their names and the institution in which they trained are disguised, they know who they are. Whether in person in their office or home or on the telephone, through many hours of taped interviews they candidly revealed intimate situations that affected their professional lives, and conversely exposed how their professional work affected their private homes and families. Several also served as informants, confidants and critics of their peers and the medical profession as a whole.

More than anything I admire their tenacity and resilience as they built rewarding careers in spite of disappointments and challenges at various stages. At the time of the last interviews in 2016, a third of them were retired, sometimes reluctantly and sometimes with one foot still in the medical world. The rest were still in their practice settings with retirement in their near or distant future. Sadly, one of the cohort passed away in the latter phase of his career with unfinished business to be told at the time. I hope my interpretation of their individual and collective careers does them justice.

And finally to my family—my sister Phyllis Cohen, who was always there for me. To my daughter, Eve Madison Rodsky, and son, Josh Madison, to whom I dedicated my first book in 1986. Josh always keeps me grounded. Eve continues to be my anchor, champion, supporter who also challenges and encourages me to go beyond my comfort zone and has made me a better writer and more importantly, better person.

Notes

1. The name of the actual school and the city and state are concealed to protect anonymity of the institution. All of the physicians' names are pseudonyms to help protect their anonymity.

2. The general structure for the physicians as they completed school and began their careers was the following: medical school usually four years, and then a residency period consisting of an internship in year one, and then junior and senior residency in years two and three. After that, there were fellowships after house staff training for those who went into subspecializations, and a fourth year post residency for those six who were selected as chief residents.

3. In actuality, the SAMS house staff at the time I began my observations were almost all White, with one man of color, and about 75 percent male. I regret I did not interview the only Black male or the few White female residents at the time to ascertain whether race or gender had any impact on their attitudes or behavior.

4. The study was approved by the Institutional Review Board of Hunter College of the City University of New York. All interviews were taped with permission of the participants and transcribed. They were told that their names and institutions would be disguised and indeed they were. After the publication of my book in 1986, they were mailed a copy which several commented on in subsequent years. In all these years, I have not revealed their names or the actual city and institution where they trained in any public forum. One physician refused any additional interviews after the entry phase (1979–1980) because he did not like my portrayal of the house staff. Five additional physicians, four of whom had chosen cardiology as a sub-specialization coincidentally or not, declined further contact after the early phase (1980–1984) despite repeated attempts to convince their staffs and themselves to participate. One told me he did not appreciate the tone of my book. Others praised it or said they found it compelling. Twenty were interviewed by phone or in person an additional four times—fifteen years (1994), twenty-five years (2004), thirty-plus years (2011), and thirty-five-plus years (2016) since they completed their SAMS residency.

5. After having interviewed the physicians in four time frames, I invited two other researchers to join me in conducting a deeper analysis of the data. Each of us independently coded the transcripts to increase the credibility of the findings. We created the Satisfaction Index to assess their positivity or negativity toward their career each phase. The team's collective task included reconciling differences in order to achieve a high degree of inter-rater reliability (Padgett, Mathew, et al., 2004). A peer debriefing process

highly recommended by qualitative methodologists was utilized (Corbin and Strauss, 2008; Padgett, Mathew, et al., 2004). This meant rotating as primary and secondary readers, the latter filling in data on the agreed-upon coding grid that the primary coder may have omitted. The third person was available when there were significant differences in interpretation, which happened on occasion. Regular meetings were held with the goal of locating commentary in the transcripts to illustrate a theme and puzzling for a long while at several stark contradictions and cyclical responses that often emerged within and between timeframes. There were rarely identical perspectives on the same circumstances, although there clearly were trends at the cohort level over time. We discovered Saldana's framework to apply to these data and answer these questions among others: "What is cumulative, what surges, what decreases, what remains constant, what is idiosyncratic and what is missing over time?" (2003, pp. 163–167).

6. Other scholars have made similar findings in other studies (Arnetz, 2001; Bury, 2004; Chehab, Panicker, et al., 2001).

CHAPTER 3 — SATISFACTION AND STRAINS

1. The entry phase (1979–1980) is captured in my earlier book (Mizrahi, 1986). As a result, this section is abbreviated and summarized here, whereas the later phases, which present new material with additional questions, are explained in more detail, including in-depth discussions of Satisfaction Index, satisfaction and dissatisfaction themes, components of satisfaction, and anticipating the future. In almost every chapter, discussions of the entry phase (1979–1980) are either omitted or abbreviated.

CHAPTER 8 — VULNERABILITY FROM WITHIN

1. Policy makers, scholars, and critics of medicine are increasingly seeing the relationship between the subjective feelings of physicians and objective outcomes, not just in the United States, but in other countries as well (Kenny and Shelton, 2006; Linzer, Gerrity, et al., 2002; Williams and Skinner, 2003; Zuger, 2004). Those few studies use in-depth interviews, journals, and narrative approaches to bring out personal meanings and context (Dunstone and Reames, 2001; Elliott, 2006; Meier, Back, et al., 2001). These sometimes hidden or secret sentiments appear in the international literature as well. Lupton (1997) conducted semistructured interviews with twenty physicians in Australia. She found evidence of cynicism partly as a result of changes in perspectives on expert knowledge and the changing status of the medical profession. While she (and I) found that many of these physicians said they were still shown respect and granted an air of authority by their own patient cohort or local community, at the same time, they articulated that patients were becoming more assertive and more willing to challenge them. Lupton concluded that the micro politics and power dimensions of medical practice adversely affected physician-patient relationships. Loneliness was identified as a consequence of medical arrangements found in German physicians by Kuhlmann (2006). She concluded that there is a need to build a shared trust among physicians and patients and a new way of reframing the doctor-patient relationship. One study (Testerman, Morton, et al., 1996) tested whether cynicism was transmitted intergenerationally

as part of medical socialization during graduate and postgraduate training among students, residents, and faculty, or whether it was a temporary by-product of that socialization known as "professional identity." The authors found that medical students were the most cynical and attending faculty the least, confirming the latter hypothesis.

2. These questions are described in more detail in my earlier book in the chapter titled, "A Retrospective View of House Staff Training from Practice" (Mizrahi, 1986).

CHAPTER 9 — THE PERSONAL AND THE PROFESSIONAL

1. These questions included a speculative query for the first time in the ending phase: "Do you think your wife sacrificed for your career? What do you think she would say if asked her that question?" Most publications that focused on physician-related marriage and family issues appeared since 2000 (Read and Addington, 2011). Before then, there were very few publications that had interviewed the wives of physicians; Gerber (1983) was an exception.

CHAPTER 10 — PHYSICIANS' HAPPIEST AND UNHAPPIEST TIMES, AND THEIR WISHES AND MISSES THROUGHOUT THEIR CAREERS

1. As discussed in earlier chapters, most of the physicians continued to use the concept of "fun" to indicate a sense of joy and even exhilaration in their work. On the other hand, they also used it to signal the reverse by noting it as being absent or missing.

CHAPTER 11 — CONCLUSION

1. My 1986 book was one of the few references identified in the New York State Department of Health report known as the "Bell Commission." Additionally, I have a personal note from Bertram Bell (dated August 1, 1987) thanking me for the research and the book, noting it was instrumental in shaping the recommendations of the commission to curtail the hours residents could work a week and addressing other professional issues (NYS Department of Health, 1987).

References

Abbott, A. (1995). *The system of professions; an essay on the division of expert labor.* Chicago, IL: University of Chicago Press.

Adler, P. P., Kwon, S-W., and Heckcher, C. (2007). Professional work: The emergence of collaborative community. *Organization Science.* https://www.mbs.ac.uk/newsevents /documents/Pauladler.pdf

Agency for Health Care Research and Quality. (2019, September). *Medication errors and adverse drug events.* Patient Safety Network. https://psnet.ahrq.gov/primer/medication -errors-and-adverse-drug-events

Al-Lamki, L. (2009). Peer review of physicians' performance: Is it necessary quality assurance activity? *Sultan Qaboos University Medical Journal,* 109–112.

American Hospital Association. (1992). *The patient care partnership.* https://www.aha .org/other-resources/patient-care-partnership

American Medical Association. (2001). *Code of ethics.* https://www.ama-assn.org/sites /ama-assn.org/files/corp/media-browser/principles-of-medical-ethics.pdf

Annas, G. J. (1975). *The rights of hospital patients: The basic ACLU guide to hospital patients' bill of rights.* New York, NY: Discus Books.

Antiel, R. M., James, K. M., Egginton, J. S., Sheeler, R. D., Liebow, M., Goold, S. D., and Tilburt, J. C. (2013). Specialty, political affiliation, and perceived social responsibility are associated with U.S. physician reactions to health care reform legislation. *Journal of General Internal Medicine, 29*(2), 399–403.

Appold, K. (2016, June 17). *Three patterns of self-reflection from physicians.* https://www .physicianspractice.com/patient-relations/three-patterns-self-reflection-physicians

Arnetz, B. B. (2001). Psychosocial challenges facing physicians today. *Social Science & Medicine, 5*(2), 203–213.

Association of American Medical Colleges. (2017, December). *2017 Application and matriculation tables.* Retrieved February 8, 2020, from https://www.aamc.org/system/files/d /1/5-2017_applicant_and_matriculant_data_tables.pdf

Bailie, R., Sibthorpe, B., Douglas, B., Broom, D., Attewell, R., McGuiness, C. (1998). Mixed feelings: Satisfaction and disillusionment among Australian GPs. *Family Practice, 15*(1), 58–65.

Beckers Hospital Review. (2014, February 11). *A brief history on the road to health care reform: From Truman to Obama.* https://www.beckershospitalreview.com/news-analysis/a-brief -history-on-the-road-to-healthcare-reform-from-truman-to-obama.html

Beeson, P. B. (1986). One hundred years of American internal medicine: A view from the inside. *Annals of Internal Medicine, 105*(3), 436–444.

Bloch, A. L. (1989). The post-Bell Commission on residency: Sleep or care? *Journal of the American Medical Association, 261*(22), 3243–3244.

Blumenthal, D., and Morone, J. A. (2010). *Heart of power with a new preface: Health and politics in the Oval Office.* Berkeley, CA: University of California Press.

Boisaubin, E. V., and Levine, R. E. (2001). Identifying and assisting the impaired physician. *American Journal of Medical Sciences, 322*(1), 31–36.

Bollier, D. (1991). *Citizen action and other big ideas: A history of Ralph Nader and the modern consumer movement.* Washington, DC: Center for the Study of Responsive Law.

Boothman, R. C., Imhoff, S. J., and Campbell Jr., D. A. (2012). Nurturing a culture of patient safety and achieving lower malpractice risk through disclosure: lessons learned and future directions. *Frontiers of Health Services Management, 28*(3), 13–28.

Borges, N. J., Navarro, A. M., Grover, A., and Hoban, J. D. (2010). How, when and why do physicians choose careers in academic medicine. *Academic Medicine, 84*(4), 680–686.

Bosk, C. L. (2003). *Forgive and remember: Managing medical failure* (2nd ed.). Chicago, IL: University of Chicago Press.

Boston Health Collective. (1970). *Our bodies ourselves: A book of and by women.* New York, NY: Touchstone Publishers.

Boyd, J. W. (2015). Deciding whether to refer a colleague to a physician health program. *AMA Journal of Ethics*, 888–893.

Brill, S. (2015). *America's bitter pill: Money, politics, backroom deals and the fight to fix our broken health care system.* New York, NY: Random House.

Buckley, L. M., Sanders, K., Shih, M., and Hampton, C. L. (2000). Attitudes of clinical faculty about career progress, career success and recognition, and commitment to academic medicine. Results of a survey. *Archives of Internal Medicine, 160*(17), 2625–2629.

Bury, M. (2004). Researching patient-professional interactions. *Journal of Health Services Research and Policy, 9*(1 Suppl), 48–54.

Bushnell, B. B. (2013). The evolution of the DRGs. *American Association of Orthopedic Surgeons.* https://www.aaos.org/AAOSNow/2013/Dec/advocacy/advocacy2/?ssopc=1

Carrier, E. R., Reschovsky, J. D., Katz, D. A., and Mello, M. M. (2013). High physician concern about malpractice risk predicts more aggressive diagnostic testing in office-based practice. *Health Affairs, 32*(8), 1383–1391.

CFA Institute. (2014). *Code of ethics & standards of professional conduct.* https://www.cfainstitute.org/en/ethics/codes/code-of-ethics-and-standards-of-professional-conduct

Charles, S. C., Wilbert, J. R., and Franke, K. J. (1985). Sued and non-sued physicians' self-reported reactions to malpractice litigation. *American Journal of Psychiatry, 142*, 437–440.

Charon, R. (2008). Narrative medicine: New York: Oxford University Press.

Chassin, M. (2019). To err is human: The next 20 years. Joint Commission. https://www
.jointcommission.org/resources/news-and-multimedia/blogs/high-reliability-healthcare
/2019/11/to-err-is-human-the-next-20-years/

Chehab, E., Panicker, N., Alper, P. R., Baker, L. C., Wilson, S. R., and Raffin, T. A. (2001).
The impact of practice setting on physician perceptions of the quality of practice and
patient care in the managed care era. *Archive of Internal Medicine, 161,* 202–211.

Chen, B. K., and Yang, C. Y. (2014). Increased perception of malpractice liability and the
practice of defensive medicine. *Journal of Empirical Legal Studies, 11*(3), 446–476.

Chimonas, S., DeVito, N. J., and Rothman, D. J. (2017). Bringing transparency to medicine: Exploring physicians views and experiences of the Sunshine Act. *American Journal of Bioethics, 17*(4), 4–18.

Chirba, M. A., and Noble, A. (2013, May 14). Medical malpractice, the Affordable Care
Act & state provider shield laws: More myth than necessity? *Bill of Health Blog at Harvard Law.* https://blogs.law.harvard.edu/billofhealth/2013/05/14/medical-malpractice
-the-affordable-care-act-and-state-provider-shield-laws-more-myth-than-necessity/

Chowkwanyun, M. (2011). The new left and public health: The Health Policy Advisory
Center, community organizing, and the big business of health 1967–1975. *American
Journal of Public Health, 101,* 238–249.

———. (2018). The war on poverty's health legacy: What it was and why it matters.
Health Affair, 37(1), 47–53.

Coburn, D., Rapport, S., and Bourgeault, I. (1997). Decline and retention of medical
power through restratification: An examination of the Ontario case. *Sociology of
Health & Illness, 19*(1), 1–22.

Cole, T. R., and Carlin, N. (2009). The suffering of physicians. *The Lancet, 374*(I 9699),
1414–1415.

Collins, S. R., Rasmussen, P. W., Doty, M. M., and Beutel, S. (2015). *The rise in health care
coverage and affordability since health reform took effect.* Washington, DC: Commonwealth
Fund.

Conover, C. (2014, October 30). *Critiquing US health care critics.* Forbes.

Cooch, N. (2020, June 2). The impact of COVID-19 on physicians: Lessons from previous
outbreaks. Practice Update. https://www.practiceupdate.com/content/the-psychological
-impact-of-covid-19-on-physicians-lessons-from-previous-outbreaks/100995

Corbin, J., and Strauss, A. (2008). *A basics of qualitative research* (3rd ed.). Thousand Oaks,
CA: Sage Publications.

Coulehan, J., and Williams, P. C. (2001). Vanquishing virtue: The impact of medical
education. *Academic Medicine, 76,* 598–605.

Croner, A. (2015, December 3). Is there a doctor in the marriage? *The New York Times.*

Crowley, R.A. and Bornstein, S.S. (2019). Improving the Patient Protection and Affordable Care Act's Insurance Coverage Provisions: A Position Paper from the American
College of Physicians. *Annals of Internal Medicine, 170* (9), 651–653.

Curlin, F. A., Chin, M. H., and Sellergren, M. A. (2006). The association of physicians' religious characteristics with their attitudes and self-reported behaviors regarding religion and spirituality in the clinical encounter. *Medicare Care, 44*(5), 446–453.

Dellinger, E. P., Pellegrini, C. A., and Gallagher, T. H. (2017). The aging physician and the medical profession: A review. *JAMA Surgery, 152*(10), 967–971.

Deyo-Svendsen, M. E., Phillips, M. R., Albright, J. K., Schilling, K. A., and Palmer, K. A. (2016). A systematic approach to clinical peer review in a critical access hospital. *Quality Management in Health Care, 25*(4), 213–218.

Dingwall, R. and Lewis, P. (1983). *Sociology of the professions: Lawyers, doctors and others.* London: Macmillan.

Dittmer, J. (2009). *The good doctors: The medical committee for human rights and the struggle for social justice in health care.* London, UK: Bloomsbury Publishing.

Diverse Medicine Recruitment Center. (2018, March 15.) *Dr. Dale: How to have fun during medical school.* https://www.diversemedicine.com.

Domagalski, T. (2005). *Physician discontent: Dissent or co-optation in response to capitalist initiatives?* Critical Studies Conference #4. Cambridge University, UK.

Dumelow, C., Littlejohns, P., and Griffiths, S. (2000). Relation between a career and family life for English hospital consultants: Qualitative, semi-structured interview study. *British Medical Journal, 320,* 1437–1440.

Dunstone, D. C., and Reames, Jr., H. R. (2001). Physician satisfaction revised. *Social Science & Medicine, 52,* 825–837.

Durrington, D. A., Western, J. S., Haynes, M., and Dwan, K. (2006). Characteristics and benefits of professional work: Assessment of their importance over a 30 year career. *Journal of Sociology, 42*(2), 165–188.

Edwards, N., Kornaki, M. J., and Silversin, J.(2002). Unhappy doctors: What are the causes and what can be done. *British Medical Journal, 324*(7341), 835–838.

Ehrenreich, B., and Ehrenreich, J. (1970). *The American health empires: Power, profits and politics.* New York, NY: Random House.

Elliot, C. (2006). Disillusioned doctors. In N. Kenny and W. Shelton (Eds.), *Lost virtue: Professional character development in medical education* (Vol. 10, pp. 87–98). Amsterdam, Netherlands: Elsevier.

Emanuel, E. J. (2020). *Which country has the best health care in the world?* New York, NY: PublicAffairs.

Emanuel, E. J., and Steinmetz, A. (2013). Will physicians lead on controlling health care costs? *Journal of the American Medical Association, 310*(4), 374–375.

Erdmann, J. B., Jones, R. F., and Xenier, T. (1978). *A.A.M.C. longitudinal study of medical school graduates of 1960.* Washington, DC: A.A.M.C.

Evett, J. (2003). The sociological analysis of professionalism: Occupational change in the modern world. *International Sociology, 18*(2), 395–415.

Fargen, K. M., Leslie-Mazwi, T. M., Klucznik, R. P., Wolfe, S. Q., Brown, P., Ansari, S. A., Dabus, G., Spiotta, A. M., Mokin, M., Hassan, A. E., Liebeskind, D., Welch, B. G., Siddiqui, A. H., and Hirsch, J. A. (2020). The professional and personal impact of the coronavirus pandemic on US neurointerventional practices: A nationwide survey. *Journal of Neuro-Interventional Surgery.* 12(10). https://jnis.bmj.com/content/12/10/927

Freidson, E. (1970). *Profession of medicine: A study of the sociology of applied knowledge.* Chicago, IL: University of Chicago.

———. (1984). The changing nature of professional control. *Annual Review of Sociology, 10,* 1–20.

———. (1995). The power of physicians' autonomy and balance in a changing system. *American Journal of Medicine, 16*(3), 579–586.

———. (2001). *Professionalism: The third logic.* Chicago, IL: University of Chicago Press.

Funk, C., and Gramlich, J. (2020). Amid coronavirus threat, Americans generally have a high level of trust in medical doctors. https://www.pewresearch.org/fact-tank/2020 /03/13/amid-coronavirus-threat-americans-generally-have-a-high-level-of-trust-in -medical-doctors/

Furrow, B. R. (1998). Doctors' little secrets: The dark side of medical privacy. *Washburn Law Journal, 37,* 283–316.

Furst, L. R. (1998). *Between doctors and patients: The changing balance of power.* Charlottesville, VA: University Press of Virginia.

Gawande, A. (1999, February). When doctors make mistakes. *The New Yorker,* 40–43.

———. (2017, October). Is health care a right? *The New Yorker,* 48–51.

Geer, M. A. (1983). Mental health-Pennhurst State School and Hospital v. Haldeman: Back to the drawing board for the developmentally disabled. *North Carolina Law Review, 60*(5), 1116–1125.

Geiger, H. J. (2017). The political future of social medicine: Reflections on physicians as activists. *Academic Medicine, 92*(3), 282–284.

Gerber, L. A. (1983). *Married to their careers: Career and family dilemmas in doctors' lives.* London: Tavistock Publications.

Ghalandarpoorattar, S. M., Kaviani, A., and Asghari, F. (2012). Medical error disclosure: The gap between attitude and practice. *Postgraduate Medical Journal, 88*(1037), 130–133.

Gingrich, N. (1994). *Contract with America.* http://www.rialto.k12.ca.us/rhs/planetwhited /AP%20PDF%20Docs/Unit%2014/CONTRAC7.PDP

Goode, D., Hill, D., Reiss, J., and Bronston, W. (2013). *The history and sociology of the Willowbrook State School.* Washington, DC: American Association on Intellectual and Developmental Disabilities.

Gorin, S., & Mizrahi, T. (2013, November 4). Health Care Reform. *Encyclopedia of Social Work.* Retrieved October 20, 2020, from https://oxfordre.com/socialwork/view/10 .1093/acrefore/9780199975839.001.0001/acrefore-9780199975839-e-175

Gossman, W., Robinson, K. J., and Nouhan, P. P. (2019). *Expert witness*. https://www.ncbi.nlm.nih.gov/books/NBK436001/

Gouveia, V. V., Barbosa, G. A., Andrade, E. O. and Carneiro, M. B. (2005). Measuring life satisfaction among physicians in Brazil. [In Portuguese] *Jornal Brasileiro de Psiquiatria, 54,* 298–305.

Greenhalgh, T., Potts, HW, Wong, G., Bark, P., and Singlehurst, D. (2009). Tensions and paradoxes in electronic patient record research—A systematic literature review using meta-narrative methods. *Milbank Quarterly, 87*(4), 729–88.

Gref, S., Gildemeister, S., and Wasem, J. (2004). The social transformation of American medicine: A comparative view from Germany. *Journal of Health Politics, Policy & Law, 29*(4/5), 679–699.

Grober, E. D., and Bohnen, J. M. A. (2005). Defining medical error. *Canadian Journal of Surgery, 48*(1), 39–44.

Gunderman, R. (2016, September 21). Hospitalists and the decline of comprehensive care. *New England Journal of Medicine, 375,* 1011–1913.

Hafferty, F. W. (2006). Definitions of professionalism. *Clinical Orthopedic and Related Research, 449,* 193–204.

———. (1988). Cadaver stories and the emotional socialization of medical students. *Journal of Health and Social Behavior 12,* 344–356.

Hagar, J. P. (2012). *At least you'll be married to a doctor: Managing your intimate relationships through medical school.* Denver, CO: Outskirts Press.

Hall, H. (1971). *Unfinished business in the neighborhood and nation. A first-hand account by the former director of Henry Street Settlement.* New York, NY: Macmillan.

Harris, D., and Puskarz, K. (2017). An observational study of provider perspectives on alternative payment models. *Population Health Management, 20*(5), 402–410.

Harris, L., and Associates. (1981). *Medical practice in the 1980's: Physicians' look at their changing profession.* Henry J. Kaiser Family Foundation. https://www.kff.org/wp-content/uploads/2013/01/highlights-and-chart-pack-2.pdf

Harris, R. (1969). *A sacred trust: The story of organized medicine's multi-million dollar fight against public health legislation.* New York, NY: Pelican Books.

Hartley, H. (2002). The system of alignments challenging physician professional dominance: An elaborated theory of countervailing powers. *Sociology of Health and Illness, 24*(2), 178–207.

Haskell, H. (2014, June 1). *Patient advocacy in patient safety: Have things changed?* Patient Safety Network. https://www.psnet.ahrq.gov/perspective/patient-advocacy-patient-safety-have-things-changed

Health Affairs. (2020, February 19). Evolving opinion about the Affordable Care Act 2010–2019. *Blog.* https://www.healthaffairs.org/do/10.1377/hblog20200219.654090/full/

Henry, J. (2004). OMA membership survey results confirm overwhelming level of frustration among Ontario physicians. *Ontario Medical Review, 71,* 1–6.

Heriot, J. (2017). *Riding the second wave: How feminism changed women's psychology and mine*. North Charleston, SC: Create Space Independent Publishing Platform.

Hershey, N. (1972). The defensive practice of medicine: Myth or reality. *The Milbank Memorial Fund Quarterly, 50*(1), 69–97.

Hilfiker, D. (1984). Facing our mistakes. *The New England Journal of Medicine, 310*(2), 118–122.

Hinckle, W., and Simon, J. J. (1995). *Do no harm: The Libby Zion case: How doctors killed her and then blamed the victim*. Madison, WI: Argonaut Press.

Hinko, A. (2012). The AMA and health care reform. *The Pharos, Winter*, 24–30. https://alphaomegaalpha.org/pharos/PDFs/2012/1/Hinko.pdf

Hojat, M., Gonnella, J. S., Veloski, J. J., and Xu, G. (1995). Primary care and non-primary care physicians: A longitudinal study of their similarities, differences, and correlates before, during and after medical school. *Academic Medicine, 70*(1 Suppl), S17–S28.

Holzman, I. R., and Barnett, S. H. (2000). The Bell Commission: Ethical implications for the training of the physicians. *Mt. Sinai Journal of Medicine, 67*(2), 136–139.

Horowitz, C. R., Suchman, A. L., Branch, Jr., W. T., and Frankel, R. M. (2003). What do doctors find meaningful about their work? *Annals of Internal Medicine, 138*(9), 772–776.

Hunter, K. M. (1993). *Doctors' stories: The narrative structure of medical knowledge*. Princeton, NJ: Princeton University Press.

Jacobs, L. R., and Skocpol, T. (2010). *Health care reform & American politics: What everyone needs to know*. New York, NY: Oxford University Press.

Jasso-Aguilar, R., Waitzkin, H., and Landwehr, A. (2004). Multinational corporations and health care in the United States and Latin America: Strategies, actions, and effects. *Journal of Health and Social Behavior, 45*, 136–157.

Jauhar, S. (2014). *Doctored: The disillusionment of an American physician*. New York, NY: Farrar, Strauss & Giroux.

Jennett, P. A., Kishinevsky, M., Bryant, H., and Hunter K. L. (1990). Major changes in medical careers following medical school graduation: when, how often, and why. *Academic Medicine, 65*(1), 48–49.

Johnson, H., and Broder, D. S. (1996). *The system: The American way of politics at the breaking point*. Boston, MA: Little Brown & Co.

Johnson, T. M. (1988). Physician impairment: Social origins of a medical concern. *Medical Anthropology Quarterly, 2*(1), 17–33.

Jovic, E., Wallace, J. E., and Lemaire, J. (2006, May). The generation and gender shifts in medicine: an exploratory survey of internal medicine physicians. *BMC Health Services Research, 5*(6), 55.

Kass, J. S., and Rose, R. V. (2016). Ethical challenges for medical expert witness. *AMA Journal of Ethics, 18*(3), 201–208.

Kassirer, J. P., and Cecil, J. S. (2002). Inconsistency in evidentiary standards for medical testimony: Disorder in the courts. *Journal of the American Medical Association, 288*(11), 1382–1387.

Kelly, E. L., Moen, P., Oakes, J. M., Fen, W., Okechukwu, C., Davis, K. D., Hammer, L.B., Kossek, E., King, R. B., Hanson, G. C., Mierzwa, F., and Casper, L. M. (2014). Changing work and work-family conflict: Evidence from the work, family and health network. *American Sociological Review, 79*(3), 485–516.

Kenny, N. and Shelton, W. (Eds). (2006). *Lost virtue—Professional character development in medical education.* Amsterdam, Netherlands: Elsevier.

Kirsch, R. (2011). *Fighting for our health: The epic battle to make health care a right in the United States.* Albany, NY: Rockefeller Institute Press.

Klitzman, R. (2008). *When doctors become patients.* New York, NY: Oxford University Press.

Kohn, L. T., Corrigan, J. M., and Donaldson, M. S. (1999). *To err is human: Building a safer health system.* Washington, DC: National Academy Press.

Konrad, T., Williams, E., Linzer, M., McMurray, J., Pathman, D., Gerrity, M., Schwartz, M. D., Schleckler, W. E., Van Kirk, J., Rhodes, E., and Douglas, J. (1999). Measuring physician job satisfaction in a changing workplace and a challenging environment. *Medical Care, 37*, 1174–1182.

Kraman, S. S., and Hamm, G. (1999). Risk management: Extreme honesty may be the best policy. *Annals of Internal Medicine, 131*(12), 963–967.

Kuhlmann, E. (2006). Traces of doubt and sources of trust: Health professions in an uncertain society. *Current Sociology 54,* 607–620.

Landon, B. E., Reschovsky, J. D., Pham, H. H., and Blumenthal, D. (2006). Leaving medicine: The consequences of physician dissatisfaction. *Medical Care, 44*(1), 234–242.

Lawthers, A., G., Laird, N. M., Lipsitz, S., Hebert, L., and Brennan, T. A. (1992). Physicians' perceptions of the risk of being sued. *Journal of Health, Politics, Policy, and Law, 17*(3), 463–482.

Leaf, P. (1977). Wyatt v. Stickney: Assessing the impact in Alabama. *Hospital and Community Psychiatry, 5,* 351–356.

Leape, L. L. (1994). Error in medicine. *Journal of American Medical Association, 272*(23), 1851–1857.

Leigh, J. P., Kravitz, R. L., Schembri, M., Samuels, M., and Mobley, S. (2002). Physician career satisfaction across specialties. *Archives of Internal Medicine, 162*(14), 1577–1584.

Light, D. W. (1980). *Becoming psychiatrists: The professional transformation of self.* New York, NY: W. W. Norton & Co.

———. (2004). Ironies of success: A new history of the American health care "system." *Journal of Health and Social Behavior, 45,* 1–24.

———. (2005). Countervailing power: The changing character of the medical profession in the United States. In P. Conrad (Ed.), *Sociology of health and illness: Critical perspectives,* (7th ed., pp. 189–215). New York, NY: Worth Publishers.

Linzer, M., Gerrity, M., Douglas, J., McMurray, J., Williams, E., and Konrad, T. (2002). Physician stress: Results from the physician worklife study. *Journal of Stress and Health, 18,* 37–42.

Lipp, M. (1980). *The bitter pill*. New York, NY: Harper and Row.

Lipsenthal, L. (2007). *Finding a balance in medical life: A guided program to help you reclaim your sense of balance in your busy life in medicine*. Lee Lipsenthal: printed by author.

Lockwood, L. E., Luker, A., Ascherman, L. I., and Bukelis, I. (2018). Human side of medicine: Understanding physician burnout at the University of Alabama Department of Psychiatry. *Child and Adolescent Psychiatry, 57*(10 Suppl), S264.

Lupton, D. (1997). Doctors on the medical profession. *Sociology of Health & Illness, 19*(4), 480–497.

Makary, M. A., and Daniel, M. (2016). Medical error—the third leading cause of death in the US. *British Medical Journal, 353*(2139). https://doi.org/10.1136/bmj.i2139

Manchikanti, L., Helm, Li S., Benyamin, R. M., and Hirsch, J. A. (2017). A critical analysis of Obamacare: Affordable care or insurance for many and coverage for a few? *Pain Physician, 20*(3), 111–138.

Markel, H. (2009, August 17). A book doctors' can't close. *The New York Times*. https://www.nytimes.com/2009/08/18/health/18house.html

Marmor, T. (2000). *The politics of Medicare*. (2nd ed.). Hawthorne, NY: Aldine de Gruyter.

Mawardi, B. H. (1979). Satisfaction, dissatisfaction and causes of stressing medical practice. *Journal of the American Medical Association, 241*, 1483–1486.

Maxwell, A., and Shields, T. (2017, June 26). *The impact of "modern sexism" on the 2016 presidential election*. Fayetteville, AR: Blair Center of Southern Politics & Society.

McCormick, D., Himmelstein, D. U., and Woolhandler, S. (2004). Single-payer national health insurance: Physicians' Views. *JAMA Internal Medicine. 164* (3), 300–304.

McGreevey, S. (2015, February 19). Doctors and divorce. *Harvard Medical School News and Research*.

McKinlay, J. B., and Marceau, L. D. (2005). The end of the golden age of doctoring. In P. Conrad (Ed.), *Sociology of health and illness: Critical perspectives* (7th ed., pp. 215–224). New York, NY: Worth Publishers.

McMurray, J. E., Williams, E., Schwartz, M. D., Douglas, J., Van Kirk, J., Konrad, T. R., Gerrity, M., Bigby, J. A., Linzer, M., and SGIM Career Satisfaction Study Group. (1999). Physician job satisfaction: Developing a model using qualitative data. SGIM Career Satisfaction Study Group. *Journal of General Internal Medicine, 12*, 711–714.

Mechanic, D. (1996). Changing medical organization and the erosion of trust. *The Milbank Quarterly, 74*(2), 171–189.

Medical Ethics Advisor (2006). Critics charge physician peer review misused. *Medical Ethics Advisor*. 2006. http://www.accessmylibrary.com/coms2/summary_0286-18035554_ITM

Medicine Net. (n.d.). *Medical definition of defensive medicine*. Retrieved March 10, 2019, from https://www.medicinenet.com/script/main/art.asp?articlekey=33262

Meier, D. E., Back, A. L., and Morrison, S. (2001). The inner life of physicians and care of the seriously ill. *Journal of the American Medical Association 286*(23), 3007–3014.

Melish, T. J. (2010). Maximum feasible participation of the poor: New governance, new accountability and 21st century war on the sources of poverty. *Yale Human Rights and Development Journal, 13,* 101–234.

Merritt Hawkins. (2015). *The aging physician workforce: A demographic dilemma.* https://www.hasc.org/sites/main/files/link1mhawhitepaperaging.pdf

Mizrahi, T. (1984a). Managing medical mistakes: Ideology, insularity and accountability among internists-in-training. *Social Science and Medicine, 19*(2), 135–146.

———. (1984b). The outpatient clinic: The crucible of the doctor-patient relationship in graduate medical education. *Journal of Ambulatory Care Management, 7*(2), 51–68.

———. (1986). *Getting rid of patients: Contradictions in the socialization of physicians.* New Brunswick, NJ: Rutgers University Press.

Monteiro, A. R. (2015). *Sociology of professions.* New York, NY: Springer.

Mostashari, F., Sanghavi, D., and McClellan, M. (2014). Health reform and physician-led accountable care: the paradox of primary care physician leadership. *Journal of the American Medical Association, 311*(18), 1855–1856.

Muhammad, M., Wallerstein, N., Sussman, A. L., Avila, M., Belone, L., and Duran, B. (2014). Reflections on researcher identity and power: The impact of positionality on community based participatory research processes and outcomes. *Critical Sociology,* 1–19.

Murphy, J. W. (2018). The role of reflection in narrative medicine. *Journal of Medical Education & Curricular Development.* https://journals.sagepub.com/doi/full/10.1177/238 2120518785301

Murphy, M. (2018, July 13). Medical errors: Causes and solutions. *Medical Scribe Journal.*

Murray, A., Montgomery, J. E., Chang, H., Rogers, W. H., Inul, T., and Safran, D. G. (2001). Doctor discontent: A comparison of physician satisfaction in different delivery system settings, 1986 and 1997. *Journal of General Internal Medicine, 16,* 451–459.

Newman, M. C. (1996). The emotional impact of mistakes on family physicians. *Archives of Family Medicine, 5*(2), 71–75.

Nickon, C. (2010, December 7). William Osler's humor, and finding fun in medicine. *KEVINMD BLOG.* https://Kevinmd.com/blog/2010/12

Nixon, R. L., and Jaramillo, F. (2003). Impact of practice arrangements on physicians' satisfaction. *Hospital Topics, 81*(4), 19–25.

N.Y.S. Department of Health. (1987, October). *Final report of the New York State AD HOC Advisory Committee on emergency services.*

Ochsner, J. (2003). The Code of Medical Ethics of the American Medical Association. *The Ochsner Journal, 5*(2), 6–10.

Ofri, D. (2013a). *What doctors feel: How emotions affect the practice of medicine.* Boston, MA: Beacon Press.

——— (2013b, July 2). The epidemic of disillusionment. *Time.*

Omotosho, A., and Emuoyibofarhe, J. (2014). A criticism of the current security, privacy, and accountability. *International Journal of Informational Systems* 7(8), 11–18.

O'Rourke, M. (2014, November). Doctors tell all and it's bad. *The Atlantic.* https://www.theatlantic.com/magazine/archive/2014/11/doctors-tell-all-and-its-bad/380785/

Padgett, D. K. (1998). *Qualitative methods in social work research: Challenge and rewards.* Thousand Oaks, CA: Sage Publications.

Padgett, D. K., Mathew, R., and Conte, S. (2004). Peer debriefing and support groups: Formation, care, and maintenance. In D. K. Padgett (Ed.), *The Qualitative Research Experience,* (pp. 229–239). Belmont, CA: Wadsworth/Thomas Learning.

Pantilat, S. (2006, February). What is a hospitalist? The hospitalist. *Society of Hospital Medicine.* https://www.the-hospitalist.org/hospitalist/article/123072/what-hospitalist

Pearl, R. (2014a, March 6). *Malcolm Gladwell on American health care: An interview.* Forbes.

———. (2014b, March 13). *Malcolm Gladwell: Tell people what it's really like to be a doctor.* Forbes.

Pearson, R. (2019, December 25). "The House of God": A book as sexist as it was influential, gets a sequel. *The New Yorker.* https://www.newyorker.com/books/under-review/the-house-of-god-a-book-as-sexist-as-it-was-influential-gets-a-sequel

Peckham, C. (2012a, February 22). *Profiles in happiness: Which physicians enjoy life the most?* https://www.medscape.com/viewarticle/760127_1

———. (2012b, March 22). *Are physicians happily married?* https://wbww.medscape.com/viewarticle/760127_6

Perlman, R. L., Ross, P. T., and Lypson, M. I. (2014). Understanding the medical marriage: Physicians and their partners share strategies for success. *Academic Medicine,* 1–6.

Pololi, L. H., Krupat, E., Civian, J. T., Ash, A. S., and Brennan, R. T. (2012). Why are a quarter of faculty considering leaving academic medicine? A study of their perceptions of institutional culture and intentions to leave at 26 representative US medical schools. *Academic Medicine,* 87(7), 859–869.

Potter, W. (2010). *Deadly spin: An insurance company insider speaks out on how corporate PR is killing health care and deceiving Americans.* New York, NY: Bloomsbury Press.

Quality Interagency Coordination Task Force (2000). *Doing what counts for patient safety: Federal actions to reduce medical errors and their impact—A report of the QICTF.*

RAND (2020). *The future of health care: Replace or Revise the ACA?* RAND Health Care. https://www.rand.org/health-care/key-topics/health-policy/in-depth.html

Rawal, P. H. (2016). *The Affordable Care Act: Examining the facts.* Santa Barbara, CA: ABC-CLIO.

Read, D., and Addington, S. (2011). *Prescription for the doctor's wife: Hope and health for your unique marriage.* Colorado Springs, CO.

Reames, H. R., Jr., and Dunstone, D. C. (1989). Professional satisfaction of physicians. *Archives of Internal Medicine,* 149, 1951–1956.

Reference MD. (n.d.). *Medical definition of medical errors*. Retrieved from http://www
.reference.md/files/D019/mD019300.html

Renkema, E., Broekhuis, M., and Ahaus, K. (2014). Conditions that influence the impact
of malpractice litigation risk on physicians' behavior regarding patient safety. *BMC
Health Services Research, 14*(1), 38. https://doi.org/10.1186/1472-6963-14-38

Roberts, D. L., Shanafelt, T. D., Liselotte, N. D., Dyrbye, L. N.,and West, C. P. (2014). A
national comparison of burnout and work-life balance among internal medicine hospitalists and outpatient general internists. *Journal of Hospital Medicine, 9*(3), 176–181.

Robertson, S. L., Robinson, M. D., and Reid, A. (2017). Electronic health record effects
on work-life balance and burnout within the population collaborative. *Journal of
Graduate Medical Education, 9*(4), 479–484.

Robins, N. S. (1995). *The girl who died twice—Every patient's nightmare: The Libby Zion case
and the hidden hazards of hospitals*. New York, NY: Delacorte Press.

Robinson, K. A., Cheng, M. R., Hansen, P. N., and Gray, R. J. (2017). Religion and spiritual beliefs of physicians. *Journal of Religion & Health, 56*(1), 205–225.

Rodsky, E. M. (2019). *Fair play*. New York, NY: Random House.

Rodwin, M. A. (1993). *Medicine, money & morals: Physicians' conflicts of interest*. New York,
NY: Oxford University Press.

Ross, S. (2003). Identifying the impaired physician. *AMA Journal of Ethics, 5*(12), 420–422.

Ruspini, E. (2000). Longitudinal research in the social sciences. *Social Research Update,
20*. https://www.soc.surrey.ac.uk/sru/SRU28.html

Saldana, J. (2003). *Longitudinal qualitative research: Analyzing changes through time*. Walnut
Creek, CA: AltiMira Press.

Sample, S. (2011). Vulnerability in physicians' narratives. *Medicine and Society, 13*(7), 494–498.

Sargent, D. A. (1985). The impaired physicians' movement: An interim report. *Hospital
& Community Psychiatry, 36*(3), 294–295.

Schleiter, K. E. (2009). Difficult patient-physician relationships and the risk of medical
malpractice litigation. *AMA Journal of Ethics*. https://journalofethics.ama-assn.org
/article/difficult-patient-physician-relationships-and-risk-medical-malpractice
-litigation/2009-03

Schlesinger, M. (2002). A loss of faith: The sources of reduced political legitimacy for the
American medical profession. *The Milbank Quarterly 80*(2), 185–235.

Seabury, S. A., Chandra, A., Lakdawalla, D. N., and Jena, A. B. (2013). On average, physicians spend nearly 11 percent of their 40-year careers with an open, unresolved malpractice claim. *Health Affairs, 32*(1), 111–119.

Sekhar, M. S., and Vyas, N. (2013). Defensive medicine: A bane to healthcare. *Annals of
Medical and Health Sciences Research, 3*(2), 295–296.

Serafini, M. (2018, January 17). Why physicians support single-payer health insurance:
Who will win and who will lose? *NEJM (New England Journal of Medicine) Catalyst*.
https://catalyst.nejm.org/doi/full/10.1056/CAT.18.0278

Seys, D., Wu, A. W., Gerven, E. V., Vleugels, A., Euwema, M., Panella, M., Scott, S. D., Conway, J., Sermeus, W., and Vanhaecht, K. (2013). Health care professionals as second victims after adverse events: a systematic review. *Evaluation & the Health Professions, 36*(2), 135–162.

Shanafelt T. D., Boone, S. L., Dyrbye, L. N., Oreskovich, M. R., Tan, L., West, C. P., Sloan, J. A., and Sotile, W. M. (2013). The medical marriage: A national survey of the spouses/partnership of US physicians. *Mayo Clinic Proceedings, 88*(3), 216–225.

Shanafelt, T. D., Hasan, O., Dyrbye, L. N., Sinsky, C., Satele, D., Sloan, J., and West, C. P. (2015). Changes in burnout and satisfaction with work-life balance in physicians and the general US working population between 2011 and 2014. *Mayo Clinic Proceedings, 90*(12), 1600–1613.

Shanafelt, T. D., Sloan, J. A., and Habermann, T. M. (2003). The well-being of physicians. *American Medical Journal, 114*, 513–517.

Shem, S. (1978). *The House of God.* New York, NY: Marek.

Siddiqui, S. (2017, March 23). *Doctors are not God, no matter that the public expects miracles from them.* Womensweb. https://www.womensweb.in/2017/03/doctors-are-not-god/

Skocpol, T. (1995). The rise and resounding demise of the Clinton Plan. *Health Affairs, 14*(1), 66–85.

———. (1997). *Boomerang: Clinton's health security effort and the turn against government.* New York, NY: W. W. Norton & Co.

Sohn, D. H. (2013). Negligence, genuine error, and litigation. *International Journal of General Medicine, 6*, 49–56.

Sotile, W. M., and Sotile, M. O. (2011). *The medical marriage: Sustaining healthy relationships for physicians and their families* (Rev. ed.). American Medical Association.

Srivastava, A. B. (2018). Impaired physician: Obliterating the stigma. *American Journal of Psychiatry, 13*(3), 4–6.

Starr, P. (2004). Precis of Paul Starr's "The Social Transformation of American Medicine" in special issue on transforming American medicine: Retrospective on social transformation of medicine. *Journal of Health Policy, Politics and Law, 29*(4/5), 575–620.

———. (2013). *Remedy and reaction: The peculiar American struggle over health care reform.* New Haven, CT: Yale University Press.

Statista. (2020). *Statistics & facts on physicians in the U.S.* Retrieved February 8, 2020, from https://www.statista.com/topics/1244/physicians

Stevens, R. A. (2001). Public roles for the medical profession in the United States: Beyond theories of decline and fall. *The Milbank Quarterly, 79*(3), 327–353.

Stroman, D. (2003). *The disability rights movement: From deinstitutionalization to self-determination.* Lanham, MD: University Press of America.

Strong, E. A., De Castro, R., Sambuco, D., Stewart, A., Ubel, P. A., Griffith, K. A., and Jagsi, R. (2013). Work–life balance in academic medicine: Narratives of physician-researchers and their mentors. *Journal of General Internal Medicine, 28*(12), 1596–1603.

Sturm, R. (2002). Effect of managed care and financing on practice constraints and career satisfaction in primary care. *Journal of the American Board of Family Practice, 15,* 367–377.

Summerton, N. (1995). Positive and negative factors in defensive medicine: A questionnaire study of general practitioners. *British Medical Journal, 310,* 27–29.

Surowiecki, J. (2016, December 19 and 26). How doctors could thwart health-care reform. *The New Yorker.*

Taylor, J. W. (2014, February 11). A brief history of health care reform: From Truman to Obama. *Becker's Hospital Review.* https://www.beckershospitalreview.com/news -analysis/a-brief-history-on-the-road-to-healthcare-reform-from-truman-to-obama .html

Testerman, J. K., Morton, K. R., Loo, L. K., Worthley, J. S., and Lamberton, H. H. (1996, October). The natural history of cynicism in physicians [Suppl.]. *Academic Medicine,* 71(10), 843–845.

Tilburt, J. C., Wynia, M. K., Sheeler, R. D., Thorsteinsdotir, B., James, K. M., Egginton, J. S., Liebow, M., Hurst, S., Danis, M., and Goold, S. D. (2013). Views of US physicians about controlling health care costs. *Journal of the American Medical Association, 310*(4), 380–389.

Thompson, F.J., (2020, October 9). Six ways Trump has sabotaged the Affordable Care Act. Brookings. https://www.brookings.edu/blog/fixgov/2020/10/09/six-ways-trump -has-sabotaged-the-affordable-care-act/

Transue, E. R. (2013). *On call: A doctor's days and nights in residency.* New York, NY: St. Martin's Griffin.

Tucker, D. (2018). Self-doubt in medicine and the imposter syndrome. https://www .linkedin.com/pulse/self-doubt-medicine-imposter-syndrome-danny-tucker

Tyrance, P. H., Sims, Ma'luf, N., Fairchild, D., and Bates, D. W. (1999). Capitation and its effects on physician satisfaction. *Cost & Quality, 5,* 12–18.

Tyssen, R., Palmer, K. S., Solberg, I. B., Voltmer, E., and Frank, E. (2013). Physicians perceptions of quality of care, professional autonomy and job satisfaction in Canada, Norway, and the United States. *BioMed Central Health Services Research, 13,* 516–525.

Ubel, P. (2014, January 30). Medicare and the desegregation of American hospitals. *Forbes.*

Vaillant, G. E. (1977). *Adaptation to life.* Boston, MA: Little, Brown & Co.

Vyas, D., and Hozain, A. E. (2014). Clinical peer review in the US: History, legal development and subsequent abuse. *World Journal 20*(21), 6357–6363.

Watson, K. (2011). Gallows humor in medicine. *The Hastings Center Report, 41*(5), 37–45.

Weiner, S. (2017, November 7). *What happens when doctors become patients? Renown writer Anna Quindlin "Jumped at the chance" to find out.* AAMC. https://news.aamc.org/patient -care/article/what-happens-when-doctors-become-patients-quindlen/

Weissert, W. G., and Weissert, C. S. (2020). *Governing health: The politics of health policy* (5th ed.). Baltimore, MD: Johns Hopkins University Press.

Westervelt, S. D., and Cook, K. J. (2012). *Life after death row: Exonerees' search for community and identity.* New Brunswick, NJ: Rutgers University Press.

Wiener, J. B. (1998). *Managing the iatrogenic risks of risk management.* https://heinonline.org/HOL/LandingPage?handle=hein.journals/risk9&div=11&id=&page=

Williams, E., Konrad, T., Linzer, M., McMurray, J., Pathman, D., Gerrity, M., and Douglas, J. 1999). Refining the measurement of physician job satisfaction. Results from the Physician Worklife Survey. SGGIM Career Satisfaction Study Group. Society of General Internal Medicine. *Medical Care, 37,* 1140–1154.

Williams, E., Konrad, T., Linzer, M., McMurray, J., Pathman, D., Gerrity, M., Schwartz, M. D., Scheckler, W. E., and Douglas, J. (2002). Physician, practice and patient characteristics related to primary care physician physical and mental health: Results from the physician worklife study. *Health Services Research, 37,* 120–143.

Williams, E. S., and Skinner, A. C. (2003). Outcomes of physician job satisfaction: A narrative review, implications and directions for future research. *Health Care Management Review, 28*(2), 119–140.

Witzig, S. M., and Smith, S. M. (2019). Work-life balance solutions for physicians—It's all about you, your work, and others. *Mayo Clinic Proceedings, 94*(4), 573–576.

Yamey, G., and Wilkes, M. (2001). Promoting well-being among doctors. *British Medical Journal, 322,* 252–253.

Zhao, Q. and Wichman, A. (2015). *Incremental beliefs about ability ameliorate self-doubt effects.* Thousand Oaks, CA: Sage Publications.

Zuger, A. (2004). Dissatisfaction with medical practice. *The New England Journal of Medicine, 350*(1), 69–75.

Index

About the Author

TERRY MIZRAHI is a sociologist and a social worker. She has been a professor at the Silberman School of Social Work at Hunter College of the City University of New York since 1980. She is the author of dozens of scholarly and professional articles and five books in the fields of health policy and practice, community organizing, interdisciplinary and interprofessional collaboration and coalition-building, and social work-physician relationships. Her first book, *Getting Rid of Patients: Contradictions in the Socialization of Physicians* (1986), is the predecessor to *From Residency to Retirement: Physicians' Careers over a Professional Lifetime.*

Available titles in the Critical Issues in Health and Medicine series:

Laura E. Gómez and Nancy López, eds., *Mapping "Race": Critical Approaches to Health Disparities Research*

Janet Greenlees, *When the Air Became Important: A Social History of the New England and Lancashire Textile Industries*

Gerald N. Grob and Howard H. Goldman, *The Dilemma of Federal Mental Health Policy: Radical Reform or Incremental Change?*

Gerald N. Grob and Allan V. Horwitz, *Diagnosis, Therapy, and Evidence: Conundrums in Modern American Medicine*

Rachel Grob, *Testing Baby: The Transformation of Newborn Screening, Parenting, and Policymaking*

Mark A. Hall and Sara Rosenbaum, eds., *The Health Care "Safety Net" in a Post-Reform World*

Laura L. Heinemann, *Transplanting Care: Shifting Commitments in Health and Care in the United States*

Laura D. Hirshbein, *American Melancholy: Constructions of Depression in the Twentieth Century*

Laura D. Hirshbein, *Smoking Privileges: Psychiatry, the Mentally Ill, and the Tobacco Industry in America*

Timothy Hoff, *Practice under Pressure: Primary Care Physicians and Their Medicine in the Twenty-first Century*

Beatrix Hoffman, Nancy Tomes, Rachel N. Grob, and Mark Schlesinger, eds., *Patients as Policy Actors*

Ruth Horowitz, *Deciding the Public Interest: Medical Licensing and Discipline*

Powel Kazanjian, *Frederick Novy and the Development of Bacteriology in American Medicine*

Claas Kirchhelle, *Pyrrhic Progress: The History of Antibiotics in Anglo-American Food Production*

Rebecca M. Kluchin, *Fit to Be Tied: Sterilization and Reproductive Rights in America, 1950–1980*

Jennifer Lisa Koslow, *Cultivating Health: Los Angeles Women and Public Health Reform*

Jennifer Lisa Koslow, *Exhibiting Health: Public Health Displays in the Progressive Era*

Susan C. Lawrence, *Privacy and the Past: Research, Law, Archives, Ethics*

Bonnie Lefkowitz, *Community Health Centers: A Movement and the People Who Made It Happen*

Ellen Leopold, *Under the Radar: Cancer and the Cold War*

Barbara L. Ley, *From Pink to Green: Disease Prevention and the Environmental Breast Cancer Movement*

Sonja Mackenzie, *Structural Intimacies: Sexual Stories in the Black AIDS Epidemic*

Stephen E. Mawdsley, *Selling Science: Polio and the Promise of Gamma Globulin*

Frank M. McClellan, *Healthcare and Human Dignity: Law Matters*

Michelle McClellan, *Lady Lushes: Gender, Alcohol, and Medicine in Modern America*

David Mechanic, *The Truth about Health Care: Why Reform Is Not Working in America*

Richard A. Meckel, *Classrooms and Clinics: Urban Schools and the Protection and Promotion of Child Health, 1870–1930*

Terry Mizrahi, *From Residency to Retirement: Physicians' Careers over a Professional Lifetime*

Manon Parry, *Broadcasting Birth Control: Mass Media and Family Planning*

Alyssa Picard, *Making the American Mouth: Dentists and Public Health in the Twentieth Century*

Heather Munro Prescott, *The Morning After: A History of Emergency Contraception in the United States*

Sarah B. Rodriguez, *The Love Surgeon: A Story of Trust, Harm, and the Limits of Medical Regulation*

David J. Rothman and David Blumenthal, eds., *Medical Professionalism in the New Information Age*

Andrew R. Ruis, *Eating to Learn, Learning to Eat: School Lunches and Nutrition Policy in the United States*

James A. Schafer Jr., *The Business of Private Medical Practice: Doctors, Specialization, and Urban Change in Philadelphia, 1900–1940*

David G. Schuster, *Neurasthenic Nation: America's Search for Health, Happiness, and Comfort, 1869–1920*

Karen Seccombe and Kim A. Hoffman, *Just Don't Get Sick: Access to Health Care in the Aftermath of Welfare Reform*

Leo B. Slater, *War and Disease: Biomedical Research on Malaria in the Twentieth Century*

Piper Sledge, *Bodies Unbound: Gender-Specific Cancer and Biolegitimacy*

Dena T. Smith, *Medicine over Mind: Mental Health Practice in the Biomedical Era*

Kylie M. Smith, *Talking Therapy: Knowledge and Power in American Psychiatric Nursing*

Matthew Smith, *An Alternative History of Hyperactivity: Food Additives and the Feingold Diet*

Paige Hall Smith, Bernice L. Hausman, and Miriam Labbok, *Beyond Health, Beyond Choice: Breastfeeding Constraints and Realities*

Susan L. Smith, *Toxic Exposures: Mustard Gas and the Health Consequences of World War II in the United States*

Rosemary A. Stevens, Charles E. Rosenberg, and Lawton R. Burns, eds., *History and Health Policy in the United States: Putting the Past Back In*

Marianne Sullivan, *Tainted Earth: Smelters, Public Health, and the Environment*

Courtney E. Thompson, *An Organ of Murder: Crime, Violence, and Phrenology in Nineteenth-Century America*

Barbra Mann Wall, *American Catholic Hospitals: A Century of Changing Markets and Missions*

Frances Ward, *The Door of Last Resort: Memoirs of a Nurse Practitioner*

Jean C. Whelan, *Nursing the Nation: Building the Nurse Labor Force*

Shannon Withycombe, *Lost: Miscarriage in Nineteenth-Century America*